ALSACE TO THE ALSATIANS?

Studies in Contemporary European History

Editors:
Konrad Jarausch, University of North Carolina, Chapel Hill
Henry Rousso, Institut d'histoire du temps présent, CNRS, Paris

Volume 1
Between Utopia and Disillusionment: A Narrative of the Political Transformation in Eastern Europe
  Henri Vogt

Volume 2
The Inverted Mirror: Mythologizing the Enemy in France and Germany, 1898–1914
  Michael E. Nolan

Volume 3
Conflicted Memories: Europeanizing Contemporary Histories
  Edited by Konrad H. Jarausch and Thomas Lindenberger with the Collaboration of Annelie Ramsbrock

Volume 4
Playing Politics with History: The Bundestag Inquiries into East Germany
  Andrew H. Beattie

Volume 5
Alsace to the Alsatians? Visions and Divisions of Alsatian Regionalism, 1870–1939
  Christopher J. Fischer

Volume 6
A European Memory? Contested Histories and Politics of Remembrance
  Edited by Małgorzata Pakier and Bo Stråth

Volume 7
Experience and Memory: The Second World War in Europe
  Edited by Jörg Echternkamp and Stefan Martens

Volume 8
Children, Families, and States: Time Policies of Childcare, Preschool, and Primary Education in Europe
  Edited by Karen Hagemann, Konrad H. Jarausch, and Cristina Allemann-Ghionda

Volume 9
Social Policy in the Smaller European Union States
  Edited by Gary B. Cohen, Ben W. Ansell, Jane Gingrich, and Robert Henry Cox

Volume 10
A State of Peace in Europe: West Germany and the CSCE, 1966–1975
  Petri Hakkarainen

Volume 11
Visions of the End of the Cold War
  Edited by Frederic Bozo, Marie-Pierre Rey, Bernd Rother, and N. Piers Ludlow

Volume 12
Investigating Srebrenica: Institutions, Facts, Responsibilities
  Edited by Isabelle Delpla, Xavier Bougarel, and Jean-Louis Fournel

Volume 13
Samizdat, Tamizdat, and Beyond: Transnational Media During and After Socialism
  Edited by Friederike Kind-Kovács and Jessie Labov

ALSACE TO THE ALSATIANS?

Visions and Divisions of
Alsatian Regionalism, 1870–1939

Christopher J. Fischer

berghahn
NEW YORK • OXFORD
www.berghahnbooks.com

First published in 2010 by
Berghahn Books
www.berghahnbooks.com

© 2010, 2014 Christopher J. Fischer
Paperback edition published in 2014

All rights reserved.
Except for the quotation of short passages
for the purposes of criticism and review, no part of this book
may be reproduced in any form or by any means, electronic or
mechanical, including photocopying, recording, or any information
storage and retrieval system now known or to be invented,
without written permission of the publisher.

Library of Congress Cataloging-in-Publication Data

Fischer, Christopher J.
  Alsace to the Alsatians? : visions and divisions of Alsatian regionalism, 1870-1939 / Christopher J. Fischer.
     p. cm. — (Contemporary european history ; v. 5)
  Includes bibliographical references and index.
  ISBN 978-1-84545-724-2 (hardback) -- ISBN 978-1-78238-394-9 paperback -- ISBN 978-1-84545-806-5 (ebook)
  1. Alsace (France)—History—19th century. 2. Alsace (France)—History—20th century. 3. Regionalism—France—Alsace—History. 4. Alsace (France)—Ethnic relations. 5. Alsace (France)—History—Autonomy and independence movements. 6. Group identity—France—Alsace—History. I. Title.
DC650.5.F56 2010
944'.39081—dc22   200904779

British Library Cataloguing in Publication Data

A catalogue record for this book is available from
the British Library

Printed on acid-free paper

ISBN: 978-1-78238-394-9 paperback
ISBN: 978-1-84545-806-5 ebook

To my parents

Contents

List of Figures   ix

Acknowledgements   xi

Abbreviations and Terms   xiii

Note on Places   xv

Note on Archives   xvii

Introduction   1

Chapter 1
Alsace Reborn: Emerging Visions of Alsace, 1895–1913   20

Chapter 2
Monuments, Museums, and Memory:
Commemoration in Alsace, 1900–1914   52

Chapter 3
From Disunity to Unity: The Constitutional
Debates and the Zabern Affair, 1910–1914   73

Chapter 4
War Weariness or National Reunion?
World War I and Alsace, 1914–1918   100

Chapter 5
"Ne toucher pas de choses d'Alsace":
The Return of French Rule to Alsace, 1918–1925   128

Chapter 6
Dual Cultures and Contested Memories: Alsace in the 1920s   152

Chapter 7
    The Apogee of the Autonomist Movement   179

    Conclusion: Visions and Divisions   206

Bibliography   213

Index   229

Figures

Figure 1.1. Gustave Stoskopf, *E Demonstration* — 34

Figure 1.2. Hansi, "Le Toit," *Die Hohkönigsburg und ihre Einweihung* — 38

Figure 1.3. Hansi, *L'Histoire d'Alsace* — 40

Figure 1.4. Hansi, *Mon Village* — 41

Figure 1.5. Hansi, *Mon Village* — 42

Figure 1.6. Hansi, *Mon Village* — 42

Figure 2.1. Wilhelm II visits Hohkönigsburg — 57

Figure 2.2. Hohkönigsburg — 59

Figure 2.3. Alsatian Kitchen, Musée Alsacien — 62

Figure 4.1. Hartmannswillerkopf — 102

Figure 5.1. "Le Plebiscit est fait": President Poincaré in Strasbourg, December 1918 — 129

Figure 6.1. Bastille Day 1919, Strasbourg — 172

Acknowledgements

Works of history, much like most major undertakings in life, require the help of many. This project has benefited from the insights of mentors, friends, and colleagues. Konrad Jarausch, as an advisor and teacher, imparted much timely direction and advice to this book. At the University of North Carolina, I also benefited greatly from the insights and prodding of Christopher Browning, Lloyd Kramer, Donald Raleigh, Donald Reid, and Jay Smith. I have also profited from the experience and advice of other scholars of Alsatian history. At conferences, through email, and in France as well as Germany, Laird Boswell, Ulrich Herbert, Tony Steinhoff, and Steven Harp have offered useful direction and insight.

I would also like to thank the German Historical Institute and the Friends of the German Historical Institute for support on this project through the Fritz Stern Prize. In particular, I would like to thank the Prize committee from 2004—Kees Gispen, Atina Grossman, and especially Vernon Lidtke—for passing along both their praise and, more importantly, suggestions for improving the manuscript. The late Gerald Feldman offered warm comments and suggestions at the 2004 Friends Symposium. David Lazar and Richard Wetzell gave needed advice and suggestion moving this project from dissertation to manuscript.

If intellectual support has been one pillar of this project, then institutional and financial support have stood as two others. Various organizations have provided funds for travel, research, and writing over the years The German Academic Exchange Service (DAAD), the Graduate School at UNC, and UNC's Center for European Studies all provided funds to work in France and Germany. The Humanities Center at Loyola College (Maryland) provided a summer research grant. The History Departments at UNC, Loyola, and Indiana State University have given support for research and travel. I would also like to express my deep gratitude to the knowledgeable and friendly staffs at the Archives Départementales du Bas-Rhin in Strasbourg, the Archives Départementales du Haut-Rhin in Colmar, the Archives Municipales in Strasbourg, the Bundesarchiv in Freiburg, and the Archives Nationales in Paris. The staffs at the libraries at the University of North Carolina, Indiana State, Loyola College, and the University of Freiburg, especially the Interlibrary Loan departments, for all their assistance over the years. And I offer my gratitude (and apologies) to the staff at the Bibliothèque Nationale et Universitaire in Strasbourg, in particular the staff of the microfilm room, for putting up with my incessant, large requests. Finally, I want to thank Malou Schneider of the Musée alsacien in Strasbourg who allowed me access to the museum's archive and discussed its history with me, and Monique Fuchs, conservator at the museum at Hohkönigsberg, for pointing me to the relevant files at the ADBR.

Friends and colleagues have provided additional advice and support along the way. Bernhard von Hülsen offered key advice in the ADBR; Brian Crim provided support and directions at the BA-MA in Freiburg. Sharon Kowalsky, Thomas Pegelow, Karin Breuer, and Todd Berryman at UNC, along with Barbara Skinner and Isaac Land at Indiana State, kindly read and commented upon sections of the manuscript. All defects of the manuscript remain my, and not their, responsibility.

I would also like to thank the helpful staff at Berghahn Books, especially Marion Berghahn, but also Ann Przyzycki, Melissa Spinelli, and Kristine Hunt for their help ushering this project through publication.

Finally, there are those without whose personal support this project would have never come to fruition. Elana Passman provided trenchant criticism, her indefatigable and inestimable skills as an editor, general patience, profound friendship, and so much more. And for their inexhaustible patience, support, and care, I dedicate this work to my parents, Thomas and Kathleen. This is what I have been working on all these years.

Abbreviations and Terms

ADBR	Archives Départementales du Bas-Rhin
ADHR	Archives Départementales du Haut-Rhin
AMA	Archives du musée alsacien
AMS	Archives Municipales de Strasbourg
AN	Archives Nationales (CARAN)
APNA	Action Populaire Nationale d'Alsace
BA-Freiburg	Bundesarchiv-Freiburg
BNUS	Bibliothèque Nationale et Universitaire de Strasbourg
DEW	*Die elsässische Woche*
JAL	*Journal d'Alsace et de Lorraine*
JfGSL	*Jahrbuch für Geschichte, Sprache, und Literatur*
Nddba	*Nouveau dictionnaire de biographie alsacienne*
Optants	Alsatians who "opted" for French citizenship after 1871
PCA	Parti Communiste d'Alsace
RdAL	*Revue d'Alsace et de Lorraine*
Reichsland	Designation and administrative unit for Alsace-Lorraine, 1871–1918
Revenants	Alsatians who lived in France and returned to the region after World War I.
SFIO	Section française de l'Internationale ouvrière
SPD	Sozialdemocratische Partei Deutschlands
SNZ	*Strassburger Neue Zeitung*
UPR	Union Populaire Républicaine

Note on Places

The shifting geopolitical fortunes of Germany and France brought alternating emphasis on German and French usage for city, town, and district names. As a matter of convenience, I have employed the French equivalents for most place names. This choice is meant to allow consistency and ease of reading, not express political sentiments. Two exceptions are made to this rule. First, the town of Zabern uses the German rather than the French version of the name (Saverne) as the incident in the town in 1913 often goes in English language historiography as the Zabern Affair. Likewise, the castle of Hohkönigsburg will be referred to with the German spelling of the landmark.

Note on Archives

In general, the archives used for this book are clear in their designation of file series and folders. Two exceptions must be noted. First, the Archives Départementales in Colmar has two designations for some series, especially the files relating to the French-occupied regions of Alsace during the First World War. The first designation, used in the archive guide-books, lists the files under series AJ 30; however, the files are cross-listed, and had (at the time of my research) to be cross-listed with the "Purgatoire" series (in the notes, "Purg.") Second, the Archives Municipales in Strasbourg has recategorized many of its files since the research for this project was completed. This manuscript has kept the older designations drawn from the five-volume guide *Inventaire des archives contemporaines et administratives de la ville de Strasbourg, 1789–1960* edited by Erwin Martin.

Introduction

Français ne puis-je
Allemand ne daigne
Alsacien suis-je.

[I can't be French
Won't deign to be German
I am an Alsatian]

—Saying of the Rohan Cardinals

The Alsatian feels physical and moral suffering. He loves Germany and yet does not come to hate France. He feels like a child who loves his two parents and who suffers seeing them unable to stand one other, and much worse, to see that they strike one another and they wish to go their own way. He has trust in the father, a severe, rigorous, and authoritarian man. He feels for the father very much, takes him as an example, he respects and loves him, but he does not manage to forget his beautiful mother, this woman so charming. The father knows she will try any means to retake her child. Suspicious and jealous, he watches all the deeds and gestures of the child, all the steps of his rival. This one succeeds in visiting the child, who receives her with an overly demonstrative joy so that he is punished severely by the father.

—Philippe Husser, *Un Instituteur Alsacien*

Alsace to the Alsatians. Alsace aux Alsaciens. Elsass den Elsässern. In the first three decades of the twentieth century, this motto became the rallying cry for the Alsatian regional movement. First coined by the writer and politician Charles Grad, the phrase was adopted by various Alsatian parties in the 1890s before becoming a common slogan of Alsatian regionalists

---

Notes for this section begin on page 16.

well into the 1930s. Francophile Alsatians in the decades before World War I, however, had far different motives from their autonomist brethren in the interwar period: the former group wanted to see Alsace return to the *mère-patrie*, the latter wanted Alsatian privileges safeguarded, especially in the realms of religion and language. In its many iterations, the regionalist movement befuddled both German and French authorities. German and French administrators realized that Alsatian regionalism represented a deep dissatisfaction with their respective rule. The same bureaucrats, however, were spurred on by fellow nationalists to quell Alsatian "antinational sentiments."[1]

The idea of "Alsace to the Alsatians" served as more than a convenient motto for Alsatian political interests, but what exactly did this catchphrase mean? Did it imply an Alsatian cultural particularity? Was it a cry for regional autonomy within the German Empire and, after the Treaty of Versailles, the French Third Republic? Or was regionalism merely a language with which to protest other issues?

Such questions are not easily answered. Part of the difficulty with the case of Alsace lies in its particular political circumstances. Annexed in 1871 by Germany and returned to France at the conclusion of World War I, Alsace, along with the neighboring province of Lorraine, served as a victory trophy in Franco-German conflicts.[2] Germany and France in turn sought to win over the loyalty of the region's inhabitants and in the process quite often alienated the local population. Fate, therefore, dictated that Alsatian culture in part be defined relationally to France and Germany. Therefore, regionalism could serve as a manner of protesting French and German policies, or of resisting nationalist pressures to assimilate. Alsatian regionalism did not simply serve as a convenient mode of contesting the region's fate. Alsatians also sought to define their culture, traditions, and heritage positively. Yet Alsatians, arguing among themselves about their relationship with Germany and France, hardly presented a unified front. Alsatian regionalism, therefore, took on a Janus-faced character.

Internal divisions among Alsatians exacerbated this duality. Social divisions existed between the region's workers and industrial and administrative elites; linguistic differences, in turn, overlay social divides.[3] Alsace possessed a confessionally mixed population, with a Catholic majority, a large Protestant population, and a substantial Jewish community.[4] The complexity of Alsatian society further complicated Alsatian responses to German and French rule as different social, linguistic, religious, and political groups had divergent attitudes about Alsace's future.

This study examines the phenomenon of Alsatian regionalism by asking several basic questions: What did Alsatians mean when they said "Alsace to the Alsatians?" How did Alsatians present and represent their own history, culture, and traditions? How did political developments, both within Alsace and on the larger European stage, affect Alsatian regionalism? How did the regionalism of the pre-1914 period influence and shape that of the interwar years? The answers are not simple as Alsatian regionalism proved multilayered, evolving, contingent, and contested.

The Nature of Regionalism

As regionalism is the central subject of this study, the concept of regionalism itself first needs clarification. Is regionalism primarily economic, as it often appears in its European Union variant? Is it a political-cultural nexus, as in South Tyrol, or more ominously, in the Balkan states or the Basque region?[5] Or is it a political, cultural, and economic phenomenon, as in Bavaria?[6] Much like its near relative nationalism, regionalism possesses a protean quality. Therefore, two issues arise: first, how does one define a region, and second, how does one explain the relationship between the region and regionalism?

Regions, even more so than nations, at times elude definition. They vary in function, size, and degree of popular identification. At times willed into existence by local leaders, they can be produced by administrative fiat. As Michael Keating has observed, regions are an "intermediate territorial level between the state and locality"; yet Keating also notes that regions can be defined politically, socially, economically, linguistically, or "delineated according to the sense of identity felt by citizens and political actors." The ambitions of regionalists vary as well, from demanding autonomy to economic partnerships to simply existing as an administrative unit.[7]

Rather than develop a complex taxonomy of regions, this study analyzes a number of factors that allow for the development of a region. They include (but not necessarily all simultaneously) geographic unity, economic cohesion, a shared cultural heritage, an administrative apparatus, and popular identification with the region as a community unto itself. Regions result from a variety of economic, cultural, political, and social vectors. Rarely are they uncontested in their construction. A broad definition allows us to consider regionalism in its multiple forms, while still defining it in relationship to other forms of territorial organization such as supranational organizations, nation-states, or localities.[8]

Given the multiple possible incarnations of regions, it is necessary not to become overly wed to a narrow conception of what it means to be a regionalist. Regionalism can best be understood as a movement that seeks to promote the political, social, economic, and/or cultural interests of a particular region. Regionalists therefore consider the region unique for cultural, linguistic, and historical reasons, but not necessarily separate from the nation. Since regions usually must operate within the framework of the nation-state, their representatives often do not have the political leeway to pursue their goals with complete liberty. Therefore, politics should be defined not simply as the realm of political parties and formal movements, but should also include such diverse activities as terrorism and cultural revivals as part of regionalist efforts.

With regard more specifically to the cases of Germany and France, regionalism has gained prominence in recent scholarship for its role in shaping national belonging in both countries. For example, though differing on the dynamics of the relationship between region and nation, both Celia Applegate and Alon Confino have explored how the Heimat (home or homeland])[9] movements catalyzed the process of identification with the nation. Local history, culture, and traditions slowly became intertwined with national meaning, thus promoting belonging to both region and nation.[10] Other scholars have explored the role of German regionalism, pointing not only to its importance before unification and thereafter, but also suggesting that it could be modernizing and forward thinking.[11] In a similar vein, scholars have increasingly argued for the importance of local and regional community for shaping French identity in the Third Republic.[12]

These trends point to the importance of the locality or region in the imagining of the national community. A willingness to consider regionalism not solely as conflicting with but also as complementary to nationalism further allows a clearer understanding of the dynamics of regionalism at the local level. A group that wants to promote the relationship between the nation and the region may well choose to emphasize those elements of a particular locality's history, traditions, and customs that connect it more closely to the nation. Conversely, a group seeking to elevate the place of the region relative to the nation might stress those aspects of regional culture that point to the uniqueness, or at least particularity, of the region within the nation.

To pursue the particular nature of Alsatian regionalism, this study examines the phenomenon along three vectors. The first, *political*, is itself divided into several categories. For a regionalist who finds local values, traditions, and culture compatible with those of the nation-state, regionalism may take the form of a federalist movement. This means, in effect, that the region exists within a federated system, maintaining its own distinctive cultural heritage while perhaps enjoying some political or economic freedom within a larger political unit. Particularism, as a form of regionalism, takes a more solipsistic turn; particularists view their community as more distinct from the nation; moreover, they may try to push for a great deal of autonomy within the framework of a given nation-state. At the far end of the spectrum exists separatism. Separatists understand the nation as antithetical to the region, see a great cultural and historical opposition between the two, and therefore seek to secede from the nation-state. In a given region more than one form of regionalism may exist depending on how local rivals understand the nature of their community and how they choose to express such regional conceptions politically.[13]

Second, the *social* basis of a regional movement also plays an essential role in defining its character. For example, in parts of Brittany, local lower clergy and their lay allies tried to address the social needs of Bretons in the face of Third Republic attempts at secularization; their efforts led to the rise of a Christian Socialism rooted in the culture of Lower Brittany.[14] The use of regional imagery and rhetoric heightened the appeal of Breton Christian Socialism, while the social appeal of this form of regionalism increased attachment to the region. Thus, confession and class can each serve to define the character of regionalism; moreover, the marriage of social and regional interests can potentially strengthen both. Conversely, diverse social interests within the region can weaken regionalism's appeal or divide its political strength.

Culture constitutes the third major element of regionalism. At its most basic level, regional culture involves honoring local traditions and customs, writing local history, commemorating important sites and people, and perhaps upholding a local dialect or literary tradition. Regional culture, like that of the nation, is not uniformly defined. Differences in political, social, or economic leanings can translate into multiple conceptions of the region. Additionally, as regions rarely exist outside of nation-states, these contestations over the meaning of the region are not simply horizontal, i.e. among the local population, but also vertical, between the region and the nation. Therefore, the region is constituted at two levels culturally. First, the customs, images, history, and other such intellectual and cultural products that serve as the representational form of the region need to be articulated. Second, and more broadly, the region as a form of community imbued with (often contested) meaning must be developed in conjunction with and in relation to other types of community.

The fact that regionalists seek to shape and draw upon feelings of belonging to the regional community points to the importance of identity to this project. After all, how can one claim to speak for Bavaria, Alsace, South Tyrol, or the Basque region without feeling Bavarian, Alsatian, Tyrolean, or Basque? Like the nation, the region can be defined as a particular territorial space whose inhabitants share historical and cultural traits that privilege the development of a sense of community among the region's inhabitants.

The vast literature on nationalism is suggestive of how one might approach understanding regionalism and regional identity,[15] yet as Celia Applegate has argued, one must take care as some approaches, such as those relying on modernization theory, may actually obscure processes contributing to the formation of regional identities. Conversely, regional identities may warp or alter the nature of national identities.[16]

This project draws upon a cultural constructionist view of national identity to offer guidance in the study of regional identity. First, identity is formed when regionalists, investing meaning in symbols and imagery through a process of selective remembrance and forgetting, shape memory. This does not mean that regional identity is "invented," but it must be cultivated and disseminated. Those regionalists—politicians, local historians, preservation groups, or literary societies—who engage in active remembrance of local history and customs help create a sense of regional community. Yet these very activities are limited by a given set of symbols and imagery that may be drawn upon; remembering the region, or even imagining it, does not mean that it is fabricated.[17] Second, cultural constructionists point to the changing and contested nature of communal identities; regional identities develop, change, and become the object of struggle, whether between institutions of the nation and the region, or among the competing representatives of the local community. Third, a regional identity does not have to exist as the primary form of identification. Regionalists may also feel strong attachment to a nation, religion, social class, or gender.[18] In other words, worrying about the primacy of one form of identity offers an oversimplified, if not essentialized, conception of belonging to a community.

Regional community, however, should not be taken simply as a national community writ small. Although sharing many of the same qualities as the national community, the regional community also has its distinct features. First, given the prevalence of the nation-state, the regional community rarely claims a predominant place among other forms of allegiance. Rather, the region must develop in concordance, or perhaps in variance, with the national community. More importantly, the regional community has an immediacy often lacking from imaginings of the nation. The prominence of local quotidian traditions, proximity of sites of memory, use of a dialect, or particularities of local culture make regional identities more subtle and intimate than their national analogues.

The Complex Case of Alsace

Alsace presents a particularly complicated case for the scholar interested in regionalism. Like many other borderlands in Europe, Alsace experienced not only successive, alternating occupations, but its inhabitants were expected to transform themselves into good citizens of a different country with each turning of the geopolitical tide. Alsace's mixed cultural and political heritage, the product of standing for centuries at a major European cultural and political crossroads, complicated the situation further. Some regionalists argued that Alsace should be allowed to maintain its complex heritage not just for its own sake, but also so that the region could serve as a bridge between France and Germany. Yet such arguments held little weight under either the German or French regimes. Instead, German and French nationalists sought to shape the loyalties of Alsatians by seeking to eliminate vestiges of the other country's culture when in control of the region, and would encourage when possible their own culture even when Alsace was foreign territory.

In many ways then, Alsace's fate as a borderland shaped its regionalism, not to mention the lives of local inhabitants. On a practical level, the events of 1871 and 1918 altered the region's economy, interrupted the careers of civil servants, forced Alsatians to acclimate themselves to new legal standards, and even led to the changing of street names. German then French nationalists, each believing their own myths about Alsatian loyalties, culture, language, and society, sought with varying degrees of intensity to inscribe their own vision of national belonging on the region. Yet despite ambitious hopes to bring the Alsatians back into the national fold, neither the Germans nor the French fully trusted their newly found countrymen. Thus, the Alsatians found themselves in the difficult position of often trying to define their regional culture positively as a complex mélange of their competing neighbors' (and would-be masters') cultures, when neither side wholly accepted the legitimacy of Alsace's frontier identity.

One of the great ironies of Alsatian history is the degree to which German and French administrators made similar mistakes in their respective treatment of the Alsatians. After the Franco-Prussian War, firebrand German nationalists came to Alsace bearing the banner of German nationalism only to meet a lukewarm response. French armies after World War I, in contrast, found cheering throngs; yet within a year of the French repossession of the region, both Alsatians and French administrators spoke of a *"malaise alsacien."* German and French administrators managed to alienate the Alsatians through a combination of means. Both viewed the Alsatians as long-lost brothers, but treated the Alsatians as a quasi-colonial people whose loyalty was not altogether assured. Both national governments made the mistake of impinging upon Alsatian Catholicism, first in the form of the *Kulturkampf* against German Catholics, and later in the Herriot government's attempt to complete the secularization of the French state. Both governments sought to impose the national tongue upon a linguistically diverse Alsace in schools, administrative offices, and the courts.[19] Such efforts, in combination with other obvious attempts to nationalize the region, forced the Alsatians into a greater awareness of their own regional loyalties and of the difficulties of living in a border region.

The social and cultural diversity of Alsatian society, in turn, made Alsatian responses to German and French initiatives all the more complex. Linguistic differences coincided with social divisions. The bulk of the upper classes spoke French, controlled Alsatian industry, and dominated the cultural life of Alsatian urban centers before 1871. Despite the emigration of a large portion of this segment of the population following the 1871 Treaty of Frankfurt, these elites maintained a prominent position in Alsatian society.[20] This predominantly urbanized group of industrialists and landowners had both the means and the drive to maintain its ties to France. Others, such as the German-speaking Protestants of

Lower Alsace, viewed German rule more benignly. For the vast majority of Alsatians—many of whom spoke Alsatian (a German dialect) and only a smattering of French—the question of national belonging was less pressing as a major political theme. They conditioned their support for the cause of Alsace based upon other important issues, notably religion, language, and the economy.

Finally, World War I profoundly altered the dynamics of Alsatian regionalism. While heated exchanges took place in the decades preceding the war between French and German nationalists in the region, and scandals such as the 1913 Zabern Affair did nothing to improve the atmosphere in Alsace, a new level of acrimony entered regionalist and nationalist discourse in the years after the war. For some regionalists, France appeared to have reneged on its promises to respect Alsatian rights; therefore, they pinned their hopes for a separate autonomy within France. From the standpoint of pro-French regionalists and French administrators, autonomists at best ignored the sacrifices made to regain Alsace; more often, these malcontents were viewed as subversive German agents bent on twisting Alsatian minds against the *mère-patrie*. The memory of the war, as well as the new Wilsonian language of self-determination, not only heightened tensions between Alsatians and the French but also brought about a change in regionalist rhetoric as more radical regionalists claimed national minority status for Alsatians and even threatened to appeal to the League of Nations.[21]

From this mix of national pressures on a borderland and a complex, local social structure sprang diverse expressions of Alsatian regionalism. The Alsatians did not idly sit by and allow the Germans or the French to imprint the nation upon them, nor did they display a monolithic opposition to German or French rule. Instead, Alsatians' conceptions of their place in the world—and more specifically, in relation to Germany and France—were expressed in a wide variety of forms, from cultural revivals to hopes for political upheaval.

The social diversity in the region helped fuel these forms of Alsatian regionalism. For the largely Francophile upper classes, pre-1914 regionalism denoted loyalty to Alsace, a desire for return to France, and a means of resisting Germanization. They became the standard-bearers of the "dual culture" of Alsace, a mix of German and French cultural influences in the region that needed protection and cultivation. For the lower classes, especially among Catholics, this prewar anti-German, pro-French regionalism played less of a role. Some Alsatians supported Germany before 1918. After 1919, the French-speaking bourgeoisie, in varying degrees, pushed for the swift (re)Frenchification of the region. Others wanted a return to Germany in the interwar years. Still others, disinclined to German rule before 1918 yet doubtful as to whether German control would be reversed, promoted a regional autonomy within Germany; many of these same Alsatians would urge the French not to pursue their goals too vigorously for fear of alienating the region. Catholic clergymen and lay leaders alike would employ the language of a dual culture to defend their conception of a devoutly Catholic, German-speaking Alsace against the French administration of the region.

Not only did the Alsatians respond to national pressures in myriad fashion, but they also pursued their goals through a wide variety of means. Some Alsatians wished to celebrate local customs, crafts, and the regional dialect through festivals, museums, plays, and children's books as a way of demonstrating their love for Alsace. Behind such efforts lay not only an admiration for the region in itself but also a form of cultural politics; these Alsatians were, in effect, trying to define what it meant to be Alsatian. Others took a more political route, arguing in the local assembly or national parliament on behalf of Alsatian rights. Some even championed Alsatian demands from afar, using Paris, Berlin, Frankfurt, Freiburg, and Nancy as bases for furthering French or German claims to the region.

Only by understanding Alsatian regionalism as a complex, multifaceted phenomenon can we understand the varied responses Alsatians had to their situation. Moreover, by not considering Alsatian regionalism as a monolithic structure, we can better understand the difficulties that the Alsatians faced in promoting their aims vis-à-vis Germany and France. The Alsatian inability to face their rulers with a united front in part frustrated their efforts to serve Alsatian interests. Moreover, the divisions within Alsatian regionalism often served to confound German and French administrators, who did not know whether they should view the Alsatians as long-lost siblings or reluctant, distantly related members of the national family.

Examining Alsatian Regionalism

This study seeks to elaborate how exactly Alsatians expressed their conceptions of regional belonging, how they fought among themselves to represent Alsace, and how such activities influenced Alsace's relationship with Germany and France. In doing so, this study situates itself within a broader literature on regionalism. The works of Confino and Applegate for Germany or the scholarship of Caroline Ford and Shanny Peer[22] for France have all pointed to the ways in which regionalism has served to integrate French regions into the greater national community. This is especially true of the German case as Germany has traditionally been conceived as a federal nation-state. Not only did Germany have a federalist structure, but Germans envisioned their nation as growing out a diversity of regions that together, bound by language, culture, and ethnicity, formed the German nation.[23] In contrast, in France the issue of regionalism has been far more contested as the idea of regionalism, or particularism, was linked to reactionary traditions; after the Revolution, France was projected as unified, centralized nation-state where regions were anathema to the unity of France "indivisible." After 1871, regionalism experienced a rebirth within the French Right, but the Jacobin vision of the centralized, unified nation-state remained predominant.[24]

In theory, Alsatian regionalism could have served to integrate the region into the nation; many regionalists before the First World War wanted equality for Alsace-Lorraine in the Reich, and many German officials hoped regionalism would stand in for lingering loyalty to France. After 1918, many regionalists hoped to preserve Alsace's unique heritage within the context of the French nation-state. Yet under both German and French rule, some Alsatians used regionalism to disrupt the process of integration. This project therefore examines the integrative and disruptive force of regionalism with regard to the forging of national community; more narrowly, the study seeks to elucidate the place of regionalism within the context of conceptions of German and French nationhood.

In order to pursue this agenda, this project focuses on the development of Alsatian regionalism from the 1870 to 1939, giving special attention to the years between the mid-1890s and the late 1920s. This chronological framework may appear arbitrary. The choice of both dates, however, lies in their importance as approximate markers of changes in Alsatian regionalism. In the 1890s, two interrelated developments marked a shift from the earlier period of the "Protestler," i.e. the first decades following German annexation when the majority of Alsatian politicians expressed their opposition to the outcome of 1871. First, a new generation of Alsatian leaders, many raised under German rule, began to come into their own. No longer seeking simply to overturn the events of 1870–71, these Alsatian leaders sought to define Alsace's place within the German Empire. The cultural life of the region shifted nearly simultaneously with the change in the region's political scene. Beginning in the mid-1890s, Alsatians such as Anselm Laugel, Charles Spindler, and Gustave Stoskopf inaugurated an "Alsatian Renaissance," a revival of Alsatian culture and traditions. Their work, in turn, would help to provide the imagery necessary for Alsatian regionalism as a political movement.

The 1939 terminus reflects the outbreak of war. Yet even before the war, beginning in the early 1930s, Alsatian regionalism had undergone a key period of transformation. After a series of important, well-publicized trials at Colmar and Besançon in 1928 and 1929, the Alsatian regionalist movement slowly broke into a variety of factions; some groups flirted with French fascism, others with Nazism, while some groups even sought to nurture a form of far-right agrarian populism. This splintering of the regional movement, combined with the dolor of the Great Depression, the ominous shadow of Nazi Germany, and most importantly, the easing of those measures deemed most injurious to Alsatian interests, slowly eroded support for regionally based politics. While regionalist, increasingly separatist groups did not fully disappear from the Alsatian political scene, altered domestic and foreign conditions rendered the cacophonous voices of Alsatian autonomism less compelling.[25]

This project adopts an exemplary approach, examining key moments and developments in Alsatian regionalism to understand how Alsatian conceptions of their own community and their relationship with France and Germany evolved. Several reasons militate in favor of the episodic approach over a more chronological one, or one more focused in its subject matter. First, Alsatian regionalism manifested itself in a variety of ways. To examine one incarnation of regionalism to the exclusion of another ignores the interrelationships among the various forms of Alsatian regionalism. Second, the exemplary approach is linked by evolving conceptions of regionalism, and more importantly, the major figures promoting its various incarnations. The major protagonists promoting Alsatian culture in the early 1900s later came to support, either directly or indirectly, political movements and parties that aimed to secure Alsatian rights within Germany or France. Likewise, some members of the regionalist movement before 1914 assumed leadership roles in the autonomist movement of the interwar decades. Finally, manifestations of regionalism can be linked discursively. Alsatians fought among themselves and with the Germans and French over the rights of the region and even over what it meant to be Alsatian. Moreover, Alsatians often debated their own recent past by seeking to appropriate some specific event or some aspect of the regional culture as a means of legitimating their own vision of the region. In this way, the various contenders for regional leadership staked a claim to authority.

To examine the development of Alsatian regionalism, this project employs methods of both cultural and political history. With regard to cultural history, the works of Alsatian intellectuals—poets, playwrights, journalists, artists—come to the fore.[26] Their cultural output, whether concerned with Alsace directly or not, helped shape popular conceptions of what it meant to be Alsatian. Thus this project examines how Alsatian intellectuals articulated their conceptions of Alsatianness.

Exploring culture solely as product of a group of intellectuals, however, offers a limited perspective on the influence such people had on the development of regionalism. Culture, then, is more broadly understood as the system of meaning through which social order is communicated, reproduced, and contested.[27] If we are to grasp how Alsatians conceived of their regional community, it is necessary that the full range of expressions of regionalism be examined. By moving culture onto this broader plain, it becomes possible to examine how and why Alsatians articulated and debated multiple conceptions of the region by adding religion, language, and class into the regional mix. This study thus focuses on how language, images, and symbols were imbued with meaning and disseminated, and how they became objects of contention among Alsatians and between Alsatians and their German and French rulers.

In a parallel manner, this is a work of political history on two levels. Here, the broader level follows logically from our understanding of culture. The attempt to define systems of meaning—in this case, the nature of the region vis-à-vis the nation—is inherently political. Alsatians sought to delimit and enforce their conceptions of the region; these articulations, however, intersected with social and religious concerns, political careers, and personal understandings of Alsace's history and culture.[28] As such, these regional visions also represented attempts by social groups and individuals to shape Alsatian society and to gain, then maintain political power.

We must also therefore examine the role of politics in the more traditional sense. Alsatian political parties did not represent the only venue for the dissemination of specific visions of the region; Alsatian intellectuals and their publications and performances contributed greatly to this process. Their newspapers, periodicals, conferences, and rallies allowed party leaders to explicate their vision of Alsace, ranging from extremely conservative Catholicism to radical Communism. And although Alsatian opportunities to alter their political situation in a radical manner remained limited, local and national legislative bodies offered Alsatian representatives convenient rostra from which to argue on behalf of the region.

Alsace 1870–1890

Long before Prussia and France made Alsace a prize of war in 1870, the region had endured the ravages and enjoyed the privileges of its location on the frontier between two cultures and two distinct political entities. The French Revolution, in particular, helped pave the path for the slow, if incomplete, integration of Alsace into France. On the eve of the war of 1870–71, the upper classes spoke French, mimicked Parisian trends, and looked to Paris as their national capital; the lower classes spoke German, or the Alsatian regional dialect thereof, and had a more tenuous relationship with France.

In the summer of 1870, French and Prussian relations entered a period of crisis; Louis Napoleon contested the succession of a distant cousin of the ruling house of Prussia to the throne of Spain. In July, propelled by the scheming of Chancellor Otto von Bismarck, hostilities broke out between France and Prussia, along with Prussia's southern German allies. After brief but fierce fighting in September 1870, Napoleon III and the bulk of the French army surrendered to combined German forces.

It would take German forces several months to subdue French resistance completely; however, calls began to be put forth early for the annexation of the French provinces of Alsace and Lorraine. For nationalists such as Heinrich von Treitschke, the two regions clearly belonged to the German nation.[29] The Prussian military leadership also pushed for the annexation of Alsace and parts of Lorraine surrounding Metz. Bismarck, yielding to public pressure and the security concerns of his generals, demanded and received the concession of Alsace and the eastern part of Lorraine from the French.[30]

Thus was born the *Reichsland* (Imperial Land) of Alsace-Lorraine. Though Alsace and Lorraine were theoretically under direct control of the emperor, German authorities toyed with various schemes of how to administer the region. From 1871–1879, Eduard von Möller, a long-time Prussian bureaucrat, served as the *Oberpräsident* (high president) of Alsace-Lorraine; however, tensions between the Protestant Möller and his largely Catholic charges, overly complex administrative structures, and a nascent autonomist movement in Alsace led Bismarck to issue a new constitution and administration for Alsace-Lorraine. In particular, Bismarck hoped to nourish Alsatian particularism as a means of weaning Alsatians from their devotion to France.[31]

The new government entailed a *Statthalter* (governor) to act as the chief executive in the region instead of an *Oberpräsident*. Legislative authority rested primarily with the Bundesrat (Federal Council) and to a lesser degree with the Reichstag, the Empire's parliament. However, a local body of indirectly elected notables, the *Landesausschuss* (territorial committee, created in 1874), had limited rights to initiate legislation and had the right to approve legislation from the Bundesrat and Reichstag. The *Landesausschuss* would later gain partial and conditional control over the regional budget.

Several features of this early period of German administration stand out, especially for the later evolution of Alsatian regionalism. First, both the *Oberpräsident* and the *Statthalter* possessed wide-ranging powers to deal with "dangers to the security of the state." The so-called "dictatorship paragraph" allowed the *Oberpräsident* and later the various *Statthalter* to curtail political activities in Alsace and Lorraine sharply. Catholics and Social Democrats, suspect in the eyes of local authorities, found their efforts to form analogues to the national parties difficult, though SPD luminaries like August Bebel took a hand at organizing regional branches of the SPD. Moreover, the government also utilized the powers of the dictatorship paragraph to harass pro-French elements of the local populace. In the wake of the Boulanger crisis and the success of Francophile Alsatians in the 1887 Reichstag elections, the German authorities went so far as to impose a stringent passport system on the region's frontier with France.[32]

Such constraints upon the development of Alsatian and Lorrainer political life reflected the limited autonomy of the region. Other *Länder* (states) of the German Empire had their own legislature, administration, and Bundesrat representatives; Bavaria, Württemberg, and Baden even possessed their own military units and postal service. In contrast, the *Reichsland* had only its *Landesausschuss*, a body of limited powers with no ministerial control over the *Statthalter*. Moreover, the *Reichsland* had no representation in the Bundesrat. Additionally, the region's administrators overwhelmingly hailed from across the Rhine.[33]

German policies did not merely imply political control over the region or political coercion of its people. Fueled by nationalistic zeal and the firm belief that Alsatians were merely Germans misguided by several centuries of French rule, German administrators, educators, and intellectuals sought to inculcate German patriotism in their Alsatian charges.[34] Often abrasive to the local population, these champions of the German nation made only limited headway, often offending local sensibilities, for example by trying to integrate children into one school regardless of confession or combining male and female students, a taboo by local standards. Parallel to their efforts to use primary education as a tool by which the local populace could be Germanized, the Germans sought to create a first-class university to similar ends. By creating a top-flight institution, Germans wanted to demonstrate their superiority to the local populace as well as to the French; moreover, Alsatians studying at the university, in theory, would deepen their loyalty to the German nation.[35] German rulers even inscribed their nationalistic vision of the region in Alsace's public spaces, filling its landscape with monuments and architectural flourishes meant to link Alsace and Germany.

For those living in Alsace, annexation meant an abrupt change in political, economic, and social fortunes and generated a complex series of responses. Several factors influenced Alsatian attitudes toward their new sovereign that paralleled the religious, social, and linguistic divides in the region. Confessionally, Alsace was overwhelmingly Roman Catholic. In Lower Alsace, the northern half of the region, 70 percent of the population was Catholic compared to 89 percent in Upper Alsace. The remainder of the populace mostly practiced some form of Protestantism (Lutheran or Calvinist), with a small Jewish minority rounding out the religious mix. The highly Catholic nature of the region would significantly shape the Alsatian response to German annexation as church leaders feared control by Protestant-dominated Germany, a concern born out during Bismarck's anti-Catholic *Kulturkampf*.[36] The Catholic clergy managed to parlay their influence into electoral success, building one of the dominant (though not always unified) parties in the region, a party that was often a thorn in the side of the German (and later French) administration.

If confession helped to shape Alsatian political life, so too did social and linguistic concerns. Here, the two elements are more difficult to disaggregate. Regional notables, whether urban industrialists or rural clergy and landowners, primarily spoke French. By dint of their superior economic position, many of these Francophile Alsatians could afford to remain Francophile. They sent their sons to French universities, enrolled their daughters in Parisian finishing schools, and maintained close relationships with kin and friends across the border. It was from this group that the principal patrons of Alsatian arts and culture as well as the most stridently vocal opponents of the German regime would come.

In contrast, the lower classes of Alsace—mostly urban workers and rural laborers—spoke a dialect of German. Not only did a shared language permit swifter assimilation of this group into German society, but the lower classes did not have the means to maintain their loyalty to France. While German administrative and religious policies may have rankled many Alsatians, they nonetheless adapted to life in Germany by attending German-run schools and serving in the German military. Moreover, their politics tended to run either toward Social Democracy, at times putting them at odds with their wealthier neighbors. Over time, though not wholly supportive of the German government, the lower classes began to be assimilated into the social and political milieu of the German Empire. Thus, as social and linguistic divides began to evolve into more formal political divides, it seems hardly surprising that divisions cropped up among Alsatians related to their needs within the German Empire.[37]

While Alsace's complex confessional, social, and linguistic demographics would gradually shape the region's relationship with Germany, annexation also brought about immediate responses to German rule. Most significantly, over one hundred thousand Alsatians left the region for France in the years directly following the Franco-Prussian War. Under the terms of the Treaty of Frankfurt, Alsatians could opt to remain French citizens, but would have to relocate to France; in all, 132,239 residents opted for France. While figures remain unclear as both to the number of Alsatians who actually departed as well as to the count of those who left without formal declaration, such responses point to the short-term dissatisfaction with the change in geopolitical circumstances in 1871. Such large-scale migration, taken in conjunction with those who emigrated over the period of German rule, represented a weakening of the Francophile milieu in Alsace. Those Francophiles who remained, however, had the financial means to remain connected to French culture and served as the principal proponents of a French vision of the region.

This presence was exhibited as early as February 1871, several months before the Treaty of Frankfurt formalized German occupation of the region. Alsatian representatives to the National Assembly at Bordeaux argued that Alsace should not be allowed to fall into German hands. Such protest, however, did not find unanimous approval among Alsatians; in the Assembly elections of early 1871, several Protestant businessmen such as Jacques Kablé and August Schneegans sought to maximize Alsace's place within the German Empire, in effect acknowledging the inevitability of German occupation.[38] These divisions remained between autonomists and the *protestaires* ("protesters," or those Alsatian leaders who protested the annexation of Alsace, for example, making a declaration similar to that of Bordeaux in the Reichstag in 1874). Well into the 1880s, when these political camps began to disband, Alsatian leaders were increasingly replaced with emergent political parties whose contours were analogous to those of the German mainstream, specifically Liberals, Social Democrats, and Catholics (Center).[39]

The basic foundations of Alsatian politics began to take shape in the late 1880s and 1890s. As internal differences began to take precedence over a unified opposition to German rule, divisions began to emerge in how Alsatians viewed their place in the German Empire. German administrators complicated these developments by at once trying to conciliate Alsatians and to compel them to renounce their attachment to France. Never strong enough to force the issue, never agreeable enough to win over the local inhabitants, these measures left Alsatians with the difficult task of defining their political, social, and cultural relationship to Germany and to one another.

Notes

1. Karl Graf von Wedel, Circular to the Bezirkspräsidenten, ADBR 247 D 23(b), AN F7/13396.
2. The idea of "Alsace-Lorraine" resulted from the simultaneous annexation and subsequent joint administration of the two areas after 1871. In addition, the provinces were traditionally paired in French in revanchist discourse. The two regions, however, had separate linguistic and religious demographics, distinct German dialects, and differing customs and traditions. Moreover, although groups from the two regions often collaborated in regionalist initiatives, contemporaries clearly viewed the two regions as separate. These differences, combined with the fact that Alsace's post-1919 regionalist movement was far stronger than its Lorraine counterpart, all militate in favor of this study's focus solely on Alsace.
3. The region's upper classes tended to speak French, while the working and rural classes spoke German, or a regional variant thereof. See Stephen Harp, *Learning to be Loyal: Primary Schooling as Nation Building in Alsace and Lorraine* (Dekalb, IL, 1998), 12–13.
4. According to the 1871 figures, Alsace-Lorraine included in its population 1,200,000 Catholics, 250,000 adherents of the Lutheran and Reformed Churches, and 40,000 Jews. Only 16,000 of the Protestants lived in Lorraine. See Daniel Silverman, *Reluctant Union: Alsace-Lorraine and Imperial Germany, 1871–1918* (University Park, PA, 1972), 223 n. 1.
5. Christopher Harvie, *The Rise of Regional Europe*, Historical Connections, ed. Geoffrey Cossick, Tom Scott et. al. (London, 1994).
6. Allan Mitchell, "'A Real Foreign Country': Bavarian Particularism in Imperial Germany, 1870–1918," *Francia* 7 (1979): 587–96.
7. Michael Keating, *The New Regionalism in Western Europe* (Cheltenham, UK, 1998), 9.
8. Ibid., 10–11.
9. *Heimat* is a difficult word to define easily, either in German or English. While "homeland" is a literal translation of the word, it fails to capture the multiple connotations and emotional resonance of the word. Anton Kaes, "Germany as Memory," in *From Hitler to Heimat: The Return of History as Film* (Cambridge, MA, 1989), 165.
10. Celia Applegate, *A Nation of Provincials: The German Idea of Heimat* (Berkeley, CA, 1990); Alon Confino, *The Nation as Local Metaphor: Württemberg, Imperial Germany, and National*

Memory, 1871–1918 (Chapel Hill, NC, 1997). This is not to say that Confino and Applegate thoroughly agree on all aspects of Heimat movements. In particular, Applegate views the identification of region to nation as a "trickle-up" effect, whereby increased attachment to the Heimat can translate into a heightened sense of belonging to the nation. Confino, in contrast, argues that a reciprocal effect exists; just as the region can serve to bond local citizens to the nation, the region can be appropriated at the national level, homogenized, and reexported back to the region, thus leading to greater similarity in how both nation and region are envisioned. See Applegate, *Nation of Provincials*, 11–19; Confino, *Nation as Local Metaphor*, 158–89 Applegate, in addition questioning national use of the local metaphor in Confino's account, also critiques Confino's understanding of the social bases of Heimat movements, his discussion of the relationship between Heimat movements and the Sonderweg thesis, and his concept of how the idea of Heimat was used in wartime propaganda between 1914–1918. See Celia Applegate, "Heimat and the Varieties of Regional History," *Central European History* 33, no. 1 (2000): 109–15.

11. Abigail Green, "The Federal Alternative? A New View of Modern German History," *The Historical Journal* 46, no. 1 (2003): 187–202; Jennifer Jenkins, *Provincial Modernity: Local Culture and Liberal Politics in Fin-de-Siècle Hamburg* (Ithaca, NY, 2003); Dan. S White, "Regionalism and Particularism," in *Imperial Germany: A Historiographical Companion*, ed. Roger Chickering (Westport, CT, 1996), 131–55.
12. Maurice Agulhon, "The Center and the Periphery," in *Rethinking France: Les Lieux Des Mémoire*. vol. 1, *The State*, ed. Pierre Nora (Chicago, 2001), 53–76; Sharif Gemie. *Brittany 1750—1950: The Invisible Nation* (Cardiff, 2007); Stéphane Gerson. *The Pride of Place: Local Memories & Political Culture in Nineteenth-Century France* (Ithaca, NY, 2003); Robert Gildea, *The Past in French History* (New Haven, CT, 1994); Kolleen M. Guy, *When Champagne Became French: Wine and the Making of a National Identity* (Baltimore, 2003); Benjamin J. Lammers, "National Identity on the French Periphery: The End of Peasants into Frenchmen?" *National Identities* 1, no. 1 (1999): 81–87; Anne-Marie Thiesse, *Ecrire la France: Le mouvement littéraire régionaliste de langue française entre la Belle Epoque et la Libération*. Collection "Ethnologies." (Paris, 1991); Anne-Marie Thiesse, *Ils Apprenaient La France : L'exaltation des Régions dans le discours patriotique* (Paris, 1997); Julian Wright, *The Regionalist Movement in France, 1890–1914: Jean Charles-Brun and French Political Thought* (Oxford, 2003); Patrick Young, "Of Pardons, Loss, and Longing: The Tourist's Pursuit of Originality in Brittany, 1890–1935," *French Historical Studies* 30, no. 2 (2007): 269–304.
13. Mitchell, "A Real Foreign Country," 589.
14. Caroline Ford, *Creating the Nation in Provincial France: Religion and Political Identity in Brittany* (Princeton, NJ, 1993).
15. Benedict Anderson, *Imagined Communities: Reflections on the Origin and Spread of Nationalism*, 2nd ed. (London, 1991); Homi Bhabha, "DissemiNation: Time, Narrative, and the Margins of the Modern Nation," in *Nation and Narration*, ed. Homi Bhahba (London, 1990; reprint, 1994), 291–322; Ernest Gellner, *Nations and Nationalism* (Ithaca, NY, 1983); Eugen Weber, *Peasants into Frenchmen: The Modernization of Rural France, 1870–1914* (Stanford, CA, 1976).
16. Celia Applegate, "A Europe of Regions: Reflections on the Historiography of Sub-National Places in Modern Times," *American Historical Review* (1999): 1157–82; David Laven and Timothy Baycroft, "Border Regions and Identity," *European Review of History—Revue européenne d'histoire* 15, no. 3 (June 2008): 255–75; Maiken Umbach, "Introduction," *European Review of History—Revue européenne d'histoire* 15, no. 3 (June 2008): 235–42.
17. Rudy Koshar, *Germany's Transient Pasts: Preservation and National Memory in the Twentieth Century* (Chapel Hill, NC, 1998), 7–9.
18. Etienne Balibar, "The Nation Form: History and Ideology," in *Becoming National*, ed. Geoff Eley and Ronald Suny (Oxford, 1996), 132–50; Prasenjit Duara, "Historicizing

National Identity, or Who Imagines What and When," in *Becoming National*, ed. Geoff Eley and Ronald Suny (Oxford, 1996), 151–78.
19. Christian Baechler, *Le parti catholique alsacien 1890–1939, du Reichsland à la République jacobine* (Paris, 1982); Stefan Fisch, "Assimilation und Eigenständigkeit: Zur Wiedervereinigung des Elsass mit dem Frankreich der dritten Republik nach 1918," *Historisches Jahrbuch* 117, no. 1 (1997): 111–28; Jena M. Gaines, "The Spectrum of Alsatian Autonomism" (PhD diss., University of Virginia, 1990); Silverman, *Reluctant Union*.
20. Daniel Silverman has explained that it is difficult to note these numbers exactly. Approximately 130,000 Alsatians officially opted to leave after 1871, but not all followed through; conversely, many Alsatians left without formally opting. In addition, numerous Alsatians emigrated to France to pursue economic activities or to avoid conscription into the German army. Silverman has suggested that approximately 450,000 Alsatians left the region under the decades of German rule. Silverman, *Reluctant Union*, 66–70.
21. Samuel Goodfellow, *Between the Swastika and the Cross of Lorraine* (Dekalb, IL, 1999).
22. Applegate, *Nation of Provincials*; Confino, *Nation as Local Metaphor*; Ford, *Creating the Nation*; Shanny Peer, *France on Display: Peasants, Provincials, and Folklore in the 1937 Paris World's Fair* (New York, 1998). For a broader discussion of the phenomenon, see Applegate, "Europe of Regions," 1157–82.
23. Siegfried Welchlein, "Saxons into Germans: The Progress of the National Idea in Saxony after 1866" (paper presented at Memory, Democracy, and the Mediated Nation. Political Cultures and Regional Identities in Germany, 1848–1998, Toronto, 18–20 September 1998).
24. Gildea, *Past in French History*, 166–213.
25. Goodfellow, *Between the Swastika and the Cross of Lorraine*, 14.
26. Geoff Eley and Ronald Suny, "Introduction," *Becoming National* (Oxford, 1996); 16–17.
27. Koshar, *Germany's Transient Pasts*, 1–15; James Gelvin, *Divided Loyalties and Mass Politics in Syria at the Close of Empire* (Berkeley, CA, 1998), 10–11; Julie Skurski, "The Ambiguities of Authenticity in Latin America: *Doña Bárbara* and the Construction of National Identity," in *Becoming National*, ed. Geoff Eley and Ronald Suny (Oxford, 1996), 371–402.
28. Keith Baker, *Inventing the French Revolution* (Cambridge, 1990), 4–5; Gildea, *Past in French History*, 8–9.
29. "These lands are ours by the right of the conqueror, and we want to dispose of them by a higher right, by the right of the German nation which cannot allow its prodigal sons to become estranged forever from the German Reich. . . . We want to restore them to their true selves, against their will. . . . We call on them—on all those strong German men who once put our spiritual imprint upon language and custom, art and life of the Upper Rhineland—and before the 19th century will have drawn to its close the world shall acknowledge that the spirit of Erwin von Steinbach and Sebastian Brandt is still alive, and that we are fulfilling merely a demand of national honor when we ignore the wishes of present day Alsatians." See Heinrich von Treitschke, "Was fordern wir Frankreich," *Zehn Jahre Deutscher Kämpfe: Schriften zur Tagespolitik* (Berlin, 1897), reprinted in Andreas Dorpalen, *Heinrich von Treitschke* (New Haven, 1957), 165–66.
30. Otto Pflanze, *Bismarck and the Development of Germany*. vol. 1, *The Period of Unification, 1815–1871*, 2nd ed. (Princeton, NJ, 1990), 484–89; Lothar Gall, "Das Problem Elsass-Lothringen," in *Reichsgründung, 1870/71. Tatsachen, Kontroversen, Interpretationen*, ed. Theodor Schieder and Ernst Deuerlein (Stuttgart, 1970), 365–85.
31. Silverman, *Reluctant Union*, 38–39.
32. Christian Baechler, *Le parti catholique*, 14–18.
33. Bernard Vogler, *Histoire politique de l'Alsace* (Strasbourg, 1995), 178–83. For an eyewitness account, see Friedrich Meinecke's description of German-Alsatian relations in Friedrich Meinecke, *Erinnerungen, 1901–1919. Strassburg, Freiburg, Berlin* (Stuttgart, 1949), 20.
34. Harp, *Learning to be Loyal*.

35. John E. Craig, *Scholarship and Nation Building: The Universities of Strasbourg and Alsatian Society, 1870–1939* (Chicago, 1984).
36. A. Wahl and J.-C. Richez, *L'Alsace entre France et Allemagne, 1850–1950* (Strasbourg, 1994).
37. Silverman, *Reluctant Union*, 66–70.
38. Ibid., 200–207.
39. Jean-Marie Mayeur, *Autonomie et politique en Alsace. La Constitution de 1911* (Paris, 1970), 25–36.

Chapter 1

ALSACE REBORN
EMERGING VISIONS OF ALSACE, 1895–1913

In the waning decades of the nineteenth century, a small band of Alsatians sought to preserve and promote the region's unique cultural heritage. The local dialect, regional customs, traditional dress, and the area's history became objects of interest for these enthusiastic regionalists. For contemporaries, these efforts to celebrate all things Alsatian represented a rebirth of Alsatian culture; thus, the movement as a whole came to be known as the Alsatian Renaissance. For some historians such as Jean-Claude Richez and Bernard Vogler, however, this period of cultural ferment represents not a rebirth of traditional Alsatian regional culture, but rather its invention in modern form.[1]

To foster a stronger regional identity, cultural leaders such as Charles Spindler, Gustave Stoskopf, and Pierre Bucher drew upon the local dialect, traditions, and architecture to elaborate multiple conceptions of Alsatianness. Such images resonated with the local populace, but also limited the freedom of such regionalists to promote a specific, politically laden vision of Alsace.[2] Francophile regionalists could not simply ignore the fact that the vast majority of the population spoke the German-based Alsatian dialect; pro-German regionalists had to deal with the region's fond remembrance of the heady days of Napoleon's rule when Alsatian generals had covered themselves in glory in the name of France.

A deep conflict over goals underlay this process of cultural revival. While many Alsatians remained to varying degrees ambivalent or even hostile to the German presence, Alsatians were divided over how to attenuate German influence. Some Alsatians promoted Alsatian culture and the region's uniqueness without engaging overtly in the question of Alsatian national belonging. Others, believing Alsace to be French, agitated to remind Alsatians of their "true" national heritage. And some Alsatians even took the opposite tack, arguing that Alsatians were German, and therefore encouraged the process of Germanization. Across the political spectrum, Alsatians began to concern themselves with the region's traditions, customs, and history; the meaning ascribed to each, however, diverged widely.

Notes for this section begin on page 47.

The efforts to revive Alsatian customs and traditions, the drive to give them meaning within the larger context of Alsace's relationship with Germany and France, and the struggles among diverse groups of Alsatians to control these activities form the subject of this chapter and much of the next. In particular, this chapter examines the context in which Alsatian regionalism developed as a cultural revival under the guidance of men such as Charles Spindler, Anselm Laugel, and Pierre Bucher. The chapter then turns to consider the careers and publications of three prominent Alsatians, Gustave Stoskopf, Jean-Jacques Waltz (better known by the diminutive form of his name in the Alsatian dialect, Hansi), and Friedrich Lienhard, each of whom promoted different conceptions of Alsace. Finally, the chapter assesses some of the explicit debates over the nature of Alsatianness in the first decade of the twentieth century. By examining these divergent visions of Alsace, this chapter argues that Alsatian regionalism, rather than monolithic in nature, emerged as diverse, at times contradictory, currents from the outset.

The "Renaissance Alsacienne"

In 1895, Charles Spindler, a young, German-educated Alsatian, drew up a prototype of a periodical entitled *Images Alsaciennes* (*Alsatian Images*). Seeking advice on the project, Spindler showed an unedited version of the journal to his friend Anselm Laugel; Laugel, in turn, queried his friend: "Images, I grant you, but why Alsatian?" Spindler later explained Laugel's confusion: "In his eyes, Alsace had no life of its own capable of justifying this appellation. There remained in his conception a combination of two, recently French departments."[3] Laugel's initial skepticism concerning the project was understandable; a veteran of the French army and member of the movement that protested German rule in the 1870s and 1880s, Laugel did not view Alsace as an independent entity, but rather as a part of France. Over time, however, Laugel become a fierce proponent and leading patron of the "Alsatian Renaissance."

The Alsatian Renaissance, in contrast to both the more politically driven protest and autonomist movements of the 1870s and 1880s, represented a form of cultural regionalism. Though the desire for greater political freedom for Alsace did not abate—nor did the hope of some for a return to France entirely wither—a small group of Alsatians sought to revive Alsatian traditions, celebrate the area's history, and highlight particular regional customs. While the love of local culture influenced the cultural revival, ulterior motives also provided impetus for the movement. By invoking the region's culture, local advocates could argue that the maintenance of the region's ties to French culture and civilization constituted an integral aspect of the Alsatian character. Moreover, by celebrating their own uniqueness, Alsatians could distinguish themselves from the Germans recently arrived in Alsace.

The cultural revival, however, should not merely be viewed as a response to German rule, nor was it unique to Alsace. Alsatian politicians, often local notables, clad themselves in a regionalist cloak to blend in with, and therefore gain the support of, their fellow Alsatians in an era of mass political participation.[4] Such efforts paralleled those of German elites in other *Länder* to revive and promote local traditions in order to buttress their place in society.[5] More generally, many regions of Europe witnessed a growth of interest in regional traditions and history; Alsace, in this way, reflected a larger pattern of development in fin-de-siècle Europe.

The Alsatian Renaissance of the 1890s rapidly expanded the range and depth of regionalist cultural activities. Charles Spindler and Anselm Laugel led a protracted and wide-ranging campaign to promote Alsatian culture. Spindler, born in 1865, had grown up in the small town of Borsch and later Strasbourg before training as an artist in Düsseldorf, Berlin, and Munich. Laugel, in contrast, had closer ties to Alsace's French past. Born in 1851, Laugel had served in the French army before returning to Alsace to oversee his investments and engage in local politics. An avid art patron, Laugel met the aspiring artist Spindler in the late 1880s. Laugel, although never fully relinquishing the idea that Alsace was a French province, nonetheless was slowly won over to Spindler's project and helped provide financial support to Spindler's vision.[6]

Spindler's initial activities were relatively modest. He began to collect Alsatian traditional dress, furniture, farm and kitchen implements, and other objects of art and daily life with the goal of placing them on display; his collection would provide the foundation for the holdings of the Musée alsacien. The pair also brought together like-minded individuals to Laugel's home in St. Leonard to discuss Alsatian culture, among them Gustave Stoskopf, later the leading playwright of the Alsatian dialect theater. And while Spindler's *Images Alsaciennes* never got off the ground, it provided the basis for one of the group's most important undertakings, the *Revue alsacienne illustrée* (*Alsatian Illustrated Review*, hereafter *RAI*).[7]

The *RAI* became one of the most important institutions of the Alsatian Renaissance. The 1898 prospectus of the *RAI* laid out the journal's goals: "Our program is to report all that which currently derives from our own heritage, all that which takes place within the patrimony of the nation, and all that which constitutes eternal Alsace."[8] Laugel wrote and Spindler illustrated some of the initial contributions. Most articles focused on Alsatian history, its landscape, and its popular art. The journal at its outset possessed an ecumenical spirit that celebrated Alsace's "dual culture" and contained articles in French and German. Moreover, the editors invited local German dignitaries deemed sympathetic to Alsatian culture to pen articles; for example, the wife of the German secretary of state for the *Reichsland*, Alberta von Puttkamer, offered an article for the first edition.

In 1901 Pierre Bucher assumed the editorship of the magazine; Spindler stepped into the background to pursue his artistic interests. Under

Bucher—a native Alsatian and Paris-educated doctor with strong Francophile leanings—the *RAI* managed to gain a consistent list of subscribers (approximately one thousand).⁹ The periodical took an increasingly anti-German tone, slowly eliminating articles in German and dialect while publishing editorials critical of German cultural policies. Bucher's sentiments concerning Alsace's national destiny were clear. In an 1899 letter to Maurice Barrès, Bucher wrote:

> No matter the state of affairs, France is its culture and having the good fortune of enjoying it. It seems insupportable to us to return to the barbarisms of a people without generosity and tact.... We thus have every right to protest against the moral annexation, while even admitting that we can do nothing about the political annexation.... When I see this invasion always aggrandizing the Germanic elements and the prodigious efforts of the administration to extirpate all that is the French essence and I sense sometimes that despite themselves [Alsatians] lose the exact notion of the French thing [*la chose française*], I have a heavy heart close to discouragement.¹⁰

Bucher used the *RAI* promote the French cause in numerous ways both subtle and obvious. For example, Bucher invited Barrès to offer occasional contributions that stressed the Alsace's "true" character. More importantly, Bucher added a section entitled *Chronique d'Alsace-Lorraine* (*Chronicle of Alsace-Lorraine*), a quarterly supplement that included book and play reviews, news of important events, and editorials, many of which were critical of the German regime. Later detached from the journal, the *Chronique* transformed into the *Cahiers d'Alsace-Lorraine*, a highly Francophile and politically charged publication.¹¹ Despite the separation, the damage was done. Less Francophile supporters of the *RAI* such as Stoskopf no longer contributed and even Charles Spindler increasingly took his distance from the project.¹²

The *RAI* did not solely focus on Francophile influences in its sixteen years of publication (1898–1914), but took a deep interest in the broad range of Alsatian culture. For example, the journal gave ample space to the examination of Alsatian popular culture, including painting, sculpture, and styles of Alsatian furniture.¹³ Other articles focused on the place of Sainte Odile, the patron saint of the region, in the area's lore and, in the form of Mt. Sainte-Odile, the region's landscape.¹⁴

Laugel laid out this element of the journal's mission in a multipart article on Alsace's popular culture. Writing in part to celebrate the opening of the Musée alsacien, the series had two goals.¹⁵ First, Laugel wished to promote the art of the people, not "of the great lords," but rather of "the small people, even the farmers, whose resources are modest" in order to increase their knowledge of their heritage and to save them from "intellectual and moral poisons" of "alcohol, the noxious atmosphere of the inn and the cabaret." Second, he argued for preservation of local culture as "one knows the vandalism committed each day, when, under the pretext of restoration or improvement, those venerable vestiges which bear witness in favor of the culture and morals of our ancestors are made to disappear." This "vandalism" referred to German efforts to imprint Alsace, especially in its urban areas, with its own art, architecture, and customs. Later, Laugel would make this point yet clearer: "Our old Alsatian popular art, which has flourished in our villages and cities for the last twenty years, is attached to the genius of our race in the most intimate fashion. All its manifestations simply reflect our national soul."[16]

In general, Laugel's work recalled an alleged heyday of Alsatian culture that had increasingly been undermined by industrialization and urbanization.[17] Laugel sought to promote specific elements of Alsatian culture. First, Alsatian architecture, with its half-timbered houses, streetside windows, and stenciled religious and philosophical sayings on the outside of buildings were emblematic of Alsatian hospitality and sociability. Second, the great care and concern that went into the creation of Alsatian traditional furniture, especially in the *Stube*, or common room, demonstrated the Alsatian concern with quality and family life. Third, the traditional female costumes, used to celebrate regional and religious festivals as well as life's important moments such as marriage and baptism, assumed a prominent position in the constellation of Alsatian popular art. Finally, the region's numerous festivals and holidays reflected the region's sociability and love of conviviality.[18]

Laugel's essay highlights two major components of the *RAI*. First, the *RAI* sought to outline what precisely it meant to be Alsatian. Not only did the Alsatians enjoy a particular architecture, mode of dress, and even lifestyle, but these customs were embedded in the very soil of the land. This conception of Alsatian culture was conjoined with a particular understanding of Alsatian history that firmly posited the Alsatians as the true and rightful inhabitants of the region. Moreover, it also demonstrates the second aim of the *RAI*: to set Alsatians apart from their French neighbors, and more importantly, the Germans who currently held sway in the area.

How, then, did the *RAI* emphasize the French, or at least non-German, elements of Alsatian history? The primary method of the journal lay in its stress on Alsace's "dual culture," i.e., the synthesis of elements of French and German culture. Articles penned by Werner Wittich, Otto Flake, and Fritz Kiener (a German-born professor, the son of a German bureaucrat, and an Alsatian lawyer respectively) explored the cultural history of the region and argued for the maintenance of both national cultures present in the region that together nourished Alsace's unique culture. Arguments for the persistence of both cultures gave the *RAI* a stake in the raging debates over the nature of region, nation, and the Alsatian character in the first decade of the 1900s. The notion of a dual culture allowed Bucher and his fellow travelers to promote French-oriented activities under the aegis of preserving Alsace's unique cultural legacy.

One means by which the *RAI*'s editors accomplished this goal was to publish short biographies of famous Alsatian men under the title "*biographies alsaciennes.*" The vast majority of the short pieces concerned artists who ranged from the famous—Gustave Doré or Jean-Jacques Henner—to the obscure, for example, the nineteenth-century Strasbourg pastor and painter, Eugen Ensfelder.[19] Most either worked in Paris or stayed in Alsace, and at least five had been inducted into the French Legion of Honor. Such a slanted view of Alsace's contribution to art history is not surprising; most of the selected artists were active in the mid- to late 1800s and therefore came in large part from the French-oriented elite. In contrast, a German understanding of Alsatian cultural history would have highlighted the great writers of the Middle Ages—for example, Gottfried von Strasbourg or Sebastian Brant—rather than nineteenth-century artists. The focus on Alsatian artists rather than Alsatian generals in Napoleon's armies served to tie Alsace to France without provoking German authorities.

Beyond the confines of the publication itself, the *RAI* gained added importance as a nexus for collaboration among various Alsatians concerned with the region's cultural patrimony. For example, regular contributors Ferdinand and Léon Dollinger, along with Bucher, took up Spindler's idea for an Alsatian museum in Strasbourg and realized the project in 1907. Moreover, Gustave Stoskopf, one of the most important writers of the Alsatian theater, and Hansi, caricaturist par excellence, received much initial support from the periodical and contributed regularly for short periods of time (Stoskopf roughly from 1898–1905, Hansi 1904–1906). Finally, Bucher used the offices of the periodical as a base of operations for founding associations geared toward maintaining French aspects of Alsatian culture.

What importance should one accord to the *Revue alsacienne illustreé*? Disregarding the issue of financial wherewithal, leisure time, and desire, the average Alsatian could not have read the *RAI*, at least not the French content, after thirty years of German education. Moreover, there existed limited crossover between the educated Alsatian and German classes; therefore, the *RAI* would have had little influence pushing Germans to a more complex understanding of Alsatian culture. Yet the journal had immense influence, especially in promoting the notion of an Alsatian dual culture. By examining Alsatian art, culture, and history, the *RAI* put forth a conception of Alsace that was at once a cosmopolitan blend of French and German culture and deeply rooted in the soil, villages, and traditions of the region. Though the *RAI* was occasionally contradictory in its conception of Alsatianness—the promotion of a cosmopolitan dual culture at times clashed with a more territorial-bound, French, and even, as Jean-Claude Richez has noted, racial conception of Alsatianness—it remained an influential periodical among the pro-French and pro-Alsatian elements of Alsatian society in defining what it meant to be Alsatian.[20]

A German Alsace?

If the *RAI* offered one vision of Alsace, Germans and some Alsatians living in the region presented a different conception of the region. Many Germans had a quite nationalistic view of Alsace; nationally minded German journalists, administrators, and professionals (such as teachers) viewed Alsatians as Germans by virtue of their culture and language. While this ethnic-cultural definition dominated German understandings of Alsatian culture and national belonging, a minority of Germans, such as the economist Werner Wittich, appreciated the mixed Franco-German heritage of the region. Yet others appreciated Alsatian culture for itself: the dialect, customs, and traditions. This attention given local culture also had much in common with the work of the *RAI*.

German interest in Alsatian culture is not surprising. Germans in Bavaria, the Palatinate, and Württemberg had created societies to study the local cultures of these respective German regions. Germans who moved to Alsace cultivated their interest in local cultures generally by examining Alsatian culture particularly. As Alon Confino has shown, such activities ranged from the preservation of local medieval ruins to the creation of *Heimat* museums to the foundation of historical societies.[21] Therefore Germans living in the *Reichsland* were following similar pursuits to their countrymen across the Rhine. The difference, however, was twofold. First, Alsatians and Germans did not easily mix. The historian Friedrich Meinecke once described his relations with Alsatians during his time at the University of Strasbourg as "formal" and noted that living in the *Reichsland*, given the lack of contact between Germans and the native population, was akin to living in a colony.[22] Second, the German interest in Alsace's charms did not extend to the region's French legacy.

Numerous journals such as *Erwinia* and *Die elsässische Monatsschrift* (*The Alsatian Monthly*) explored the Alsatian dialect, history, and customs. The most important of these journals, catering to a largely German audience in the *Reichsland*, was the *Jahrbuch für Geschichte, Sprache und Literatur* (*Yearbook for History, Language, and Literature*, hereafter *JfGSL*), published by the Historical-Literary Branch Club, a smaller club within the Vogesen Club. Unlike the *RAI* whose support came from the indigenous Francophile population, the *JfGSL*, judging from its published membership lists, drew upon the mostly German ranks of the regional administration, professional classes, and to a lesser extent, the business community. The Historical-Literary Branch Club enjoyed a membership of approximately 2,500 and published well over 3,000 copies of the journal, with extra copies being sent to like-minded organizations across Germany.[23]

The focus of the journal was Alsatian culture. One series entitled "Customs and Habits" provided annual reports on various festivals and celebrations. The journal also offered studies on dialect; indeed, some of the journal's contributors compiled a dialect dictionary. Finally, some articles focused on the ties between Germans and Alsace, discussing, for example, the sojourns of Goethe and Herder in Alsace. Missing from the journal was any mention of the French heritage of the region. Instead, the editors of the *JfGSL* projected a vision of Alsace that resonated with its readers' more general experiences with local and regional cultures across Germany.

The editors were aware, however, of the struggle to define Alsace as historically German or French. The *JfGSL* contributed to the German side of the debate by attempting to paint Alsatian history in German hues. In particular, much like the *RAI* with its *"biographies alsaciennes,"* the *JfGSL* focused on the place of important German artists, writers, and other intellectuals in the history of the region. Such Alsatians included the medieval writer Sebastian Brandt, who wrote *Das Narrenschiff* (*The Ship of Fools*) and Erwin von Steinbach, who designed the Strasbourg cathedral. Moreover, the *JfGSL* also tried to reshape the narrative of Alsatian history by arguing, for example, that the true annexation of Alsace came in 1681, when Louis XIV took possession of Strasbourg, not in 1871.[24] In a similar vein, Emil von Borries offered an apology for the bombardment of Strasbourg and the destruction of the famous library there by placing the blame on both German and French missteps during the 1870 campaign.[25]

The German vision of Alsace, however, made little inroads into the circles of the local intelligentsia; the *RAI* stood as the most important journal of the Alsatian revival among Alsatians. This is not to say that the *JfGSL* failed to influence Alsatians. One of the most ardent interwar autonomists, Karl Roos, whose politics would slide from autonomy to separatism and would eventually become tinged with Nazism, made contributions to the journal as a student at the university. Thus, while the journal never challenged the *RAI* for influence, it both introduced some young Alsatians to a Germanized version of local culture and gave a platform for Germanophile writers, such as Friedrich Lienhard.

Lienhard, born in the town of Rothbach in Upper Alsace in 1860, came from a Protestant family. The family, despite the fact his father taught French, spoke German, especially during catechization. Lienhard attended a German *gymnasium* and there, according to his own recollections, developed a desire to become a writer. He published his first poems in 1886 while at the University of Strasbourg. During a stint in Berlin, Lienhard stood vigil with a "mass of people" as Kaiser Wilhelm I lay dying in 1888.[26]

According to his memoirs Lienhard began to "cultivate his Germanness"[27] while at the university, a trend that continued in his later career. Indeed, Lienhard eventually opted to move to Germany and did not return to Alsace. Yet he was also grounded in Alsatian culture. He spoke the dialect at home and loved the *Trachten* worn on holidays. Thus he was touched personally by split loyalties and split cultural influences in Alsace. Lienhard witnessed the misunderstandings and vexations between Alsatians and Germans as the two groups groped toward a modus vivendi in the years following the Franco-Prussian War. Some of the family's relatives, including a close cousin, left the region for France. Lienhard commented that his immediate family did not "want to be a mishmash, neither meat nor fish, neither French nor German. We were too healthy for that."[28] Instead of living in the "double culture," he and his brother were raised as "good Germans." Lienhard promoted a *Hochdeutsch*, thoroughly German vision of Alsace, especially as he became immersed in German culture at the university—writing that one of his life goals was "the introduction of our Alsace into German culture."[29]

Although some historians have argued that Lienhard served as an apostle for Germany's regional diversity,[30] within Alsace he appeared as an evangelist for the German nation. With his earliest publications, Lienhard aimed not to promote Alsace, but instead saw himself as part of the larger German literary world. Indeed, one of Lienhard's first jobs was as a writer for *Die Heimat*, a journal published in Berlin. Lienhard, moreover, maintained ties with the Alsatian cultural world, at least the cultural world of German Alsace. One of his regular correspondents was Christian Schmitt, a poet who regularly contributed to the *JfGSL* and who had helped found the Alsabund, a literary society with strong support among the German populace of Alsace. And just as his German literary friends had only a limited audience among Alsatians, so too did his own work. Lienhard failed to find a local following.[31]

Following his failure in Alsace in the late 1890s and early 1900s, Lienhard moved to Weimar to pursue his art. This did not mean that he lost all contact with Alsace. His poems, novels, and plays continued to draw upon his knowledge of the region; one of his books of poems even contained drawings by Charles Spindler. Moreover, Lienhard felt strongly about developments in Alsace. In particular, he rejected the concept of a double-culture as "hermaphroditic," disliked journals like the *RAI*, and condemned the Alsatian theater for lacking artistic merit. Some of his novels likewise promoted such tendencies.[32] *Oberlin*, his most successful novel, portrayed the French Revolution as a negative development for the region.[33]

Lienhard left Alsace during the war and moved to Weimar. Michel Ertz has suggested that Lienhard, who never returned to Alsace, remembered his homeland fondly yet remained bitter that Alsace was no longer German. Lienhard may have drawn much of his material from his childhood in Alsace, but may not have understood the broader situation in the region as his upbringing, and general environment, encouraged a pro-German conception of Alsatianness. His rejection of the dialect as an artistic language and lack of empathy for French culture set him apart from many of his contemporaries. Lienhard enjoyed little fame in Alsace following the war outside the occasional mention in the autonomist press.[34] Some young men of the next generation would also adopt a love for German culture and seek to pursue this love under French rule. Yet their vision of a German Alsace, much like Lienhard's, was in the minority before the war and gained little popularity thereafter.

Gustave Stoskopf and the Denationalized Region

The *Revue alsacienne illustrée* served as a key publication for the Alsatian Renaissance; yet the Alsatian cultural revival included more than one journal and its related activities. While some historians have recently tried to separate the Alsatian theater from the broader Alsatian Renaissance, the argument does not quite hold; the theater, for contemporaries, stood as part of the revival of Alsatian culture.[35] Moreover, leaders of the theater such as Gustave Stoskopf often worked on parallel projects in the region. Thus the Alsatian theater, founded in the late 1890s and whose plays were written in the local dialect and dealt with contemporary Alsatian society, assumed a central role in defining the region. First, the theater celebrated the local dialect as essentially Alsatian. Second, the content of the plays promoted a vision of Alsace predicated on the unity of the Alsatian community and rejection of the national pretensions of France and especially Germany in the region. Yet unlike the *RAI*, the theater tended toward greater ambivalence on the issue of Alsatian national belonging. Much of this ambivalence stemmed from the works of the theater's most popular playwright and cofounder, the artist Gustave Stoskopf.

In many ways, Stoskopf's early training prepared him well for a career promoting Alsatian identity through art. Born in 1869, Stoskopf, not content to follow his father's trade of tanning, used grants from the provincial government to study art in Alsace. He spent several years in Paris learning the skills of a portrait artist as well as an additional year at time at the Royal Academy of Art in Munich to hone his abilities as a landscape artist. Portraiture and landscapes, the skills he developed in France and Germany respectively, would dominate Stoskopf's works.[36]

Stoskopf's formal introduction to the Alsatian revival came in 1894. On a train home from Paris, Stoskopf met Spindler, who invited the twenty-five-year-old painter to a meeting of Alsatian artists in Strasbourg. From this first meeting would eventually develop a group of artists and their patrons, the Société des amis des arts d'Alsace, which had as its goal the creation of a distinct Alsatian art form. Rejecting such current trends as French Neoimpressionism and German Expressionism, they adopted a realistic style of painting portraits, landscapes, and still lifes of persons and things Alsatian.[37]

It was while contributing to the planning for the *RAI* and working within at the Société des amis des arts that Stoskopf became involved in the organization of the theater along with the writers Julius Greber and Ferdinand Bastian, the actors Eugen Criqui and Adolf Horsch, as well as Alexander Hessler.[38] Stoskopf, who emerged as the theater's early key playwright, would draw on his experiences from Paris, in particular on his exposure to the to the *théâtre du boulevard*. These three-act comedies were romantic stories alluded to political and social realities. Combining the farcical style of these works with the Alsatian dialect and Alsatian settings, Stoskopf set out to present the Alsace that he knew from his childhood in Brumath on the stages of Strasbourg.[39]

The organizers of the theater faced several immediate problems. They had to find a venue for the performances and the financial backing necessary for such a project, and Stoskopf had to develop material for the stage. The director of the Strasbourg Stadttheater, Alexander Hessler, offered his theater and his contacts with Alsatian actors to help stage productions. Hessler also used his connections with Karl Hauss, a member of the Reichstag and editor of the Catholic paper *Der Elsässer*, to receive a start-up grant of three thousand marks from the provincial government for the theater.[40]

The last problem proved at first the most difficult to solve as little literature existed in the dialect. Efforts of some local scholars and writers in the nineteenth century had ameliorated this situation somewhat. Most notably, the Stoeber family, first Daniel Ehrenfried Stoeber (1779–1835), then his sons Auguste (1808–1884) and Adolphe (1810–1892) promoted dialect literature both through their own publications as well as through their creation of various literary societies.[41] Along with the writing duo of Émile Erckmann and Alexandre Chatrian, the Stoeber family provided the core of Alsatian dialect literature in the nineteenth century.[42] Seeking to create a larger corpus of works, Stoskopf wrote *D'r Herr Maire* (*Sir Mayor*) at Laugel's home in St. Leonard where he also staged readings to an interested audience.[43] Meanwhile, the Alsatian theater opened successfully in October 1898 with its first production, an adaptation of the novel by Émile Erckmann and Alexandre Chatrian, *L'Ami Fritz*.

Stoskopf's plays evolved out of the political, social, and cultural environment of Alsace in the late 1890's. The grist for Stoskopf's literary mill came from many sources: his understanding of the Alsatian dialect, his insights into contemporary Alsatian society—especially the presence of the German military and bureaucracy—as well as his knowledge of the history and culture of Alsace. Above all, Stoskopf desired to help Alsace maintain its regional uniqueness without either succumbing to assimilation by the Germans or sliding into revanchism. Stoskopf emphasized the place of language, especially the role of dialect in Alsace. Moreover, his plays mocked German attempts to win over the national loyalty of the local populace, using light-hearted humor to circumvent imperial censorship. Finally, Stoskopf's plot structures point to a common theme, the need for Alsatians to set aside their differences and come together as a unified community.

The use of dialect was one of the central aspects of the Alsatian theater. Patois offered one means of constructing a regional community from the various segments of Alsatian society, who regardless of social, economic, and religious background, could understand the dialect. The nonpartisan quality and ubiquity of the dialect could be employed to make the Alsatian community seem distinct and timeless and thus helped to forge a unique Alsatian identity.[44] By elevating the local idiom to a literary language,

Stoskopf offered not only a source of identity but also made clear distinctions between Alsatians and other national groups without offending the Germans by using French or his Francophile Alsatian compatriots by employing *Hochdeutsch*. Therefore, the use of dialect in Stoskopf's plays merits closer attention.[45]

Much as in the wider Alsatian society, Stoskopf's Alsace was multilingual, with French, German, and the dialect in prevalent use. Indeed, Stoskopf exploited the situation to great comic advantage. One example is in *D'r Hoflieferant (The Courtly Purveyor)*. The main character, a businessman by the name of Grinsinger, speaks French fluently to maintain his commercial and social ties in Paris. Born in Saxony, he can easily switch into German. And as a patriotic Alsatian, he is a master of the dialect. This balance of French, German, and Alsatian finds its expression in the final scenes of the play when Grinsinger is faced with a potentially embarrassing situation as he is hosting a French guest at the same moment as the Sachsenbund (Saxon Association) arrives to celebrate his appointment as courtly purveyor of the Saxon court. Neither the members of the Sachsenbund nor his French guest Baron de Rosa have the ability to speak the others' language. Grinsinger, therefore, is forced to mediate between the two groups, intentionally mistranslating and transforming potential slights into unintended compliments, while throughout cursing to himself in Alsatian over his fate and the potential disaster should his Francophile, Alsatian compatriots arrive and disrupt his linguistic juggling act.[46] More important, Grinsinger's character provides insight into Stoskopf's vision of Alsace as a bicultural bridge between France and Germany, not as an object of (inter-)national contestation.

Language was not the only way that Stoskopf sought to promote Alsatian uniqueness through differentiation.[47] In Alsace, social and economic concerns between Alsatians and *Altdeutsche* likewise played a role in the creation of identity, because the annexation of Alsace-Lorraine, the influx of Germans from across the Rhine, and the rise of popular political parties all undermined the economic, social, and political status of traditional local, especially Francophile, elites.[48]

These socioeconomic processes of identity formation are important, but not central to our discussion of Stoskopf's works, for here we refer to a much more deliberate form of constructing regional identity, albeit one that drew heavily upon social and economic realities. Stoskopf's adaptation of the satirical *théâtre du boulevard* gave him the opportunity to construct a view of the "Other(s)" that not only criticized current German policy but also rejected those elements of German culture which Stoskopf found antithetical to his vision of Alsace. By investing national stereotypes with undesirable characteristics and values and subsequently rejecting them through the use of satire, Stoskopf created spaces in which to develop, accentuate, or promote those images and qualities that he believed a part of "Alsatianness."[49]

German militarism was one of the more prominent elements of German rule that Stoskopf lampoons. By depicting Germans as needing to accomplish even simple, daily tasks in military fashion, Stoskopf could satirize both the German penchant for militarism, and more importantly, the immense military forces present in Alsace. For example, in *D'r Hoflieferant*, the members of the Sachsenbund are presented with an opportunity to dine at a buffet. However, they cannot simply line up and partake of the proffered victuals. Instead, one of their leaders assumes control, shouting:

> Silence! Beloved Saxons! You now have a difficult, strategic mission! (pointing to the table) This table here with the sumptuous goods is an enemy battery. . . . (laughter) Now show your courage! The Fatherland demands that each man does his duty! Army on the right flank, attack! March! March! Hurrah! [He (the leader) rushes the buffet, all follow him with loud cheers.][50]

Naturally the Alsatian host, Fritz Grinsinger, recoils in shock from this onslaught, especially as it takes place in front of his French guest, the Baron de Rosa. By veiling his criticisms of German rule in such buffoonery, Stoskopf avoided offending imperial authorities and even attracted some *Altdeutsche* to the performances with the skill of his characterizations, while simultaneously rejecting the militaristic values Germans hoped to inculcate within the Alsatian populace.

Like the military, the German bureaucracy also came under attack. In *D'r Verbotte Fahne* (*The Forbidden Flag*), the protagonist, Herr Klopfer, a mayoral candidate, asks his friends in the German bureaucracy to forbid the flying of the Alsatian flag so as to disrupt his rival's upcoming rally. When this political maneuver turns his fellow Alsatians against him,[51] Klopfer asks his bureaucratic friends to repeal the order. The bureaucrat Herr Plaschke is unequivocal in his response:

> Plaschke: Do you not know what a bureaucrat is? An imperial bureaucrat? . . . You know that if you were not from the friendly side that I would have to construe such a demand as an insult?!—What! I should allow the ban to be repealed, *I* should, so to speak, answer for a mistake!
> Klopfer: No, no, no mistake! No one is even speaking of such!
> Plaschke: Most certainly, the authority of my senior office would be rocked by the repeal of the ban, the foundations of the state would be made into a farce . . . the erroneous idea would be spread that a senior official could make a mistake! That has simply never existed! It cannot exist and it will not exist!
> Frau Plaschke: A senior official in principle makes no mistakes![52]

Stoskopf not only satirized German attempts to win over the region, but also sought to promote a positive sense of Alsatianness. Two symbols that emerged as important to his work are the red and white flag of Alsace and the "Alsatian" *Marseillaise*, the song "Hans von Schnakenloch." The flag and the song serve as objects around which the conflict of the *D'r Verbotte Fahne* and *E Demonstration* respectively revolve. In *D'r Verbotte Fahne*,

Herr Klopfer, by seeking to have the Alsatian flag forbidden, angers his Alsatian neighbors instead of disrupting his rival's meeting.[53] Klopfer, through various devices, wins approval of a different red and white flag, mending relations with his Alsatian neighbors and celebrating the flag in the closing scene of the play:

> Red and White are our colors,
> Merrily they flutter in the wind!
> Tell us, how we could find,
> A land like our Alsace?!
> From the Palatinate to Basel,
> From the Vogeskamm to the Rhine,
> The valleys bear the golden Rhine,
> The berries yield sparkling wine.
> Red and white are our colors.[54]

The second symbol, "Hans im Schnakenloch," was an old song based upon a figure of popular Alsatian culture. "Hans im Schnakenloch" served as a basis for two plays, the first of which was contributed to the Elsässisches Theater in 1899 by Stoskopf's colleague, Ferdinand Bastian; the second was written not in dialect but *Hochdeutsch* by René Schickele during World War I.[55] Stoskopf's appropriation of the local song in *E Demostration* must by viewed with a cautionary note.[56]

If the dialect offered Stoskopf one means of creating community within Alsace, and the use of the "Other" allowed him to distance Alsatians from cultural assimilation by the Germans, then the narrative aspects of his plays also served to forge a sense of Alsatian identity.[57] In particular, Stoskopf's plays each have a thread of conflict, usually based around the central character's need to ingratiate himself with the German authorities, while not simultaneously alienating his fellow, more Francophile, Alsatians. Running parallel to the main plot line are subplots, usually involving romantic pairings of young Alsatians whose amorous ambitions are disrupted by the misadventures of their protagonist fathers.

The work *E Demonstration* (see Figure 1.1) offers a clear example of this pattern. The story centers around Georg Rebholz, a local factory owner who opposes the replacement of the current mayor by German authorities and wishes to show his revanchist leanings. His political predilections unfortunately raise not only the specter of government retribution but also threaten to disrupt his domestic life. Rebholz's daughters, Jeanne and Marie, have each found true love. However, Charles Schmidt and Fritz Schreiber, their suitors, edit the local antiregime and proregime papers respectively. Rebholz first allows Schmidt's courtship to continue. When Rebholz believes that he will go to prison for singing the *Marseillaise*, he quickly changes sides, blaming Schmidt's influence for his deed and pleading with Schreiber to clear his name in his paper by calling him a "loyal citizen" and "true Alsatian." Rebholz, finally absolved of any wrongdoing, decides to refrain from political protesting and retreats instead into the safety of his Alsatian circle of friends. His daughters' suitors, Schmidt and Schreiber, also ease his situation by agreeing to combine their newspaper operations and concentrate not on political activities, but on supporting the local Alsatian community. Stoskopf then leaves us with the happy celebration of the two couples, brought together in matrimony by the acceptance on the part of their father and fiancées of their Alsatian identity.[58]

Stoskopf's plays generated a variety of responses within Alsatian society. Popular reception of the plays is the most difficult to ascertain. Although specific numbers are not available, there exists indirect evidence that many of the plays enjoyed popular appeal. First, the reviews of Stoskopf's plays often comment on the packed crowds at the Stadttheater in Strasbourg for *D'r Herr Maire*, *E Demonstration*, and *D'r Hoflieferant*.[59] Second, Stoskopf, along with fellow literati such as Jules Greber and Ferdinand Bastian, wrote and produced dozen of plays to a public ready for such fare, many of which saw repeated performances. Not only did the Alsatian theater find an audience in Strasbourg, but sentiments for these Alsatian dramas led to the foundation of similar theaters in Colmar, Mulhouse, and Sélestat between 1899–1901.[60] Not all of the theaters proved as successful as that at Strasbourg; Colmar, in particular, suffered from 1902–1906 as it neither received the government subsidies furnished to the Alsatian theaters in Mulhouse and Strasbourg nor did it possess the rights to enough works to vary its program. In 1906, a "Syndicate of Alsatian Theaters" was created to generate sufficient material in dialect and disburse the government subsidy among all of the member organizations.[61]

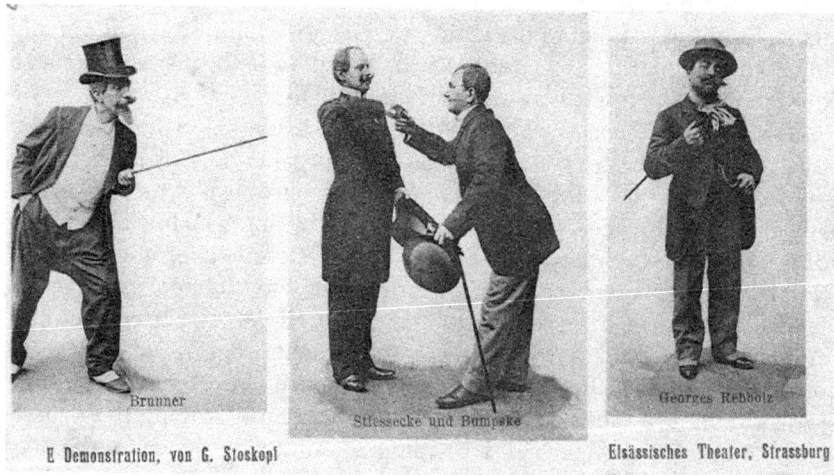

Figure 1.1. Gustave Stoskopf, *E Demonstration*

If the popular reception of Stoskopf's works in particular and of the *Heimat* theater appears positive, the critical response proved more varied. The reviewers of the *Revue alsacienne illustrée*, while sometimes criticizing the scenery, actors, or direction of the plays, not surprisingly struck a fully positive note about the literary and political qualities of the works themselves. In a more wide-ranging essay aimed at not only judging the value of the theater but also recounting the history of dialect literature in Alsace, Anselm Laugel viewed this "particularist theater" as a means of expressing the "national character" of Alsace, i.e., one dependent on both its German and French heritage.[62] Some Germans also praised the new dramas; as reported in the *Jahresbericht für neuere deutsche Literaturgeschichte* (*Yearbook for Modern German Literary History*), one critic "most joyfully welcomed the dialect literature that can best develop in the healthy realism of modern drama. The aforementioned work from Stoskopf [*D'r Herr Maire*], is recognized despite reservations about its one-sidedness."[63] Others showed themselves less enamored of the Alsatian theater but supportive of dialect literature. For example, a literary group centered around René Schickele, Youngest Alsace, strove to eschew the political overtones present in the dialect literature by writing in both German and dialect as a purely artistic endeavor.[64]

Stronger criticism came from pro-German elements of the Alsatian cultural scene. For example, one observer commented that the plays were "silly," and viewed the theater as "child's play that only serves as shallow entertainment."[65] Another commentator wrote that "particularism led to the founding of the theater" and viewed "the Alsatian Theater as a club stage that cannot truly fulfill the need for popular theater."[66] Perhaps the harshest criticism came from Friedrich Lienhard, who had little use for the dialect plays. Lienhard referred to the dialect as "urbanized, corrupted patois" and the writers of the Alsatian theater as "jokers without psychological profundity" and as "hermaphrodites between French and German art." Moreover, he named "their [Alsatian dialect writers'] tendencies and supporters fully particularist."[67] Lienhard, in railing against Alsatian particularism and its manifestation in the form of the theater, demonstrated his loyalty to his *Altdeutsche* patrons and their mission of Germanization within Alsace. As an Alsatian, his imprecations against particularism point to the uncertain status of the newly emergent Alsatian identity.

Producing numerous plays in the years between 1898 and the mid-1900s, Stoskopf also remained highly involved in the organization of the theater. In addition, he moved into new endeavors. Most notably, he established the *Strassburger Neue Zeitung* (hereafter, *SNZ*), a daily of the Strasbourg branch of the Alsatian Liberal Party; Stoskopf also served on the paper's editorial board. First printed in 1909, the paper, much like Stoskopf's plays, combined criticism of the excesses of the German government with a cautionary stance toward overly nationalistic or excessive efforts to promote the place of France in the region.

One or two examples serve to illustrate this wary attitude toward nationalistic displays. For example, in 1909 a Swiss citizen visiting Mulhouse, in the paper's words, "drank his fill" and proceeded to ask the musicians in an inn to play the *Marseillaise*. German officers in the room were insulted and departed, only to be followed by the inebriated Swiss patron to another bar where the scene repeated itself. In response, the local commander forbade his troops to patronize the two watering holes. The *SNZ* called the entire affair an "meaningless accident" and argued furthermore that restaurants were "neutral ground" where people regardless of political outlook or nationality should respect the other guests.[68]

The paper's efforts to mediate between the more extreme elements in the region brought the paper under criticism from more French-minded Alsatians as well as German nationalists. The charge of *"Deutschfeindlichkeit"* (anti-German feeling) led to a swift response from the paper. In March 1914, the *Deutsche Tageszeitung* accused the *SNZ* and Stoskopf personally of being *"deutschfeindlich."* In return, the paper and Stoskopf sued the *Tageszeitung* for slander. Although the superior court did not issue any fines against the *Tageszeitung*, the *SNZ* was delighted to report the court's decision:

> In reference to the attitude of the plaintiff Stoskopf his poem to Kléber comes under consideration. It is known both commonly and especially to the court, that the reproach of *Deutschfeindlichkeit* against Stoskopf is grounded in the comedy "D'r Hoflieferant." The "Neue Zeitung" is known as a democratic, Alsatian paper and Stoskopf is presumably of the same political line.

The report continued: "After consideration of the limited available material, the claim of conscious *Deutschfeindlichkeit*—and it concerns this point alone—in reference to the *SNZ* and the playwright Stoskopf is fully unfounded."[69]

Stoskopf's plays, and later his paper, served as vehicles to promote a particular vision of Alsace, one in which the region could be free of the pernicious and divisive influences of nationalistic strivings. This is not to say that Stoskopf refrained from criticizing the German regime for its illiberal or chauvinistic policies. Rather, Stoskopf's writings both as a playwright and as a journalist pointed to a vision of Alsace in which the region was to be drained of its nationalist strains in favor a unified Alsatian community.

The Region Nationalized: The Caricatures of Hansi

Walking down the streets of Colmar, and to a lesser extent Strasbourg, Riquewihr, or Ribeauvillé, the tourist of today is struck by the myriad postcards, pictures, and collectibles painted with scenes of Alsatian children playing gaily in the streets or in the fields. Many are the work of the artist Jean-Jacques Waltz, better known by his nom-de-plume, Hansi.

Hansi, who painted numerous such innocuous scenes, was formerly better known for his caricatures, which skewered the Germans and their presence in Alsace while simultaneously celebrating the ties between Alsace and France. Whereas Stoskopf sought to reconcile Alsatians to both their French and German neighbors, Hansi strove to keep the flames of French loyalty burning within the hearts of Alsatians. Using children's books, newspapers, and even postcards, Hansi sought to undo the outcome of 1871.

Born in 1873 in Colmar, Hansi learned his "love for France" and his appreciation for "the beauty of Alsace" from his father André Waltz, who served as both municipal librarian and the conservator of the Musée d'Unterlinden in Colmar. Hansi, an indifferent student by his own admission, took up drawing with his father's encouragement. According to his "*Notes Biographiques*," the professors at the German *gymnasium* encouraged his love of drawing with their intense program of "Germanizing us, proclaiming the greatness of Germany and downplaying that of France." Following matriculation from the *gymnasium*, Hansi, under some pressure from his parents, undertook a course of studies in industrial design rather than fine arts at the Ecole des Beaux-Arts in Lyon and later in Cernay.[70]

Hansi returned to Alsace and took a position at the Firm Herzog in Logenbach. The aspiring artist, however, wishing to pursue an alternate career and averse to the regular hours of business, did not last long at the firm.[71] Having met Pierre Bucher at local art exhibitions, Hansi began to draw for the *RAI* as well as for the periodical *Vogesenbilder*. In addition to coming into contact with Bucher and his circle, Hansi became acquainted with Emile Wetterlé, a Catholic cleric, member of both the *Landesausschuss* and Reichstag, newspaper owner and editor, and a staunch anti-German, pro-French regionalist. In 1905, Hansi began working as a correspondent and cartoonist for Wetterlé's *Journal de Colmar*, and after it closed, Wetterlé's paper *Le Nouvelliste*. Under the twin influences of Wetterlé and Bucher, he started to develop his own voice and vision for Alsace, first publishing *Die Hohkönigsburg und ihre Einweihung* (*Hohkönigsburg and its Inauguration*) (1907) and soon thereafter *Professor Knatschke* (1908).[72]

These early works laid out some of the major themes that would come to be constitutive of his more important, and more infamous, later books. In *Die Hohkönigsburg*, Hansi lampooned the festivities surrounding the inauguration of the newly restored castle of Hohkönigsburg, a reconstructed medieval fortress that was to celebrate Alsace's ties to the Holy Roman Empire. Not only did Hansi lampoon German nationalism, morals, and customs, but he also developed a particular visual style in his depiction of Germans. Figure 1.2, taken from *Die Einweihung*, demonstrates Hansi's basic image of the German: prototypical Germans are bespeckled and ruddy-faced and are often corpulent or thin and unhealthy looking. All wear green *Trachten*. This essentialized depiction of the Germans would remain a cornerstone of his works well into the 1920s.

Figure 1.2. Hansi, "Le Toit," *Die Hohkönigsburg und ihre Einweihung*

Hansi's *Professor Knatschke*, published in 1908, gained both Hansi and Wetterlé notoriety. The story, which follows the travels of a German professor and his daughter to Paris, lampoons the German view of the French in general and Paris in particular. A German-born professor at a *gymnasium* in Colmar took offence at the work. Professor Gneisse had openly pushed for the schools to accelerate their program of Germanizing the Alsatian populace. Moreover, he vociferously argued against the use of French in school. Gneisse sued the paper for slander and demanded the regional government punish both author and publisher. Though urged by his Francophile, British-born wife not to impose heavy punishments, *Statthalter* Karl von Wedel nonetheless sentenced Wetterlé to a short jail term and fined him five hundred marks.[73] Wetterlé's release witnessed him and Hansi being feted before a crowd of several thousand.

It was, however, two works of Hansi's in particular that drew the ire of German authorities. *L'Histoire d'Alsace. Recontée aux Petits Enfants d'Alsace et de France par l'Oncle Hansi* (*The History of Alsace, Recounted to the Small Children of Alsace and Lorraine by Uncle Hansi*) and *Mon Village. Ceux qui n'oublient pas; images et commentaries par l'Oncle Hansi* (*My Village: Those Who Do Not Forget; Images and Commentary by Uncle Hansi*),[74] written in 1912 and 1913, criticized German rule while simultaneously drawing clear connections between France and Alsace. Hansi drew upon his earlier works, depicting the Germans as an "Other" against which French Alsatianness could be defined. At the same time, he reaffirmed Alsace's historical, cultural, and linguistic ties to France. By stressing the "hard" boundaries between Alsace and Germany, Hansi painted the divides between Alsace and France as soft, and therefore ultimately compatible.[75] The Alsatians were separate from the French in Hansi's account, but could subsume their regional identity into the French national community. In contrast, Hansi depicts Alsatians as fundamentally separate from the Germans, intrinsically opposed to their rule, and ultimately French in their national orientation.

The depiction of Germans as inherently not Alsatian can be demonstrated through a few clear examples. In *L'Histoire*, Hansi depicts the Rhine as the natural boundary between Alsace and Germany while simultaneously demonstrating the invasive tendencies of Germans in the region.[76] In figure 1.3, German barbarians look longingly across the river upon Alsace's well-cultivated land as they await the next chance to sally forth to pillage and raid. And when the barbarians dare cross, they encounter stiff resistance. The Alsatians' will to survive the presence of the foreign German is such that even it has become an essential part of their nature.[77]

Hansi elaborates on this idea of the cruel, barbarous, and of course despised German. In almost every representation, Hansi draws the Germans with sundials or clocks slung over their shoulders. Only in Alsace can they discover civilization, as their own technological progress trailed that of the Alsatians by millennia. Finally, just as the Alsatians possess an ingrained hatred of Germans, the Germans show their inherently brutal nature in their need to raid, pillage, and burn Alsace. By depicting the Germans as invading barbarians, *L'Histoire* served not only to question the legitimacy of German rule in 1912, but also to accent Alsace's ties with benevolent rulers. Hansi examines a number of the former rulers of Alsace—the Romans, Franks, Stauffen dynasty of the Holy Roman Empire, and the various French regimes—to narrate a tale of Alsatian acceptance of foreign rulers. For example, the Romans, though limiting the political rights of Alsatians, never attempted to impose their own culture, customs, or language on Alsace, unlike, of course, the contemporary Germans.[78] Under French control, the Alsatians' cultural and linguistic rights were even expanded.[79] As such, the Alsatians had enjoyed the greatest political liberties under French rule; France thus represents a more advanced civilization and therefore should appeal to the Alsatians. Hansi then closed the circle of invasions and just administration by discussing the history

Les Germains aperçoivent l'Alsace de l'autre côté du Rhin.

Figure 1.3 Hansi, *L'Histoire d'Alsace*

of Alsace since the "Terrible Year" of 1871 when his land passed into German hands. Germans attempted to impose their culture and language in schools, thereby violating basic rights of the Alsatians that former rulers without exception respected. Moreover, "carpet-bagger" Badens, Bavarians, Saxons, and Prussians traveled to Alsace to take jobs in the government, bringing with them their attitudes of cultural and national superiority over the Alsatians. Not content to allow his description of the immorality of German rule to speak for itself, Hansi writes of their cruelties, "God denies Germany all the qualities of shrewdness and generosity that are the fruit of a long-standing civilization."[80]

The issue of the German heavy-handedness was further elaborated in *Mon Village*. As part of their program to foster acculturation in German culture, teachers taught Alsatians false history, stressing the accomplishments of Prussia's military while slighting the heritage of the French Revolution within Alsace. Moreover, children found themselves exposed solely to the German language with no chance to learn French. Figure 1.4 is emblematic of Hansi's view of German schools; the teacher reads from a history of the Kaiser, whose portrait hangs in the background between a huge map of Prussia and a blackboard proclaiming both that "Greater-Berlin is the largest city in the world" and that "2x2=5." The Alsatian children, meanwhile, poke fun at the oblivious instructor. Hansi is also quick to point out that the children had never given the old, skilled French pedagogue any sort of trouble in class.[81]

Mon Village also illustrates the natural affiliation between French and Alsatians and simultaneously the artificial place of Germans within Alsace. Two drawings of French and German tourists demonstrate this perspective. (Figures 1.5 and 1.6).[82] The French visitors are well-clad, slim, and healthy, whereas the Germans are overweight, bespectacled, and dressed in drab green hiking clothes. The French tourists move in an open square,

Figure 1.4 Hansi, *Mon Village*

Figure 1.5 Hansi, *Mon Village*

Figure 1.6 Hansi, *Mon Village*

mingling with the Alsatians, visiting their "foreign" yet familiar national brothers and sisters. Their German counterparts sit in an enclosed garden, eating *Wurst*, reading their copy of the *Strassburger Post* (the government's official newspaper), and as Hansi intimates, drinking themselves silly.[83] They refuse to fraternize with the Alsatians. Rather, they are served by a beautiful, natural-looking (compared to the German women) Alsatian woman. Alsatians remain subservient to Germans, while their French brothers and sisters greet them openly. Perhaps most indicative of the differences between Germans and the French is the place of children in the two pictures. The French women talk to Alsatian children, "passing around to all bon-bons wrapped in gold and silver paper."[84] In contrast, the Alsatian children remain at the garden's gate, removed from the German visitors. They are strangers to the youths. To the French, the children are like nieces and nephews, family members who unfortunately live across the border.

Hansi's revanchism also shines through in his treatment of two holidays. The German feast of the emperor is a boring day, filled with long-winded speeches, the awarding of trivial prizes for trivial deeds, and much parading in military garb, children included. Alsatians do not partake in the festivities as the holiday represents the founding of the German Empire and defeat of the French in 1871; the day is implicitly one of sorrow.[85] Alsatian children instead hold July 14 as their favorite day of the year when, in order to celebrate Bastille Day, they travel to Nancy. There the Alsatians are greeted warmly by their national compatriots and it is there that "they [the Alsatians] can cry to the winds of that [Germany] which oppresses their hearts.[86] And it is of these festivities that Alsatian children dream for months. The connections between France and Alsace are unambiguous—even the young Alsatian or French child being read *Mon Village* could take away the proper lesson that they belonged to the same national community.[87]

Hansi's use of French symbols, especially the *drapeau tricolore* and liberty tree along with the strong affinity of Alsatian children for French tourists, toys, and holidays show the close bonds of Alsace and France. Not satisfied to demonstrate Alsace's links to France in these multiple examples, however, Hansi proclaims Alsace's desire to return to France. Hansi describes the silence of three veterans of the Franco-Prussian war who walk the streets on Sunday as indicting "we swear, as much as for us as for our children and their descendants, to lay claim eternally to the right of Alsatians and Lorrainers to remain members of the French nation."[88] Not content with this statement of Alsatian loyalty, Hansi describes his hope for Alsace's future in the closing pages: "Better days are coming and then these brave people will be treated with justice and there will only be free and happy Alsatians in my village."[89]

Hansi's pro-French, anti-German conception of Alsace, even published under the guise of a children's book, did not sit well with the Germans in

Alsace. For *L'Histoire,* Hansi was accused of insulting both German veterans and the army and had to serve three months in jail.[90] Shortly after the publication of *Mon Village,* Hansi managed once again to draw the attention of German authorities, causing an incident at a local pub. Specifically, Hansi was accused of insulting a German officer by wiping down a chair on which the officer had been seated and proclaiming the seat "disinfected."[91] More significantly, Hansi found himself the target of prosecution for high treason for *Mon Village.* In July 1914, the Superior Court in Leipzig found Hansi guilty and sentenced the artist to a one-year prison term.[92] Fortunately for Hansi, he secured a short furlough to visit his aging father and took the opportunity to slip across the border into France, thereby avoiding certain imprisonment and allowing him to serve as a propagandist in the French army during the First World War.[93]

Hansi's works, read in both France and Alsace, became one of the central means through which the myth and partial reality of an Alsace faithful to France was propagated.[94] Whereas Pierre Bucher managed to play a more ubiquitous role in organizing specific French cultural groups, and whereas Emile Wetterlé, Hansi's sometime employer and friend, remained the leading political voice of Alsatian pro-French sentiment, Hansi packaged Alsace in attractive French wrapping. Although his conception of Alsace became the standard of French Alsatianness, contemporaries had diverse opinions as to the nature of Alsace and the possibilities for loyalty to France, Germany, and the region itself.

Debating Alsace: French, German, or Something Unique?

The differing conceptions of Alsace evident in the literary world had parallels in the larger debates over the nature of Alsatian culture, history, and claims to uniqueness. In particular, much ink was spilled trying to decide whether Alsace was German, French, or some admixture of the two. Two considerations ran through these disputes. First, writers tried to judge whether regionalism helped defend French culture or aided in assimilation to the German nation. Second, participants tried to evaluate the general utility and nature of regionalism as well as its place in the fight for the region's soul.

One of the first to write on this issue extensively was a German economics professor at the University of Strasbourg, Werner Wittich. Coming to the subject with a fairly neutral attitude, Wittich believed that in certain locations, such as colonies or world cities, "great national cultures compete in all their relationships and characteristics. The most important and interesting battle site between two cultures was currently Alsace."[95] Wittich launched into a wide-ranging discussion of the Alsatian character. For example, Alsatians were German by race, French in their political culture. Alsatian religious practice put them more in the German cultural camp, while their intellectual traditions fell on the French side. Wittich thus developed a taxonomy of the national influences on Alsatian life. He concluded by analyzing the impact of Germanization since 1870; in his judgment (not altogether unique), because the French-speaking bourgeois could resist Germanization and the *Altdeutsche* refused to mingle with the general populace of Alsace, Germanization would continue to proceed slowly.[96]

Wittich's approach, void of polemics, clearly stood against the more vicious debates that occurred in the ensuing decade. Heinrich Rulard, a Colmar-based German lawyer, argued in an extended essay that if proponents of French culture in Alsace could be silenced, and the misguided policies of intense Germanization and bureaucratic arrogance could be avoided, then Alsace could be brought into the German national fold. For example, Rulard welcomed the rise of local literary groups such as Young Alsace, of which Stoskopf was a member. The members of Young Alsace could render major dramas of German literature into dialect, thereby allowing the wider populace to become immersed in German culture, and thus hastening the growth of Alsatian loyalty to Germany.[97] Additionally, Rulard cautioned that pro-French particularism was misguided as it kept the Alsatians from joining their true nation, Germany.[98] Thus, regionalism represented a double-edged sword, capable of integrating or resisting the assimilation of Alsace into its real national community.

Other Alsatians explored the region's unique heritage. Antoine Legrand, writing in the *RAI*, pointed to important elements of French political culture in the region, especially the love of freedom, as antithetical to German "militarism, bureaucratism, nationalism, and monarchism." Moreover, Germans were simply too serious and did not understand the Alsatian sense of humor. Instead, Germans would have to "modify their attitude" and accept that

> to the Alsatian, who for centuries has been accustomed to the deep, cross-cutting conflict between Teutonic and Romance, between German and French nature, there exists no other choice than either to let himself be overwhelmed by these conflicts and quietly drown, or to adapt and cope with the new synthesis. The past of a homeland, as well as the tenacious resistance, which it (the homeland) brings against the leveling Prussian spirit, proves that the better part chooses. That is, it was strong enough to unite the disparate elements of two worlds synthetically and—this is the pertinent point—is not a noncivilization [*Unkultur*], as is claimed, but instead has covered itself with a higher, civilized culture, which the men of all nations are called to realize. National peculiarities as well as the love of the fatherland should be a means and a way [to this goal].[99]

Such sentiments, as we shall see in ensuing chapters, would be expressed repeatedly about not only the German administration, but later the French government.

Joseph Fleurent, a Francophile lawyer from Colmar, argued along more Francophile lines through his examination of the idea of *"patrie"* or homeland in Alsace. According to Fleurent, the annexation of the region in 1871 deprived the Alsatians of a *grande patrie*. Alsatians, not allowed to be French and not quite German, remained torn between two *"patries intellectuelles."* Therefore, *"la petite patrie"* or "little homeland" had become the sole object of Alsatian communal loyalties.[100]

In theory, Fleurent had no difficulty in accepting the place of particularism either within Germany or France.[101] However, for Alsace, the case was less clear. Fleurent wrote that "it seems an exaggeration that the love of the region possessed in excess" could replace the *grande patrie intellectuelle* by "constructing an Alsatian civilization influenced by those of France and Germany, but always distinct."[102] Questioning the cultural bases of Alsatian particularism, he noted that Alsace "lacks, before all, a language and a historical tradition." The dialect was "gross and improper for rendering the slightest nuance of feeling, fitted at most for depicting the life of a peasant or worker."[103] Thus, Alsatian claims to cultural independence and subsequent appeal to regional loyalty were unfounded. Fleurent wrote in part out of a concern that Alsatian regionalism would serve to both undermine the region's connections to France and strengthen its ties to Germany.[104]

While Fleurent's fears were perhaps not misplaced,[105] his condemnation of Alsatian regionalism provoked a swift response, most notably from Anselm Laugel. For Laugel, Alsatian regionalism was not a slippery slope to Germanization; rather, it was a means of defending Alsatian culture, social mores, and economic concerns. Indeed, quoting a Bavarian journalist, Laugel argued that "the Northern Germans (i.e., Prussians) with their eternal discussion of Germandom and patriotism get on the nerves of southern Germans,"[106] regionalism could be seen in part as a general trend of anti-Prussianism in Germany. Alsace, treated as an economic colony and held in a constitutionally subservient position, needed regionalism to protect itself within the Empire.[107]

More narrowly, Laugel suggested that Alsace could have its own culture by utilizing a concept of progress in which each country and era enriched humanity in its own way. Laugel argued that Alsatians took the best of Germany and France and, employing their own "particular genius," create a distinct culture.[108] Combining German philosophy and French political traditions, Alsatians could not only enjoy their dual heritage, but could also contribute to the development of their neighbors. For example, Laugel stated that the Germans could benefit from the Alsatian sense of humor as the former "always take themselves too seriously."[109]

Finally, Laugel took up the defense of those elements of Alsatian culture which Fleurent had so strongly opposed, especially the language and theater. Laugel agreed that the dialect should not be employed in "doing integral or differential calculus," but had a role to play with regard to the theater and when "one wished to strike a emotional, sentimental, or poignant note." Moreover, in the case of the Alsatian theater, "which lacked neither allure nor poetic verve . . . [it] was necessary not to forget that this theater is a popular theater, which must remain popular, and which would lose its raison d'être if it would dare to stage the fury of Orestes or the agonies of Andromache."[110] To appeal to an Alsatian public, the plays had to be in the Alsatian dialect. Marked by both French and German cultural influences, and possessing its own special genius, Alsace had the ability and reason to exist as an autonomous land.

Conclusion

In the opening decade of the twentieth century, Alsatians deeply considered the nature of being Alsatian. From the efforts of Charles Spindler and Anselm Laugel arose numerous other attempts to articulate the substance of regional culture. Beyond such pro-German Alsatians such as Friedrich Lienhard, such activities had several commonalities. All placed great value on the separation of things Alsatian from things German. True, Alsatians may have shared a common language with Germans and even had some common traditions, but the infusion of French political and social values into the region had altered Alsatian culture in such a way to make it at the very least a *"Doppelkultur,"* a so-called double culture, if not a separate and unique civilization.

Beyond a common opposition to German cultural hegemony, the chorus of voices singing the praises of Alsatian traditions and mores was not unified. The *RAI*, in many ways the principal work in this movement, demonstrated such a split. Likewise, two purveyors of popular culture, Hansi and Stoskopf, adopted divergent views toward Alsace. The former attempted to inscribe the French nation on the region, while the latter sought to denationalize the region in favor of a more unified regional community.

Taken as a whole, these activities helped to lay the basis for a long-term definition of Alsatianness. Over the short term, however, the multiplicity of voices in the debate merely divided opinion over what it meant to be Alsatian. And as it will be seen in the following chapters, such divisions over what it meant to be Alsatian led to failed attempts to unify the region politically and a divergence of goals among Alsatians over where their future lay, and what form that future should take.

Notes

1. Georges Bischoff, "L'Invention de l'Alsace," *Saisons d'Alsace*, no. 119 (Printemps 1993): 35–70; Jean-Claude Richez, "L'Alsace revue et inventée. *La Revue alsacienne illustrée*, 1895–1914," *Saisons d'Alsace*, no. 119 (Printemps 1993): 83–94.
2. Rudy Koshar argues incisively that while nationalism contains culturally constructed elements, drawing upon the work of Anthony Smith he also argues against a "collective

misreading" of the concept of the "invention" of nations, instead pointing to the limits on such activities and the concrete processes through which the nation comes to be imagined. See Rudy Koshar, *Germany's Transient Pasts: Preservation and National Memory in the Twentieth Century* (Chapel Hill, NC, 1998): 8–9.
3. Richez, "L'Alsace revue et inventée," 83.
4. James Wilkinson, "The Uses of Popular Culture by Rival Elites: The Case of Alsace, 1890–1918," *History of European Ideas* 11 (1989): 605–18.
5. Alon Confino, *The Nation as Local Metaphor: Württemberg, Imperial Germany, and National Memory, 1871–1918* (Chapel Hill, NC, 1997), 97–101.
6. A. Andreas, *Charles Spindler. Aus dem Leben und Schaffen eines elsässichen Künstlers.* (Strassburg, 1934): 17–24; *Nouveau dictionnaire des biographies alsaciennes*, 2235–36.
7. Andreas, *Charles Spindler*, 16, 35–36.
8. *Prospectus de Revue Alsacienne Illustrée*, reprinted in *Documents de l'Histoire de l'Alsace*. ed. Philippe Dollinger (Toulouse, 1972), 436.
9. ADBR AL 98–700, Letter from Karl Spindler to Gerhard Lüdtke dated 18 June 1917.
10. Maurice Barrès, *Mes Cahiers*, Tome II (Paris, 1929), 295. See also Gisela Loth, *Un rêve de France: Pierre Bucher, une passion française au coeur de l'Alsace allemand*, Editions de l'Est (Strasbourg, 2000), 71.
11. "A Notre Lecteurs," *Cahiers Alsaciens* no. 1 (Jan. 1912): 1–3.
12. Jack G. Morrison, "The Intransigents: The Alsace-Lorrainers against the Annexation, 1900–1914." PhD diss., University of Iowa, 1970, 207–12, and Bonnie Menes Kahn, *My Father Spoke French: Nationalism and Legitimacy in Alsace, 1871–1914*. Harvard Studies in Sociology (New York, 1990), 156–58; See also ADBR AL 98 700, Letter from Karl Spindler to Gerhard Lüdtke dated 18 June 1917.
13. Ferdinand Dollinger, "Que nous enseigne la terre d'Alsace," *RAI* 6 (1904): 4–13; André Girondie, "Observations sur la sculpture en Alsace," *RAI* 6 (1904): 86–98; "Elsässische Kunst," *RAI* 7 (1905): 51–52; "Maison d'art Alsacienne à Strasbourg," *RAI* 11 (1909): 63–67; André Girondie, "La tradition de la toile imprimée en Alsace," *RAI* 10 (1908): 19–26; "Trois Tapestries alsaciennes. La venture de Sainte Odile," *RAI* 10 (1908): 19–24; K. Statsman, "Elsässische Heimatkunst aus dem Fünfzehnten Jahrhundert," *RAI* 10 (1908): 24–32.
14. "Sta. Odilia," *RAI* 9 (1907): 121–59.
15. Anselm Laugel, "L'art populaire en Alsace," *RAI* 6 (1904): 125–27.
16. Ibid., 126–27.
17. Ibid, 125.
18. Anselm Laugel, "L'art populaire en Alsace," *RAI* 7 (1905): 9–23, 122.
19. "Gustav Doré, (Biographies alsaciennes XXII)," *RAI* 10 (1908): 1–15; "J. J. Henner (Biographies alsaciennes XXVIII)," *RAI* 13 (1911): 65–96; "Eugène Ensfelder (Biographies alsaciennes XVI)," *RAI* 7 (1905): 1–8.
20. Richez, "L'Alsace revue et inventée," 83–94.
21. Confino, *Nation as Local Metaphor*, 134–51.
22. Friedrich Meinecke, *Erinnerungen, 1901–1919. Strassburg, Freiburg, Berlin* (Stuttgart, 1949), 19–20.
23. The minutes of the executive council of the Historical-Literary Club's biannual meetings, at which the publishing goals for the coming year and membership levels were the main subjects of discussion, form the basis of this judgment. Records exist from 1885, the first year the journal was published, until 1917, the last year of publication due to declining membership. See also François Igersheim, *L'Alsace et ses historiens, 1680–1914. La fabrique des monuments* (Strasbourg, 2006), 333–44.
24. "Drei Lieder auf Strasburgs Übergabe 1681," *JfGSL* (1890): 5–8.
25. Emil v. Borries, "Die Zerstörung der Strassburger Bibliothek im Jahre 1870," *JfGSL* (1900): 305–44.
26. Friedrich Lienhard, *Jugendjahre. Erinnerungen von Friedrich Lienhard* (Stuttgart, 1918), 1–10, 41–45, 112–58.

27. Ibid., 116–17.
28. Ibid., 65.
29. Ibid., 95.
30. Dan. S White, "Regionalism and Particularism," in *Imperial Germany: A Historiographical Companion*, ed. Roger Chickering (Westport, CT, 1996), 143–44.
31. Michel Ertz, *Friedrich Lienhard und René Schickele: Elsässische Literaten zwischen Deutschland und Frankreich* (Hildesheim, 1990), 74–84.
32. Christiane Harter-Feist, "Le problème d'Alsace et les relations franco-allemandes dans l'oeuvre de Friedrich Lienhard" (PhD diss., Université des Sciences Humaines de Strasbourg, 1998), 180–93.
33. Friedrich Lienhard, *Oberlin: Roman aus der Revolutionszeit im Elsaß* (Hamburg, 1933).
34. Ertz, *Friedrich Lienhard und René Schickele*, 317–21.
35. Bernhard von Hülsen, *Szenenwechsel in Elsass. Theater und Gesellschaft in Strassburg zwischen Deutschland und Frankreich, 1890–1944* (Leipzig, 2003), 64–70.
36. Morrison, "Intransigents," 233–34; Kahn, *My Father*, 101–3; Charles Gustav Stoskopf, *Stoskopf, le peintre: 1896–1944* (Colmar, 1976), 9–11, 80–1, 203–7; Gustave Stoskopf, "In der Gewerej Stoskopf," *Revue alsacienne de littérature*, no. 2 (1983): 7–10; Nicolas Stoskopf, "Un étudiant alsacien à Paris," *Saisons d'Alsace*, no. 4 (1999): 32–37; Camille Schneider, "Gustave Stoskopf: zélateur, fondateur, et animateur des arts au seuil du siècle," *Saisons d'Alsace* (1954), 274–84.
37. Stoskopf, *Stoskopf, le peintre*, 9–11, 80–81, 203–7.
38. Hülsen, *Szenenwechsel in Elsass*, 71–90.
39. Wilkinson, "Uses of Popular Culture," 310–11; Schneider, "Gustave Stoskopf," 274–84.
40. Morrison, "Intransigents," 235–36.
41. Bernard Vogler, *Histoire culturelle de l'Alsace* (Strabourg, 1994), 239–40.
42. Eros Vicari, *L'histoire de la littérature en Alsace*. (Strasbourg, 1985), 293–97.
43. A. Andreas, *Charles Spindler*, 32.
44. Eric Robertson, *Writing Between the Lines: René Schickele, 'Citoyen francais, deutscher Dichter' (1883–1940)* (Amsterdam, 1995), 16.
45. Ernest Gellner, *Nations and Nationalism* (Ithaca, NY, 1983), 56–67; Eric Hobsbawm, *Nations and Nationalism since 1780: Myth, Program, and Reality*, 2nd. ed. (Cambridge, 1992; reprint, 1993), 111–15.
46. Gustave Stoskopf, *D'r Hoflieferant: elsässische Komodie in drei Aufzuge* (Strassburg, 1904), 89–94.
47. Peter Sahlins, *Boundaries: The Making of Spain and France in the Pyrenees* (Berkeley, CA, 1989).
48. Jena M. Gaines, "The Politics of National Identity in Alsace," *Canadian Review of Studies in Nationalism* 21, no. 1–2 (1994): 103–7.
49. Homi Bhabha, "DissemiNation: Time, Narrative, and the Margins of the Modern Nation," in *Nation and Narration*, ed. Homi Bhabha (London, 1990; reprint, 1994), 291–322; Linda Colley, *Britons: Forging the Nation, 1707–1837* (New Haven, CT, 1992); Liah Greenfeld, *Nationalism: Five Roads to Modernity* (Cambridge, MA, 1992); and David Morley and Kevin Robins, "No Place like *Heimat*: Images of Home(land) in European Culture," *New Formations* 12 (Winter 1990), 1–23, reprinted in *Becoming National*, ed. Ronald Suny and Geoff Eley (New York, 1996), 456–80.
50. Stoskopf, *D'r Hoflieferant*, 94.
51. Gustave Stoskopf, *D'r Verbotte Fahne* (Strassburg, 1905), 79–83.
52. Ibid., 96.
53. Ibid., 81–84, 97–98.
54. Ibid., 112.
55. Robertson, *Writing Between the Lines*, 79–80.
56. Gustave Stoskopf, *E Demonstration* (Strassburg, 1904), 90–93.
57. Anderson, *Imagined Communities*, 22–36; Hülsen, *Szenenwechsel in Elsass*, 113.
58. Stoskopf, *E Demonstration*, passim.

59. "Chronique d'Alsace," *RAI* 5 (1903): 33–34; "Chronique d'Alsace," *RAI* 6 (1904): 1–3; "Chronique d'Alsace," *RAI* 8 (1906): 2–3.
60. Georges Baumann, "Le Théâtre Alsacien, 1900 à 1950," *Saisons d'Alsace* 3 (1950): 345–47.
61. Jean-Marie Gall, "Quatre-vingts ans de theatre alsacien de Colmar," *Saisons d'Alsace* 25, no. 73 (Printemps 1981): 45–46.
62. Laugel, "Le Theatre," 172.
63. F. Curtius, "Poesie und Politik im Elsass," *Deutsche Rundschau* 100, 27–30, summarized in "Drama and Literatur Geschichte des 18./19. Jahrhunderts," *Jahresbericht für neuere deutsche Literaturgeschichte* 11 (1899): IV, 4: 442.
64. Morrison, "The Intransigents," 238.
65. J. Brand, "Das Alsabund," *Kritik* 15, 41–4. Summarized in "Drama und Theatergeschichte des 18./19. Jahrhunderts," *Jahresbericht für neuere deutsche Literaturgeschichte* 12 (1900): IV, 4:496.
66. K. Storck, "Jung Elsass," *Das litterarische Echo*, 889–97. Summarized in "Drama und Theaterschichte des 18./19. Jahrhunderts," *Jahresbericht für neuere deutsche Literaturgeschichte* 12 (1900): IV, 4:496.
67. Friedrich Lienhard, as reported in "Drama and Literatur Geschichte de 18./19. Jahrhunderts," *Jahresbericht für neuere deutsche Literaturgeschichte* 11 (1899): IV, 4:440.
68. "Ein Zwischenfall," *SNZ* (11 Nov. 1909).
69. *SNZ* (19 July 1914).
70. ADHR J 81/49a, "Notes Biographiques"; Joseph Fleurent, "Hansi. Sa vie, son oeuvre," *Saisons d'Alsace* 3, no. 1 (Hiver 1952), 17–38; Pierre Marie Tyl, *N.d.d.a.a.*, 1412–13.
71. Fleurent, "Hansi," 18.
72. Charles Haenggi, "Hansi, journaliste," *Saisons d'Alsace* 3, no. 1 (Hiver 1952): 79–82.
73. Joseph Fleurent, "Hansi. Sa vie, son oeuvre," 17–30; Marie-Joseph Bopp, "Le premier procès de Hansi," *Saisons d'Alsace* 3, no. 1 (Hiver 1952): 65–73; Hermann Hiery, "Zwischen Scylla und Charybdis: Carl Graf von Wedel als Statthalter im Reichsland Elsass-Lothringen (1907–1914)," *Revue d'Alsace* (1986): 318–21; Gisela Loth, *Un rêve de France: Pierre Bucher, une passion française au coeur de l'Alsace allemand*, Editions de l'Est (Strasbourg, 2000), 143; ADHR "Papiers Wetterlé" 27 J 10.
74. Jean Jacques Waltz [Hansi], *L'Histoire d'Alsace. Recontee aux petits enfants d'Alsace et de France par l'Oncle Hansi* (Paris, 1913; reprint 1915); Waltz, *Mon Village. Ceux qui n'oublient pas; images et commentaries par l'Oncle Hansi* (Paris, 1913).
75. Presenjit Duara, "Historicizing National Identity, or Who Imagines What and When," in *Becoming National*, ed. Geoff Eley and Robert Suny (New York, 1996), 167–69.
76. Waltz, *Histoire d'Alsace*, 5.
77. Ibid., 3.
78. Ibid., 11–12.
79. Ibid., 11–12, 36, 65.
80. Ibid., 96.
81. Waltz, *Mon Village*, 6.
82. Ibid., 17–18.
83. Ibid., 16.
84. Ibid., 19.
85. Ibid., 24.
86. Ibid., 28.
87. Ibid., 24–25, 28–29.
88. Ibid., 12. This wording is actually almost verbatim the phrasing used by Alsatian representatives at the National Assembly in Bordeaux in 1871. See Dollinger, *Documents de l'Histoire de l'Alsace*, 421.
89. Waltz, *Mon Village*, 32.
90. ADHR 9 J 81/49a, "Notes Biographiques"; Fleurent, "Hansi. Sa vie, son oeuvre."
91. ADHR 8 AL 1/9410, Report signed "Greb."

92. ADBR AL 30–131, Letter from Oberreichsgericht Leipzig to Ministerium Elsass-Lothringen dated 9 July 1914; ADHR 9 J 81/49a, "Notes Biographiques."
93. "Steckbrief und Vermögensbeschlagnahme," *Strassburger Post* (26 September 1914); ADHR J 81/49a, "Notes Biographiques." ADBR AL 30–131, Letter from Oberreichsgericht Leipzig to Ministerium Elsass-Lothringen dated 27 July 1914.
94. ADHR AJ 30/41–1 (Purg. 11700)
95. Werner Wittich, "Deutsche und Französische Kultur im Elsass," *RAI* 3 (1900): 71–92, 113–40, 176–216.
96. Ibid., 71–92, 113–40, 176–216.
97. Heinrich Ruland, *Deutschtum und Franzosentum in Elsass-Lothringen. Eine Kulturfrage*. 2. Auflage (Colmar, 1909), 155–66.
98. Ibid., 187–89.
99. A. Legrand, "Die elsässische Kulturfrage," *RAI* (1910): 30–31.
100. Joseph Fleurent, "L'idée de patrie en Alsace," *Revue politique et parliamentaire* 14 (January/February/March 1907): 327–33.
101. Ibid., 338–39.
102. Ibid., 340.
103. Ibid., 340.
104. Ibid., 341–42.
105. John E. Craig, *Scholarship and Nation Building: The Universities of Strasbourg and Alsatian Society 1870–1939* (Chicago, 1984), 173–79.
106. Anselm Laugel, "L'Avenir intellectual de l'Alsace," *Revue politique et parliamentaire* 14 (July/August/September 1908): 252.
107. Ibid., 251–52.
108. Ibid., 256–58.
109. Ibid., 262.
110. Ibid., 266.

Chapter 2

MONUMENTS, MUSEUMS, AND MEMORY
COMMEMORATION IN ALSACE, 1900–1914

Strasbourg, Alsace's capital and cultural center, served as the central site in the struggles to define what it meant to be Alsatian. Indeed, fights over cultural identity and political loyalty often became interwoven into the city's landscape. Under German rule, the Kaiserplatz (Emperor's Square, today the Place de la République) became one such center where the Germans projected their vision of German Alsace onto the physical environs. The imperial residence and university library along with other governmental buildings on the plaza represented the political and cultural power of Germany in Alsace.

Germans and Alsatians sought to use public spaces across the region to define Alsace's history, and more broadly, national belonging. Monuments and museums served as concrete representations of the larger debates over Alsace's past. Much like the articles in the *RAI*, the contributions to the *JfGSL*, or the books of Hansi, monuments framed the present and future of the region by clearly defining the region's past. Fights over history, or more precisely, collective memory, overlapped with contemporary politics. The historiography of collective memory—embodied in such works as Pierre Nora's monumental collection on French *lieux de mémoire*—is rich and diverse. Drawing on Daniel Sherman, collective memory shall be defined as "the ideas, assumptions, and knowledges that structure the relationship of individuals and groups to the immediate as well as the distant past."[1] One might add that collective memory, by shaping a present community in light of its past, has embedded within it a conception of the community's future.[2]

The ways by which collective memories can be iterated or represented are diverse. Commemoration—whether through monuments, museums, national cemeteries, holidays, or other events celebrating important dates or milestones—helps shape collective memories. Commemoration evokes a specific representation of a particular event or epoch to reaffirm or create a particular social and cultural vision made

---

Notes for this section begin on page 69.

"inherent" in the commemorated event.³ The practice of commemoration, then, in theory serves to provide a coherent narrative for a defined community, thereby inculcating a sense of belonging among the members of a given community.

While the practice of commemoration strives to create coherence, it may also open the door to discord. Groups do not always agree on the proper means, or even propriety of, dedicating a space, place, or time to a specific event or person.⁴ Internal differences, especially for events in the recent past, may exist between witnesses (or participants) and those less directly involved in the event in question. Such divergent interpretations may exist due to differences in religion, class, or political affiliation. Debates over how to commemorate properly point to a second major issue, that of power. Part of the contest over memory comes from a struggle to impose a common identity onto groups that may not feel part of, or may have variances with, a particular version of events. Therefore the act of commemoration may not become a moment of unity within a given community, but rather may serve to crystallize divisions.

In Alsace, the erection of monuments and museums brought to the fore issues of memory and belonging. For German nationalists, the architecture of the recently reestablished university, friezes on the main Strasbourg train station, or statues of Wilhelm I could visibly tie Alsace to Germany's glories of both the distant and more recent past. Francophile Alsatians, in turn, could criticize these projects, often on aesthetic grounds, to undermine efforts to impose a German past on the region. Concurrently, Alsatians like Pierre Bucher, the Dollinger brothers, and Anselm Laugel pushed for the establishment of monuments promoting a French version of Alsace's past, ranging from the Alsatian Museum to the war memorial at Wissembourg.

This chapter examines the built environment to analyze Alsatian and German strategies to define Alsace's past, present, and future. In particular, this chapter focuses on three major projects. First, it looks to the restoration of the castle of Hohkönigsburg, a medieval fortress that the Kaiser reconstructed to demonstrate the return of German power to the region. The chapter then turns to the Musée alsacien, an ethnographic museum founded by Pierre Bucher and the brothers Dollinger. Finally, it considers the creation of the war monument at Wissembourg in 1909, a memorial dedicated to Alsatians who had fallen while serving under the French flag.

The Restoration of Hohkönigsburg

Schools, the German bureaucracy, and the military (through conscription) formed important elements of the German effort to turn Alsatians into loyal Germans. Beyond such institutions, German nationalists tried to inculcate a sense of Germanness in the Alsatians through other means. For example, the University of Strasbourg, opened in 1873, was supposed to impress both Alsatians and the world with the erudition of German scholarship.⁵ Several of the *Statthalter* underwrote large artistic projects to bring first-class German art to Alsace. And private groups such as the Vogesenverein sought to use history to their advantage in promoting German-Alsatian ties.

Architecture, especially in the form of monuments, served as yet another means of putatively binding Alsace to Germany. For example, Strasbourg's Kaiserplatz had at its center a statue of Wilhelm I and was surrounded by the Imperial Residence, the main administrative buildings of the *Reichsland* government, the seat of the *Landesausschuss*, and the University Library. The last of these was adorned with busts of major German and European thinkers, writers, and artists as a means of demonstrating the importance of Germans to the European canon. Likewise, the main friezes at the newly built Strasbourg central train station depicted scenes of Friedrich Barbarossa in Alsace, thereby linking the medieval Holy Roman Empire, Germany, and Alsace together. Indeed, this medieval connection between the region and the German nation provided one of the most consistent and important themes by which German nationalists sought to evoke a sense of a common past in Alsace.⁶

The reconstruction of Hohkönigsburg was to assume a key role in representing, in concrete monumental terms, these historical ties. Hohkönigsburg itself sits atop a mountain overlooking the city of Sélestat. Originally built in the twelfth century, the castle was sacked and later rebuilt in the sixteenth century, only to suffer another siege and destruction during the Thirty Years' War.⁷ Over the next several centuries, the ruins had several French noblemen for owners, and fell further into desuetude until finally coming into the possession of the city of Sélestat in the mid-nineteenth century. In May 1899, the municipal council of Sélestat, citing patriotic reasons, decided to give the ruins to Kaiser Wilhelm II during his visit to the town.

Wilhelm II welcomed the donation as a sign of "the trusting love between myself and the *Reichsland*," and hoped the castle would "watch over a peaceful and content population."⁸ The donation itself, however, raised several questions in the local press. While the Sélestat city council presented it as a gift from loyal subjects to their monarch, accusations of ulterior motives abounded. Above all, critics accused the town of trying to rid itself of a white elephant; indeed, as numerous articles pointed out, the city council had been denied funds for the maintenance of the ruins by the *Landesausschuss* the previous year.⁹ While Sélestat's mayor protested in local papers that the town had only patriotic intentions, a letter written by the German administrator in charge of the area around Sélestat places the town's motives in a more ambivalent light.

Kreisdirektor Albert Dieckmann, an imperial official in Sélestat, shortly before the inauguration of the restored castle and in the belief he would soon succumb to illness, claimed to have been the moving presence behind the donation. Dieckmann suggested to his superiors, including the *Statthalter*, that the castle could be turned over to the kaiser by the city. His request, however, was rejected on the grounds that politics were not his bailiwick; moreover, the cost of maintaining the ruins would be immense. Undeterred, Dieckmann slyly suggested to several of the city council members that one way to maintain the castle, a continual drain on the city coffers, would be to give the ruins to the kaiser. The city council, "enthused" with the idea, agreed to offer the castle to the kaiser on his impending visit.[10] The council members' decision to donate Hohkönigsburg—or at least the pretense that they, as loyal subjects, were bestowing the ruins of the castle—allowed the imperial administration to prepare for the donation with the hope that local involvement would obviate local opposition to the move.[11]

The controversy surrounding the original intent of the Sélestat city fathers paled in comparison to the debates over whether the castle, or any castle, ought to be restored to its original, historical form (as far as such was possible) or simply preserved as historic ruins. In the late nineteenth and early twentieth century, architects, preservationists, and historians debated the issue fiercely. Preservationists argued that one could not possibly recreate a fallen building and thus rejected the idea of "restoration" in favor of preservation. In contrast, restorationists, in the firm belief that the historical integrity of buildings and monuments could be recreated, maintained that such restored "documents of stone" could continue to speak to current generations at the local, regional, and national levels.[12]

As Rudy Koshar has noted, the question of Hohkönigsburg became a central battleground in such debates, especially after Wilhelm II decided to restore the castle. Bodo Ebhardt, the Berlin-based architect chosen by the kaiser and his advisers to oversee the restoration plans, and later, the actual reconstruction, found himself the target of criticism both small and large. The director of the regional archive, for example, displayed great reticence in supporting his efforts, repeatedly delaying requests for materials that might help Ebhardt plan his reconstruction. On a larger scale, professional preservationists criticized the plans for the restoration, both in their journal *Monument Preservation (Die Denkmalpflege)* and at their annual conference (*Tag der Denkmalpflege*) in 1900 and 1901 as well as in the national press. Ebhardt was forced to defend his work personally at the 1901 conference. In particular, critics argued that the reconstruction would be flawed due to a lack of proper information, and moreover, that a restored castle would never be able to evoke accurately the past it tried to recall.[13]

These national debates trickled down to the regional level; local opponents of the project adopted this language of opposition to their own cause to criticize the restoration in the local press and local legislative assembly. While the local liberal nationalist paper, the *Strassburger Post*, generally supported the project, other local papers took a more critical stance.[14] Many questioned the possibility of ever accurately restoring the castle. One local paper even suggested that the castle might infringe upon the picturesque beauty of the region around Sélestat.[15] This is not to say that there was no local support for the project; some art historians argued in favor and some local businessmen saw potential for a reconstructed castle, especially in long-term gains from tourism.[16]

Financial concerns surrounding the castle's restoration also caused an uproar. As it became clear that the *Reichsland* would be asked to bear part of the costs of reconstruction, local papers linked the potential financial difficulties of the project to its dubious aesthetic goals. For example, one of the local Catholic papers strongly opposed the project. The paper argued Sélestat had only donated the property to absolve itself of the costs of maintaining the ruins; moreover, as the castle was "the personal possession of the kaiser and not a responsibility of the German people, both the Reichstag and *Landesausschuss* should reject the projected 1.5 million-mark project."[17] The *Strassburger Zeitung* echoed such calls, and argued that both legislative bodies should reject the castle project because instead of creating beauty, the restored castle would create "a false romanticism that threatened the true poignancy of the ruins."[18] Other papers were more direct, stating that "we view it as an insult from the kaiser that the pennies [*Grotschen*] of the poor taxpayers of Alsace-Lorraine be demanded for the restoration of the castle."[19]

Opposition to the project in the press was reflected in the debates of the *Landesausschuss*. Although this body possessed limited powers in terms of legislative initiative and ministerial responsibility, it did have the ability to confirm the annual budget for Alsace-Lorraine. In 1901 and 1902 the *Landesauschuss* was asked to approve an annual expenditure of 150,000 marks to help underwrite approximately half of the restoration costs. The Alsatian legislative body had numerous members whose support for Germany in general, and the emperor in particular, was at best lukewarm; therefore, the request for sizeable donations to the emperor's own possession, a castle that was to stand as a clear symbol of German predominance in the region, received a cold welcome.

The *Landesaussschuss* deputies marshaled several arguments against matching the Reichstag's financial support of the project. Some of the arguments were aesthetic in nature. For example, Laugel opined, "Restoration . . . [is] simply impossible, because no one can know how things were earlier." Yet he was "pleased with the plans . . . though it [the restoration] was a difficult task." Laugel, despite his aesthetic misgivings, stated he was "prepared to approve [the project] in light of considerations of a political nature."[20] In other words, Alsace-Lorraine would begrudgingly support the project in the hope that the *Diktatur* would be lifted. Others conceded this point, and even noted that the project might have a historical significance, but queried whether the ruins held importance for Alsatians. Others, angered at the political situation, questioned the project and its links to political progress. For example, Deputy Ditsch argued, "Today as we have thirty years of annexation behind us, we also have to our immense regret thirty years of *Diktatur*. How long will this yet last? Only the gods and the government in Strasbourg know."[21] Finally, some deputies, such as Emile Wetterlé, questioned whether the body would have provided such funds if Sélestat or a preservation society had put forth the request for the project. Moreover, he questioned the "public use or necessity" of such a project to be underwritten by regional taxpayers.[22]

Despite vocal and public opposition, the *Landesausschuss* approved the budgetary measures for funding the castle. The reason for the seeming opposition between word and deed lies in the peculiar political circumstances of Alsace-Lorraine. Alsace-Lorraine, unlike the other German states of the federal empire, found its political rights severely limited. The region had no voting rights in the German Federal Council. The *Landesausschuss* had only limited rights to initiate legislation, and the regional

Figure 2.1 Wilhelm II vists Hohkönigsburg

executive, the *Statthalter*, was named by the emperor and had no ministerial responsibility to the *Landesausschuss*. More importantly, under the region's constitution, the German governor could exercise emergency powers to squelch potential security breaches within the border region, powers enumerated under the *"Diktatur"* paragraph of the constitution of Alsace-Lorraine. The *Landesausschuss*, by approving of the budget for the castle's restoration, hoped for an improvement in the political status of Alsace-Lorraine.[23]

Although Wilhelm II lifted the *Diktatur* in 1902 while visiting Hohkönigsburg (See Figure 2.1), the castle continued to provoke controversy. When the project ran over budget and more support was requested from the *Landesausschuss*, Alsatian and Lorrainer deputies responded with skepticism.[24] Wetterlé, for example, criticized the architect Ebhardt as either "incompetent" or a liar, stating further that "the Thiersteiner[25] Castle is not at all being rebuilt, it is not a restoration of the old castle. More accurately, it is a new construction in the view of Herr Ebhardt, a complete work of fantasy."[26] Laugel echoed such criticisms; he, along with numerous other deputies, asked who exactly would foot the bill for maintaining the newly restored castle. Daniel Blumenthal, a liberal deputy from Colmar, went so far as to argue that a rejection of the measure would serve "as a demonstration on behalf of the *Land*." But some deputies, reasoning that inflation had driven up costs, supported the measure; moreover, deputies Hoeffel and Goetz suggested tax funds from both Alsace and the Reichstag would thereby remain in Alsace. Despite the vocal opposition of Blumenthal, Laugel, and Wetterlé as well as the interwar autonomist Eugen Ricklin, the appropriation of additional funds was approved by a vote of thirty-nine to ten.

Beyond the political and aesthetic debates surrounding the restoration of the castle, several minor problems arose. One issue was the question of how to use the interior of the castle. The Hohkönigsburgsverein (Hohkönigsburg Society), which supported the restoration, wanted to install a small museum dedicated to the popular art and ethnography of Alsace within the castle walls. To this end, the group gained a concession to conduct a lottery to outfit the interior.[27] At first criticized in the press for wanting a museum far removed from most of its likely visitors, the association ran into another problem. The best examples of the art that the club wanted to collect—ornate stoves, pottery, traditional dresses, and items emblematic of Alsatian culture and traditions—had already been gathered by the founders of the Musée alsacien. Rather than staking a claim to represent Alsatian culture and history within the symbolically important castle, the society had to defer to the *musée* and instead chose to collect arms and armaments representative of the castle itself.

The official unveiling of the castle in May 1908 (See Figure 2.2) sparked renewed criticism of the project. The gala included a luncheon, a pageant of Germans in late medieval dress, and a poem written and recited by

Figure 2.2. Hohkönigsburg

Friedrich Lienhard. The festivities were aimed, much like the castle, at symbolically linking Alsace and Germany as well as the Hohenzollern lineage with that of the Hohenstaufen and Carolingian dynasties.[28] Keeping in line with their seemingly pathological need to annoy the Alsatians with the castle, the Germans left the members of the *Landesausschuss* off the list of dignitaries asked to attend the ceremonies. Invited belatedly, many members of the body chose not show up at all.

Reactions to the event were mixed. Many papers across the political spectrum praised the festivities themselves (though some took delight in the impact that a steady rain had upon the occasion). Most critics, however, found the speeches a disappointment.[29] The kaiser, while praising the people of Alsace for both the gift of the castle and the funds for its restoration, also tried to tie the castle to the region's past and future, saying:

> The castle is again in the possession of the German kaiser and it will, God willingly, remain ever so. . . . May Hohkönigsburg here in the West as Marienburg[30] in the East stand as a symbol of German culture and power for all time, and let it serve as a pious reminder of the past to the edification and joy to all those thousands and thousands who journey to this imperial seat.[31]

The kaiser's avoidance of some sort of conciliatory gesture to the Alsatians—for example, many hoped that the kaiser would offer Alsatians and Lorrainers the chance to write a new constitution—overshadowed his efforts to link German and Alsatian history. Instead of symbolizing the historic ties between Alsace and Germany, then, the castle became yet another symbol of the rather heavy-handed attempt of the Germans to assimilate the region's population.[32]

After its inauguration, the castle faded from view as an object of controversy. It did, however, become a popular tourist site. As gleaned from the guest books from the years 1909–14, the castle was well visited by Germans and Alsatians, though numerous entries indicate visitors from the neighboring French departments. Moreover, tourists from as far away as Cleveland and Lublin visited the site.[33] The castle was closed during the war, passed into French hands in 1919, and later became a French national monument. It did not, however, successfully inculcate a greater sense of patriotism among Alsatians for Germany; and indeed, it serves as a reminder of the nationalist pretensions of Wilhelm II.[34]

The Musée alsacien

In contrast to Hohkönigsburg, the Musée alsacien was a far more modest institution: a small, urban museum dedicated to the popular art, traditions, and history of Alsace. Yet the simplicity of the *musée* and the virtual lack of controversy (though not lack of attention) surrounding its foundation belie its importance in shaping regional identity and conceptions of Alsatian history. Moreover, while the collections of the *musée* resembled similar museums established across Germany in the decades before World War I, the activities sponsored by the museum revealed the ulterior aims of its founders. The wider context of Alsatian regionalism of the pre-1914 period afforded the *musée's* organizers the opportunity to promote a pro-French vision under the guise of celebrating local culture.

The founders of the Musée alsacien included a familiar group of Alsatian activists: Charles Spindler, Anselm Laugel, Gustave Stoskopf, Pierre Bucher, Jules Greber, and the brothers Dollinger.[35] Members of the Groupe St. Leonard, the founders traced the idea for the museum to a shared interest in Alsatian traditional dress. Indeed, at the turn of the century, Stoskopf and Spindler began to travel around Alsace to collect examples of Alsatian *Trachten*,[36] and Spindler and Laugel wrote an illustrated guide to Alsatian traditional dress in 1902. Stoskopf, according to the *Strassburger Bürgerzeitung*, hoped to use the costume collection as a complementary way of promoting the Alsatian theater.

A small, poorly documented controversy seemed to infuse the project in its early stages. Bucher took on the main responsibility for the project around 1900, and by 1902, was fully in control of it. It appears, however, that Gustave Stoskopf was edged out of the picture. Stoskopf and Greber on one side, and Bucher and his compatriots on the other, disagreed on whether or not official state support for the museum should be sought. The Stoskopf camp lost, and the museum was established as a private, limited liability corporation.[37]

Calling on fellow Alsatians to join in a "common homage to the *patrie*," the founders of the museum wanted to create a museum dedicated to the region's art and popular traditions.[38] The prelude to the organization's statutes made its goals clear: "The aim of this enterprise is the creation of an Alsatian ethnographical museum, destined to hold objects of any nature that belong to Alsatian art or popular traditions, to group these objects, and to display and maintain [them] for exposition to public curiosity at a locale especially appropriate to this usage."[39] In this way, the museum both symbolized and propagated the Alsatian Renaissance.

The foundation of a museum of Alsatian popular art received unequivocally high praise from the Alsatian press whether liberal, Catholic, or German nationalist. Most journals, claiming that it was high time for such a institution to be created in Strasbourg, praised the museum's creation. The Catholic paper, *Der Elsässer*, called upon "wider circles to take advantage of" the museum, while the liberal papers wished the museum "fullest support and great success." Even the nationalist *Strassburger Post* hoped that the planned museum "would be passionately supported" to help offer the city a "complete picture of the old Alsatian popular life."[40] With such benedictions, the museum's founders set about actually establishing the institution.

Using the materials gathered by Stoskopf and Spindler as starting points, the brothers Dollinger, along with Bucher, scoured the Alsatian countryside for artifacts of Alsatian culture. As Léon Dollinger recounted in 1910, the farmers and artisans from whom the materials were collected met the project with amusement.[41] Why, after all, would anyone want to collect old furniture, clothes, and kitchen utensils for a museum? Despite the skepticism encountered by Bucher and Léon Dollinger, the collection slowly came together. Moreover, Bucher and Ferdinand Dollinger, acting as the museum's directors, purchased a house on the Quai St. Nicolas in 1904, hired an architect to upgrade the sixteenth-century home, and began to install the exhibits of the future museum.

Bucher utilized his position as editor of the *RAI* to promote the museum, for example, by inviting Maurice Barrès to contribute articles on the importance of the museum to the preservation of Alsatian uniqueness.[42] Bucher, again utilizing the resources of the *RAI*, began publishing a series entitled "Images from the Alsatian Museum," photographs depicting classic examples of Alsatian dress, architecture, and furniture. Beyond items earmarked for the museum proper, Bucher included pictures of Alsatians in their hometowns in traditional dress, houses deemed emblematic of the Alsatian architectural style, and furniture in its normal setting.[43] Although subscriptions for the "Images" seemed never to have surpassed 250, subscribers included numerous prominent members of Alsatian society, including members of the Schlumberger family (whose financial interests were far-flung and successful) and Hugo Zorn von Bulach, an Alsatian noble who held several important posts in the regional administration.[44]

Moreover, the "Images" found praise in the local press, which heightened the impact of the serial.[45]

The museum finally opened its doors to the public in May 1907. Ensconced within a traditional half-timbered Alsatian house, its three stories contained examples of Alsatian wood carving and metalwork, displays on Alsatian dress, kitchen implements, toys, household religious objects, and even an example of a wine press in honor of the region's signature industry.[46] Indeed, the museum put forth an image of Alsace as an idealized rustic, rural culture, celebrating popular traditions as a part of a seemingly timeless and unchanging Alsace.(See Figure 2.3) The founders were so skillful in their presentation of Alsatian popular art that the museum received almost universal praise in the local press. Indeed, the *Strassburger Post*, usually a critic of the *RAI* and of the indigenous Francophile elite in general, closed its glowing review of the museum with the call, "go, ladies and gentleman, go to the Alsatian Museum."[47]

Such universal displays and public support, however, belied the ulterior motives of Bucher and his collaborators. Sprinkled through the museum were indications of Alsace's French past; for example, French soldiers stood among the toys, French draft notices were among a collection of documents, and a banner dedicated to Napoleon hung in the special section celebrating Jewish culture in Alsace. In a similar, if far more muted fashion than the *RAI*, the Musée alsacien provided Bucher and his cohort with the means of projecting two images of Alsace: one timeless, rustic, and intimately tied to the quotidian habits of Alsace's inhabitants; the other inherently French.

Figure 2.3. Alstaian Kitchen, Musée Alscien

For example, the museum served as a host for several fêtes that raised funds to send lower-class Alsatian children to French-language camps.[48] The first event celebrated Alsatian traditional dress. The second, the Fête d'Erckmann-Chatrian, saw the museum's supporters decked out in the attire of the characters of the Émile Erckmann and Louis-Alexandre Chatrian play *Madame Thérèse*, set in the time of the French Revolution. By employing a play by a pair of local writers, the museum managed to hold an event that recalled the French past in the region without arousing the suspicions of the German authorities.

The regional papers, consistent with earlier attitudes, praised both events.[49] The *Journal d'Alsace-Lorraine*, a Francophile periodical, commended the collection of funds for the summer camps.[50] The following year, the journal lauded the revolutionary costumes as "rare, original, and artistic," the setting a "familial home of Alsace, a reminder full of emotion and charm."[51] The liberal *Strassburger Bürgerzeitung* also waxed effusively, reporting, "The courtyard offered a picture that one might have seen 120 years ago. . . . Each costume is a work of art," and concluding, "I can counsel all readers, to—hopefully!—visit the Bazaar today or tomorrow."[52] Even the *Strassburger Post* praised the museum's activities, writing that Ferdinand Dollinger gave the paper's representative a personal tour of the festival; even the rain that day "much as it did not hinder the Revolution, neither did it this memorable fest."[53]

German fascination with the museum should have come as no surprise. As we have seen in the previous chapter, German groups studied the same Alsatian cultural and physical artifacts as the founders of the *musée* and, by extension, the *RAI*. Such "popular art or folklore museums" [*Volkskunst/Volkskunde*], moreover, were common to the *Kaiserreich*; as Alon Confino notes, at least 371 such museums sprang up between 1871 and 1918.[54] Thus, the Alsatian Museum was likely viewed as promoting a Germanic culture to Germans, Alsatian culture to Alsatians, and a veiled French Alsace to the museum's founders.

During the Great War, German authorities confiscated the museum as part of their actions against many of the museum founders, including Bucher and the brothers Dollinger.[55] While German authorities decided what to do with the institution, the interim and later interwar curator of the museum pressed for the sale of the museum to the city. He wrote in a memo:

> In our opinion, the city of Strasbourg would fulfill an honorable duty through the takeover of the museum. It is urgently necessary that every political tendency be eliminated from every organization that engages in cultural efforts, and that they safeguard only the common good. The earlier managers of the Alsatian Museum did not support such basic ideas in every respect, although their activities in the expansion of the museum merited much recognition.[56]

The city did assume control of the museum in 1917 and named Adolph Riff as curator. After the war, the town council voted to compensate the museum's original founders, many of whom had fled to France during the war, for their investment and adopted a twenty-year repayment schedule.[57]

The museum also seems to have maintained its importance in the years following the Armistice. Judging by the correspondence of the museum's interwar curator, who requested additional help for cleaning, the coat-check, and for overseeing visiting guests, the museum enjoyed a popularity similar to that of the prewar years.[58] Moreover, according to the museum's guest book, the museum appears to have become regular destination for visiting luminaries: notable visitors included Edouard Herriot, Marshalls Joffre and Lyautey, Louis Barthou, and Alexandre Millerand, as well as Rudyard Kipling and the Prince of the Netherlands.

Celebrating the region's popular art and architecture, dress, and rustic lifestyle, the Musée alsacien embodied many of the central concepts of the Alsatian Renaissance. Moreover, by presenting Alsatian culture and history, tied to the peasant tradition and lifestyle, the museum offered a vision of Alsace as timeless and lacking any particular national overtones, in any case as not at all German. The occasional references to the region's French heritage remained muted amid the baker's tools and chairs, traditional dress, and reconstructed Alsatian parlors. The museum thereby served to contrast the region's history with the more politically minded Hohkönigsburg and, in 1909, the monument erected in Wissembourg to Alsatian soldiers fallen under the French flag.

"Morts Pour la Patrie": The War Monument at Wissembourg

Wissembourg had been the site of a French defeat in August 1870 during the opening stages of the Franco-Prussian War. The "cult of the dead" did not simply materialize in 1909 and assume an immediate importance. The German government for years had allowed the erection and maintenance of gravesites dedicated to the fallen French soldiers of 1870–71.[59] Both French and German veterans had for decades maintained gravesites, visited battlefields, and at times, such as at Noisseville in Lorraine in 1908, even commemorated their fallen comrades together.[60]

The inauguration of the monument at Wissembourg, in contrast, saw issues of national belonging assume a new level of acrimony as the German press roundly denounced the presence, however minor, of French flags at the ceremonies. The attendance of Souvenir Française members at the ceremonies, an association founded by Xavier Neissen in France in 1887 to commemorate the loss of one hundred thousand troops during the Franco-Prussian war, also provoked ire, especially as the group was also dedicated to remember the lost provinces, had supporters throughout France, and enjoyed semiofficial status as an organization recognized by the French state. Thus, the celebration of the monument reinvigorated nationalist debates over the region and even forced the usually open-minded *Statthalter*, Karl Graf von Wedel, to take steps to curb the influence of French nationalists.[61]

If Hohkönigsburg represented the most ambitious efforts by the Germans to tie the region to the nation, and if the Musée alsacien served as an emblem of a muted French Alsatianness, then the monument erected at Wissembourg in 1909 stood as the most prominent attempt to tie the region's history directly to that of France. Yet the Wissembourg monument was not the first attempt of Francophile Alsatians to commemorate their French past under German auspices. For example, in May 1908, under the direction of André Kiener, a local industrialist, and Daniel Blumenthal, Colmar's mayor and a member of the *Landesausschuss*, a monument was erected in honor of the sculptor Auguste Bartholdi.[62] German authorities were concerned about the use of French at the ceremonies, but relented, noting that Bartholdi's widow did not speak German. The speeches therefore were delivered in both languages. Likewise, the use of French inscriptions on the monument was opposed by some bureaucrats, but again the inscription "A Auguste Bartholdi" passed muster as "the sculptor's native language was French." Finally, the mention of Bartholdi's military service in 1870 and his work on the "Lion of Belfort," dedicated to the same conflict, raised some eyebrows, but not enough to merit official sanction.[63]

The monument at Wissembourg first emerged as a project in 1907 when a committee appealed for financial support for the project, which it renewed the ensuing year. Using an office in Wissembourg as one base of operations, and the space at the *RAI* in Strasbourg as another, the committee for the monument laid the groundwork for the project. Local politicians, for example, endorsed the project, including Reichstag deputies Delsor, Hauss, Hoeffel, Preis, Ricklin, Vonderscheer, Wetterlé, Will, and Wiltberger. A subcommittee was formed in 1908, led by Anselm Laugel, to conduct a competition among sculptors, with Albert Schultz gaining the honor of creating the monument.[64]

As the day of the unveiling of the monument approached, expectations ran high among the participants in the ceremony. The festivities surrounding the inauguration, however, also caused great consternation among German authorities. Indeed, *Statthalter* von Wedel took the occasion to consider the place of regionalism and nationalism in Alsace in a circular to the *Bezirkspräsidenten*, revealing not only German attitudes toward Alsatians but of the political landscape in Alsace in general. Wedel, as both the circular and his activities in general reveal, tended to take a less nationalistic approach toward the Alsatians than many of his underlings in the *Reichsland* or colleagues across the Rhine.[65]

At the crux of Wedel's circular was the question of how the *Reichsland* administration should handle the upcoming festivities. Wedel had grave concerns about the intentions of the planners. An "increase in the number of demonstrations" by a "small, but powerful group" with the goal of "maintaining the memory of the region's former attachment to France" was an issue. Moreover, the Souvenir Français was without doubt a "questionable institution" that required "urgent" surveillance. Therefore, parades with French music, processions to and from the French border, and open displays of the French flag were to be "absolutely forbidden." Wedel, however, also wanted the gendarmes and civil servants present to treat the participants "calmly and cautiously" to avoid any major demonstrations; in any case, the honoring of fallen comrades was to be respected. By not squelching the demonstration outright but also by curbing the more pro-French demonstrations at the unveiling, Wedel hoped to avoid the appearance that the Germans "wanted to stamp Frenchness into the grave out of blind and trivial hate." For the monument, Wedel's administration sought to allow the festivities to take place without angering German nationalists while simultaneously also denying pro-French Alsatians further grist for their anti-German mill.[66]

The ceremonies dedicating the monument began on October 16, 1909, with a service at the Catholic church in Wissembourg. Abbé Meuley, priest from the Invalides in Paris, gave the first sermon in French, largely praising the fallen, but also tying their sacrifice to that of the fallen of 1793 and the sacrifice of Joan of Arc. Abbé Delsor of Strasbourg followed with a speech in German, largely focused on the religious aspect of sacrifice for "the homeland" [*Heimat*]. After a brief service at the local synagogue, and a break for lunch, the ceremonies proceeded to the mausoleum of General Abel Douay, a French officer killed in action in August 1870. There, Emile Wetterlé gave a rather restrained speech hinting at "the past glories of our province" and praising the French general "not a son of this land [*pays*], but we consider him one of ours, as he died while defending our soil." The participants then placed wreaths on an isolated set of graves in the forest before returning to Wissembourg for an evening banquet.[67]

Sunday's activities began with a service at a local Protestant church where A. Gérold praised the fallen for "remaining faithful, faithful to the flag and faithful to the fatherland [*patrie*] unto death." Following the services, the participants, among them both French and German veteran groups, local musical clubs, Alsatian women in traditional dress, and thousands of bystanders, proceeded to the new monument for the actual inauguration ceremonies. There, the president of the committee for the monument, Antoine Spinner, opened the commemoration "to the French soldiers fallen for the fatherland," and then extolled the Alsatian heroes of the Revolution (Kléber, Broglie, etc.) who "have always given to the *mère-patrie* without reservation." Continuing in the same vein, and clearly linking region and nation, Spinner finished, "French soldiers who died for the *patrie*! to you, immortality, to us, the memory!" The rest of the day's speeches proceeded largely without incident, though Jacques Preiss, an Alsatian deputy to the Reichstag, commented in a speech that evening upon "the bereavement of France and the bereavement of Alsace. It is not possible to separate France and Alsace in the veneration of their common children fallen for a common cause;" he thereby explicitly linked France and Alsace but drew no official censure.[68]

For the Alsatian press, the monument's dedication served as a cause célèbre. All of the major papers across the political spectrum devoted the bulk of their front pages to coverage of the festivities. The Catholic *Elsässer Kurier*, for example, commented upon the bedecked streets of Wissembourg formed "a wonderful and colorful picture," although they were packed with "an immense mob." Indeed, the paper estimated that between veteran organizations and music groups, members of the Souvenir Français, and simple onlookers, over fifty thousand people participated in the dedication ceremonies.[69] The *Elsässer Volksbote* and the local *Weissenburger Zeitung* likewise wrote extensively on the size of the crowds present, and all three papers made careful mention of the fact that the *Marseillaise* was sung at the end of the dedication ceremony, though the *Kurier* noted that "few sung quietly at first, then many joined in" before applauding the draping of the *drapeau tricolore* over the monument.[70]

Other papers offered more direct commentary on the festivities. For example, the *Strassburger Neueste Nachrichten* provided a highly detailed account of the festivities, including transcripts of all of the speeches of the day. This liberal paper indicated that the day held a "neutral character," in part due to the permission granted for the various speeches by German censors. The speeches, especially of Spinner, seem to belie this "neutral character," with their references, both direct and oblique, to Alsace's ties to France. Other papers took a decidedly more Francophile stance. For example, the *Freie Presse*, a socialist daily under the leadership of Jacques Peirotes, one of the most consistently Francophile papers, connected the fallen of 1870 to volunteers of 1793 by noting that the men had not fallen for "great lords," but "fought for a beautiful cause, great and just; they died as heroes. . . . We salute the valiant troops, who even as they fell, sacrificed their life for the *patrie*, spilling all their blood for the native land [*terre*]."[71] In contrast, Wetterlé's Colmar-based *Nouvelliste* refrained from taking advantage of the situation. Instead the paper merely provided detailed coverage of the event, offering sparing commentary on the vast number of Alsatians, French, and Germans who participated in the weekend's events, praising the speeches, and lamenting the end of the ceremonies.[72]

In official circles, the initial perspective on the monument's dedication was relatively benign. Graf Bissingen-Nippenburg, *Kreisdirektor* of Wissembourg, expressed qualms about some of the comments by Spinner and the head of the Souvenir Français, Niessen. He also put the total of participants at approximately thirty thousand, a number significantly lower than proclaimed in the Alsatian press. He noted in his report to the *Bezirkspräsident*, however, that "the local population of the *Kreis* Wissembourg, as far I could observe and heard from many quarters, behaved quietly and correctly, and the well-represented local population of the *Reichsland* did not participate in the demonstrations heavily laced with French sympathies."[73] This initial acceptance, however, was belied by subsequent developments. From the Francophile side, Spinner made it abundantly clear in later recollections that he felt the event had served its purpose, "linking local, regional, and national [French] history," his goal from the inception of the project.[74]

More importantly, the deep resonance of the event aroused the concern of the local administration as well as the ire of nationalists across the Rhine. In addition, speeches by several Alsatians in Paris, among them Wetterlé, disturbed *Reichland* administrators. As a result, the Alsatian branch of the Souvenir Français was branded a political organization and disbanded in 1912. Not content to allow the organization to die out, Spinner, along with other notables such as Laugel and Henri Zislin reorganized the Souvenir and renamed it Souvenir Alsace-Lorraine. German authorities were less than impressed and set about trying to prove that the organization remained political, and moreover, that "traitorous activity" is "the aim, to awaken *an exclusive inclination to France* [underscored in original text] in the population of the *Land* through a one-sided glorification of the French character and French fame."[75] Although the administration lost its original case against the group in court, and Alsace's liberal papers vociferously protested the legality of the investigation, the *Reichsland* government realized a ban against the organization in 1913.[76] Indeed, the regional administration instructed its local officials to keep close tabs on the former organization to stamp it out root and branch.

Conclusion

The restoration of the castle at Hohkönigsburg, the creation of the Musée alsacien, and the inauguration of the monument at Wissembourg all served as key moments in the debate over Alsace's past. At least in the fight over memory in public spaces, the Germans, despite their grandiose notions and hopes, could not awaken the same enthusiasm that Francophile Alsatians, with the support of the Souvenir Français, generated for their monument for the fallen in French wars. And neither castle nor monument captured the apparently essential, timeless nature of Alsace as found in the Musée alsacien. Hohkönigsburg later became, narrated through the German loss of WWI, the symbol of failed German ambitions.

The erection of the monument at Wissembourg, in contrast, assumed a major role as part of the effort to keep the French memory alive in France, but would be quickly overshadowed in the interwar decades by new monuments dedicated to the memory of the fallen of the Great War. The short-term success of the Wissembourg monument was also less than its heavy press coverage might otherwise indicate. The proponents of the project, many of whom also supported the *RAI*, as we shall see in the following chapter, had difficulties translating the cultural vision of a French Alsace into political success.

The debates over the various monuments helped keep Alsace's view of past, present, and future in a state of turmoil. The restored castle at Hohkönigsburg did not capture the imagination of Alsatians as people with a Germanic past; the monument at Wissembourg had limited impact. However, as they celebrated the festivities of October 1909, most Francophile Alsatians could not foresee, barring war (an idea that most categorically rejected), the possibility of a return to France. Between these two poles lay a widely defined common ground. Alsace's past was unique, partially grounded in its French past, partially in the region's own allegedly timeless traditions. This vision of an independent Alsatian past in turn fueled the drive by Alsatians for their region, along with Lorraine, to attain the status of a full-fledged Land within the German Empire. Differing conceptions over Alsace's past, overlaid with local politics and religious concerns, would play into the debate over the form of Alsace's new constitution.

Notes

1. Daniel Sherman, *The Construction of Memory in Interwar France* (Chicago, 1999), 2.
2. Jay Bodner, "Public Memory in an American Society: Commemoration in Cleveland," in *Commemorations: The Politics of National Identity*, ed. John R. Gillis (Princeton, NJ, 1994), 76.
3. Sherman, *Construction of Memory*, 6.
4. Bodner, "Public Memory," 76; Sarah Farmer, *Martyred Village: Commemorating the 1944 Massacre at Oradour-sur-Glane* (Berkeley, CA, 1999); Charlotte Taacke, *Denkmal im sozialen Raum: Nationale Symbole in Deutschland und Frankreich im 19. Jahrhundert* (Göttingen, 1995).
5. John E. Craig, *Scholarship and Nation Building: The Universities of Strasbourg and Alsatian Society, 1870–1939* (Chicago, 1984), 35–66.
6. Klaus Nohlen, *Baupolitik im Reichsland Elsass-Lothringen, 1871–1918* (Berlin, 1982), 13–17; Niels Wilcken, *Architektur im Grenzraum: das öffentliche Bauwesen in Elsass-Lothringen, 1871–1918* (Saarbrücken, 2000), 23, 50–51, 148–59.
7. Laurent Baridou and Nathalie Pintus, *Le Château du Haut-Koenigsburg. À la recherche du Moyen Âge* (Paris, 1998).
8. ADBR AL 27–840a, Letter from Wilhelm II to the Ministry of Alsace-Lorraine dated 9 May 1899.
9. "Die Hohkönigsburg und der Reichstag," *Elsässer Kurier* (14 Nov. 1900); "Der Streit um die Hohkönigsburg," *Strassburger Zeitung* (2 Feb. 1901).
10. ADBR AL 27–840c, Letter marked "Darstellung der Dieckmann um die Schenkung der Hohkönigsburg," dated 1907.
11. ADBR AL 27–840a.
12. Rudy Koshar, *Germany's Transient Pasts: Preservation and National Memory in the Twentieth Century* (Chapel Hill, NC, 1998), 55–60.
13. Ibid. See also "Die Wiederherstellung der Hohkönigsburg," *Frankfurter Zeitung*; "Die Denkschrift des Reichsamtes des Innern um Hohkönigsburg-Projekt," *Frankfurter Zeitung* (4 Jan. 1901); "Die Hohkönigsburg," *Frankfurter Zeitung* (13 May 1902).

14. "Zur Hohkönigsburgsfrage," *Strassburger Post* (22 Feb. 1902).
15. C. Krollman, "Zur Wiederherstellung der Hohkönigsburg," *Strassburger Zeitung* (19 Feb. 1901); Otto Piper, "Die Hohkönigsburg," *Strassburger Zeitung* (14 Sept. 1901): *Schlettstadter Tagesblatt* (24 Jan. 1901); "Hohkönigsburg," *Strassburger Neueste Nachrichten* (23 Apr. 1901); "Der Streit um die Hohkönigsburg," *Strassburger Zeitung* (15 Jan. 1901).
16. C. Krollman, "Zur Wiederherstellung der Hohkönigsburg," *Strassburger Zeitung* (19 Feb. 1901); *Petition des Vogesen Hotel-Besitzer Vereins und die Bewilligung des Wiederaufbaus der Hohkönigsburg*, Bibliothèque Nationale et Universitaire (BNUS) (1901)
17. "Elsass-Lothringen: Die Hohkönigsburg und der Reichstag," *Elsässer Kurier* (14 Nov. 1900); "Die Hohkönigsburg," *Der Elsässer* (14 February 1901).
18. "Der Streit um die Hohkönigsburg," *Strassburger Zeitung* (15 Jan. 1901).
19. "Die Hohkönigsburg," *Elsässische Landeszeitung* (15 Nov. 1900).
20. *Stenographisches Protokoll des Landesausschusses*, XXXVIII Session, 6 Sitzung, 28 February 1901, 156.
21. *Stenographisches Protokoll des Landesausschusses*, XXXVIII Session, 2 Sitzung, 5 February 1901, 31.
22. *Stenographisches Protokoll des Landesausschusses*, XXXVIII Session, 6 Sitzung, 28 February 1901, 161.
23. Daniel Silverman, *Reluctant Union: Alsace-Lorraine and Imperial Germany, 1871–1918* (University Park, PA, 1972), 87–88.
24. *Stenographisches Protokoll des Landesausschusses*, XXXIII Session, 21 Sitzung, 25 April 1906, 470, 483. Wetterlé was not the only deputy to raise the aesthetic issue of preservation. For example, Deputy Preiss stated, "As with the many aestheticists, I must also state my opinion, that with historical monuments, from an aesthetic point of view only conservation, or maintenance, not reconstruction or restoration can come under consideration."
25. The Thiersteins were nobles in the Holy Roman Empire who took possession of the castle in the sixteenth century and rebuilt the fortress. Their castle was the one to be restored.
26. *Stenographisches Protokoll des Landesausschusses*, XXXIII Session, 21 Sitzung, 25 April 1906, 471.
27. "Satzungen des Hohkönigsburgsverein," 1903. BNUS M 20521. ADBR AL 27–840a, "Letter from Bodo Ebhardt to Baron von Geymueller," (20 January 1903). See also ADBR AL 27–840g.
28. Jean-Claude Richez, "Le château du Haut-Koenigsburg: Frontière, mémoire, et illusion," *Revue des Sciences Sociales dans la France de l'Est*, no. 18 (1993): 249–54.
29. "Einweihung der Hohkönigsburg," *Strassburger Korrespondenz* (22 May 1908).
30. A castle in East Prussia restored in the nineteenth century.
31. Quoted in "Die Einweihung von Hohkönigsburg," *Strassburger Neueste Nachrichten* (14 May 1908).
32. "Die Einweihung Hohkönigsburg," *Die Elsässische Volksbote* (14 May 1908); "Die Hohkönigsburgfeier," *Der Elsässer* (14 Mai 1908); "Enttäuschung," *Der Volksfreund* (22 May 1908). "L'inauguration du Haut-Koenigsbourg," *Journal d'Alsace-Lorraine* (14 May 1908).
33. ADBR W 1146/23–24.
34. Richez, "Le Château," 249–54.
35. James Wilkinson, "The Uses of Popular Culture by Rival Elites: The Case of Alsace, 1890–1918," *History of European Ideas* 11 (1989): 605–18.
36. Bernard Vogler, *Histoire culturelle de l'Alsace* (Strasbourg, 1994).
37. "Un musée ethnologique alsacien," *Elsässer Kurier* (21 Dec. 1902); "Elsässisches Museum," *Strassburger Bürgerzeitung* (20 Dec. 1902); *Der Elsässer* (24 Dec. 1902).
38. AMA. Box entitled "Articles de presses alsaciennes."

39. AMS Div. IV 326/1799. Statutes du Musée Alsacien, AMS Div. IV 326/1799 Bulletin du Musée Alsacien.
40. "Das elsässische Museum," *Der Elsässer* (24 Dec. 1902); *Strassburger Burger Zeitung* (20 Dec. 1902); "Un musée alsacien," *L'Express de Mulhouse* (3 Jan. 1903); "Elsässische Museum," *Strassburger Post* (19 Dec. 1902). Clips found in the archives of the Musée alsacien.
41. Léon Dollinger, "Das Elsässische Museum in Strassburg und seine Bestrebungen," *Das Neue Elsass* 11 (1910), 181–83.
42. Maurice Barrès, "Sur la conscience alsacienne," *Revue alsacienne illustrée* 6 (1904): 41–44.
43. The collection of the *Images du Musée Alsacien* consulted in the archives of the Musée alsacien.
44. The subscription records for the *Images du Musée Alsacien* are held in AMS D IV 326/1799.
45. Articles held in the AMA: *Strassburger Bürgerzeitung* (12 March 1904); *Elsässische Volksbote* (14 March 1904); *Strassburger Post* (13 March 1904); *Der Elsässer* (19 March 1904); *Strassburger Neueste Nachrichten* (11 March 1904); *Journal d'Alsace-Lorraine* (11 March 1904); *Strassburger Post* (29 Jan. 1905); *Der Elsässer* (11 Feb. 1905); *Der Elsässer* (29 July 1905); *Der Elsässer* (8 March 1905).
46. "Rapport des Gérants: L'activité de la societé pedant les années 1906, 1907, et 1908," AMS Div. IV 326/1799.
47. *Strassburger Post* (31 May 1907).
48. AMS Div. IV 326/1799, "Programme du Kermesse de 1907"; AMS Div. IV 326/1799 Fête du Erckmann-Chatrian (Strasbourg, 1908); Suzanne Herrenschmidt, *Mémoires pour la petite histoire. Souvenirs d'une Strasbourgeoise* (Strasbourg, 1972): 83–84.
49. *Der Elsässer* (7 June 1907), *Strassburger Bürgerzeitung* (10 June 1907), *Journal d'Alsace-Lorraine* (12 June 1907).
50. *Journal d'Alsace-Lorraine* (12 June 1907); see also *Der Elsässer* (7 June 1906).
51. *Journal d'Alsace-Lorraine* (24 May 1908).
52. *Strassburger Bürgerzeitung* (23 May 1908).
53. "Der Bazar des elsässisches Museum," *Strassburger Post* (27 May 1908).
54. Alon Confino, *The Nation as Local Metaphor: Württemberg, Imperial Germany, and National Memory, 1871–1918* (Chapel Hill, NC, 1997), 134–52. See also Hanswilhelm Haefs, *Die deutsche Heimat-museen* (Frankfurt, 1984); Erika Karasek, *Die volkskundlich-kulturhistorisch Museen in Deutschland. Zur Rolle der Volkskunde in der bürgerliche-imperialistischen Gesellschaft* (Berlin, 1984); Martin Roth, *Heimatmuseum: zur Geschichte einer deutscher Institution* (Berlin, 1990).
55. ADBR AL 98–700, AMS D IV 326/1799.
56. AMS IV 326/1799, "Luedtke an Bürgermeister Schwander."
57. AMS D IV 326/180, Note of 6 September 1929.
58. AMS D IV 326/1799, IV N 409/20, Letter from Riff to municipal administration dated 10 February 1920; AMS D IV. N. 310, Letter to municipal administration dated 26 June 1922.
59. ADBR AL 71–21, File marked "Monuments—der auf dem Schlachtfelder bei Worth a.V. liegende Denkmäler im Krieg 1870–1871 gefallenene französichen Off. u. Sold."; ADBR AL 27–371 Errichtung von Denkmälern fuer französischen Soldaten durch die Gesellschaft Souvenir Française."
60. Annette Maas, "Kriegerdenkmäler und Gedenkfeiern um Metz: Formen und Funktionen kollektiver Erinnerung in einer Grenzregion," in *Stadtentwicklung im deutsch-französisch-luxemburgischen Grenzraum (19. u 20. Jh.)*, ed. Rainer Hudemann and Rolf Wittenbrock (Saarbrücken, 1991), 115–18.
61. Ibid.
62. ADBR AL 71–21, "Festprogram des Bartholdi-Denkmals."

63. See the correspondence between Under-Secretary for the Interior (Alsace-Lorraine) Karl Mandel and Bezirkspräsident Puttkamer, ADBR AL 71–21, as well as ADHR 3 AL 1/834, "Einweihung des Bartholdi-Denkmals."
64. "Chronique d'Alsace-Lorraine," *RAI* 12 (1910): 1–2; ADBR AL 71–21, Letter from Kreisdirektor Bissingen to the Ministry of Alsace-Lorraine dated 21 April 1921; ADHR AJ 30/40–1 (Purg. 11699).
65. Herman Hiery, "Zwischen Scylla und Charybdis: Carl Graf von Wedel als Statthalter im Reichsland Elsass-Lothringen (1907–1914)." *Revue d'Alsace* (1986): 299–328.
66. ADBR D 247–23b, Circular from Wedel to Bezirkpräsidenten dated 14 Oct. 1909.
67. *Elsässer Kurier* (18/19 Oct. 1909); *Le Nouvelliste* (18/19 Oct 1909); ADBR D 247–23(b), "Die Feierlichkeiten anlässlich der Einweihung des französichen Kriegerdenkmals bei Weissenburg"; ADHR Purg. 11699 (AJ 30/40–1).
68. *Elsässer Kurier* (18/19 Oct. 1909); *Le Nouvelliste* (18/19 Oct 1909); ADBR D 247–23(b) "Die Feierlichkeiten anlässlich der Einweihung des französichen Kriegerdenkmals bei Weissenburg"; ADHR Purg. 11699 (AJ 30/40–1).
69. *Elsässer Kurier* (18 Oct. 1909).
70. *Weissenburger Zeitung* (18 Oct. 1909); *Elsässische Volksbote* (18 Oct. 1909).
71. *Freie Presse* (18. Oct. 1909).
72. *Elsässer Kurier* (18/19 Oct. 1909); *Le Nouvelliste* (18/19 Oct 1909); ADBR 247 D 23(b) "Die Feierlichkeiten anlässlich der Einweihung des französichen Kriegerdenkmals bei Weissenburg"; ADHR Purg. 11699 (AJ 30/40–1).
73. ADBR D 247–23(b) "Die Feierlichkeiten anlässlich der Einweihung des französichen Kriegerdenkmals bei Weissenburg."
74. ADHR Purg. 11699 (AJ 30/40–1), Note from A. Spinner dated 1917.
75. ADBR AL 27–180, Report of Regierungsrat Unckell dated 31 Jan. 1913.
76. *Freie Presse* (4 Nov. 1913); *Le Nouvelliste* (11 Aug. 1913); *Strassburger Neue Zeitung* (30 Jan. 1913); *Strassburger Neue Zeitung* (24 May 1913); *Strassburger Post* (13 Feb. 1914); Also see correspondence between the Bezirkpräsidenten for Unter-Elsass and Ober-Elsass, ADBR D 247–23(b).

Chapter 3

FROM DISUNITY TO UNITY
THE CONSTITUTIONAL DEBATES AND THE ZABERN AFFAIR, 1910–1914

In October 1909, *Statthalter* von Wedel sent a circular to high-ranking *Reichsland* administrators concerning the dedication of the monument at Wissembourg. The memorandum proved not only descriptive of the situation at that time, but in many ways delimited and predicted the course of developments in Alsace-Lorraine. Wedel had been concerned about the rising activities of a pro-French minority. Yet while warning of the threat of the Francophile elements of Alsatian society, he also counseled German bureaucrats and military authorities to stop treating Alsatians as if they were a conquered people and instead remain focused on their responsibility to protect the region's interests. Wedel in fact foresaw the possibility of a healthy, potentially pro-German regionalism in Alsace, which he hoped to cultivate. In particular, Wedel commented, "I recognize, with certain caveats, the demand of 'Alsace-Lorraine to the Alsatians and Lorrainers' as justified. . . . The people of the *Land* have, as do other German tribes, the right to maintain their own special character." Wedel decried the pernicious influence of contending nationalisms in the area because German nationalists and pro-French locals both represented a disruption in the smooth administration of the *Reichsland*. In this way, his more nuanced understanding of the situation in Alsace helped usher in a new phase in the development of Alsatian regionalism.[1]

Between 1910 and early 1914 three events in particular affected the development of regionalism in the area and confirmed the hopes, concerns, and fears contained in Wedel's memo. First, in March 1910, Chancellor Theobald von Bethmann-Hollweg announced a new project to reform the constitution of Alsace-Lorraine. Alsatian political parties debated internally, among each another, and with the government—at times with great acrimony at each level—over the future form of the region's constitution, which did not become law until May 1911. Second, the *Landtag* (regional parliament) elections of October 1911—a result of the new

---

Notes for this section begin on page 95.

constitution—gave birth to a political organization purporting to represent the interests of all Alsatians, the Nationalbund (l'Union nationale or National Union). This group's emergence forced Alsatian parties to take stock yet again of their goals vis-à-vis the future of Alsace. Finally, the transformation of a minor military training incident into a regional crisis, national debate, and international media event—the so-called Zabern Affair—renewed the debate over Alsace's place within the German Empire.

This chapter in part treads over familiar historiographical terrain. Within the narrow context of Alsatian history, Jean-Marie Mayeur, for example, has detailed the deep political and cultural divisions that emerged within Alsace during debates over the constitution.[2] David Schoenbaum has analyzed the Zabern Affair, though he gives more attention to how the entire imbroglio marked a minor step toward greater ministerial responsibility and democratic principles within the German Empire rather than a retrograde moment in German-Alsatian relations.[3]

Both the constitutional debates and the Zabern Affair also touch upon a larger strand of historiography concerning German history, the nature of the German Second Empire. That the German Empire had autocratic features uneasily mixed with some elements of a constitutional system in a rapidly modernizing society is not in question; rather, the degree of autocracy versus liberalizing tendencies is the focus of the debate. Scholars such as Hans-Ulrich Wehler have argued that the Second Empire, backed by a highly conservative military, bureaucracy, and industrial elite, used a variety of stratagems to mobilize support against the forces of liberalism, socialism, and democracy. In contrast, historians such as Geoff Eley, David Blackbourn, and Margaret Anderson have criticized the more negative assessment of the *Kaiserreich* as too dismissive of the swelling undercurrents of democratic and liberal forces at local and regional levels of politics; outside of politics, the influence of more liberalizing tendencies demonstrated a slow but steady change in the nature of the Second Reich.[4]

Alsace presents a particular case in this discussion for it enjoyed an ambiguous position in the empire constitutionally, and the people of the *Reichsland* were not fully trusted; Alsatians chafed under the restrictions of the local constitution and the broader German political culture. The constitutional debates would therefore reveal much about the ability, or lack thereof, of the German government to reform. The Zabern Affair, in contrast, brought tensions between an autocratic, militaristic regime and forces of constitutionalism in Germany to the fore, with immense consequences for Alsatians' conception of their place in Germany.

This chapter seeks to understand the German Empire through developments in Alsace between 1909–1914. More centrally, the chapter looks at these events in terms of the long-term development of Alsatian regionalism. First, the chapter takes Alsatian disunity as its starting point. The many fractures of Alsace's sociopolitical world came to the fore during the constitutional debates only to be effaced, temporarily, by the Zabern

Affair. Thus, this chapter examines how the disunity of 1910–11 gave way to a unified sense of indignation, outrage, and disappointment over the outcome of the Zabern Affair. Second, this chapter examines the clear intertwining of Alsatian cultural regionalism and its political regionalism, thereby demonstrating the importance of the cultural activities of the earlier chapters to attempts to forge a political place for Alsace within the German Empire. Finally, the chapter reexamines these heretofore studied developments with one eye fixed on their importance for Alsatian regionalism in the ensuing decades.

Reforming the Constitution

Since Bismarck helped create the Alsace-Lorraine constitution in 1879, the *Reichsland* had exercised exceedingly weak powers, especially compared to the independence enjoyed by the other German states. The kaiser named the *Statthalter*, real legislative authority lay in the Reichstag and Bundesrat, and the *Landesausschuss* had limited control over the regional budget. The *Landesausschuss* could propose legislation, but had no guarantee its wishes would be followed; moreover, the *Statthalter* could prorogue the assembly and even pass recess ordinances subject to later *Landesausschuss* approval. As a final indignity, the region possessed no representation in the Bundesrat.

Several attempts had been made to alter this situation. Charles Grad, an early autonomist who coined the motto "Alsace-Lorraine to the Alsace-Lorrainers," had urged the reform of the region's status in the early 1880s.[5] In 1903–04, in 1905, and early in 1910, a new generation of Alsatian politicians championed greater regional autonomy. Their efforts failed in part due to opposition by imperial authorities, and in part because of divisions among Alsatians over voting procedures for a future regional legislature.[6] Yet in the years before 1910, the political terrain shifted. New leadership—embodied in *Statthalter* Karl von Wedel (1907), Alsatian-born *Staatssekretär* (Secretary of State) Hugo Zorn von Bulach (1910), and Chancellor Theobald von Bethmann-Hollweg (1909)—proved willing to consider altering the *Reichsland's* constitutional status. Moreover, ongoing antagonism between pro-French nationalist and Pan-Germanists, for example over the monument at Wissembourg or during the Gneisse trial, gave renewed impetus to the government to resolve the constitutional issue of Alsace-Lorraine. Locals and officials hoped thereby to dispel the "nationalist agitation" that had plagued the region.[7]

The desire to ameliorate the situation in Alsace-Lorraine led to Bethmann-Hollweg's announcement of a project to change the constitution of the *Reichsland* in a speech before the Reichstag on 14 March 1910. The Reichstag session generated a complex response on the part of Alsatian leaders. Karl Hauss, Reichstag and *Landesausschuss* deputy, later noted it was one of the only two times he left the Reichstag building happy.[8] The local papers likewise greeted the announcement with a sense of joyous relief that Alsace-Lorraine could finally become a regular state within the German Empire. The local press also sounded a cautious note as Bethmann-Hollweg had not submitted a very detailed plan: Would the *Reichsland* actually gain full autonomy? What sort of legislature would Alsace-Lorraine receive? And, of great importance to all parties involved, what sort of electoral system would be put in place? The devil remained to be found in the details.[9]

The proposal touched off nine months of bitter and contentious debate among the political parties of Alsace. Two major questions lay behind some of the fiercest arguments. First, to what degree should Alsatians be willing to compromise with the government on the issue of Alsace's future? Should the Alsatians adopt an "all or nothing" attitude, or should they take those concessions offered by the government as steps in the right direction? The issue of compromise relates then to the second major question: what sort of autonomy should Alsace-Lorrainers demand? Suggestions among local representatives ranged from the elevation of the *Reichsland* to full *Bundesstaat* status to a willingness to accept something less than full parity with the other German states on the condition that the *Reichsland* gain a larger degree of control over its own affairs.

In addition to the questions of compromise and future status, two other considerations influenced the development of the constitution. First, Alsatian parties had to decide to what degree they could garner support from their broader German analogues (for example, the larger Center and SPD organizations). The national parties had proved poor partners, neither aligning their goals with nor spending political capital for their Alsatian brethren. Second, the German government—prodded by the army, reproached by the German nationalist press, and watched over by a skeptical kaiser—was limited in the extent to which it would sacrifice its security concerns in the border region.

Within this larger framework, several specific issues had to be determined. First, what form would the local legislature take? The government proposal had suggested a bicameral legislature. Second, what sort of executive would lead the Alsace-Lorraine government and would he be responsible to the local legislature? A regent chosen from one of the ruling houses of southern Germany? Or would the status quo prevail? Third, would Alsace-Lorraine receive voting privileges in the Bundesrat, and if so, who would control such votes?

An examination of the positions of the various Alsatian political parties offers the best means of gauging the Alsatian response to Bethmann-Hollweg's proposal and points to deep divisions both within and among the various political organizations. At stake was not just the national future of Alsace, nor the status of the *Reichsland*, but also more mundane considerations of local political power.

The Liberals, a loose organization garnering support from Alsatian Protestants and *Altdeutsche*, took a relatively open stance.[10] Led by, among others, Strasbourg mayor Rudolf Schwander and George Wolf, with Stoskopf's *SNZ* serving as one of the party's papers,[11] the Liberals remained optimistic, though with specific concerns. The party objected to the proposal of an unelected First Chamber. The *Statthalter* should enjoy greater independence from Berlin. On the electoral system, the Liberals remained less open. Polling approximately 22 percent of the electorate, yet consistently losing to the stronger Center Party, Liberals pushed for proportional representation.[12] Finally, the *SNZ* blasted the "nationalism" of the "agitation" of the Francophile "Colmar trio"—Daniel Blumenthal, Jacques Preiss, and Emile Wetterlé—whose efforts undermined the entire process of constitutional revision.[13]

While some historians have recently pointed to the relative ideological unity of liberals in Alsace, the issue of nationalism, and the debates over the constitution more general, suggest deep divides within the liberal camp.[14] Daniel Blumenthal's democratically minded Elsass-Lothringische Volkspartei (Alsace-Lorraine People's Party), took a more intransigent stance, for example demanding a democratically elected unicameral legislature, elevation to full status as a republican *Bundesstaat*, and even the use of French in Alsace's schools.[15] Yet more audacious was liberal-minded journalist Léon Boll. He used his paper, the *Journal d'Alsace-Lorraine*, to promote a Francophile, republican view of Alsace's future.[16] His basic demands echoed those of Blumenthal; more shockingly, he suggested Alsace-Lorraine be made a neutral state only nominally under German control, thus hinting, though not openly claiming, that Alsace-Lorraine's status remained open.[17] He opined that a neutral, autonomous Alsace-Lorraine would satisfy regional desires, and more importantly, would both dash the hopes of French revanchists and quell French fears of a German invasion.[18]

In contrast to the divided liberal camp, the Socialist Party, especially as embodied in Jacques Peirotes' *Freie Presse*, remained a touchstone of political consistency and coherency throughout the debates over the constitution and into the subsequent *Landtag* elections. The party wanted no regency, much less the kaiser, at the head of the Alsace-Lorraine government. Indeed, the Social Democrats demanded a republic be created with a universally elected legislature. The Social Democrats opposed the suggestion of the Center Party that voters have three years' residency in Alsace; such a provision would exclude significant portions of working-class voters. The party, therefore, also steadfastly objected to the idea of a First Chamber, especially in its suggested form with not only religious representatives but also deputies named by the kaiser. Finally, the party, much like the Liberals, wanted a separation of church and state in the region.[19]

The Center Party tried to maintain a common front despite deep conflicts within its ranks. For the Center Party, the stakes were especially high: constitutional changes could potentially diminish the party's dominant role in the region. On some issues, the party was united; specifically, the party wanted to maintain current church-state relations (i.e., the maintenance of the Napoleonic Concordat) and guarantee the place of religion in school. Beyond that, the party was divided. Wetterlé, for example, wavered between an "all or nothing" stance and concessions. Ricklin, highly critical of the First Chamber and limited suffrage for the Second Chamber, nonetheless rejected a stance of intransigence. Yet another faction allowed for even a greater degree of compromise.[20]

Such differences became apparent at a plenary meeting of the party in late October 1910. Karl Hauss opened the meeting with a speech calling for full autonomy; he cautioned, however, that the current proposal left Alsace weak and ominously hinted that the entire constitution could be disregarded if the Alsatians did not act properly after its passage. During another session, Wetterlé and Laugel demanded a republic and furthermore argued that Alsatians should unite to defend Alsatian rights; embedded in such an idea, as Hauss noted, was the creation of anti-Liberal/Social Democratic bloc meant to preserve the religious status quo in the region. The more conciliatory faction led by Charles Didio rejected the idea of a republic, remained flexible on the status of the *Statthalter*, and urged the Alsatians and Lorrainers, as supplicants in the situation, to adopt a moderate attitude. Despite such internal differences, the party came together to demand full autonomy and universal suffrage for the Second Chamber.[21]

The flammable mix of hopes for autonomy, the ambition of political parties, and personal rivalries in these debates often exploded into heated, acrimonious exchanges, as seen, for example, in the discussions of the *Landesausschuss* from 29 June 1910. In particular, deputies sparred over the electoral procedure for the new *Landtag*'s elections, debating whether a February 1910 resolution was binding. Liberal and Catholic deputies exchanged verbal barbs. Liberal Georges Wolf, after querying Wetterlé's altered stance against proportional voting, then launched into a vicious attack by calling the "nationalist" tactics of Wetterlé, Preiss, and Blumenthal "poisoning" and "goading," and accusing them of not wanting to compromise with other parties. Wetterlé and Blumenthal then defended themselves against the charge of nationalism by suggesting that they merely wanted to fight for Alsatian "particularity" (*Eigenart*) and stated that they did not want to receive another "*provisorium*" for a constitution.[22]

Such bitter exchanges found parallels in the local press. The heated exchanges between Stoskopf's Liberal *SNZ* and Emile Wetterlé's *Nouvelliste* serve to highlight the nature of such debates. These two papers also underscore the importance of differing cultural visions of Alsace to politics. Though Stoskopf did not usually pen his paper's editorials, his vision of Alsace—critical of German nationalism, yet also conciliatory to well-intentioned "Old Germans," and at all times celebratory of

Alsace—permeated the journal. Wetterlé, the principal author of the *Nouvelliste's* editorials, reflected a highly Francophile—though not openly revanchist—view of Alsace; not surprisingly, Hansi was a close friend and occasional contributor to the paper. Thus the *SNZ* and the *Nouvelliste* promoted political agendas that had close analogues to the cultural visions of Alsace found in chapter 1.

Some of the acrimony between the two journals sprang from the issue of whether the new constitution should secularize the region. The papers, as with their respective political parties, also differed on how far the Alsatians should compromise with the Germans. Wetterlé charged the *SNZ* with being a "government newspaper" while the *SNZ* attacked Wetterlé's changing positions as ploys to gain support for a Catholic-friendly republic.[23] The debates between the *SNZ* and *Nouvelliste* at times, however, took on a more personal character. In an exchange over some minor issue in the *Landesausschuss*, René Schickele, the political editor for the *SNZ* in 1911–12, and Wetterlé engaged in ad hominem attacks. Wetterlé attacked Schickele's literary journal, *Der Stürmer* by questioning its literary value and readability. Schickele countered by insinuating that it required a certain "intelligence and education" to handle literature and suggested that Wetterlé's own readers would have a difficult time tackling the works of Maurice Barrès.[24]

Wetterlé's criticism of the *SNZ* extended from the front page of his newspaper to the privacy of his personal reflections.[25] Wetterlé thought Stoskopf had "exhausted all the resources of his spirit on his *Herr Maire*, a legitimate and considerable success." His submissions to the salons in Paris did not "pass the limits of mediocrity, as Stoskopf, a ardent Alsatian nationalist, continued to paint Corot landscapes with a distressing poverty of design and color." Wetterlé opined further that Stoskopf was "not prepared for the work of journalists" and his "incommensurable vanity" led him to "pass into the camp of the Germanophiles" to the point where he accepted the awarding of the "Order of the Red Eagle from William II."[26] Varying political and cultural visions for Alsace could translate into deep animosity.

Such attacks were brought temporarily into abeyance as the Alsatian parties paused to consider the official proposal for the constitution in mid-December 1910. The First Chamber remained; half of the members were nominated by the kaiser, the other half either derived their position by virtue of their office (e.g., the representatives of the Catholic, Lutheran, and Jewish ecclesiastic organizations) or were chosen by Alsatian communes and various professional societies. Alsatians would not control their Bundesrat votes. The *Statthalter* would have no parliamentary responsibility to the *Landtag*. The electoral law foresaw less than universal suffrage with limits imposed on the basis of both age and residency; yet suffrage requirements were to be broad enough to pose a challenge to the local "notables" who had relied on their position in Alsatian society, personal influence, and indirect voting to secure their political positions. The new constitution, therefore, was aimed at both notables and Social Democrats alike. In addition, the Reichstag and Bundesrat were excluded from legislating for Alsace-Lorraine. The proposal introduced direct elections for the Second Chamber of the *Landtag* and gave the Alsace-Lorrainers a good deal of control over the region's budget.[27]

Alsace's politicians responded with varying levels of criticism of the new project. The Liberals were less than enthused about the composition of the First Chamber, lack of firm Bundesrat representation, and unclear electoral system, but still viewed the proposals as overall progress.[28] Their Francophile brethren such as Blumenthal and Boll found much in the new constitution lacking.[29] The Social Democrats opposed the program as it meant the continuation of the *Reichsland* and committed Alsace-Lorraine to a path of "Prussianization"; moreover, the lack of true universal suffrage hurt their party the most. As a result, the Social Democrats staged a number of minor demonstrations in protest.[30]

The Center's response proved moderate but further revealed deep divisions within the party; Ricklin savaged some elements of the project, Wetterlé lamented the limited reach of the proposal.[31] Center deputies remained restrained, however, as they calculated any desired changes could be made when the draft went before the Reichstag. There the broader Catholic Party could lend its support. Immediately, the Alsatian Center Party ran into difficulties. Unauthorized negotiations between party leader Léon Vonderscheer and his German counterparts created tensions within the party between hardliners and more conciliatory representatives.[32] Within the Reichstag, only minor changes were made; the *Reichsland*, for example, was given three votes in the Bundesrat, but they were ultimately subject to *Statthalter* control. The failure of the Reichstag to enact major changes in the constitution led to protests both within and outside of the party.[33] Indeed, disappointed with the results of the Reichstag's actions, the Alsatian Center Party threatened to break all ties with the larger party. Instead of a full rupture the Alsatians issued a severe admonition of the German Center and agreed to allow individual representatives to decide if they had to adhere to the larger organization's parliamentary votes.[34] The region's other parties experienced some difficulties with their German counterparts, but none felt pushed to the breaking point like the Catholic Center.

At the end of May, the constitution came before the Reichstag for final approval. Several Alsatian deputies made last-ditch efforts to insert French-language guarantees, or more importantly, gain the region full autonomy. These attempts failed, and the draft was voted into law by a large majority comprised of National Liberals, Social Democrats, and a sizeable segment of the Center Party. The same majority passed the final constitution on 26 May, and the constitution became official with its publication on 31 May 1911.[35]

The final draft hardly met all Alsatians' expectations. A bicameral chamber would have the right to legislate and exert greater control over the budget. The body also gained the right to question the local ministry, but could not overturn its decisions. The choice of *Statthalter*, moreover, remained under the control of the kaiser. Still nominated, the First Chamber could only pass or reject, not amend, legislation passed in the Second Chamber. Finally, elections for the *Landtag* were to be uninominal with two rounds; suffrage was extended to all males over age twenty-five and resident in Alsace for three years.[36] The constitution was weak, but represented progress. Historians have noted that the constitution left the region in legal limbo as it was no longer a *Reichsland* but also not a fully confederated state.[37]

The Alsatian press in general greeted the passage of the constitution with relief touched with cynicism. The *SNZ* displayed the greatest ebullience, stating that "Alsace was on the path to a democratic state" and suggesting that 26 May should become a "national holiday" to mark the progress of Alsace-Lorraine. Nonetheless, the paper criticized the First Chamber and the electoral law, noting that the constitution represented a "national beginning, not an end." In contrast, Léon Boll argued that the constitution "masked fallacious guarantees of full independence," attacked the First Chamber, and laid the blame for the weak constitution at the feet of the German SPD and Center, a line paralleled by Wetterlé's *Nouvelliste*. The Socialist Democrats demonstrated more relief than happiness, thanked Preiss and Ricklin for their last-minute efforts, and warned that the kaiser could intervene and overturn undesirable decisions of the *Landtag*. Finally, the Catholic press, while praising the efforts of its deputies in the Reichstag, also criticized both certain aspects of the document and Liberal and SPD support for an imperfect constitution.[38] In sum then, Alsatian reactions to the constitution were divided between happiness over increased autonomy and the desire for yet greater independence.

The "National Union" and the *Landtag* elections

Even as the ink dried on the new constitution, the October elections for the new *Landtag* become the focus of local political life. The impetus for such an early push for the relatively far-off electoral contests came from the formation of a new political organization in the region, the Union Nationale/ Nationalbund [National Union] in early June 1911. Under the guidance of Democrats Léon Boll and Daniel Blumenthal, the independent Jacques Preiss, as well as the Center Party's Emile Wetterlé and Anselm Laugel, the Union hoped to act as an overarching organization to bind together Alsatian parties in a common, regional program in order to secure the rights gained under the new constitution.

The idea of creating a pan-Alsatian party was not new; indeed, the new party grew out of a particular set of circumstances in Colmar. Daniel Blumenthal had called for such an organization as early as 1895 when he created the Elsässische-Lothringische Volkspartei (Alsace-Lorraine People's Party). In the program for the party, Blumenthal called for the lifting of the dictatorship paragraph, the introduction of French into the curriculum of the regional education system, and, under the mantra "Alsace-Lorraine to the Alsatian-Lorrainers," the right of Alsatian-Lorrainers to occupy local civil service posts. Blumenthal also demanded the end of noble titles, a democratically elected *Landesausschuss*, and the separation of church and state.[39]

At the time, Emile Wetterlé judged the idea of a pan-Alsatian party positively and drew parallels among the situations of Alsace-Lorraine and the annexed provinces of Denmark and Poland, all of which defended "their national life, their customs, their mores, and their language" from the "invasion . . . of a foreign *esprit*." As for the Volkspartei in particular, Wetterlé viewed it as "a stage on the path of progress." Referring to the issue of the separation of church and state, however, the cleric Wetterlé wrote that, the Volkspartei's "founders are wrong not to avert irritating questions that are impractical at the present time."[40] For this reason, Wetterlé did not heed Blumenthal's call, and Jacques Preiss would leave the party to become an independent.

Further laying the foundation for the National Union, Wetterlé sounded the trumpet for Alsatians to marshal under one banner in 1909. Wetterlé called for a "necessary union." While he realized that the local parties might not reconcile their divergent programs, he nonetheless pleaded for Alsatians to stand strong against the "*divide et impera*" tactics of the German authorities. More specifically, Wetterlé asked, "is it not the shared interest of all to form a provisional union that will never surrender until complete victory for our autonomy under the motto 'Alsace-Lorraine to the Alsace-Lorrainers' has been realized?" His pleas for unity, however, came to naught.[41]

During the constitutional debates, both Blumenthal and Boll called for Alsatians to put aside their differences to achieve a better constitution. Boll, in particular, wanted to end the condition of "dependence, subjugation, and indignity" under which the Alsatians had suffered for over forty years. He saw the possibility of Alsatians from across the political spectrum—from "well-intentioned socialists" (mostly local representatives such as socialist Jacques Peirotes) to Centrists "of good faith" (such as Emile Wetterlé)—to put aside party politics and rally to the Alsatian cause. Liberal politicians skeptically questioned whether Alsatian parties could overcome their political differences, or in the case of the Center Party, its internal divisions.[42]

Blumenthal, Boll, and Wetterlé would constitute, along with other Francophile notables such as Anselm Laugel and Jacques Preiss, the core of the eventual National Union.⁴³ Not surprisingly, the members of the National Union largely supported the concept of an Alsatian "double culture." Laugel, as we have seen, promoted the Alsatian theater, the *Revue alsacienne illustrée*, and the Souvenir Français along with the subsequent Souvenir Alsace-Lorraine. Wetterlé likewise had thrown his moral weight behind the monument celebrations at Wissembourg. He had also engaged in debates with local German officials over the use of French in Alsatian schools. The other members of the eventual Union wished to keep alive the memory of France; all wanted to reintroduce French into the regional educational system as a part of this "dual culture."

Given the Francophile leanings of many of the Union's leaders such as Wetterlé, Blumenthal, Boll, and Laugel, the meaning of "national" in National Union would remain ambiguous. The Union wished to promote the interests of Alsace-Lorraine. Yet all had known ties with France and were sharply critical of the German regime. To German authorities, therefore, the leaders of the Union were little better than agents of French nationalism. For more moderate Alsatians such as the Liberal Georges Wolf, these leading figures created more problems than they solved through their obstinate nationalist line. The heads of the National Union, though unwavering in their vision of a French Alsace, were not separatist; a return to France would necessitate a war. The effort to create a regional-wide organization to promote Alsatian interests can therefore be considered an attempt to shape the debates in the elections and, more importantly, to maximize the French elements and latent French loyalties in Alsatian society.

On 4 June 1911, forty representatives from Upper and Lower Alsace as well as Lorraine met in Strasbourg. The group's opening appeal argued that the constitution "in its entirety did not mark progress but rather a step backward." The group therefore urged all "good Alsatians" to come together to fight in the *Landtag* and Reichstag for "the creation of an equal, independent state of Alsace-Lorraine." The proclamation urged parties to join together in the pending *Landtag* elections.⁴⁴

Although the National Union had not put forth its statutes or formalized its organization, this initial call generated strong reactions across the political spectrum. Some Catholic politicians such as Hauss and Ricklin considered but declined to join; others, such as Center politician Nicholas Delsor, refused to join because they believed their party's confessional agenda trumped regional issues. The broader Catholic press questioned whether the Union could overcome its internal divisions, much less win over Liberals or Social Democrats.⁴⁵

The Socialist and Liberal press viewed the idea even more dimly than their Catholic counterparts. The Socialist *Freie Presse* viewed the new party as a "clerical campaign device" and noted that the Liberals and Socialists would have little place in such a political cartel.⁴⁶ The *SNZ* viewed the bloc as an alliance between the "National Party (the eventual union) and the Center" along with Daniel Blumenthal. The paper showered its critiques liberally. The Catholics wanted to form an electoral bloc against the "Socialists, Democrats, and Liberals." Blumenthal was simply a political schemer. In sum, the *SNZ* saw the party of as a coalition of the "clerics" and "nationalists" whose intolerance the *SNZ* could not support.[47] Charles Frey, a Liberal and collaborator on the *SNZ*, expanded this critique in *Das Neue Elsass*, questioning the political bases of the party, its ability to bridge individual parties' "world views," its potential to accomplish anything legislatively, and its apparent pro-Catholic orientation. "Good Alsatians" should support the general goals of the Union, but not the organization itself.[48]

Despite such wide-ranging and probing criticisms, at the end of June the National Union was put on firmer footing with its first formal meetings and promulgation of an official platform. The group met in Strasbourg on 29 June under the leadership of Jacques Preiss. Recalling the motto "Alsace-Lorraine to the Alsace-Lorrainers," the Union's program asserted the rights of Alsace-Lorraine in a number of areas. The *Reichsland* should be elevated to the status of a full state. Half of all civil servants should be Alsatian, and be conversant in the local languages. Furthermore, the party argued that regional revenues not be sent to Prussia or used to underwrite military expenditures. The party also desired a reduced role for the military in the region with greater civilian control over military authorities. In the realm of education, the Union called for the introduction of French language instruction alongside German as well as a "nonbiased" (i.e., not a German nationalist) approach to the teaching of history.

In the final section of the program, the party demanded that the Alsatian national "peculiarity" be preserved "as it, through the use of two languages and the heartfelt contact between two cultures, has developed." In particular, the party defended the Alsatians' right to develop their art and literature as they wished, a right that was to be extended to both Alsatians residing in the region and those living abroad. Finally, the group "desired respect for the living and the dead who did their duty, irrespective of the side for which they fought." By doing so, their opened the door for members of the Union to continue their pro-French activities without harassment. For example, the group opposed the need for Alsatians like Pierre Bucher to petition the government for permission to produce plays in French. And the last of these goals was a clear reference to the "cult of the dead" and the memory of France in the region as embodied in the banned Souvenir Français and the soon-to-be-banned Souvenir Alsace-Lorraine.[49]

Reaction to the National Union's program paralleled that of the original party proclamation. While critical, local parties also began to develop their own platforms for the election. Liberals, for their part, praised elements of the Union's program, but viewed the organization as intentionally dividing Alsatians from "Old Germans"; Alsace-Lorraine would continue develop within the political and cultural framework of the *Kaiserreich*.[50] More specifically, the party sought greater changes to the constitution, especially with regard to the First Chamber and the Bundesrat. In addition, Liberals demanded greater guarantees for the inclusion of Alsatians in the local civil service as well as greater protection for the local economy from German competition. Though open to French language instruction, the party did not make it a central component of its program.[51]

The Socialist Party, in contrast, took a harsher line toward the National Union and offered a more radical political program. For the *Freie Presse*, even the title "National Union" was a lie; the Democrats, Liberals, and the paper noted "above all" the Social Democrats had been excluded. More critically, the paper argued that the members of the Union were cowards for not specifying what Alsatian autonomy meant. Indeed, the local SPD went so far as to demand the right to self-determination because the war of 1870–71 had been a "war of conquest" that disregarded "the two-hundred-year-long assimilation process with the spirit, the culture, the interests, and the legal system of France." Like the German Social Democrats of 1871, the local party still demanded the right of Alsace to self-determination; the Union's failure to demand the same demonstrated their timidity.[52] Beyond its normal social and economic demands, the SPD also sought greater democratization of the region, including female suffrage, less restrictive age and residency requirements for voters (to expand the SPD base), revisions to the First Chamber, more control over the *Statthalter*, and control of Bundesrat votes. Finally, in a move that clearly set the party against the Center, the Social Democrats called for the complete division of church and state in the region, especially in budgetary matters and in education.[53]

If the Liberals and Social Democrats reacted negatively to the National Union's program—while furthering a regional agenda in their respective fashions—the Center response was more mixed. Some party members theoretically agreed with the Union, but questioned its virtually nonexistent stance on practical issues. Others continued to critique its stand on confessional issues.[54] Some politicians took issue with the Union's allegedly pro-French bias. Those in support included signatories to the National Union's founding manifesto, such as Wetterlé and Pfleger, as well as ardent regionalists such as the editor of the *Elsässer Kurier*, the priest Xavier Haegy.[55] These divisions complicated Center plans for the election. While the Colmar branch, led by Wetterlé, pushed for a formal alliance, the Strasbourg branch remained opposed.[56] Ricklin offered a compromise, but one with tight strictures on cooperation to maintain the character and independence of the party.[57]

When the Center laid out its program in August, it too claimed to have steadfastly defended Alsatian rights. The program, much like that of the other regional parties, then turned to demand full state status for Alsace-Lorraine. The platform claimed—under the motto "Alsace-Lorraine to the Alsace-Lorrainers"—the right for Alsatians and Lorrainers to occupy the majority of the civil servant posts within the region. While the program also addressed a number of other issues ranging from tax policy to road improvement, the most important platform was its firm stand on the importance of confessional schools, which clearly set it against its regional counterparts.[58]

The months leading up to the elections thus descended into arguments over the respective visions for Alsace's future and sharp criticism of the respective political programs. Heated debates and rousing pleas for support became a regular feature of the front pages of the regional papers. Their content, however, remained greatly unchanged. The National Union promoted itself as the best representative of Alsatian interests while it charged the alliance of Social Democrats and Liberals with being overly friendly with the German government.[59] The Liberals and Socialists criticized the sectarian regionalism of the Center and false pretensions of the Union as a mask for Catholic regionalism.[60] The Liberals further argued that the National Union was too extreme in its understanding of Alsatian particularism and suggested that Alsatians and Germans could work together as Liberals did both locally and in the wider empire.[61] And the Center maintained its argument that it remained the best defender of Alsatian values, especially in the realm of religion, in the face of a Socialist-Liberal threat to Alsatian Christian values.[62] In this way, the National Union was attacked from both ends of the political spectrum.

As the elections approached, the National Union's inability to cement firm alliances with the other regional political parties aside from the followers of Blumenthal began to assume a greater importance. Whereas the Center could rely on its campaign machine, and whereas the Social Democrats and Liberals had made an electoral pact to support each other's candidates against the Center, the National Union had to depend on name recognition and overlapping candidates from the Center. The Strasbourg branch of the Union—centered around men such as Pierre Bucher and the Dollinger brothers—was particularly disorganized, only offering its candidate lists in early October.[63] In all, the National Union only offered sixteen candidates independent of the Center in forty Alsatian electoral districts.

The elections, which took place in late October 1911, turned out poorly for the Union. In the first round, the party managed to get fourteen candidates through; however, those who remained either were Center stalwarts or faced difficult campaigns. The second set of elections proved less kind. Preiss, Laugel, and Blumenthal, among the established candidates of the party, all met defeat, although Blumenthal would later be chosen as one of Colmar's representatives to the First Chamber of the *Landtag*. Among those deputies who ran as Center candidates in association with the National Union, Wetterlé and his associates found themselves among a small minority within the Center Party. Overall, the Center had twenty-six representatives, the Liberals and Social Democrats eleven apiece, the Lorraine Bloc ten, and two deputies were independent; only five Union supporters were elected, but all ran as Center candidates.[64]

Why did the Union fail? What influence did it have on Alsatian politics and the course of the election? One primary source of difficulty for the party, noted by contemporaries and historians alike, was the Union's inability to organize effectively and to articulate a clear political program. The Union lacked the strong organization of the Center and Social Democrats; in the estimation of Jean-Marie Mayeur, "Well before the elections, the National Union had already failed." Prominent candidates such as Blumenthal, Preiss, and Laugel did not capitalize on their names and lost to better-organized opponents. The National Union's program remained vague on bread and butter concerns. In contrast, the Social Democrat, Center, and Liberal parties all staked claims on economic and social issues as well as regional ones. The National Union, then, failed to garner adherents outside of its narrow base of the Francophile Alsatian elite.[65]

Part of the National Union's failure with regard to a definitive program resulted from the stress of joining all Alsatians together under one umbrella organization. The Union's principal leaders remained divided on some of the central questions in Alsatian politics. Wetterlé's defense of religious issues and conception of the group as a bloc against the left clashed with the more democratic, secularizing tendencies of fellow union members such as Daniel Blumenthal and Léon Boll. Mayeur nicely summarized the Union's difficulties: the party was "clerical in the eyes of the democrats, anticlerical in the eyes of a part of the Center."[66] Or as the Center Reichstag deputy Nicolas Delsor noted, "Our duty [is] 'above all Catholic' and not 'above all Alsatian.'"[67] Religious, regional, and national identities could exist simultaneously and in conjunction with one another, but for some Alsatians, "Catholic" was the more important appellation.

The Union also suffered from a general sense of unease in light of the international situation. The second Moroccan crisis in particular—and the potential for a Franco-German clash—cast a pall over the fringe elements of the National Union. If the participation of the pro-French group banned in 1911, the Cercle des étudiants, brought to mind Bucher, and if Wetterlé suggested Hansi, then the National Union seemed particularly French oriented. Added to that, the adherence of the Mulhouse caricaturist Henri Zislin and such Francophiles as Léon Boll, Jacques Preiss, and Daniel Blumenthal gave the party a particularly French cast. Such nationalist undertones virtually precluded any support for the group among the region's *Altdeutsch* and may have unsettled the wider Alsatian polity.[68]

What, then, was the importance of the Union? According to Wetterlé, "The creation and its activity of several months produced appreciable effects as all the political parties were constrained to adopt its program fully. Even the Liberals themselves could not avoid this obligation."[69] Such claims need to be doubly qualified. First, such attention by the other Alsatian parties to regional issues undermined the very raison d'être of the National Union. Second, while the other parties did promote Alsatian rights, their conception of what this meant did not coincide with that of the Union. The Social Democrats and especially the Liberals remained convinced that Alsatians and Germans could reconcile their differences; the National Union, and Wetterlé in particular, did not hold out such hopes. Likewise, significant fractions within the Center Party, most notably under the leadership of Hauss and Ricklin, rejected the "all or nothing" tactics of the National Union, instead opting to push for steady if incomplete progress.[70]

The debates over the merits of the National Union demonstrated not only the political divisions among Alsatians, but also reflected the cultural fractures. The more Francophile elements of Alsatian society, such as Wetterlé, Laugel, Blumenthal, and Bucher, who played a key role in the National Union, pushed harder to maintain Franco-Alsatian cultural links. The history lessons of Hansi, the exposés and articles of the *RAI*, and the remembrance of France in the Souvenir Français all found echo within the National Union's push for the Alsatian double culture as part of a formal political program. Their brand of regionalism proved more nationalistic and less compromising. The Liberal Party was more conciliatory both politically and culturally. The *SNZ*, under the leadership of René Schickele and Stoskopf, criticized the intransigence and nationalism of the likes of Wetterlé and Hansi. Karl Hauss and Eugène Ricklin of the Catholic Party—politicians who both came of age under the German Empire—also saw the possibilities of compromise and reconciliation.[71]

Finally, the debates over the constitution as well as the elections illuminate two other developments in Alsace. First, the region's inhabitants became even more conscious of their region and its unique place within the German Empire. The better part of two years had been focused on expanding the rights of Alsace-Lorraine within the empire; the political discussions around the elections revealed divergent conceptions of what it meant to be Alsatian. These differences point to a second development within Alsatian politics, the clefts within various Alsatian parties. In particular, members of the Liberal/Democrat Parties and especially the Center Party found themselves set against not only other parties but against their putative political comrades. Over the better part of the next decade, these internal differences would be effaced by the Zabern Affair and World War I only to reemerge in the 1920s.

The Zabern Affair

With the passage of the new constitution and the subsequent elections for the *Landtag* came a brief period of simmering agitation in Alsace. Alsatian politicians, especially Francophile ones, continued to harp on the incomplete status of Alsace-Lorraine within the German Empire. In opposition, German nationalists continued to call for the thorough Germanization of Alsace. Further actions stoked such antagonisms. For example, in one of its first actions, the *Landtag* rejected contributing local monies to the kaiser's *Gnadenfond* (discretionary fund), a move that led to charges that Alsatians were ungrateful for the beneficence shown them by the German government.[72] German nationalists also could create problems. Led by the *Rhein-Westfälische Zeitung*, the German nationalist press inveighed against the selection of allegedly Francophile Théophile Heyler as head of the Elsässische Maschinenbaugesellschaft (Alsatian Machine Construction Company). Objecting vociferously in both the Reichstag and *Landtag*, local deputies could not shield Heyler. Both the Alsatian and French press called for a boycott of items manufactured under the label "Made in Germany"; yet Heyler and the controlling group of the Maschinenbaugesellschaft bowed to German pressure and Heyler resigned in May 1912.[73]

Wedel's administration also came under renewed pressure to clamp down on allegedly pro-French organizations by the German nationalist press. Wedel did not believe that every little provocation needed to be answered, and often he ignored the philippics of the nationalist German press; indeed, he recognized their maladroit and misplaced efforts to force authorities to end the French presence in Alsace actually hurt that cause. The *Statthalter*, however, did push for the suppression of groups deemed overtly and politically French.[74] The repression of the French-oriented Souvenir Français and Souvenir Alsace-Lorraine was followed by the crackdown on already "nationalist" (i.e., French) groups such as Lorraine sportive or the Cercle des etudiants.[75] In addition, Anselm Laugel was forced to resign as head of the Society for the Preservation of Historical Monuments, and Jacques Preiss and Emile Wetterlé were sharply attacked for speeches made in France concerning the past—and present—relationship of the region to its two neighbors.

In the difficult German-Alsatian relationship, the German military assumed a particularly benighted role. In many ways, the military suffered a poor reputation merely by its heavy presence in the region with large garrisons based in the major towns of Alsace-Lorraine.[76] German officers, who received a great deal of deference throughout Germany, viewed themselves as the ultimate defenders of imperial authority in Alsace, a land that some considered virtual enemy territory. Groups such as Souvenir Français, politicians such as Wetterlé, and caricaturists such as Zislin all fed this perception. The people of Alsace and Lorraine, in contrast, felt as if they were under a quasi-occupation and disliked the attitudes of the German officers.[77]

This combination of Alsatian indifference or at times antipathy to the army and German suspicion and arrogance made clashes virtually inevitable. Some incidents such as the Wegerlin Affair were rather comic in nature; in this case, the German commander in Mulhouse forbade his officers from frequenting two local establishments because a Swiss citizen, fortified by a good deal of liquid courage, had called upon the house musicians to play the *Marseillaise*.[78] In 1912, Alsatian deputies noted that a group of German officers had decided to sing several patriotic songs, to which the deputies took no issue; rather, the deputies asked whether the officers needed to do so at 2 AM in the middle of the street as the hardworking people of Mulhouse slept.[79]

Such incidents, at least in the eyes of Alsatian deputies, were neither exceptional nor represented the most serious infractions by the military. In 1912, for example, an apprentice in Mulhouse made the mistake of trying to pass between two companies of the Mulhouse garrison as they marched down the street; the move was a violation of the law. A German officer blocked the apprentice with his saber, or in the eyes of numerous witnesses, he stabbed the young miscreant. The officer was formally excused of any wrongdoing by a military court, thus sparking outrage in the *Landtag*. In a heated session, numerous stories of military abuse against Alsatian and Lorrainer civilians came to the fore. These ranged from officers refusing to frequent establishments in which they heard French spoken to a farmer being assaulted because his broken cart could not be moved for a unit on the march, to Jewish shopkeepers being insulted by German officers. Three fundamental questions emerged in these debates: Why was the German military so hostile toward the people of Alsace-Lorraine? Why had the local government not done more to represent the region vis-à-vis the military? And why was the military accorded deference by the civil government over the wishes of the local population?[80]

Although the leaders of the *Reichsland* government, led by Wedel, at times sought to attenuate the actions of the regional military leaders, even appealing to Berlin for support, their efforts were not made public. Moreover, they were rarely successful, and even the successes required enormous effort for little tangible, enduring gain.[81] Thus, neither the imperial government nor the elected legislature of the *Reichsland* had much authority over the military. This situation, indeed, was not atypical of German civil-military relations; without overstating the case, the military enjoyed a high degree of public support, had the firm backing of the monarch, and—along with the *Reichskanzler* (Chancellor)—was subject to parliamentary review only insofar as it relied on the Reichstag for appropriations. Even here, despite the reticence of some parties, especially the SPD, to give the military its funding carte blanche, the military normally received most of the support it requested.[82]

The volatile relationship between region and nation, and between civilian and military authorities, was set aflame by a thoughtless young German officer with the help of the press. Lieutenant Gunther Baron von Forstner, a junior officer of the 99th Infantry Regiment of the XV Army Corps, garrisoned in Zabern, was known as a harsh disciplinarian. In late October 1913, Forstner, while berating a group of recruits, referred to Alsatians as *Wackes*, a term literally meaning "lazy bum" or "tramp." The word, however, also possessed an explosive connotation not unlike modern racial epithets. Approximately one week later, the Strasbourg

Catholic daily *Der Elsässer* published a brief report on the incident. The story quickly spread among the local press, and from there, to the French and German papers, turning a training field incident into an international cause célèbre.[83]

The incident slowly generated shockwaves in the region. In Zabern itself, Forstner faced harassment by local youths, which he at times countered by laughingly smoking outside his residence. More ominously, crowds of protesters had to be broken up by gendarmes and the fire department. In response, the local military commander Colonel Adolf von Reuter became increasingly incensed and told the *Kreisdirektor* of Zabern, Mahl, that he was poised to take strong measures to defend the dignity of the military.[84]

The local press took this opportunity to express its outrage at the military, the apparent lack of action by the *Reichsland* government, and the general insult to the Alsatian people. The discordant notes of partisan politics from the preceding several years were transformed into a unified chorus of protest. The Liberal *Strassburger Neue Zeitung* criticized not only the attitude of the military but of the German press in general, which had not questioned the military's explanation of events. The paper, however, also pleaded for *Altdeutsche* and Alsatians to find a modus vivendi.[85] The socialist *Freie Presse* wrote: "The behavior of the military officials and the government of Alsace-Lorraine with regard to the regrettable incidents is becoming increasingly incomprehensible. It seems that the government has no idea and no understanding of the seriousness of the situation."[86] The Catholic press also took a strong line against Wedel's regime. The *Elsässer* asked: "Is the government mute? Where is the feeling of duty? Do they have no heart for the land with whose interests they have been entrusted?"[87] The paper further pointed to the military's lack of understanding of the insulting quality of the word *Wackes*.[88] Soon thereafter the paper called for Wedel's resignation.[89] *Die elsässische Volksbote* grew concerned with rumors that soldiers in Zabern had been outfitted with live ammunition in case civil authorities could not maintain control.[90]

The local *Reichsland* officials were, in actuality, intensely cognizant of the dangers posed by the incident to the German cause and tried to ameliorate the situation. Kreisdirektor Mahl, for example, tried both to curb the hectoring of Forstner and to get the military under control. In a letter to his superiors, Mahl pleaded: "I hold it in the most urgent interest of Lt. Freiherr Forstner that he go in the street so little as possible for the time being. The best would be if he took an apartment on the military base."[91] Likewise, Wedel appealed to the local military leaders, the chancellor, and the kaiser to resolve the situation, to little avail.[92] The military did transfer the recruits in question, and Forstner was given six days' house arrest. He remained, however, stationed in Zabern.[93] Unfortunately for the local situation, neither Forstner's punishment nor the efforts of Mahl and Wedel were made public.

On the local level, the population of Zabern renewed its harassment of Forstner. Colonel Reuter, Forstner's commander, had grown tired of the harassment of his officers and threatened to take action as early as 12 November, but was forestalled by the intervention of Kreisdirektor Mahl. General Deimling, Reuter's superior, encouraged stronger measures by the army. On the evening of 28 November Forstner again found himself the target of Alsatian verbal barbs. Forstner returned to base where Reuter ordered soldiers with bayonets to clear the streets and arrest anyone interfering with the military action; several dozen Alsatians, including several judges from the local court who had tried to make the military see reason, were arrested. Reuter seized control in Zabern for the next several days by asserting that "civil authorities" had failed and by claiming the preeminence of military authorities in times of emergency under a Prussian law from 1820.[94]

While Colonel Reuter cleared the streets of Zabern, Alsatian representatives sought to defend the region's interest. War Minister Erich von Falkenhayn met the deputies, but laid the blame upon the Alsatian soldiers who had reported the incident to the press.[95] The German government's intransigence continued during several days of contentious interpellations in the Reichstag. Under attacks by deputies from both Alsace and Germany more generally, Falkenhayn and Chancellor Bethmann-Hollweg sought to defend the army without effectively placating the outraged deputies. Hollweg, in particular, failed to mention that an investigation was underway regarding the activities of Forstner and Reuter. The government then received a verbal broadside from Alsatian deputies as well as members of the National Liberal, Center, and Social Democratic parties.[96]

When Alsatian and other deputies addressed Zabern as well as broader issues, the debate had moved beyond a simple discussion of an insensitive lieutenant or combative colonel. At stake were the issues of military authority versus civilian control and imperial prerogative versus ministerial responsibility. Bethmann-Hollweg gamely defended the importance of the army and the legality of its actions, but to the increasing dissatisfaction of the Reichstag. Indeed, so outraged was the German parliament that it voted to censure the chancellor by an overwhelming vote of 294 to 54.[97]

The contentious sessions of the Reichstag in December gave way to a relative period of calm. Reuter's regiment was sent to an outlying garrison for winter quartering to help pacify the local populace. The government of the *Reichsland*, however, was in a state of bitter disarray. Wedel had argued for swift, public measures against the military through official, nonpublic channels; the lack of support from Berlin led him to consider resignation, only to be persuaded to stay by Bethmann-Hollweg. Zorn von Bulach, the Alsatian state secretary, expressed his disappointment with the situation in Berlin newspapers. Adding to their difficulties were the attacks of German conservatives in both the Reichstag and national press; conservatives blamed the situation on the Alsatians and on the local administration, which had not cracked down firmly enough upon the local malcontents, thereby leading to the insult to the military.[98]

Meanwhile, Alsatian political parties prepared for the reopening of the *Landtag* for its 1914 session. The Center meeting of December 1913 was one of the most highly attended ever; party members called for greater guarantees against such abuses by the military in the future and for the strengthening of the *Reichsland* constitution.[99] The military trials of Forstner and Reuter in early January 1914—during which the former was given a mild reprimand for his training-ground abuses, and the latter was fully cleared of wrongdoing for his imposition of martial law—fueled Alsatian anger in the days leading up to the opening of the *Landtag*. Indeed, the office handling seating in the *Landtag*'s chamber expected an overflow crowd and requested instructions for how to prioritize requests for entrance into the chamber.

The *Landtag* debates themselves allowed the Alsatian deputies to reprimand the local government (though Kreisdirektor Mahl received praise for his attempts to limit the military's actions), the military, and the imperial government sharply. After each of the major factions of the *Landtag* submitted formal inquiries to the local government,[100] the representatives dove headlong into heavy critiques of the government. First, the deputies repeatedly decried the military usurpation of civil authority. Zorn von Bulach's flaccid defense of the military's actions—specifically, that the insults to the soldiers necessitated a vigorous response as the "uniform of the kaiser had to respected"—earned him derision and led several deputies to comment that the kaiser's uniform would be given respect when its wearer had earned it. Second, the representatives critiqued the *Statthalter* and his ministers for not engaging in a vigorous defense of Alsatian and Lorrainer rights. Third, the deputies attacked the original insult to the Alsatian people. Finally, the Alsatian representatives asked why they were treated as second-class citizens within the German Empire.

Despite these sharp critiques of the government, neither Alsatian nor Lorrainer deputies called into question Alsace-Lorraine's place as a part of the German Empire. Indeed, the concern among all the deputies, as well in the broader press, centered on the transgression of Alsatian rights within the German Empire and the need for better guarantees for those rights. The Democratic deputy from Mulhouse, Edouard Drumm, ended the final day of debates over Zabern as follows:

> If the Zabern Affair was something for Alsace-Lorraine that we all regret ... so is it something for us Alsace-Lorrainers over which our hearts have rejoiced, namely, that we Alsace-Lorrainers have found ourselves again. Alsace-Lorraine is reawakened. The many differences that have existed in this house must disappear so that there are no longer Centrists, Social Democrats, and Progressivists, but only Alsace-Lorrainers who take up the holy fight for our beloved Fatherland [*Vaterland*] hand-in-hand, shoulder-to-shoulder. The [Affair] is in such a way good news. It is within this context that I close, so that we are in agreement, with the words: Long live Alsace-Lorraine![101]

The Alsatian deputies may have had their differences in the past, but in the wake of the Zabern Affair, they spoke with a common voice.

Although the political spotlight turned from the Zabern Affair to other concerns, it nonetheless continued to have repercussions in the region. Throughout 1914, officials reported incidents between soldiers and the local inhabitants. One major in Forstner's division wrote that his daughters had been denigrated with words such as "dirty pig" by "shameless rascals" [*Lümmel*] in Zabern. Another officer, along with Forstner, found himself the object of youthful invective. Both incidents led to talks with the parents and stern warnings to the children involved.[102] Outside of Zabern, Hansi found opportunity to poke fun at the German military: in the dining room of the Central Hotel in Colmar, as two German officers left the establishment, Hansi lit a piece of alcohol-soaked sugar on their chairs and pronounced, in French, to his companions, that the seats had been disinfected.[103]

From a broader perspective, the Zabern Affair left a bitter aftertaste for Alsatians. They had been insulted, their calls for justice ignored. Indeed, the officers involved only received minor punishments, if any at all. In terms of national politics, the Zabern Affair demonstrated the relative lack of power of the Alsatian-Lorrainer government. Ironically, the inability of *Statthalter* Wedel and his ministers to defend Alsatian rights led them to resign (with the exception of the minister in charge of finances), and a hard-line nationalist, Johann von Dallwitz, was appointed as *Statthalter*. Most importantly, the Zabern Affair brought Alsatians together, at least temporarily, after a period of intense partisan politics, thereby strengthening Alsatian regionalism while souring, without destroying, the relationship between region and Reich.

Conclusion

The constitutional reform and Zabern Affair reveal much about the nature of the German Empire. The limited, begrudgingly granted constitution points to a limited ability on the part of the German Empire to reform itself, a problem hardly restricted to Alsace-Lorraine. The Zabern Affair demonstrated at both the local and national level the inherent weaknesses of German parliamentary rule. Neither the *Landtag* nor the Reichstag, however vociferous their denunciations of the military's actions, could exert power over Wedel or Hollweg, much less alter the government. And yet even if the actions of local and national politicians during the Zabern Affair were mostly sound and fury, the lively debates over the regional constitution did signify something. A political culture was alive and well in the German Empire even if the highest echelons of the government and constitution remained mired in autocracy.

The tensions between reform and stagnation, between constitutionalism and autocracy profoundly marked the development of Alsatian regionalism. Alsatians gained with the constitution a modicum of autonomy, yet not enough to satisfy local demands. The issue, however, served as a focal point of Alsatians for the better part of four years. From the constitutional reform emerged a region better able to articulate and defend its interests. Indeed, the constitution, however disappointing to some local leaders, would become the benchmark of Alsatian independence within the German Empire and serve as the basis for later claims for a regional administration under the French government.

The constitutional debates and *Landtag* elections also revealed the deep cultural divisions among Alsatians about what it meant to be Alsatian in the realm of politics. A younger generation of Alsatian politicians raised in the decades following the German annexation of Alsace and Lorraine, though disappointed by the 1911 constitution, nonetheless adopted a compromising line in the hope that Alsatian aspirations could be realized in subsequent revisions. The National Union, a largely Francophile organization, sought to enshrine the memory of France and French culture within the local political system, thus demonstrating the close links between people such as Hansi and Wetterlé. Its failure and the recriminations of its leaders left deep scissions among Alsatians and within Alsace's political establishment.

The Zabern Affair, imposed upon a relatively strengthened *Reichsland* and divided Alsace, had a double impact. With regard to the constitution, the Affair demonstrated the rather severe limits of regional power in Alsace and Lorraine. The failure of the local administration under Wedel to act decisively on the *Reichsland*'s behalf or to achieve clear results, combined with the *Landtag*'s inability to initiate action against the military or hold the *Statthalter* responsible, reawakened Alsatian fears that they were indeed no more than second-class citizens within the German Empire. Ironically, the German actions served to unite a fragmented community of Alsatians against a common enemy of German rule. Such unity and such discontent with the German administration would make German efforts to rally the Alsatians to their cause during First World War all the more difficult.

Notes

1. ADBR D 247–23b, Circular from Wedel dated 14 Oct. 1909.
2. Jean-Marie Mayeur, *Autonomie et politique en Alsace. La Constitution de 1911* (Paris, 1970), passim.
3. David Schoenbaum, *Zabern1913: Consensus Politics in Imperial Germany* (London, Boston, 1982), passim.
4. For the generally negative view of the *Kaiserreich*, see Volker Berghahn, *Imperial Germany: 1871–1914* (Providence, RI, 1994); Wolfgang Mommsen, *Imperial Germany,*

1867–1918: Politics, Culture, and Society in an Authoritarian State (London, 1995); Hans-Ulrich Wehler, *The German Empire, 1871–1918* (New York: 1985). For a more positive evaluation, see Margaret Anderson, *Practicing Democracy: Elections and Political Culture in Imperial Germany* (Princeton, NJ, 2000); David Blackbourn, *The Long Nineteenth Century: A History of Germany, 1780–1918* (Oxford, 1997); David Blackbourn and Geoff Eley, *The Peculiarities of German History* (Oxford, 1985).

5. Mayeur, *Autonomie et politique*, 16.
6. Ibid., 36–39.
7. Baechler, *Le parti catholique alsacien 1890–1939, du Reichsland à la République jacobine*, (Paris, 1982), 108–14; Mayeur, *Autonomie et politique*, 41–51; for the issue of local desires to resolve nationalist tensions through a constitutional solution, see also *SNZ* (11 February 1910).
8. Hauss's other felicitous departure from the building came when the dictatorship paragraph was formally lifted in 1902. See "Erster Parteitag des Elsass-Lothringischen Zentrums," *Elsässer* (24 Oct. 1910).
9. "Die Reichstagdebatten über Elsass-Lothringen," *Elsässer* (15/16/17 March 1910); "Berlin und Wir," *Freie Presse* (15 March 1910); "Die elsass.-lothr. Verfassungsfrage vor dem Reichstag," *SNZ* (15 March 1910). See also Mayeur, *Autonomie et politique*, 52–69.
10. Almost 300,000 Germans lived in Alsace-Lorraine in 1910 (out of a population of approximately 1.5 million), with heavy concentrations in administrative/military centers such as Metz and Strasbourg, where Germans made up about 41 percent and 23 percent of the population respectively. See Daniel Silverman, *Reluctant Union: Alsace-Lorraine and Imperial Germany, 1871–1918* (University Park, PA, 1972), 69.
11. Claude Lorentz, *La presse alsacienne du XXe siècle. Répertoire des journaux parus depuis 1918* (Strasbourg: BNUS, 1997), 378–9; Mayeur, *Autonomie et politique*, 24–25, 31–35.
12. "Autonomie," *SNZ* (9 April 1910); "Zur elsass-lothringischen Verfassungsrevision," *SNZ* (12 June 1910); P. Jakob "Zur elsass-lothringischen Verfassungsfrage," *SNZ* (17 June 1910); "Eine Kundgebung" *SNZ* (21 June 1910).
13. "Die Verfassungsreform im Landesausschuss," *SNZ* (23 June 1910); Ernest Theodor, "Das elsässische Volk und sein Parlement," *SNZ* (26 June 1910).
14. While Kurlander does show some of the convergences of various streams in the liberal camp, he underplays the divisions over issues such the place of the National Union. Moreover, many within the liberal camp were deeply at personal odds with one another. Eric Kurlander, *The Price of Exclusion: Ethnicity, National Identity, and the Decline of German Liberalism, 1898–1933* (New York, 2006), 152–62.
15. Mayeur, *Autonomie et politique*, 65–66.
16. Boll's paper sometimes featured the political cartoons of Henri Zislin, whose drawings were far more critical of German rule and those who cooperated with Germans than even the works of Hansi.
17. *Journal d'Alsace Lorraine* (27 Nov. 1910); Mayeur, *Autonomie et politique*, 61. See also Fernand Stehelin, "La protestation," *Journal d'Alsace-Lorraine* (November 1910); Frédéric Eccard, "Le problème de l'autonomie," *Journal d'Alsace-Lorraine* (16 November 1910).
18. *Journal d'Alsace-Lorraine* (27 Nov. 1910).
19. "Berlin und Wir," *Freie Presse* (15 March 1910).
20. Baechler, *Le parti catholique*, 215–16.
21. Baechler, *Le parti catholique*, 217–18. See also *Elsässer* (23/24/25 October 1910).
22. *Verhandlungen des Landesausschusses* (29 June 1910), 889–922; Charles Frey, "Nationalismus und Demokratie in Elsass-Lothringen," *Das Neue Elsass* (28 April 1911).
23. Jacques Goetz, "Die Politik Wetterlés," *SNZ* (22 April 1910); "Evolutionniste," *SNZ* (30 Oct. 1910); "Vivat Wetterlé," *SNZ* (31 Dec. 1910).
24. "L'homme aux petits papiers," *Nouvelliste* (28 Oct. 1910); "Un organe alsacien," *Nouvelliste* (29 Apr. 1911); René Schickele, "Nouvelliste," *SNZ* (29 May 1911). See also the massive collection of clippings in ADBR AL 132–21.

25. The Archives Départementales in Colmar contain Wetterlé's personal papers, the bulk of which, unfortunately, consist of the drafts of his wartime speeches and articles.
26. ADHR 27 J 3/8, "Journalists."
27. Mayeur, *Autonomie et politique*, 73; Joseph Rossé et al., *Das Elsass von 1870–1932. I Band. Politische Geschichte* (Colmar, 1938), 137.
28. Mayeur, *Autonomie et politique*, 78; See also Frédéric Eccard, "Die erste Kammer im Verfassungsentwurf für Elsass-Lothringen," *Das Neue Elsass* (6 Jan. 1911), 17–21; Ernst Theodor, "Das Neue Elsass," *Das Neue Elsass* (1 Jan. 1911), 1–2; Georges Wolf, "Die Aufgabe des Oberhauses im Zweikammersystem," *Das Neue Elsass* (20 January 1911), 51–55.
29. Daniel Blumenthal, "Die Freistaat Elsass-Lothringen. Die elsass-lothringische Frage und die Frage der elsass-lothringische Verfassung," *Das Neue Elsass* (20 Jan. 1911), 49–51; Léon Boll, "Vers la coalition nationale pour l'autonomie républicaine, I," *Das Neue Elsass* (24 February 1911), 129–31; Léon Boll, "Vers la coalition nationale pour l'autonomie républicaine, II," *Das Neue Elsass* (3 March 1911), 145–48.
30. Mayeur, *Autonomie et politique*, 74–75.
31. Baechler, *Le parti catholique*, 119–20.
32. Baechler, *Le parti catholique*, 121–24; Mayeur, *Autonomie et politique*, 81–83.
33. Baechler, *Le parti catholique*, 121–22; Mayeur, *Autonomie et politique*, 82–87. See also Emile Wetterlé, "Nous sommes roulés," *Nouvelliste* (1 Feb. 1911). For a succinct description of the Liberal criticism of the Center Party, see Charles Frey, "Die Haltung des Zentrums in der Verfassungsfrage," *Das Neue Elsass* (10 Feb. 1910), 97–100; Charles Frey, "Die Haltung des Zentrums in der Verfassungsfrage," *Das Neue Elsass* (17 Feb. 1910), 113–15.
34. Baechler, *Le parti catholique*, 122–27.
35. Mayeur, *Autonomie et politique*, 110–13.
36. Ministers, teachers, clergy, and civil servants were exempt from the residency requirements.
37. Mayeur, *Autonomie et politique*, 113; Wehler, *German Empire*, 27–54.
38. "Ein Nationalfest?" *SNZ* (27 May 1911); "La Fin de Cauchemar," *Journal d'Alsace-Lorraine* (27 May 1911); "Verfassungsreform im Hafen," *Freie Presse* (27 May 1911); "Parteikundgebungen zur Verfassungsfrage," *Elsässer* (31 May 1911); "Die Verfassungsreform im Bundesrat angenommen," *Elsässer Kurier* (29 May 1911).
39. ADBR AL 69–462(139), Program of the Elsässische-Lothringishe Landespartei dated 28 June 1895.
40. ADBR AL 69–462(139), Clip of the *Journal de Colmar* (15 August 1895).
41. ADHR 27 J 10.
42. Léon Boll, "Vers la coalition nationale pour l'autonomie républicaine, I," *Das Neue Elsass* (24 Feb. 1911), 129–31; Léon Boll, "Vers la coalition nationale pour l'autonomie républicaine, II," *Das Neue Elsass* (3 March 1911), 145–48; Franz Weidenreich, "Demokratie und Verfassungspartei," *Das Neue Elsass* (3 March 1911), 148–51.
43. It is important to note that Preiss, Wetterlé, and Blumenthal, much like Hansi, all came from Colmar. This "Colmar milieu," as Christian Baechler has called it, tended toward a more Francophile and intransigent regionalism. See Baechler, *Le parti catholique*, 128. The trio had also worked together before. For example, in the Gneisse trial, Blumenthal and Preiss served as representatives in the defense of Hansi and Wetterlé. See ADHR 27 J 6, Untitled manuscript, p. 16.
44. *Journal d'Alsace-Lorraine* (6 June 1911); *Le Nouvelliste* (6 June 1911).
45. *Elsässer* (6 June 1911).
46. "Nach Annahme der Verfassungsreform," *Freie Presse* (7 June 1911).
47. "Die Partei ist fertig, ihr Programm kommt nach," *SNZ* (7 June 1911); "Nationalpartei in Elsass-Lothringen und ihre Aufgabe," *SNZ* (21 June 1911).
48. Charles Frey, "Die Elsass-Lothringische Nationalpartei" *Das Neue Elsass* (16 June 1911).
49. "L'Union nationale d'Alsace-Lorraine," *Journal d'Alsace-Lorraine* (30 June 1911); "Die Gründung des elsass-lothr. Nationalbundes," *Elsässer Kurier* (30 June 1914).

50. Mayeur, *Autonomie et politique*, 139–40.
51. Ibid., 146. See also Ernst Theodor, "Der Stunde der Entscheidung," *SNZ* (21 July 1911).
52. "Der Bund der Feiglinge," *Freie Presse* (1 July 1911).
53. "Unsere Landes Versammlung," *Freie Presse* (24 July 1911); "Aktionsprogram," *Freie Presse* (24 July 1911).
54. Letter cited in Baechler, *Le parti catholique*, 133.
55. Baechler, *Le parti catholique*, 131–35.
56. Die Elsass.-Lothring. Nationalbund," *Elsässer* (30 June 1911); Baechler, *Le parti catholique*, 133.
57. Baechler, *Le parti catholique*, 134; See also "Delegiertentag für Els-Lothr. Zentrumspartei," *Elsässer* (4 August 1911).
58. "Elsass-Lothringische Zentrumspartei. Aufruf zu den Landtagswahlen in Jahre 1911," in Rossé et al., *Das Elsass*, 4:474–84.
59. "Leurs arguments," *Nouvelliste* (6 Aug. 1911); "Gouvernementaux et socialistes," *Nouvelliste* (24 Oct. 1911); "Pas fiers," *Nouvelliste* (25 Oct. 1911). Also, at the Strasbourg and Mulhouse meetings of 10 October, Jacques Preiss asserted that the Liberals had too many Germans in their party and were too willing to compromise to be considered "true Alsatians." See "Réunion générale de l'union nationale à Strasbourg," *Journal d'Alsace-Lorraine* (11 Oct. 1911); "Elsass-Lothringischer Nationalbund: An die Strassburger Wähler," *Journal d'Alsace-Lorraine* (15 Oct. 1911); "Pauvre Blumenthal!" *Journal d'Alsace-Lorraine* (18 Oct. 1911).
60. "Der 'Nationalbund' in eigener und fremder Beleuchtung," *Freie Presse* (16 Aug. 1911); "Wahlprogramme," *Freie Presse* (22 Aug.1911); "Zentrums Partikularismus," *Freie Presse* (25 Sept. 1911).
61. Mayeur, *Autonomie et politique*, 158–59.
62. Ibid., 154.
63. Ibid., 152; Gisela Loth, *Un rêve de France: Pierre Bucher, une passion française au coeur de l'Alsace allemand*, Editions de l'Est (Strasbourg, 2000), 151–52.
64. Mayeur, *Autonomie et politique*, 166–78.
65. *Carnets du Thomas Seltz* cited in Baechler, *Le parti catholique*, 128–29; Mayeur, *Autonomie et politique*, 172–73; Rossé, *Das Elsass*, 1:142.
66. Mayeur, *Autonomie et politique*, 150.
67. *Revue Catholique d'Alsace* (June 1911).
68. Carnet du Thomas Seltz cited in Baechler, *Le parti catholique*, 128–29, 172–73; Rossé, *Das Elsass*, 1:142.
69. ADHR 27 J 2, Untitled tract; See also *Nouvelliste* (24 Oct. 1911); Léon Boll, "Aujourd'hui et Demain," *Journal d'Alsace-Lorraine* (24 Oct. 1911).
70. Mayeur, *Autonomie et politique*, 187–90.
71. Ibid., 187–90.
72. *Stenographisches Protokolle des Landtages der zweiten Kammer des Landtages*, 21 Sitzung, 28 March 1912. See also Herman Hiery, "Zwischen Scylla und Charybdis: Carl Graf von Wedel als Statthalter im Reichsland Elsass-Lothringen (1907–1914)," *Revue d'Alsace* (1986): 314–15; Igersheim, 167. Not only did the press express disappointment at the continued intransigence of Alsatians and Lorrainers, but the kaiser himself felt, as he told the mayor of Strasbourg in May 1912, that the rejection of the funds was a gesture of "thanklessness."
73. Igersheim, *Alsace des Notables (1870–1914)*, 167–68; Rossé, *Das Elsass*, vol. I, 159–60.
74. Joseph Fleurent, "Hansi. Sa vie, son oeuvre," *Saisons d'Alsace* 3, no. 1 (Hiver 1952), 17–38; Marie-Joseph Bopp, "Le premier procès de Hansi," *Saisons d'Alsace* 3, no. 1 (Hiver 1952), 65–73; Hiery, "Zwischen Scylla und Charybdis, "318–21; Loth, *Un rêve de France*, 143. ADHR "Fonds Wetterlé" 27 J 10.
75. See correspondence of Wedel, Polizeikommissar Baumberg, Bezirkspräsident Zepplin, and Unterstaatssekretär des Innern Mandel in ADBR 27 AL 180.

76. Alsace-Lorraine had some 82,276 soldiers in the region in 1910, about 4.47 percent of the population, as compared to 1.1 percent in most of the other parts of the empire. See Silverman, *Reluctant Union*, 73.
77. ADHR 27 J 1, Untitled Tract.
78. Cf. Chapter 2, 30–31.
79. *Stenographisches Protokolle der zweiten Kammer des Landtags*, 50 Sitzung, 6 February 1913, 2827–31.
80. Ibid., 2827–62.
81. Hiery, "Zwischen Scylla und Charybdis," 324–25; Igersheim, 174–77.
82. Schoenbaum, *Zabern 1913*, 47–58; Wehler, *Krisenherde des Kaiserreiches: Studien zur deutschen Sozial- und Verfassungsgeschichte* (Göttingen, 1970; Second edition, 1979); Gordon Craig, *Politics of the Prussian Army, 1640–1945* (New York: 1955; reprint 1964), 238–54.
83. *Elsässer* (6 November 1913); *Zaberner Tageblatt* (7 November 1911); Schoenbaum, *Zabern 1913*, 98–100.
84. ADBR D 388–677, Mahl, "An der königlichen Kommando der Infanterie Regiment Nr. 99," dated 9 November 1913; ADBR D 388–677, Bericht des Kreisdirektors dated 12 November; ADBR D 388–677, Unruhe im Zabern, 1913 Report dated 13 November.
85. *Strassburger Neue Zeitung* (10/12 Nov. 1913).
86. *Freie Presse* (11 Nov. 1913).
87. "Schläft die Regierung?" *Elsässer* (12 Nov. 1913).
88. *Elsässer* (20 Nov. 1913).
89. *Elsässer* (22 Nov. 1913).
90. "Der Krawall von Zabern," *Der elsässische Volksbote* (15 Nov. 1913).
91. ADBR AL 388–677, Unruhe im Zabern, 1913, Report dated 13 November. Mahl would later be replaced, though the mayor of Zabern, in conjunction with members of the *Kreistag* for Zabern and a local agricultural organization, wrote to the regional authorities praising his work on behalf of the town and laying the blame on the military. See AMS Événements historiques 19/65, Letter from North to Statthalter.
92. Hiery, "Zwischen Scylla und Charybdis," 299–328.
93. Schoenbaum, *Zabern 1913*, 103–6.
94. Ibid., 106–10. See also ADBR 388 AL 677, Mahl, Unruhe in Zabern—28 Nov.
95. Baechler, *Le parti catholique*, 149–50.
96. Schoenbaum, *Zabern 1913*, 121–28.
97. Baechler, *Le parti catholique*, 150; Schoenbaum, *Zabern 1913*, 121–28.
98. Schoenbaum, *Zabern 1913*, 128–31.
99. Baechler, *Le parti catholique*, 151.
100. See *Verhandlungen der zweiten Kammer des Landtags für Elsass-Lothringen* (13 January 1914), 131–32.
101. *Verhandlungen der zweiten Kammer des Landtags für Elsass-Lothringen* (15 January 1914), 287. Emile Wetterlé expressed similar sentiments about the entire affair in his personal papers, though perhaps with greater intransigence, stating, "Just as with the Grafenstaden affair, that of Zabern revived the spirit of irreducible opposition, not just among the population, but in parliament. It was necessary to see these tumultuous days, in the passages of the *Landtag*, realize the profound irritation provoked by the excesses of the military leadership, even among their supporters. The Nationalists in the chamber then knew beautiful days. No longer did we fight among ourselves; on the contrary, one sought our society and we were able to provoke new conflicts." See ADHR 27 J 2, "L'affaire de Saverne."
102. ADBR AL 388–677. See especially the correspondence of Kleiboehme, Knoepffler and Meyer to the Bezirkspräsident for Unterelsass.
103. ADHR 8 AL 1/9410, Report signed "Greb."

Chapter 4

WAR WEARINESS OR NATIONAL REUNION?
WORLD WAR I AND ALSACE, 1914–1918

Entering the summer of 1914, Alsatian-German relations had undergone almost five years of redefinition, a process marked by mutual recrimination and tinged with bitterness. Numerous minor incidents had robbed the luster from the gains of the new constitution. In the wake of the Zabern Affair, German officers had been hectored while Alsatian political leaders again renewed their complaints about Alsace's incomplete and second-class status within the German Empire. It is not surprising that the "Spirit of 1914" found little purchase in the region outside of those areas dominated by the *Altdeutsche*.[1]

November 1918 stood in marked contrast to the summer of 1914. The declaration of the Armistice on 11 November 1918, and the ensuing entrance of French troops into Alsace in the following weeks, sparked great excitement among the Alsatian populace. Cheering crowds thronged into the public spaces of Alsace's major cities—Strasbourg, Colmar, Mulhouse—to greet *poilu* and general alike.[2] Yet these celebrations were not simply a de facto plebiscite of Alsatian national loyalties as developments of the 1920s would prove. Rather, to understand Alsatian joy at the coming of French *poilus*, one must ask: how did the First World War shape Alsatian attitudes?

For Alsatians, the war presented a triple burden. First, they suffered the normal privations of war, sacrificing bodily at the front and materially at home. Second, the ambivalent national loyalties of Alsatians led to numerous problems: Alsatian sons fought in both armies; German authorities, in the belief that the region's dependability was suspect, instituted strict martial law; at the front, Alsatian soldiers under the German banner endured special measures designed to enforce loyalty and inhibit desertion. Third, the region's proximity to the Western Front meant that the local inhabitants faced the war more directly than either most Germans or French in the interiors of their respective countries. Alsatians, both those in territory captured by the French in 1914 as well as those in

---

Notes for this section begin on page 121.

German-held areas, were evacuated, forced to billet troops, and subjected to occasional shelling.

This chapter assesses the role of the war along several lines. First, the experiences of soldiers at the front will be analyzed; how did military service and the treatment by the German and French military influence Alsatian attitudes toward their respective nations and the region's future? Turning from the trenches to the home front, this chapter then asks how the German administration of the region, taken in conjunction with the material suffering that came with the war, influenced Alsatian attitudes. Likewise, developments in French-occupied Alsace and the French treatment of interned civilians are considered. Finally, the chapter examines the plans for Alsace's postwar future; how did Alsatians working in Paris, Strasbourg, and Berlin foresee the status of the region when hostilities finally ceased?

A Flight from the Fatherland? Alsatians at the Front

In the tension-filled summer of 1914, numerous pro-French Alsatians slipped across the border into France. Hansi fled to serve in the French army as a translator and propaganda specialist. Emile Wetterlé, Daniel Blumenthal, and Anselm Laugel likewise departed to serve the French government as advisers on the future reintegration of Alsace and Lorraine into the French state. And Pierre Bucher fled Strasbourg on the last train to Switzerland on 30 July 1914; he would serve the French government in Paris, Basel, and in French-occupied Alsace.[3] Several thousand additional Alsatians crossed over the border to serve under the *drapeau tricolore*.[4]

For the rest the Alsatian populace, mobilization proceeded without hitches. Trying in vain to raise enthusiasm for the German war effort, local German officials and generals praised the large numbers of volunteers from the region.[5] Despite reports of one hundred thousand volunteers, only approximately eight thousand Alsatians volunteered for the German war effort.[6] Outside of areas heavily populated by *Altdeutsche* such as Strasbourg or in garrison cities, Alsatians did not join in the "spirit of 1914." As an interwar history of this period noted, Alsatians were "thoroughly loyal" but "did not consider the French the enemy, much less the hereditary enemy."[7] Alsatian teacher Phillipe Husser similarly noted the smooth but decidedly unenthusiastic manner in which the Alsatians went to war,[8] a conflict that would see over 220,000 Alsatians mobilized in 1914, and close to 380,000 in German uniform over the course of the conflict.[9]

While German troops ploughed through Belgium into France under the Schlieffen Plan, French soldiers, following their own Plan XVII, attempted to retake Alsace with a quick strike. German units in the region, strengthened at the behest of neighboring provinces, pushed French troops back to the Vosges ridgeline after a brief occupation of parts of southern Alsace, including Mulhouse.¹⁰ Some of Alsace remained under French control throughout the war, including the towns of Thann, Masevaux, and St. Amarin. Despite occasional hard fighting, especially around the mountain of Hartmannswillerkopf (See Figure 4.1), the frontlines in Alsace had been fixed by late September 1914.¹¹

French incursions into Alsace had several consequences. For the long term, Alsatians would recall the words of Marshall Joffre in a speech he made at Thann in September 1914: "We have come back for good and all. Henceforth you are and ever will be French. Together with those liberties for which her name has stood throughout the ages, France brings you the assurance that your own liberties will be respected. Your Alsatian liberties, traditions, and ways of living. As her representative I bring you France's maternal embrace."¹² For the short term, the Alsatians in the occupied regions greeted the first French entrance warmly.¹³ Reports of this reception naturally made it back to German authorities, and, although Alsatians did not display a similar enthusiasm for the French on their second abortive advance into Mulhouse, German military authorities took the affair as yet further proof of the untrustworthiness, if not disloyalty, of the Alsatians.

Indeed, German military authorities had grave misgivings about Alsatian soldiers. The Zabern Affair had exacerbated difficult civil-military relations. Likewise, the attitudes of Alsatians such as Bucher, Hansi, Wetterlé—and their flight to serve France during the war—colored German perceptions. Pro-French sentiments found in Alsatian letters to home, added to reports that French officials were trying to win over Alsatian

Figure 4.1. Hartmannswillerkopf

POWs in French detainment camps, confirmed the suspicion among German military leaders that Alsatians did not merit trust.[14] Finally, reports of Alsatians betraying German troops, in conjunction with reports of mass Alsatian desertions and their privileged status in French POW camps, led German commanders to single out Alsatian troops for special treatment.[15]

German commanders, beginning in early 1915, began to implement a series of measures aimed at obviating the perceived Alsatian threat. First, most Alsatian soldiers were shipped to the Eastern Front to discourage them from deserting. Second, Alsatian soldiers, again for fear that they would flee the German flag, were placed in secondary and tertiary roles; rarely did Alsatians find themselves on the front line. Third, Alsatian troops had their furloughs sharply curtailed and, even when granted leave, could not always return to their homes in Alsace.[16] Finally, as German authorities grew increasingly concerned with the perceived strength of Alsatian perfidy, they began to contemplate punishing the families of deserters.[17]

Some military officials praised Alsatian soldiers in their reports.[18] Moreover, local military commanders, such as *Landwehr* (territorial militia) commander Delévièleuse, argued that most of the troops suspected of deserting were out of the country at the beginning of the war and could not return; indeed, Delévièleuse noted if such men were taken out of the calculation Alsace probably had equal numbers of desertions to those of other German lands.[19] Christopher Jahr has largely backed such claims, demonstrating that Alsatian desertion rates remained similar to those of Germans from the rest of the Empire.[20]

The war and German treatment of Alsatians in German uniform eroded further Alsatian affection for the empire. Copies of censored letters from Alsatian soldiers reveal a twin process; as Alsatians wearied of the war effort and their part in it, they also grew increasingly critical of Germany. For example, letters from Russian POW camps make it clear that soldiers were tired of Germany. One Eugen M. wrote to his aunt that "I thank God that despite all the pain, hunger, thirst, and suffering, I have maintained my health. . . . Immediately after the war I will probably go to Paris. I will not, however, remain in Germany where I have suffered so much." Another soldier, Valentin B., wrote from Russia asking for a French primer so that he could return prepared to a French Alsace.[21] Some soldiers did write of "doing their duty" for "God and Fatherland"; indeed, one soldier did so despite being wounded several times, but unsurprisingly also expressed his longing to be at home, especially during the holidays.[22] Reports by French military attachés in Eastern Europe reflected such despondency among the Alsatian troops in the German army as they described Alsatians unhappy with both their poor material conditions but also the special regulations that applied to only them.[23]

Alsatian troops at times took direct action to demonstrate their dislike of their special treatment. In March 1918, some seventy members of Infantry Regiment 353 were placed under armed guard for mass insubordination;

the Alsatian troops responded to the regimental commander with a rendition of the *Marseillaise*. Two months later, a small group of Alsatian troops mutinied at a camp in Belgium. The action was quashed but Alsatian soldiers tried on several occasions in August–September 1918 to repeat their earlier feat; better planning on the part of the military hierarchy quelled the unrest before it attained any momentum.[24]

The convocation of the *Landtag* due to the need for the region's representatives to raise taxes gave Alsatian politicians the chance to protest the mistreatment of Alsatians in the army, although, in theory the *Landtag* was restricted from speaking on the war. The imperial government, then, faced severe criticism in the spring sessions of 1916, 1917, and 1918 in the *Landtag*, and more specifically, in the closed sessions of the budgetary commission. For example, in 1917 Deputy Michel Diebolt-Weber of the Liberal Party, along with Eugen Ricklin of the Center Party and Eugen Imbs of the Social Democrats, questioned the government's estimate of twenty thousand Alsatian deserters.[25] Likewise, Deputy Robert Schlumberger asked in 1918 if the military had false statistics and cited the case of three soldiers presumed to be deserters but later found to have been killed in action.[26] Perhaps the most impassioned plea, however, came from Deputy Rieffel in 1918:

> Everywhere Alsatians do their duty. Wherever they are deployed, in the West or East, in the Balkans or at sea, they stand behind their comrades. The medals that decorate their chests prove this. The Iron Cross [Second Class] has been earned by thousands of native Alsatians; hundreds [have earned] the Iron Cross [First Class], apart from the other medals for courageous behavior before the enemy. The courageous behavior of Alsace-Lorrainer soldiers is stressed in numerous field reports expressly and clearly, the names of many are inscribed on the honor roll [*Ehrentafel*] in gold letters. And yet they must live with the reproach as "unreliable sorts" who have been withdrawn from the Western Front. More than a year ago the sickening regulations went into effect. At first only a several units were affected; later the regulations were generally enforced and often in a damaging manner. How embittering these regulations have been, each of us knows. Our soldiers have the feeling, as if one pressed a mark to their forehead before the gathered unit and dressed them down in disgrace because one mistrusts them, although the graves of thousands of our compatriots [*Landsleute*] serve as an example for how the Alsatians and Lorrainers in the German army have fulfilled their duty.[27]

Despite the protests of Alsatian deputies, the army made only minor changes in their policies and granted, for example, some concessions on the issue of leave.

The dejection of Alsatian troops in the German army contrasted greatly with the apparent enthusiasm of Alsatian volunteers under French arms. Approximately 17,500 Alsatians served as volunteers in the French army. In addition to the 3,000 soldiers who fled to France at the war's outbreak, 12,000 Alsatians already in France donned French uniforms. And over

1,500 Alsatian POWs from the German army were induced to join the French army during the war.[28]

This last group received close attention from the French authorities. Alsatian POWs were divided into several groups according to rank and to their "disposition in favor of France." Alsatian soldiers were dressed in French uniforms, plied with generous rations of tobacco and alcohol, and asked to participate in flag-raising ceremonies as part of a larger effort to win them over to the French cause. Likewise, POWs who worked received bonuses; French language courses were offered to soldiers who wished to improve their command of the language.[29] French authorities even tried to extend such treatment of Alsatians to POW camps in Russia.[30]

Given the negligible number of Alsatians willing to volunteer for service in the French army, the special treatment served as one element in larger strategy of winning Alsatian loyalty. In theory, these well-treated POWs could serve to promote the reintegration of the region into France at the end of the war. Alsatians would remember their time in French hands fondly and would have had French language training (with attention to patriotic French values thrown in for good measure), thereby allowing the soldiers to assimilate more easily into the French nation while simultaneously promoting the French nation among their fellow Alsatians. Such efforts, however, did not always succeed. At the St. Genest camp, reserved for those Alsatian POWs who wished to be treated like their German peers, a French colonel bitingly referred to the POWs as "poor Alsatians and Lorrainers" and threatened to blacklist the soldiers and hound them out of the region if their attitudes did not improve. The soldiers responded by singing the colonel the *Wacht am Rhein*.[31]

Once in the army, many Alsatians did not go directly into battle. French authorities kept most Alsatians in noncombat roles, often deploying them to French colonial territories. French authorities knew that Alsatian soldiers ran the risk of being tried for treason if captured.[32] Moreover, the French authorities feared how the Alsatian troops might be treated by other French soldiers since many Alsatians, especially in the French POW camps, lacked a firm command of the French language. Therefore, French authorities saw a benefit in colonial service, where Alsatians could maintain order and simultaneously allow other French troops to fight at the front, or volunteering in factories, thereby helping to cover manpower shortages.[33]

Alsatian volunteers seemed more positive about their experience in the French military than their counterparts in the German army. In part, this difference may be attributed to the difference between conscripts and volunteers. The letters of these volunteers in the French army, unsurprisingly, reflect a high degree of patriotism for France and an attendant degree of hatred for Germany. For example, one J. W. observed that "the best for all would be if all of the Prussians who are in Alsace would be tossed in the Rhine." Another soldier wrote, "I have hated this [Prussian] race since childhood, they are barbarians. . . . Vive la France! Vive l'armée française!"[34] Similar letters are numerous; intercepted by German military authorities, such language further fueled the perceptions of German authorities that the Alsatians were untrustworthy comrades-in-arms.

French policies keeping many Alsatians from the Front evoked mixed reactions from Alsatian soldiers. Some of the Alsatians stationed in southern France, Algeria, or Indochina expressed enjoyment at the situation: one soldier, in particular, praised the weather in Marseilles as well as the generous rations of wine. Many, however, expressed their desire to fight on the Western Front.[35] One Louis R. wrote to Emile Wetterlé in Paris to express his disappointment at this situation: "I volunteered at the mobilization . . . but I have not had the good fortune to go to combat and to do my duty before the enemy." Louis R. continued that he would at least like to serve as an interpreter at the front, if not as a soldier.[36]

The treatment of Alsatian soldiers in the armies of Germany and France demonstrates a marked contrast in policy. From the outset of the war, German officers generally considered Alsatian soldiers decidedly untrustworthy. The measures taken to contain this perceived Alsatian threat served to fuel a greater ambivalence among Alsatians toward the German Empire. As Alan Kramer has argued, the exceptional treatment of Alsatian troops fed perceptions of Alsatian uniqueness, if in a negative fashion, as Alsatians turned to a regional identity as a means of coping with their inferior standing within the German army. In contrast, while the French military at times was reluctant to use Alsatians possessing German citizenship in combat roles, it nonetheless made a great effort to win their trust and loyalty. It should be noted that Alsatians in French POW camps were also accorded a particular status that highlighted their unique position, in this case, as the "long-lost" brothers of the French nation. On the whole, then, the war only heightened the patriotism of pro-French Alsatians and undermined any support Alsatians in the German army may have had for the German Empire.

At Home

The First World War also posed great difficulties for civilians. In addition to the normal hardships of war, many Alsatians, especially in the southwestern districts of Upper Alsace, lived with the daily sound of warfare in the distance. In both German and French-controlled Alsace, locals faced restrictions on their movement, material hardship, and even at times the direct threat of war. More importantly, Alsatians in German areas found themselves subject to strict martial law under the auspices of the highly suspicious German army.

The imposition of martial law gave German authorities license to proceed with an intensified program of Germanization paired with a campaign of uprooting French culture in the region. The former goal was pursued by encouraging pro-German stances in the local press as well as by emphasizing patriotism in Alsatian schools, when they could be properly staffed. German authorities endeavored to stamp out French culture largely by attacking the language: French signs, street names, and topographical designations were removed in favor of their German equivalents. Business correspondence could no longer be carried out in French.[37] Even the display labels in the Musée alsacien had to be solely in German.[38] Speaking French was itself seen as a threat to the German cause; those who chose to speak French came under official suspicion and were at times denounced. Freedom of assembly and the press, moreover, were both sharply curtailed.

Despite criticism in German nationalist newspapers of the lack of patriotism among Alsatians in August 1914, local officials did praise the smooth mobilization in Alsace in the hope of inspiring greater support for the war effort.[39] Likewise, in addition to censorship, German authorities tried to promote their cause through newspapers and pamphlet literature.[40] Local writers volunteered their services to the German cause. Gymnasium professor Emil von Borries, a regular contributor to the *JfGSL*, promoted the idea that Alsatian regional privileges had suffered after the French Revolution and it should therefore remain a part of Germany. Friedrich Lienhard, who urged Alsatians to give up the French language, also tried pamphleteering. His publisher, deeming him "among the greatest champions of Germanness" in Alsace, decided that Lienhard's short book *Où appartient l'Alsace-Lorraine?* (*Where does Alsace belong?*) should be in French under the banner of a Swiss printing house to hide its partisan origins.[41]

Christian Baechler has written that the impact of such propaganda was difficult to judge. Censorship obviated the possibility of criticism in the press. Restrictions on the *Landtag* kept open political opposition to German claims to a minimum, with several exceptions.[42] Private judgments are likewise hard to ascertain. Charles Spindler generally expressed skepticism about German propaganda in his journal. More specifically, Spindler challenged Lienhard's claim about the spontaneous rejection of French among locals by arguing that people gave up French due to the "idiotic decrees" of the military. He continued, "These German sentiments, if they truly manifested themselves, are purely superficial. . . . Due to all the vexatious measures that are imposed [on us], due to all the insults that are presented in newspapers, the Alsatians have only one desire, that is to see the Germans defeated and humiliated."[43] More generally, some reports of German officials describe apathy, or at least lack of patriotic fervor, among the general populace.[44]

Alsatian indifference to the German war effort sprang from several sources. Soldiers, both during their limited visits and in their correspondence, passed on their irritation at the measures aimed to ensure discipline and safety among Alsatian troops.[45] Likewise, German efforts to maintain or even augment loyalty among the local populace struck a similar chord to the Pan-German din that had deafened Alsatian ears in the years before the war.

Another source of discontent among the local populace was material privation. In this realm, Alsatians suffered much as did the citizens of the broader German Empire.[46] Bread rations fell from 2 kg/day in 1916 to 160 g/day in July 1918.[47] A *Landtag* report from spring 1916 presented a similar if not quite as drastic picture. Food prices were rising, but retailers could not afford prices charged by farmers. Strasbourg and the other large cities suffered, despite the creation of special organizations to ensure the delivery of grain, milk, eggs, and meat.[48] Representatives of rural regions complained of the necessity of killing livestock due to inadequate fodder. Farmers, struggling not only to maintain prewar levels of production, but also to offset the net loss of agricultural products to Alsace, further had to cope with the loss of draft animals and employees, as well as fathers and sons, to the war effort. Even when some items, such as potatoes, were in abundance, as with the potato harvest of 1914–15, transportation and storage difficulties hindered the fair and timely distribution of the crop. Finally, the region's proximity to the front made the military, through both purchases and requisitions, a direct competitor with the civilian population.[49]

Despite such privations, the beleaguered region probably suffered no more than other areas across the Rhine. David Harvey has suggested that food prices in the early stages of the war in Strasbourg were actually much lower than in cities such as Cologne. Alsatian cities organized early and well to provide food.[50] And as the war progressed, conditions with regard to fuel, food, and housing deteriorated across Germany, not just in Alsace as some *Landtag* deputies alluded.[51] Yet, however relatively good or poor their situation, Alsatians filtered their experience of war through the lens of special regional suffering, a feeling exacerbated by the imposition of martial law in the *Reichsland*.

No exhaustive study on Alsatian reactions to the social and economic aspects of war exists.[52] One can, however, point to several disparate sources to grasp the overall dissatisfaction and suffering of the region's populace. Charles Spindler, for example, reported taking foodstuffs, especially butter, to his friends in Strasbourg from his home in the country.[53] Urban centers, in contrast, felt greater stress. In July 1917 and again in August 1918, the women of St. Marie-aux-Mines (Markirch) protested against the bread rations; their riot led local officials to impose a curfew on the town.[54]

Alsatian representatives, during *Landtag* debates over the issue of the economy, lodged numerous complaints about the decline in the Alsatian situation and suffering of the local population since the beginning of the war. While the *Landtag* deputies agreed that Alsace in particular had suffered greatly, and while they wished to assure that damages to the area caused by the war would be covered after an eventual peace, they argued among themselves as to whom the war had burdened more, the rural or urban populace.[55]

While economic dislocations sapped morale, requisitioning and quartering of troops served as a source of irritation between local residents and the military. Charles Spindler reported that not only his wine cellar, but also those of his neighbors, including that of an absent Anselm Laugel, had been thoroughly pillaged by German troops.[56] Likewise, the constant presence of German troops in Alsatian towns along the Front provoked vexation and anxiety among the indigenous population. Though some officers tried to be friendly, most soldiers billeted at Charles Spindler's house behaved rudely, damaged furniture, and, in one case, took the only key for the house's main bathroom to have for his own personal use.[57]

Even more damaging to German legitimacy in the region was the persecution of persons suspected of being pro-French and anti-German. German authorities began to draw up such lists of people whose political mindset on the basis of their "prior attitudes" appeared "dubious."[58] From these lists sprang a variety of measures. Some individuals, for example Charles Spindler, found themselves under surveillance.[59] Alsatians who had welcomed the short-lived French incursion into the region around Alsace were questioned about their attitudes and actions.

Such policies gave rise to denunciations. One of Spindler's neighbors accused his wife and daughter of speaking French, and attributed comments praising the German loss of Tsing-Tao to Spindler himself. The charges came to nothing, but another neighbor was caught with "anti-German" postcards in his possession and sentenced to nine months of *Schutzhaft* (preventative custody).[60] Even returning hostages and civil POWs faced potential persecution.[61]

More seriously, some Alsatians found themselves charged with high treason and faced confiscation of property and the possibility of prison. Most in this category, however, had already fled to France. Several of them lost their property, and even the Musée alsacien and the offices of the *Revue alsacienne illustreé* were seized due to their proximity to Bucher.[62] Those Alsatians of "anti-German sentiment" who remained in Alsace faced internment or removal from militarily sensitive areas; others were shipped across the Rhine and forbidden from returning to Alsace for a set duration, usually three months.[63] German authorities even began cracking down on the religious teaching orders in the area, especially among the sisters, as they were seen as possessing an "anti-German tendency."[64] Over the course of the war, more than 1,900 Alsatians were expelled or taken into custody, with the majority (1,640) put into "preventative custody." Moreover, military courts found 49 people guilty of high treason (many in absentia), 45 guilty of aiding desertion, 1,850 cases of desertion itself, and 365 cases of "anti-German sentiment."[65]

German troops at times handled the local population in a most brutal fashion, and there were occasional reports of civilians firing upon German troops; the military often responded quickly.[66] For example, the German 28th Reserve Infantry Brigade found itself under fire in November 1914. Several alleged culprits—a man named Philbert, Philbert's seventeen-year-old son, and Emile Naeger—were dragged outside and shot while a local official pleaded for their release.[67] In his account of the affair, Reitz argued, "I know these people, and while I won't claim that all are of a good German mindset, I can say that all are too fearful to do anything to German troops" and noted that he thought the shots came from the woods.[68] Local German officials, cognizant of the military's mistake, sought compensation for Naeger's widow and children.[69] The attitude of the reporting officer, in contrast, was in many ways more telling of German attitudes and points to the intense friction between the Alsatian population and the German military. Lieutenant General Stein wrote of the local commander that "he does not remember the incident. Higher officers in battle have other things to do, rather than worry about every little triviality." He continued, "It can be assumed from the results of the investigation that Naeger was innocent. No one, however, is to be reprimanded. In war such incidents cannot be avoided."[70]

The vicious cycle of Alsatian ambivalence, German suspicion, German repression, and further Alsatian demoralization is reflected in the attitudes of common Alsatians. Phillip Husser, a teacher in Upper Alsace who considered himself a patriotic German, wrote in his diary, "I want to shout at the Germans that not everyone has anti-German sentiments," later noting that the "war council has punished [people sympathetic to France] severely. These lamentable incidents have had a demoralizing effect, even on Germanophile Alsatians."[71] Alsatian deputies in the *Landtag* as well as the Reichstag argued that the imprisonment and expulsion of Alsatians were both unfair and illegal.[72] And German reports about the populace in general pointed to a disaffection with the war. As one regional administrator explained, the Alsatians displayed "an entire lack of internal participation in the war that the German people are currently experiencing"; in addition, they bought fewer war bonds and volunteered in smaller numbers than their counterparts across the Rhine.[73]

The French occupation of the region, albeit limited to the areas around Thann, Masevaux, and Altkirch,[74] differed greatly both in intent of the authorities and in the nature of the regime. In contrast to the German military, the French viewed the war as a chance to win over the populace. General Joffre wrote in December 1914, "We must above all watch that we do not at all wound the feeling of particularism and that we have assured in Alsace . . . the maintenance of the individuality of the race, the affection for our country and the use of our language." Moreover, Joffre recognized the need to respect Alsatian religious sensibilities and further argued that the assimilation of the local population would be "long and difficult."[75] Some, such as the Alsatian lawyer Paul Helmer, pushed for outright annexation, a demand rebuffed by French officials in the foreign ministry who argued that from the standpoint of international law, France's claims to the region would be enhanced if they did not violate the Hague Conventions.[76]

How did such goals translate into practical experience? The region's populace did experience a number of clear difficulties. Certain communes were subject to frequent and occasionally heavy bombardment. Provisions had to be delivered through the Vosges by the French army because some valleys were not self-sufficient, a situation exacerbated by the removal of several thousand men of arms-bearing age from the region. This lack of manpower also crippled local industry in the opening months of the war. Moreover, proximity to the Front meant that circulation of civilians in the militarily sensitive region was restricted, unregistered possession of firearms and the sale of alcohol to soldiers were forbidden, and use of photographic equipment required permission. And though compensated, Alsatians were subject to requisitions as well as the quartering of French troops.[77]

In spite of these disruptions, the French administration sought to maintain schools in the area with the hope of preparing Alsatian youth for the return of French power to the region. Using soldier-instructors, teaching orders of local nuns, and local teachers deemed loyal, French authorities kept primary schools open for approximately 8,200 students, though secondary schools, which mostly had been located in German-held regions of Alsace, remained closed. In addition, over three thousand students were enrolled in adult classes. The aim of both primary schools and adult courses was the cultivation of the French language. The primary schools, in particular, used the "direct method" of language education (i.e., immersion in the French language), thereby paralleling French methods with foreign students elsewhere and establishing a principle for the Alsatian educational system in the interwar period. In addition, schools were to teach French values—for example, the meaning of *liberté, egalité, fraternité*—as well as French history. It is also interesting to note that, despite laws concerning secular instruction, religious education was retained in Alsace so as not to upset the local population.[78] Success was limited; older Alsatian students did not react well to the direct method, French teachers had difficulties communicating with the local populace, and schools were occasionally forced to close due to wartime conditions.[79]

While the French sought to win over locals, the military need for a secure operational area also influenced the administration of French-occupied Alsace. The most important element of military control of the region was the forced evacuation of certain areas and segments of the local population. Two types of evacuations were undertaken. The first group included those removed from the region for military reasons, for example, to keep a local population safe from bombardments. The second group concerned the removal of those unwanted or suspect individuals from the operations area including functionaries in the German government, men of arms-bearing age, foreigners from neutral countries, and Germans or Alsatians taken as hostages.[80]

The group of men who were eligible for service comprised over eight thousand people.[81] Alsatians evacuated for security reasons were first sent to triage camps near Besançon to be vetted in terms of perceived loyalty to France; locals originally from other German *Länder* were likewise separated from "natural" born Alsatians. Those evacuees whose status was indeterminate or in question were then shipped onward to new camps spread throughout France, though a good number of Alsatians found themselves in depots located near Marseilles and Avignon.[82] French authorities did seek to take advantage of this segment of the population; offering anyone who agreed to five years of military service automatic French citizenship; few took advantage of the possibility.

The evacuation and internment of Alsatians mixed Alsatians and Germans together. Some Alsatians, due to their public-sector jobs, familial relations, or denunciations by Francophile Alsatians, were mistakenly confined by French authorities. A special committee, the *Commission des Alsacien-Lorrains et Otages* (Commission of Alsatians, Lorrainers, and Hostages), was created in November 1914 to rectify mistakes from the triage camps and to assign levels of national trustworthiness to Alsatians. The committee made rounds in POW and civilian internment camps in order to classify people into groups. Most Alsatians, if not deemed German, fell into two categories: category 1 for Alsatians deemed suspect and relegated to a guarded depot; category 2 for Alsatians considered of French origin, who were accorded a *"carte tricolore,"* the right to work and move about, and, with the permission of the military, to return to French-occupied regions of Alsace.[83] Starting in late 1914 and through early 1915, women, children, the elderly, and the infirm were allowed to return to Alsace, or in the case of those wishing to return to Germany, were repatriated via Switzerland. All who remained suspect were considered hostages or were of military age and remained in the special depots.[84]

For Alsatians consigned to the camps, the experience could be trying. Transport to the various camps often left much to be desired.[85] Along the way, they found themselves the object of acrimonious invective because many French citizens viewed them as Prussians.[86] Even when they arrived, became settled in a camp, and came to terms with their situation, problems cropped up: they lacked funds, could not get packages or mail without facing censors, and in any case had restrictions placed on their liberty. Even those who had obtained the coveted *"carte tricolore"*—in theory giving them liberty of movement and the ability to work—could not work as they only spoke the Alsatian dialect. Others languished in French rural hospitals.[87] Not all complained: Albert Schweitzer, for example, claimed that he tried to make the best of the situation.[88]

As the war progressed, some Alsatians were allowed to return to French- controlled regions. Men of military age in most cases received permission to return as long as they were not on a "suspect" list and were necessary for the local economy. The records of the ADHR suggest that requests by local factory owners or local municipal officials were the surest bet for gaining reentry.[89] The military, however, had to remind industrialists and officials alike that they would not proceed pell-mell with the return of Alsatian men and that the process would take time.[90] Moreover, many departed for Germany via repatriation, though men of arms-bearing age could only do so in significant numbers until 1918.[91]

Such returns and repatriations at times generated ill-will among the Alsatians as they did not proceed at an even pace. An inspector of an Alsatian camp in the department of Ardêche, for example, noted that the April 1915 repatriations caused unhappiness among those who still remained in the camps. Even those who bore the *carte tricolore* seemed distraught not to be included, although the card afforded them great liberty; returning home was more important than freedom in the French interior.[92] Individuals also wrote authorities asking to return to Alsace or repatriate to Germany, citing the need to support their families, the desire to be with family elsewhere, or their dissatisfaction with their current circumstances.[93]

For Alsatians removed from their homes for military reasons, the shock could likewise be great. Poor material conditions, the inability to speak French, and religious differences, especially for Protestant Alsatians, all served to create friction between the evacuees and the local French populace and administration. For example, a group of approximately 3,500 Protestants from the Fecht Valley in the department of Vosges came under official scrutiny when French authorities learned that a petition addressed to the Spanish ambassador was circulating among the refugees. The petitioners hoped either to receive permission to return to their homes or be allowed to repatriate to Germany. In reports by French authorities, multiple causes were cited as grounds for Alsatian complaints. Bourgeois youths, offered only work in heavy labor to which they were not accustomed, complained. The removal of a popular Protestant pastor, suspected of being pro-German and therefore sent to another region, caused anxiety. Likewise, concerns about their property, "harassment" by local officials, and the "hostile attitude" of the local populace all stood as the major issues with the Alsatian populace. To deal with the complaints, French authorities proposed a series of negative and positive measures. The negative measures included the "removal of malcontents" either through repatriation or relocation, greater surveillance over mail, and seizure of German newspapers. Positive actions included servicing the population's religious needs through the French Protestant Church, bringing in notable, patriotic Alsatians to speak to refugees, and promising that damage to their properties in Alsace would be compensated after the war.[94]

The local French citizenry also took issue with the Alsatians in their midst, especially when they seemed to shun military service at the same time French soldiers were dying. Alsatians—soldiers, evacuees from the Front, and civilian POWs—were already viewed as Germans for their use of that language.[95] The reticence of some Alsatians to fight, especially given that most did not man the trenches, in combination with the horrendous casualties among French citizens, caused tensions in regions where Alsatians were housed. As one report read, "The French population itself understands with difficulty the abstention of several hundred Alsatians who have still not done their duty; one sees the emotion that is already manifest in some departments on this subject."[96] Many did not understand the Alsatian reluctance, especially as they could achieve French citizenship by volunteering for a mere five-year tour of duty.[97] Sometimes, these tensions gave way to minor incidents, such as when a group of French conscripts scuffled with a group of Alsatian youths in a small village near Remiremont.

For Alsatians in both the German and French occupied regions of Alsace, the war proved hardly idyllic. The martial law established in the German-ruled areas ruined any goodwill that the German government may have accrued with the local populace during nearly five decades of rule. The military dictatorship, combined with the loss of loved ones and the material privations of the war, served to make the potential return of French power at the end of the war all the more desirable. The French government, in contrast, followed a more ambivalent course. While seeking to win over the local population, the French military administration also had to subjugate long-term political goals to military security and the necessities of war. Though the experience of Alsatians interned in France, or forced there as refugees, was not uniformly negative, it also pointed to areas of conflict between Alsatians and the French, especially with regard to language and religion. As a report on the military administration concluded, "Our troops started by occupying the regions whose populations reckoned among the French of Alsace. . . . It will not be the same in the other parts of Alsace where the immigrant elements are more numerous or more active, or where Germanization will have had the most profound effect."[98]

Planning for the Future

Throughout the war, Alsace's leaders not only worried about the impact of the conflict, but also had to peer through the fog of war to plan for the eventual disposition of the region. Alsatian leaders exiled in Paris acted with an unwavering vision; France would reclaim its lost province and reintegrate Alsace into the French state. For Alsatian leaders in Germany, the future remained shrouded by the vicissitudes of war and the indecision of

German authorities. Moreover, the changing conditions of the war, especially in the waning stages of the conflict, made the political calculus of Alsatian leaders all the more variable as they had to decide whether to side with a collapsing Germany, declare quasi-independence, or simply await the outcome of the war and peace negotiations.

Beginning in 1915, Alsatian leaders in Paris such as Emile Wetterlé, Daniel Blumenthal, and Anselm Laugel participated in a commission, the Conférence d'Alsace-Lorraine, to organize French control of Alsace during the war and the return of the two regions to France thereafter. The question of the reclamation of the regions never stood in doubt. It was an avowed goal of the French government and only grew in importance as the war progressed. Likewise, the members of the commission, especially the Alsatian representatives, never wavered in their belief that their long-sought goal, *l'Alsace française*, would be realized at war's end.

The bulk of the commission's work focused on such fundamental yet complex questions as the transition from German to French rule, which would necessitate easing Alsatians from the German legal and financial system to the French legal code. While important, it was other issues—administration, the religious question, and schools—that proved more contentious both within the Conference and in Alsace after the war. On a number of substantive issues, nearly unanimous agreement existed. For example, the Alsatian representatives all pushed for swift incorporation of Alsace into France after the war to avoid any transitional situation that might encourage notions of Alsatian autonomy—let alone the idea of a plebiscite—which could in turn allow the expression of anti-French or pro-German sentiments. Moreover, all concurred that Germans residing in Alsace should, in general, be expelled, though those married to Alsatians or wishing to naturalize might have the chance to stay. The representatives also pushed for the retention of German social laws until they could be squared with French law; representatives feared the immediate repeal of the more comprehensive German laws would cause a backlash against the French. And they all agreed that the "customs and traditions" of Alsace should be respected, although what this would mean in practice was never precisely defined.[99]

Alsatian representatives also delved into other potential sources of awkwardness between the "lost sisters." Schools presented one area of concern. All the members of the commission believed that French language instruction should be immediately introduced; some representatives also pressed for allowing education in German to remain as well, if for no other reason than to avoid appearing "less liberal than German legislation."[100] More contentiously, Blumenthal pushed for the implementation of "French laws of free, obligatory, and lay primary education."[101] The question of a secularized education system, in turn, pointed to a larger issue. What would be the role of religion in Alsace, where the Napoleonic Concordat still regulated church-state relations? After much consideration and some apparent wrangling—Wetterlé went so far as to invoke Joffre's promise at Thann—the commission agreed that it would be better not to apply French laws immediately.[102] It is telling, however, that the majority of the commission, comprised of French officials, foresaw the eventual implementation of lay laws, and that the Alsatian representatives, outside of Wetterlé, did not strongly object to such plans.[103]

The concerns over potential problems of church-state relations and expulsions, not to mention thorny issues of the place of Alsatian civil servants and the reintroduction of French laws, all point to a definitive ambivalence about the short-term prospects of the *désannexion* (deannexation) of Alsace. The highly pro-French Alsatian delegates and French officials all ultimately misjudged the possibility of rapid acceptance of their plans in Alsace.

For Alsatian representatives in Berlin and Strasbourg, planning for the region's future could not proceed along such clear lines as in Paris. The economic situation in the region, arrests of civilians, military dictatorship, and poor treatment of Alsatian soldiers had generated protest, if not antipathy, among both the region's representatives and the populace in general. Within Alsace, several events only served to highlight the region's precarious position within the German Reich. First, a 1917 speech in the Upper Alsace *Bezirkstag* (district assembly) in memory of the representative Jacques Preiss, who had passed away in Munich while under Schutzhaft for his Francophile attitudes, led to the call by imperial officials for several members of said body to resign (which they did not). Second, the favored candidate among Alsatians to take over as head of the university was rejected under pressure from the military and by the opposition of Pan-German elements in the faculty.[104] Finally, in March 1917, the Bundesrat decided to liquidate French properties in Germany, especially in Alsace. Several of the local papers, in the belief that these properties would be sold to Germans, argued that such seizures merely set the stage for a German colonization of Alsace.[105]

Against such measures, and within the limits imposed by the military dictatorship, Alsatian representatives tried to defend the region's interests. German planners, especially within military circles, had little love for the region, a fact born out in the treatment of Alsatian soldiers and civilians. It is not surprising that from early in 1915, military leaders, with the support of Pan-Germanists, Prussian officials, some members of the faculty at the University of Strasbourg, and with the strong endorsement of *Statthalter* von Dallwitz, wished to see either the partition of the *Reichsland* among various German states, or better still, the annexation of Alsace-Lorraine by Prussia.[106] Alsatian representatives sought to steer such discussions in a positive direction for the region.

Alsatian representatives did not have great power to counter such maneuvers alone; they could only protest such plans. Even then, there were limits as the subject could not be discussed in the local press. The

Reichstag, likewise, offered only a moderately effective tribunal as Alsatian deputies did not want to provoke military authorities in control of the region. The opposition of parts of the Center Party and the SPD, along with that of some of the southern German states, however, disrupted plans for Prussia to annex or to dismember the *Reichsland*. The future of Alsace-Lorraine thus remained unresolved throughout the early years of the war.[107]

In the summer of 1917, focus returned to the eventual legal status of the region. In conjunction with the peace resolution of July 1917, some parliamentary leaders such as Matthias Erzberger viewed a grant of full autonomy to the *Reichsland* as a necessary step in removing one of the French casus belli. Such efforts failed, meeting opposition from several quarters. Some factions within the Center Party as well as the leadership of the south German states no longer supported autonomy for Alsace-Lorraine, especially as the latter began to see the division of Alsace-Lorraine as a more attractive alternative to elevation to full *Land* status. The change in attitude was also influenced by the intransigence of Alsatian representatives in the *Landtag*; urged by their allies in Germany and forcefully enjoined by Pan-Germanists to swear an oath of loyalty to the empire, the Alsatian deputies refused. Indeed, when Eugène Ricklin, Center deputy and president of the Second Chamber of the *Landtag*, unilaterally and without permission from his party made a declaration in favor of Alsace remaining a part of the German Empire, he met with grave disapproval.[108]

Imperial authorities also lobbied hard against full autonomy for the *Reichsland*. A series of memos from December 1917 makes the common position of the various imperial authorities clear. All argued that giving the region full autonomy did not represent German interests and that Reichstag deputies who thought otherwise did not realize that such independence would only foster the pro-French tendencies of the region. Moreover, stern measures were necessary. French no longer could serve as a language of instruction. Steps had to be taken to ensure loyalty among civil servants and teachers. French economic interests in the region had to be obviated. All called for the continuation of martial law in the region. While memos of the interior ministry, German High Command, and *Statthalter* had considered the partition of Alsace-Lorraine among several other German states, the near universal conclusion was for the annexation of the region by Prussia. Alsace, due to its internal divisions, inability to provide for its own financial and economic needs, and above all, its unreliability, was not to be given its autonomy.[109]

Few notes of official protest to this treatment were sounded. Vice-Chancellor Payer remained a firm supporter of autonomy for the *Reichsland*. Rudolf Schwander, mayor of Strasbourg and a member of the *Reichsland* administration, also wrote a long memo on the issue. The idea of a partition was rejected out of hand. While he did argue that the Prussian solution "corresponds to the best interest of all of Germany," he also noted that such a choice would be highly unpopular. Therefore, he strongly promoted the idea of Alsace-Lorraine as a full *Bundesstaat*, averring that the loss of the "worst elements" to France during the war, the return of loyal troops, and natural regional evolution all pointed to a beneficial development for Alsatian regionalism and for autonomy for Alsace-Lorraine.[110]

The debates of the second half of 1917 also found some play in both the local and national press, the former allowed by a slight easing in the censorship regime. In May 1917, the *Mulhäuser Zeitung* called for an "Alsace-Lorraine to the Alsace-Lorrainers" within the context of Germany and its federalist structure; it contended that the centralizing tendencies of the French state would not satisfy the wishes of the Alsatians. Professor Laband from the University of Strasbourg, reflecting the position taken in numerous other articles by opponents of Alsatian autonomy, argued that the many internal differences among Alsatians and Lorrainers made partition a desirable solution; in any case, Alsace-Lorraine lacked the internal strength to be a fully autonomous *Land*. Such attitudes met criticism from local papers such as the *Elsässer* and *Elsässer Kurier*. Georges Wolf of the Liberal Party, in contrast, took the position that the democratically natured Alsatians would clash with the monarchically minded Prussians. The *SNZ* also entered the fray to promote the viability of the *Reichsland* as a *Bundesstaat* by noting that the area had a sound, if not strong, economy, that the German and Alsatian populations had slowly begun to meld, and that in any case the internal differences among Alsatians and Lorrainers were not nearly as great as those among German states at the outset of the nineteenth century.[111]

The question of Alsace's future status remained open into 1918 for several reasons. First, and most importantly, the outcome of the war would decide the fate of the region, a fact appreciated by all parties concerned in the debates. Second, among Alsatian leaders, the question of the war's outcome created divisions over what line should be taken. Some politicians wished to await the outcome of an eventual peace settlement. Others, such as Deputies Hauss, Ricklin, and Brom of the Center Party, saw a push for autonomy as doubly advantageous. Elevated status for the *Reichsland* would either secure the region's place favorably within the German state or would allow the region's representatives room to negotiate Alsace's final status at a peace conference.[112]

Such divisions among Alsatians came to the fore in the autumn of 1918 when both German war efforts and the German government collapsed. In a last-ditch effort to win over Alsatian loyalties, the German government named Rudolf Schwander as the first Alsatian to hold the position of *Statthalter* on 8 October 1918. With peace obviously in sight, and Alsace's eventual status very much unknown, local parties wrestled over whether to participate in Schwander's government. The Liberal Party urged support in the view as a means to secure guarantees for the region from

France.¹¹³ The Center representatives were divided. Karl Hauss joined the government over his party's objections. Other members of the party pushed for a more neutral stance, and some even advocated embracing a return to France.¹¹⁴

Calls by Eugen Ricklin for all Alsatian representatives to define a common position before the Reichstag in late October 1918 likewise failed to generate broad support. Ricklin, in particular, hoped to secure a better place for Alsace at the postwar negotiating table. Others within his own party still pushed for participation in both the regional and national German governments out of the belief that Alsace would have little say in the eventual settlement. Yet other members of the Center such as Joseph Pfleger, with the support of Social Democrats such as Jacques Peirotes, argued for neutrality with their eyes on a French return to the region.

The local press reflected such divisions. While all wanted to guarantee Alsatian rights, little consensus existed over how to secure them. The Liberal papers generally gave support to the local government; Catholic papers remained silent or polyvalent, reflecting an array of positions within the party. And the socialist press pushed the *Landtag* to assume a larger role in determining the fate of the region. Likewise, when the idea of a plebiscite was bandied about in the press, the local papers remained at odds with one another. The creation of the neutralist Elsässer Bund (Alsatian Union) that called for a neutral Alsace with ties to Germany also drew the press's attention; generally the press criticized this group as an effort by Germans—as one paper pointed out, the same Germans who months before roundly criticized regional autonomy—to defend their interests in Alsace.¹¹⁵

Such debates were largely overrun by events. The abdication of the kaiser, the Armistice, and the beginnings of a revolution among German soldiers in Alsace, combined with the expected arrival of French troops to the area, gave rise to two major concerns: the maintenance of order and the need to prepare the region for the French return. To these ends a broad range of politicians—in the theory that the kaiser's abdication had ended German control over the region—convened the Second Chamber of the *Landtag* as a *Nationalrat* (National Council) for Alsace. Here again internal differences undermined any potential action the body may have taken vis-à-vis France. Pfleger and Peirotes again vigorously pushed for the acceptance of French rule; Ricklin and his supporters wanted to wait for the issue to be decided at the peace conference; and still others wanted guarantees from France for Alsace's special situation. A pro-French tenor dominated the coverage, though already concerns about language and religion had begun to crop up in the region's papers. For a time, the enthusiastic welcome of the French troops to the region and general relief at the war's end overwhelmed these concerns. The *Nationalrat* passed from the scene in the ensuing weeks, in Christian Baechler's words, "almost unnoticed."¹¹⁶

Conclusion

In the tense years leading up to the First World War, especially in the aftermath of the Second Moroccan Crisis, Alsatian representatives sought to promote a peaceful resolution to Franco-German enmity. Many realized that their land remained at the center of French and German mutual antipathy; even Francophile, anti-German deputies wanted calm, not war, in the wake of the Moroccan crises.[117] Some representatives believed that an improved situation in Alsace-Lorraine would reduce these tensions. Other representatives went to international conferences. In 1910, several Catholic deputies including Wetterlé and Ricklin attended a conference of the Union Interparlementaire where a motion was passed, which in reference to Alsace-Lorraine read, "a decisive step on the road to rapprochement between Germany and France consists of according Alsace-Lorraine its full autonomy among the confederated states of Germany, conforming to the conditions desired by Alsace-Lorraine."[118] Likewise, Alsatian socialists attended a conference in Basel in March 1913 that called for the rejection of increased spending on German armaments and opposition to the French three-year conscription law. And within Alsace, the politicians of Mulhouse, including Socialists, Center representatives, and Democrats, convened in March 1913 to affirm the claims of "Alsatian-Lorraine to the Alsatian-Lorrainers"; some representatives even went so far as to denounce the antagonist caricatures of Hansi and Henri Zislin as well as the politics of Wetterlé and Laugel.[119] Alsatians, even the most dedicated Francophiles, did not want to return to France at the cost of war.[120]

The outbreak of the war changed the situation greatly. Men such as Bucher, Wetterlé, Laugel, and Hansi fled to France to support the French war effort and to prepare measures aimed at reintegrating Alsace into the *mère-patrie*. Thousands of Alsatians manned the trenches to the same end, fighting the Germans, and many like Laugel's son, died in the blue uniform of the *poilu*. For those Alsatians who remained in Alsace or fought in German *feldgrau*, the war represented a more ambivalent test. Their generally lukewarm response to the war turned to antipathy for the German army in particular and the German regime in general.

Embedded in these divergent experiences were widely varying expectations for the postwar period. For Alsatians who served in France as soldiers and advisors, Alsace would return to France after a French victory. For Alsatians in the region, German plans for the war undercut hopes for the elevation of Alsace-Lorraine to full *Land* status; as the war continued with its attendant suffering and martial regime, Alsatian faith in Germany, already worn thin from the Zabern Affair, slowly faded. Distaste for Germany was not, however, in most cases replaced by an automatic love for France, but rather by a general ambivalence. Last-ditch efforts to grant Alsace-Lorraine more freedom within the German Empire were both too late and too inadequate to appease Alsatian needs. The Alsatians cheered the end of the war not because of a love for France, but rather out of a relief for the war's end and a desire to be no longer in Germany.

The shift to an anti-German sentiment among most Alsatians, or even a welcoming attitude toward the French, was not foreordained. The First World War played a key role in this shift. In the words of the socialist deputy Hermann Wendel of Lorraine:

> If, before the war, one had held a referendum on the question of Alsace belonging to Germany or to France, four-fifths of the population would vote, with reason, for Germany. But today, the immense majority of Alsatians would vote for France, not because of love for the *tricolore*, but solely for the bitterness, the hate that has been done to Alsace-Lorraine since 31 July 1914.[121]

The First World War, then, did not make Alsatians into Frenchmen. The bold declarations of Alsatian representatives in Paris represented the extreme of national sentiments among Alsatians. The majority of Alsatians welcomed the return of French control to the region; however, they did so out of a desire for peace and order after a long war and out of a sense that their land had suffered disproportionately under German rule.

The influence of the war upon Alsatian national loyalties points to the ambivalent nature of identity formation in a border region. The war discredited Germany, thereby making France appear more attractive, and to judge by the *Landtag* records, heightened Alsatians' sense of a unique identity.[122] It was little surprise that Alsatians welcomed French troops in November 1918; they did so, however, not simply because they wished a return to the *mère-patrie* after decades of loyalty to the French nation, but more importantly, because the *poilus* represented order, represented an end to the war, and in any case, were distinctly not German.

Notes

1. The "Spirit of 1914," the enthusiastic, nationalistic response to the outbreak of war, was partly myth and partly reality. Among the educated middle class of Germany's urban centers one can speak of a truly spontaneous and ardent support for the war; yet border regions, working-class districts, and rural areas evinced little of this spirit. In Alsace, outside of large cities and garrison towns, few openly rejoiced at the war's outbreak. See Jeffrey Verhey, *The Spirit of 1914: Myth, Militarism, and Mobilization in Germany* (New York, 2000), 6–7, 91–97, 112–13. The lukewarm response of the Alsatians to the war also parallels the reactions of the French. See Jean-Jacques Becker, *1914: Comment les Français sont entrés dans la guerre* (Paris, 1977), 259–344.
2. "Der Einzug der Franzosen in Strassburg," *Strassburger Neuste Nachrichten* (23 Nov. 1918) clipped in ADHR 2 J 231, "Collection Heitz."
3. See Gisela Loth, *Un rêve de France: Pierre Bucher, une passion française au coeur de l'Alsace allemand, Editions de l'Est* (Strasbourg, 2000), 179–184.

4. Approximately three thousand Alsatians crossed the border to serve in the French army in the opening stages of the war. Christian Baechler, "L'Alsace entre la guerre et la paix. Recherches sur l'opinion publique (1917–1918)," vol. 1 (Thèse de troisième cycle, Université de Strasbourg, 1969), 131; Christoph Jahr, *Gewöhnliche Soldaten: Desertion und Deserteure im deutschen und britischen Heer, 1914–1918* (Göttingen, 1998), 270; See Bernard Vogler, *Histoire culturelle de l'Alsace* (Strasbourg, 1994), 379.
5. Alan Kramer, "*Wackes* at War: Alsace-Lorraine and the Failure of German National Mobilization, 1914–1918," in *State, Society, and Mobilization in Europe during the First World War*, ed. John Horne (New York, 1997), 107.
6. Joseph Rossé et al., *Das Elsass von 1870–1932, I Band, Politische Geschichte.* (Colmar, 1938), 301–20.
7. Ibid.; Charles Spindler, *L'Alsace pendant la guerre* (Strasbourg, 1926), 12.
8. Philippe Husser, *Un Instituteur Alsacien. Entre France et Allemagne, journal, 1914–1951*, ed. Alfred Wahl (Strasbourg, 1989), 31–35.
9. Rossé, *Das Elsass*, I Band, 296–301.
10. Lancelot Farrar, *The Short War Illusion: German Policy, Strategy, and Domestic Affairs, August–December 1914* (Santa Barbara, CA, 1973), 11–18.
11. Rossé, *Das Elsass*, I Band, 296–301.
12. "Address by Marshall Joffre at Thann," cited in *The Annexation of Alsace-Lorraine and its Recovery* (Paris, 1918), 5. Joffre's speech would cause no end of difficulties after the war as Alsatians were used to several decades of German rule and highly cognizant, and protective, of their apparently unique cultural heritage. The promise of Joffre later echoed, if vaguely, in French postwar planning sessions, would mean something quite different to Alsatians than it would to the French.
13. Georges Ritleng, *Souvenirs d'un vieux strasbourgeois, L'alsatique de poche* (Strasbourg, 1973), 155–56. Ritleng, an artist and teacher convalescing in the town of Thann, observed, "The seventh of August 1914 is an unforgettable date. For 44 years no French uniform has appeared in the streets of Thann. All of a sudden, a rumor ran rapidly through the valley of Thann: . . . 'They' are at Wesserling. . . . a cyclist saw them in St. Amarin—'There they are! There they are! They are coming.' At the head of the advanced guard was the 11th Cavalry Regiment, [which] preceded the 133st Infantry Regiment. . . . Then, this created a great joy and tumult! The immigrants, German functionaries, did not believe their eyes! In my bed near the street, windows opened, eyes brimming with emotion, I listened to all this noise! . . . everywhere, the population threw flowers and packets of cigarettes to the soldiers. Alas, they soon had to turn back. The German troops returned en masse on the twelfth of August without difficulty, threatening 'Watch out, Französlinge!'"
14. ADBR AL 22-77 Vol. 1 "Bericht über die Elsässer in Frankreich und deren Einreihung in des französischen Heer" dated 14 November 1914; ADBR AL 22-77, Vol. 2 Report of Unteroffizier Schopp dated September 1915. See also generally Kramer, "*Wackes* at War," 107–20.
15. Alsatians had had the reputation of being deserters; the desertion rates of Alsatians, though twice that of the national average, had nonetheless fallen precipitously in the decades before the First World War. Moreover, most deserters fled to Switzerland and not France. See Jahr, *Gewöhnliche Soldaten*, 253–55.
16. Klaus Hofer, writing to his friend Hans Karl Abel, often noted his irritation, and later anger, at the necessity of waiting for permission to return to Alsace, especially when other soldiers, who had received leave more recently than he, were able to go on leave again before him. See Hans Karl Abel, ed., *Briefe eines elsässische Bauernburschen aus dem Weltkriege an seinem Freund 1914–1918* (Stuttgart, 1922), 57ff, 93ff. See also ADHR AJ 30/40-1 (Purg. 11699), "Résultats de l'interrogation de prisonniers alsaciens à Jassy." Such measures were not put into place in the eastern border regions of Germany for the Polish minority. See Jahr, *Gewöhnliche Soldaten*, 263.

17. BA-Freiburg PH 5/IV, *Elsass-Lothringen im Kriege. Erfahrungen und Vorschläge der Armee-Abteilung Falkenhausen*, 2–12; BA-Freiburg PH 5 I/75, "Heeresgruppen Herzog Albert. Desertionen elsass-lothringischer Kriegsangehöriger;" ADBR AL 22–77, vol. 1, "Liste der angeblich zur Französischen Armee übergetretenen Elsass-Lothringen" (20 October 1915). ADBR AL 22–77, vol. 2, "Seydewitz an VIII Armee Kommando," (25 June 1915); Jahr, *Gewöhnliche Soldaten*, 258–59; Vogler, 211–13.
18. ADBR AL 22–77, vol. 1. There is a series of reports in this file, most of which either praise or do not reply negatively to requests over the behavior of Alsatian troops.
19. ADBR AL 22–77, vol. 1, "Bericht: Landwehrinspektion Strassburg."
20. Jahr, *Gewöhnliche Soldaten*, 278.
21. ADBR AL 22–77, vol. 1.
22. ADBR AL 47–29/1, "Auszüge aus Briefen von junger Leute aus Wilderbach."
23. ADHR AJ 30/40–1 (Purg. 11699), "Résultats de l'interrogation de prisonniers alsaciens à Jassy."
24. Kramer, "*Wackes* at War," 118–19.
25. ADBR AL 39–470, "Protokolle über die vertraulichen Verhandlungen der Budgetkommission," (1917), 24, 52–54.
26. ADBR AL 39–470, "Protokolle über die vertraulichen Verhandlungen der Budgetkommission," (1918), 87.
27. ADBR AL 39–470, "Protokolle über die vertraulichen Verhandlungen der Budgetkommission: Politische Debatte." (9 May 1917), 267.
28. Kramer, "*Wackes* at War," 110–11; Rossé, *Das Elsass*, I Band, 296, 328.
29. ADHR AJ 30/85 (Purg. 11745), "Régime des prisonniers de guerre alsaciens-lorrains" signed Ed. Ignace; circular on the treatment of Alsatians, signed Verand; report entitled "Traitement reservé en France aux prisonniers de guerre alsaciens-lorrains: dépots spéciaux."
30. Reinhard Nachtigal, "Loyalität gegenüber dem Staat oder zur *Mère-Patrie*? Die deutschen Kriegsgefangenen aus Elsass-Lothringen in Russland während des Ersten Weltkrieges," *Zeitschrift für die Geschichte des Oberrheins* 154 (2006): 395–428.
31. ADHR AJ 30/85 (Purg. 11745), "Régime des prisonniers de guerre alsaciens lorrains" signed Ed. Ignace; circular on the treatment of Alsatians, signed Verand; report entitled "Traitement reservé en France aux prisonniers de guerre alsaciens-lorrains: dépots spéciaux." This particular incident also found its way back to German authorities in 1918, when an interned German officer managed to send them a lengthy report on the special treatment of Alsatians. See ADBR 22 AL 59, "Die Behandlung der els.-lothr. Kriegsgefangnen in Frankreich: Die Speziallläger," signed Gabriel Welter (June 1918).
32. ADHR AJ 30/84 (Purg 11744), Packet marked "Pièces d'identité Joseph Dubois, 'Rapport sur l'envoi de papiers d'identité aux alsaciens-lorrains, naturalisés française, prisonniers de guerre en Allemagne' pour Service d'Alsace-Lorraine du Ministère de guerre." French officials in the Service d'Alsace-Lorraine debated at length the merits of sending documents such as naturalization records to German authorities to assure protection for Alsatian soldiers in French uniform; some officials even suggested manufacturing such records, but such an idea was rejected as it could jeopardize all French soldiers of Alsatian origin. See generally ADHR AJ 30/85 (Purg 11744), Packet marked "Pièces d'identité."
33. ADHR AJ 30/85 (Purg. 11745), "Etude sur la Question des engagements des alsaciens-lorrains dans l'armée française," and ADHR AJ 30/85 (Purg. 11745), "Rapport à Général en chef," signed "Masselin."
34. ADBR AL 22–77, vol. 1.
35. ADBR AL 22–77, vol. 1, "A. Messerlin an seinen Eltern," dated 21 September 1914.
36. ADHR 27 J 11, "Louis R. à l'Abbé Wetterlé," dated 3 April 1915; similar sentiments are expressed in another letter to Wetterlé concerning Alsatians stationed in Morocco; see ADHR 27 J 11, "Joseph Buehl à l'Abbé Wetterlé," dated 9 April 1915.

37. Bundesarchiv Freiburg PH 5 VI/4, Report signed "Mundra"; ADBR AL 22–84, Memo from Hindenburg to the Reichskanzler, 1917. See also Baechler, *L'Alsace entre la guerre et la paix*, 1:53–77; Stephen Harp, *Learning to be Loyal: Primary Schooling as Nation Building in Alsace and Lorraine* (Dekalb, IL, 1998), 174–77; Kramer, "*Wackes* at War," 110.
38. AMS D IV 326/1799, Letter from Polyczech dated 28 June 1917, letter from Riff to Mayor dated 28 June 1917.
39. Kramer, "*Wackes* at War," 106.
40. Baechler, *L'Alsace entre la guerre et la paix*, 1:113–28.
41. Emil v. Borries, *Die deutsche Seele des Elsass* (Basel, 1918); Friedrich Lienhard, *Où appartient l'Alsace-Lorraine?* (Zurich, 1915), See also ADBR AL 22–79.
42. Baechler, *L'Alsace entre la guerre et la paix*, 128.
43. Spindler, *L'Alsace pendant la guerre*, 86–87.
44. ADHR 4 AL 1/1, Incomplete report "Anlage zum Verwaltungsbericht für das Vierteljahr 1915," dated 10 January 1916.
45. Abel, *Briefe*, 53–59.
46. Jürgen Kocka, *Klassengesellschaft im Krieg. Deutsche Sozialgeschichte, 1914–1918* (Göttingen, 1978); Jay Winter and Jean-Louis Robert, *Capital Cities at War: Paris, London, Berlin, 1914–1919*, vol. 1 (New York, 1997).
47. Baechler, *L'Alsace entre la guerre et la paix*, 1:128.
48. Ibid.; David Allen Harvey, *Constructing Class and Identity in Alsace, 1830–1945* (Dekalb, IL, 2001), 119–21.
49. Drucksache N. 10. reprinted in *Verhandlungen der 2. Kammer des Landtags fuer Elsass-Lothringen: Drucksache und Vorlage* (1916): 100–208.
50. Ibid., 120.
51. See generally Winter and Robert, *Capital Cities at War*.
52. Harvey, *Constructing Class and Identity*, 118.
53. Spindler, *L'Alsace pendant la guerre*, 254.
54. Harvey, *Constructing Class and Identity*, 120.
55. *Stenographisches Protokolle des Landtages der zweiten Kammer des Landtages*, 5 Sitzung, 25 Mai 1916. 115–74; *Stenographisches Protokolle des Landtages der zweiten Kammer des Landtages*, 6 Sitzung, 26 Mai 1916, 177–221.
56. Spindler, *L'Alsace pendant la guerre*, 30, 251; François Laurent, *1914–1918. Des Alsaciens-Lorrains ôtages en France. Souvenirs d'un Lorrain interné en France et en Suisse pendant la guerre*, ed. Camille Maire (Strasbourg, 1998), 40–41.
57. Spindler, *L'Alsace pendant la guerre*, 30, 189, 193.
58. ADHR 8 AL 1/9140.
59. Spindler, *L'Alsace pendant la guerre*, 59–62.
60. Ibid., 151–52, 168, 172.
61. Laurent, *Des Alsaciens-Lorrains ôtages*, 40–41, 171.
62. "Steckbrief und Vermögensbeschlagnahme," *Strassburger Post* (26 September 1914) clipped in ADBR 22 AL 9. For Bucher and the *RAI*, see the series of reports from Gerhard Luedtke for the Bezirkspräsident in ADBR AL 98–700. For the Musée alsacien, see AMS D IV 326/1799. See also Loth, *Un rêve de France*, 194–95.
63. ADBR AL 116–9, "Reichsgesetzblatt N. 275: betreffend die Verhaftung und Aufenthaltsbeschrankung auf Grund des Kriegeszustandes und des Verlagerungszustandes"; ADBR AL 116–9, Report Nr. 121999 "Fall Wilhelm Zuber," signed "v. Mootz."
64. ADHR 4 AL 1/1, Incomplete report, "Anlage zum Verwaltungsbericht für das Vierteljahr 1915," dated 10 January 1916.
65. ADBR AL 47–29/1. See also Baechler, *L'Alsace entre la guerre et la paix*, 1:53–65.
66. Kramer, "*Wackes* at War"; ADHR AJ 30/40–2 (Purg 11699).
67. ADBR AL 22–29, Report of Wachtmeister Horst, dated 28 August 1914. Report of the Forest Ranger Bell, dated 15 September. Bell had tried to argue with the officer in command that Naeger could not have been guilty as witnesses had seen him elsewhere, but Naeger had already been shot.

68. ADBR AL 22–29, Note from Oberzensurkontroller Reitz, dated 26 November 1914.
69. ADBR AL 22–29, "Antrag auf Bewilligung von Witwen- und Waisengeldern sowie von Kreigswitwen für hintergeblieben von Militärpersonen vom Fedwebel abwärts und von Personen der freiwilligen Kränkenpflege auf dem Kriegsschauplatz," dated 22 May 1916; ADBR AL 22–29, Letter from Naeger to Kreisdirektor, dated 13 April 1915.
70. ADBR AL 22–29, Folder marked "Vorkommnisse bei Grandfontaine."
71. Husser, *Un Instituteur Alsacien*, 40–41, 67, 80–84.
72. ADBR AL 22–14, Verhandlungen des Reichstages, 69 Sitzung, 28 October 1916; ADBR AL 39–470, Protokolle über die vertraulichen Verhandlungen der Budgetkommission, 9 May 1917; *Stenographisches Protokolle des Landtages*, 24/25 May 1916. See also Baechler, *L'Alsace entre la guerre et la paix*, 1:63–65.
73. ADHR 4 AL 1/1, Incomplete report, "Anlage zum Verwaltungsbericht für das Vierteljahr 1915," dated 10 January 1916.
74. By a 1916 count, the population of the 91 occupied communes came to 62,527 inhabitants. Most of the communes had fewer than one thousand people, and many had populations under five hundred. In addition, eight communes were evacuated for military reasons, and sixteen were regularly subject to bombardment, leading to occasional, partial evacuations. See *Administration Militaire de l'Alsace. Rapport sur l'organisation des territoires (1914–1916)* (Thann, 1917), 181–83.
75. Le général commandant en Chef à M. le Général Com. Ière Armée, reproduced in ibid., 11–12.
76. Ibid., 50–53; *Procès Verbaux de la Conférence d'Alsace-Lorraine* (Paris, 1917).
77. ADHR AJ 30/77 (Purg. 11737), "Projet d'ârrete sur la circulation en Alsace," dated 1917; ADHR AJ 30/53 (Purg. 11713), "Reglementation vente armes," signed "LaCapelle" dated 1916; "Reglementation vente armes" signed "Clemenceau" dated 1918. ADHR AJ 30/53 (Purg. 11713), Letter to Commander Henri Poulet dated 1918. *Administration Militaire de l'Alsace*, 141–46.
78. *Administration Militaire de l'Alsace*, 186–97.
79. Harp, *Learning to be Loyal*, 166–67.
80. *Administration Militaire de l'Alsace*, 293–94; Jean-Claude Farcy, *Les camps de concentration français de première guerre mondiale (1914–1920)* (Paris, 1995), 51–60.
81. *Administration Militaire de l'Alsace*, 293–94.
82. ADHR AJ 30/74 (Purg. 11734), "Conseiller d'état président de la commission des otages et de la commission des Alsaciens-Lorrains à Général Commandant en Chef des armées de l'est," signed "Loius Blanc"; Farcy, *Les camps de concentration*, 51–60.
83. ADHR AJ 30/74 (Purg. 11734), "Conseiller d'état président de la commission des otages et de la commission des Alsaciens-Lorrains à Général Commandant en Chef des armées de l'est," signed "Louis Blanc."
84. The Commission des Alsaciens-Lorrains, traveling to camps around France and working at the triage camps, processed approximately ten thousand people between November 1914 and July 1915. The results were as follows: 5,247 Alsatians of category 2 ("*carte tricolore*"), 219 Alsatians in class 1 (suspect), 936 Alsatians were freed before the commission arrived at the camps, and 219 were considered hostages. In addition, 58 people remained to have their status defined, 415 people considered Alsatians had their status as such revoked, and some 4,214 people were classified as Austro-Germans. See ADHR AJ 30/74 (Purg. 11734), "Conseiller d'état président de la commission des ôtages et de la commission des Alsaciens-Lorrains à Général Commandant en Chef des armées de l'est" signed "Louis Blanc" and ADHR AJ 30/74 (Purg. 11734) Report signed "Van Merlen" dated 28 July 1915.
85. Laurent, *Des Alsaciens-Lorrains otages*, 54, 71–73.
86. ADHR Purg. 11699 (AJ 30/40–1), "Evacuées alsaciens," Report dated 17 November 1917.
87. ADBR AL 22–77, vol. 1, Letter from Joseph Richter to his son, dated 24 July 1915; ADBR AL 22–77, vol. 2, Report of Unteroffizier Schopp, dated September 1915. ADBR 22 AL

77, vol. 1, "Max aus Romans to his Parents," dated February 1915. This last letter is also interesting as it stands as one of the few instances among hundreds of letters and postcards in which an Alsatian criticizes French propaganda efforts, with the author commenting, "The French newspapers lie shamelessly and tell entirely absurd fairy tales [*Märchen*]. . . . A prisoners' newspaper given to us prisoners talks about our rulers, our army, and our officers in an entirely mean fashion. One can scarcely read it and laugh about it."
88. Albert Schweitzer, *Out of My Life and Thought* (New York, 1933; trans. 1949; reprint 1950).
89. ADHR AJ 30/74 (Purg. 11734), Letter from the "Directeur de la Sureté Général" to the "Général Commandant de l'armée de l'est," dated 24 March 1915.
90. ADHR AJ 30/74 (Purg 11734).
91. Farcy, *Les camps de concentration*, 114–24.
92. ADHR AJ 30/75 (Purg. 11735), "Extrait d'un rapport" signed "Molitor."
93. ADHR AJ 30/77 (Purg. 11737), Letter signed "Fritz Bennett."
94. ADHR AJ 30/77 (Purg. 11737), Report signed "Boussoudy"; Rapport sur la situation des refugies alsaciens dans le Dt. des Vosges dated 25 July 1917; Report signed "de Castelnau."
95. ADBR 22 AL 77, vol. 1, "Brief an Frau Sengel, Mulhäusen."
96. ADHR AJ 30/85 (Purg. 11745), "Etude sur la Question des engagements des alsaciens-lorrains dans l'armée française."
97. Ibid.
98. *Administration Militaire de l'Alsace*, 618–19.
99. *Procès Verbaux du Conference d'Alsace-Lorraine*, vol. 1 (Paris, 1917), 2–4, 13–17, 233–35.
100. Ibid., 46.
101. Ibid., 163–71.
102. Ibid.
103. Christian Baechler, "L'Abbé Wetterlé, un prêtre patriote et libéral (1861–1931)," *Archives de l'Eglise d'Alsace* (1986): 271–72.
104. Baechler, *L'Alsace entre la guerre et la paix*, 2:223–31.
105. See *SNZ* 1/7/17 and *Elsässer Kurier* 29/6/17, both under the title "Deutsche Ansiedler für Elsass-Lothringen" cited in Baechler, *L'Alsace entre la guerre et la paix*, 2:272–81.
106. Baechler, *L'Alsace entre la guerre et la paix*, 2:272–81.
107. Ibid.
108. Rossé, *Das Elsass*, I Band, 319. Baechler, *L'Alsace entre la guerre et la paix*, 2:236–39; Baechler, *Le parti catholique*, 223. Baechler has observed that the reasons behind Ricklin's statements "are difficult to judge" and suggested that he did so in order to "assure all sides" in the debate over Alsace's future, perhaps after speaking with local imperial officials about future guarantees. Baechler further notes that the protest of the other Catholic deputies sprang not from a desire to return to France but because they placed Alsatian interests before those of the greater Reich and, in any case, were not prepared to concede to the German administration since they suffered under martial law. The speech would haunt Ricklin after 1918 as pro-French Alsatians and opponents to the autonomy movement pointed to this occasion as proof that Ricklin was pro-German.
109. ADBR AL 22–84, Abschrift of letter to Reichskanzler signed "Hindenburg"; Report entitled "Über die zukünftige staatsrechtliche Gestaltung von Elsass-Lothringen," Report signed "Wallruf."
110. ABDR AL 22–84, "Die Zukunft des Reichslandes" signed "Schwander." Schwander's memo, often cited for calling the Prussian solution the best one, has at times been misquoted and ignores the larger context of Schwander's argument. This mistaken reading of the memo stems from the reliance of some historians on *Das Elsass* by Joseph Rossé, which misattributed an overly strong pro-Prussiann view to Schwander. See, for example, Hans-Ulrich Wehler, *Krisenherde des Kaiserreiches: Studien zur deutschen Sozial- und*

       Verfassungsgeschichte (Göttingen, 1970), 61–70; Baechler, *L'Alsace entre la guerre et la paix*, 2:282–83.
111. Baechler, *L'Alsace entre la guerre et la paix*, 2:285–99.
112. Ibid., 2:302–4.
113. Ibid., 3:327–30.
114. Baechler, *Le parti catholique*, 3:332–40.
115. Baechler, *L'Alsace entre la guerre et la paix*, 3:342–51. As many of those known to be active in the Bund were Germans, the group's activities were met with great skepticism.
116. Ibid., 3:377–87.
117. The Center Party went so far as to have one of its deputies make a formal statement in the Reichstag. Eugen Ricklin stated, "We are hostile to all war, also that which would be undertaken for our political belonging. One does not say it solely to Paris, but here in Berlin also. . . . We Alsace-Lorrainers wish with ardor nothing more than decent relations between Germany and France. Moreover, we desire the establishment of amicable relations between the two people. We think that Alsace-Lorraine does not have to be an object of discord between the two states, but indeed to the contrary, can be a link between Germany and France," *Stenographisches Bericht des Reichtags*, 2nd session, 12 December 1905, cited in Baechler.
118. Cited in Igersheim, *Alsace des Notables (1870–1914)*,, 170.
119. Ibid., 170–74.
120. Baechler, *L'Alsace entre la guerre et la paix*, 39; Joseph, 1:178–82.
121. Igersheim, *Alsace des Notables (1870–1914)*, 182.
122. Alan Kramer has argued that this was the case for Alsatian soldiers within the army; judging from the records of the home front, however, this phenomenon was constitutive of the more general Alsatian experience of the war. See Kramer, "*Wackes* at War," 120–21.

Chapter 5

"Ne toucher pas de choses d'Alsace"
The Return of French Rule to Alsace, 1918–1925

In the weeks following the November 1918 Armistice, windows and balconies were bedecked in blue, red, and white bunting and Alsatians poured into the streets to greet French troops. In Strasbourg, municipal and regional leaders, led by interim mayor Jacques Peirotes, welcomed the French as liberators. The local press echoed such sentiments.[1] Charles Frey—the erstwhile Liberal journalist, later mayor of Strasbourg and member of the French Chamber of Deputies—wrote, "We are again French, returned to the Fatherland, which we never stopped loving. We are freed and saved ... in liberty, equality, and fraternity: We are French!"[2] The happiness over the return of French troops resonated across the indigenous political spectrum.

French president Raymond Poincaré offered his interpretation of this enthusiastic welcome in a speech on 9 December 1918 (See Figure 5.1):

> The plebiscite is done. Alsace has thrown itself into the arms of its regained mother. Even before the peace was signed, the long-restrained love for France burst out in moving demonstrations. French prisoners have been freed. *Drapeaux tricolores,* leaving their hidden refuges, have suddenly adorned the facades of your houses. Committees are formed among you to receive and celebrate the victorious troops. . . . Certainly, France has no need of these spontaneous and splendid manifestations to know your aspirations and wishes. It never doubted your hearts, and the years that have passed removed neither faith nor hope.[3]

Poincaré's observations of Alsatian attitudes should not come as a surprise. Other than the weak objections of the National Council, and the lukewarm reception of French troops in a smattering of heavily Protestant towns, Alsatians had welcomed French authorities with near unanimity. The reasons for this enthusiastic greeting, however, were not nearly as straightforward as Poincaré may have thought or suggested. Moreover, Poincaré expected that the *désannexion* of Alsace and subsequent

---

Notes for this section begin on page 148.

assimilation of the region would proceed with relative ease.⁴ Events of the next decade would prove such assumptions wrong.

Many of the difficulties that arose between French authorities and the Alsatian populace sprang from myriad, often mutual, misunderstandings and misconceptions. For almost five decades, Alsace, along with Lorraine, had been the focus of French myth. The declarations made by the representatives at the National Assembly at Bordeaux, the literary works of Daudet and Barrès, and the activities of Alsatians such as Zislin, Hansi, and Wetterlé—joined to wartime propaganda—all fed the perception that Alsatians had remained French, valiantly resisting the efforts of Germans to coerce Alsatians into loyalty to the German nation. Such conceptions of Alsace did not quite square with reality. While some Alsatians had vociferously opposed German rule, many had acclimated themselves to the German administration and had worked to reform the place of the region within the Kaiserreich. In addition, the majority of Alsatians spoke German (and little French), were more religious than the French, and had grown accustomed to administratively adept (if politically incompetent) civil servants.⁵

If the French had a mistaken image of Alsace, then the Alsatians also misunderstood what it meant to return to the French fold. The France that reclaimed sovereignty over the region in 1918 was not that of 1871. The French nation-state was far more unified spiritually, culturally, and administratively—especially following the war—than in 1871, and thus greatly different from the federalist German Empire under which Alsatian regionalism had come of age.⁶ In addition, regional representatives

Figure 5.1. "Le Plebiscit est fait": President Poincaré in Strasbourg, December 1918

possessed only a vague awareness of the implications of the French separation of church and state for Alsatian affairs. Finally, Alsatians believed the wartime promises of Joffre and Poincaré, among others, to respect Alsatian customs and traditions would implicitly protect the status quo in church-state relations, preserve German laws deemed more beneficial (e.g., social welfare provisions and municipal administration) than the French equivalents, and maintain the German language as a constituent element of Alsatian culture.

The debates of the Conférence d'Alsace-Lorraine, the concerns of the National Council, and the advice of French military administrators had augured the potential for Franco-Alsatian conflict in the realms of language, religion, and economic transition. Two factors further complicated matters in Alsace. First, despite the warnings of pro-French Alsatians such as Wetterlé and Laugel, French officials were determined to push through a program of assimilation in Alsace as quickly as possible following the cessation of hostilities.[7] French authorities, however, did so without giving due consideration to the strength of Alsatian regionalism forged by several decades of running battles with German authorities and sharpened to a keen edge in the years before and during World War I.

Mutual misperceptions, French administrative blunders, and existing Alsatian regionalism led to a double irony. First, in their haste to reassimilate Alsatians, French officials committed many of the same errors with regard to religion and language as the German leadership had in the decade following the Franco-Prussian War. Furthermore, French authorities managed to irk the Alsatians with their condescending attitude, lack of respect for local customs, fumbling over the administration of the region, and unfavorable arrangements for local civil servants. The second irony stemmed from the law of intended consequences: the French government found itself confronting a refractory Alsatian regionalism that it itself had encouraged in the decades prior to World War I.

This chapter examines the effects of French administration upon Alsatian regionalism—including the development of the so-called *malaise alsacien* [Alsatian malaise]—between the end of World War I and mid-1925. The first section of the chapter looks at the policies the French government employed to secure and ensure the loyalties of the local populace. The chapter then explores Alsatian regionalism in the years immediately following the war; some Alsatians turned to regionalism as a language of protest, others envisioned a region compatible with the French nation. The final section of the chapter then turns to a consideration of the importance of the *Cartel des Gauches*, whose announced intent to introduce the full panoply of French laws, including the *lois laïques* in the region, sparked general outrage and provided the context for the development of a radical, vociferous Alsatian regionalism.

Purges, Assimilation, and Centralization: The French Administration of Alsace

The French administrators who began to replace the military administration in the regained provinces—much to the regret of sympathetic local observers such as Emile Wetterlé—came mainly from the French interior, viewed Alsace as French, and had little knowledge of or sympathy for local particularities. French authorities did not simply want to bring Alsace (as well as Lorraine) back into the French state, but also desired to purge the region of its Germanic elements, whether through the direct elimination of Germans or through the reintroduction of French culture and law to Alsace. Karl-Heinz Rothenberger has argued that the region underwent a process of purging, centralization, and assimilation that profoundly marked the early years of French control over the region.[8]

The presence of approximately three hundred thousand Germans in Alsace and Lorraine after the Armistice raised large problems for the French administration. Some members of the Conférence d'Alsace-Lorraine had demanded the immediate expulsion of Germans and their Alsatian supporters. Such individuals, it was argued, if allowed to remain would merely serve as malcontents who would undermine the authority of the French state and give Germany a putative claim on the region.[9] Such a straightforward solution, however, ignored the fact that many so-called Germans actually wanted to stay in Alsace for a combination of personal and professional reasons.

The French were partially aided by the decisions of many Germans and some Alsatians living in the region to depart. High-ranking civil servants and state employees, Germans with few ties to the area, and Germanophile Alsatians left of their own accord. French authorities, led by the military, established *commissions de triage* [triage commissions], committees whose purpose was to sort through the local population to determine national loyalties and in some cases expel potential troublemakers. Laird Boswell has called these commissions the first French *épuration* (purge) of the twentieth century that had as its goal "to expel those with German blood to establish racial purity, purge collaborators, and categorize based upon ethnic background."[10]

Each commission operated with two civilians and one military member, all of whom where supposed to have some knowledge of both Alsace and the German language. The former need was covered by drawing upon Alsatians who had opted to live in France; significantly, many of these Alsatians came from industrialist families. This demographic, in turn, David Harvey has argued, biased the commissions against leaders of Alsatian workers' organizations. The prerequisite for fluency in German often fell by the wayside.[11]

The flawed commissions compounded problems by following dubious procedures. Although witnesses could testify against those summoned before the commissions, the accused could bring neither legal representation nor their own witnesses. Even the process of identifying potential troublemakers was arbitrary. The populace had undergone an initial sorting by nationality, yet the potential number of suspects remained immense.[12] The focus of the commissions therefore fell upon four groups. First, German labor leaders came under scrutiny. Second, former civil servants and state employees were brought before the commissions. Third, Laird Boswell has argued that French authorities targeted "cultural mediators" such as teachers, religious leaders, and known regionalists. Finally, some Alsatians were summoned before the commission based upon denunciations by other Alsatians.[13]

Between November 1918 and October 1919 the commissions processed over eleven thousand cases, meting out punishments that ranged from surveillance to exile into the French interior,[14] or even expulsion into Germany. Laird Boswell, in analyzing the commission records from the northern areas of Lower Alsace, has noted that almost one-half of the cases were dismissed due to lack of evidence. One quarter of the suspects were placed under local surveillance.[15] Such treatment rankled Alsatians and left long, bitter memories of the transition from German to French rule.

Some regionalists, deemed potentially disloyal by French authorities, found themselves in exile, if temporarily. Eugène Ricklin, for example, was interned in Kork, a village in French-occupied Germany just across the Rhine. French officials in Alsace argued, largely on the basis of Ricklin's putatively pro-German 1917 speech before the *Landtag*, that his return could "cause difficulties" for the French administration. Ricklin, citing his desire to see his ill wife and to participate in the 1919 parliamentary elections, wrote repeatedly to the French High Commissioner in Strasbourg asking for his release. In addition, his wife pled his case by writing to the mayor of Strasbourg, Jacques Peirotes. Ricklin's pleas, for the short term, were rejected. He was finally released in December 1919 and immediately published a lengthy, angry, and open letter to Commissioner General Alexandre Millerand. This letter presaged Ricklin's turn to militant regionalism in the latter half of the decade.[16]

Such efforts to sweep unwanted elements out of Alsace did not stop at the commissions de triage. Alsatian industries, especially those owned or controlled by Germans, were put under French trusteeship or sold outright. Alsatian mines also fell under French control, as did the railway and public transportation systems of Alsace's major cities.[17] These changes in management coincided with a worsening of the Alsatian economy—partially a result of a postwar slowdown, and partially due to the need for Alsatian industries (especially textiles and wine production) to adjust to the French market. These economic changes fueled an increasing resentment of the new French role in Alsace.

In 1919, worker frustration gave way to strikes, with miners taking the lead. The miners' strike, however, was quashed by the French military.

Worker action continued and a general strike occurred in April 1920. After 1921 labor unrest generally subsided, at least for several years. The strikes, however, had several important consequences. French sequestration of industries in Alsace remained a sore point throughout the interwar years. The nationalization of the Alsatian railroad system in particular continued to rankle the local population because they believed local rates to be higher than in the rest of France and Alsatian railroad workers earned less than their coworkers from the interior.[18] Such discontent in part was framed in the language of *Heimatrechte* (Homeland rights); this rubric could be interpreted broadly to include issues of language, culture, religion, economic protection, a regional administration, or the continuation of beneficial German social laws. In addition, the Socialists in the region, who enjoyed positions of authority (for example, in Strasbourg, where Jacques Peirotes served as mayor) and tended to take an assimilationist, pro-French line, lost support among workers to Alsace's nascent but growing Communist Party. This shift in working-class political loyalties would, in turn, play an important role in interwar regionalism as the Communist Party under Karl Hueber adopted a strong proregionalist, intensely anti-French line.[19]

The negative consequences of the transition of the Alsatian economy from the German to the French market were not limited to industry and the working class. The French decision to introduce the French franc at a rate determined by politicians (rather than economists, or simply the economy) in late November 1918 led not to quick conversion of Alsatian wealth into French currency, but rather to resentment at losses in wealth made by such a forced exchange. Although Alsatian civil servants found themselves reinstated, they often lost their positions, seniority, and pay to counterparts from the interior. In addition, the issues of civil servant pensions and pension rates bedeviled French authorities throughout the 1920s.[20]

The French policies of purging Alsace of German sympathizers and attempting to integrate the Alsatian economy expeditiously into the French market created numerous tensions between the French government and its charges. French administrative policy also generated additional problems. French plans originally called for Alsace and Lorraine to be simply reintegrated into the French state as three separate *départements* (Bas-Rhin, Haut-Rhin, and Moselle). Thus, at the end of 1918, three high commissioners were sent to the three *départements* as forerunners to "redepartmentalization," with the commissioner in Strasbourg enjoying nominal authority over his colleagues in Colmar and Metz. In taking this direct, forced route to reintegration, Georges Clemenceau chose the zealous Jacobin and Protestant bureaucrat Jules Jeanneney, who had little feel or tolerance for the peculiarities of Alsace, to oversee Alsatian affairs from Paris.[21]

The administrative integration of Alsace swiftly ran into difficulties. Instead of drawing upon Alsatian leaders—or even experts from the military who had served in French-occupied Alsace during the war and had attempted to respect Alsatian traditions and customs but had been tasked to the Rhineland occupation—the government relied upon new administrators from the French interior. Such administrators had little experience or knowledge of the Alsatian situation. They found themselves bogged down by the complexities of the transition from German to French law and confronted by increasing Alsatian dissatisfaction over poorly thought-out initiatives such as the sequestration of German property, the commissions de triage, and inadequate food supplies. Jeanneney and his team were therefore replaced in March 1919; Alexandre Millerand assumed the newly created position of commissioner general based in Strasbourg.[22]

As commissioner general, Millerand served as an intermediary authority between the departmental prefects and the Parisian administration. Millerand, in contrast to Jeanneney, saw some value in maintaining a special status for the newly regained provinces. In part, Millerand viewed such a configuration as a means to promote greater decentralization within the whole of France. In addition, Millerand—often with Pierre Bucher at his side[23]—believed that some of the local laws inherited from the German administration should remain in place. In particular, he thought the laws regarding the independence of municipal governments and some of the social welfare provisions of German law should be retained. Millerand's administration, however, proved short lived as he stayed in Alsace only until early 1920, when he returned to Paris to fight successfully for the presidency of the French Republic.[24]

Millerand's successor, Georges Alapetite, a career bureaucrat with less vision, less political acumen, and less-skilled aides than his predecessor, faced mounting difficulties in Alsace. Growing labor tensions, cultural clashes over language and religion, decreasing support among leading Francophile Alsatians, difficulties in implementing French law, as well as the vexatious problem of Alsatian civil servants plagued Alapetite's tenure as commissioner general. Like Millerand, Alapetite was willing to effect compromises with Alsatian sensibilities. Neither Alapetite nor his subordinates, however, could satisfy local expectations; the piecemeal removal of specific areas of responsibility of the commissioner general back to Parisian ministries did nothing to elevate the office in local eyes.[25]

The final removal of any local, special administration occurred under Edouard Herriot's government in 1924 and 1925 when the office of commissioner general closed and the Service d'Alsace-Lorraine opened in Paris under the direction of Paul Valot. While this centralization of Alsatian affairs followed closely the plans of the Herriot government to do away with any special privileges for the region, it also had the backing of some Alsatians who had viewed the commissioner general office as ineffective. Criticism of the office came from several directions. Some Alsatians such as Hansi and Wetterlé criticized the commissioner general for slowing the assimilation of Alsatians; this sentiment was echoed among many French administrators. From a regionalist perspective, many locals viewed the regional administration as pushing a hard assimilationist line while failing to preserve local laws and customs, in effect reneging on General Joffre's and subsequent promises to respect Alsatian rights.[26]

In addition to purging German elements from Alsace and centralizing—however unevenly and against the will of the locals—the regional administration, the French implemented a program of intense assimilation aimed at transforming Alsatians into good and proper French citizens. The French government, for example, transformed the German university in Strasbourg into a first-class French university by replacing virtually the entire faculty with French professors.[27] Likewise, street names and public squares underwent a process of renaming, one element of struggle over public memory to be discussed in the following chapter. The most contentious French measures, however, came in the realms of language and religion.

Despite the popular image in France of Alsatian fidelity to the *mère-patrie*, the vast majority of the population in 1919 did not speak French; indeed, only 6.1 percent of Alsatians in Haut-Rhin (Upper Alsace) and 3.8 percent in Bas-Rhin (Lower Alsace) spoke French as their primary language. The changeover in language, especially in the civil administration and judicial system (though municipalities such as Strasbourg allowed bilingual internal correspondence), presented numerous difficulties. White-collar workers such as lawyers and clerks, not to mention civil servants and other state employees who spoke little or no French, saw their careers potentially threatened.

Teachers were especially open to potential dismissal as part of the transition to French rule. Many Alsatian teachers, above all those considered Germans or Alsatians loyal to the previous regime, had already undergone a vetting process under the triage commissions. The transplantation of teachers from the French interior caused friction within the school system; the new teachers often earned better pay (in the form of bonuses paid for moving to Alsace) and were viewed by local teachers as receiving favorable treatment by the new school inspectors, many of whom also came from the interior. In addition, as the government decided to hold almost all classes in French, many native teachers had scramble to acquire the appropriate linguistic proficiency to keep their jobs.[28]

French policies also had a profound influence on Alsatian students. The government wished to inculcate knowledge of the French language as swiftly as possible among Alsatians. Much as military teachers had done during the war, French teachers sought to teach via the *méthode directe*, immersing Alsatian children, many of whom could only speak the dialect, directly into French. Alsatian parents and representatives alike feared that such a teaching style would impair the language abilities of Alsatian pupils in two languages. Moreover, many resented the apparent arrogance with which the program of linguistic assimilation was implemented. Local resistance to the *méthode directe* earned only limited concessions.

Beginning in 1920, students in the third year of primary school would receive several hours of German education per week. According to Stephen Harp, the changeover in educational language and system did have a minor if appreciable effect on Alsatians. For example, Alsatians in the military had higher literacy rates than their counterparts from the rest of France, but their rates were lower than in the pre-1914 period. Moreover, many Alsatians spoke French poorly in the interwar years,[29] a fact borne out in the winter of 1939–40, when many Alsatian civilians were evacuated to the south of France for fear of a German invasion. There, they clashed with the locals who believed Alsatians, with their strange accents and poor French, to be Germans.[30]

The imposition of the French education system on Alsace raised the specter of French separation laws. While the National Bloc governments of the early 1920s neither altered nor abrogated the Concordat regulating church-state relations, and thus did not remove religious instruction from the schools, such possibilities nonetheless worried Alsatian leaders, at least outside of the Socialist Party. Indeed, the Union Populaire Républicaine (hereafter UPR), the successor to the Alsatian Center Party, expended much effort vainly seeking guarantees from the French government against the dismantling of confessional schools in Alsace.[31]

The disparate woes and concerns that beset the return of Alsace to France destroyed much of the goodwill France enjoyed in the heady days of November 1918. The discontent that followed in the wake of the commissions de triage, the economic slowdown, botched centralization, and attempted cultural assimilation did not, however, lead in a straight line to a militant Alsatian regionalism. As we will see in the following two sections, Alsatians tried to find a moderate solution to their particular problems within the French state in the years leading up to 1924. The social, economic, and cultural tensions of the early 1920s would later fuel the popularity of both moderate regionalists and hard-line autonomists in the late 1920s, groups that often included plans to redress these issues in their party programs.

Alsatian Regionalism under French Rule, 1918–1924

Alsatian regionalism, though strong in the early years of French rule, remained largely quiescent. The shock of French administration created a widespread malaise, yet before 1924 sustained opposition barely existed. Those groups that demanded full-fledged autonomy, or even the separation of Alsace from France, remained isolated. Those movements that did arise, however, attracted the close attention of French authorities. On the whole though, Alsatian regionalism—defined primarily in the political programs of the region's parties and their respective newspapers—sought to maintain certain Alsatian rights, customs, and institutions within the bounds of the French state.

The prospects for success of such movements in interwar France were dim. While men such as Maurice Barrès, Charles Maurras, and Jean-Charles Brun, founder of the Fédération Régionaliste Française, argued in favor of decentralization and regionalism for France out of a variety of ideological motives, their efforts found little purchase. For example, Deputy Jean Henessey, influenced by Brun, had repeatedly introduced plans for administrative reorganization only to see the proposals tabled. Some Alsatians such as Eugène Muller, deputy and later senator, even had close ties to groups such as the Fédération Régionaliste. However, the regionalist conception of the French nation was not in the ascendant in the 1920s.[32]

French attitudes toward regionalism in the 1920s were instead marked by a general antipathy, especially among leaders such as Edouard Herriot, Georges Clemenceau, or Raymond Poincaré. In the Jacobin, centralized vision of a unified French state, regionalism served little if any purpose. Radicals and Socialists, dominant in the 1920s, especially espoused such a view. In the shadows of the recently ended conflict and in fear of a potentially resurgent Germany, they had little inclination to support regionalist, much less the later autonomist, ambitions of Alsatians.[33]

Organized movements pushing for Alsatian autonomy within France, or even separation from the French state, were few in number and poorly organized. For example, during the Paris Peace Conference, the Executive Committee of the Free Republic of Alsace-Lorraine formed under the leadership of René César Ley, Henri Muth, and Charles Rapp. The group—based in Baden-Baden and partially funded by the German government—pushed for an autonomous Alsace within France.[34] The trio demanded the exclusion of French civil servants and military from the region, protection of local customs and language, exemptions from military service for Alsatian youth, and a "North American" guarantee for the region's independence.[35]

Ley, Rapp, and Muth gained the attention of French authorities, and in May 1920 they were found guilty of trying to undermine the security of the French state. Several Alsatians tried with the trio, however, were found innocent. The intense interest in the trial—known as the "Neutralist Affair"—quickly dissipated, yet the incident would continue to influence French views of Alsatian regionalism through the 1920s. The French political police in the region continually concerned themselves with the ties of Ley, Rapp, and Muth not only to former Alsatians living in Germany such as Rudolf Schwander (former mayor of Strasbourg and short-lived Statthalter) but to Germans such as Robert Ernst.[36] More worrisome yet to French authorities were the potential ties between "neutralists" and other prominent leaders within Alsace such as Karl Hueber (later head of the regional Communist Party), Karl Hauss, Georges Wolf, and Xavier Haegy, a priest and major regional publisher.

Several other smaller, ephemeral parties and individuals also garnered the attention of French authorities. For example, Joseph Hummel founded the Parti Fédéraliste d'Alsace-Lorraine (Alsace-Lorraine Federalist Party), which wanted to protect Alsatian linguistic, political, and social rights within the French state. While police officials took note of the organization's "Germanophile" tendencies, the party received little attention and passed away quietly.[37] Klaus Zorn von Bulach, (the younger son of the former secretary of state under German rule) founded the autonomist Oppositionsbloc in 1922. Although over eight thousand individuals showed up to a rally, including UPR deputy Michel Walter, the movement—in reality, a loose collection of people dissatisfied with French rule—collapsed by the end of 1922. For Bulach, however, the Elsässerpartei represented merely the first of several quixotic attempts to found an Alsatian autonomist movement.[38]

If the neutralists of 1919–20 and such short-lived groups as the Elsässerpartei represented one extreme of Alsatian politics with regard to regionalism, then at the other extreme of Alsatian politics stood the so-called "assimilationists" who desired to see Alsatians absorbed into the French nation as quickly as possible. At their most extreme, assimilationists pushed for the immediate implementation of French laws, the creation of three separate departments out of Alsace-Lorraine (Bas-Rhin, Haut-Rhin, and Moselle), the rapid linguistic and cultural integration of Alsace, and the removal of German elements from the region. Few Alsatians, however, were fully assimilationist, at least in 1919.

In the years immediately following the war, the resurrected *Journal d'Alsace-Lorraine* (soon retitled the *Journal d'Alsace et de Lorraine* [*JAL*] to reflect the cultural, economic, and political differences between the two regions) represented the extreme of assimilationist tendencies in the local press. In the years before the war, the *Journal*, edited by Léon Boll, had stood at the forefront of the effort to resist German efforts to win over the region, and had even advocated the creation of an independent Republic of Alsace-Lorraine in the constitutional debates of 1910–11; it is unsurprising that the newspaper celebrated the years of resistance.

For the *JAL*, the assimilation of Alsace did not mean the destruction of Alsatian traditions, but rather the obliteration of the remnants of forty-eight years of German rule. To accomplish these goals, Alsatians needed to become "French in spirit" by undergoing a process of "interior colonization" of French values and mores. The quickest and surest path to assimilation was the school system; however, the paper did see value for continued education in German to defend local interests and to ease the transition to French rule. Daniel Blumenthal, former mayor of Colmar and member of the Conférence d'Alsace, argued that a transition period, with some tolerance for German-language instruction, could ease the process of reintegration.[39]

Between 1919 and 1924, the *JAL* often blamed the difficulties of transition, such as strikes in Strasbourg, on German-oriented malcontents who should be expelled from the region. Indeed, the paper was one of leading the press organizations to support the work of the triage commissions, at least until the measures grew too onerous. The *JAL* increasingly turned its vitriol on the Catholic UPR; it blamed Catholic opposition to the full introduction of French laws for the numerous problems in the region.[40]

The *Revue d'Alsace et de Lorraine* promoted a generally assimilationist line, though the paper also supported a mildly regionalist agenda. Politically, the paper lay close to the Parti républicain-démocratique (Republican-Democratic Party) and more distantly to the local branch of the Radical-Socialist and Radical Parties.[41] As such, the *Revue*, edited by Lucien Coquet, tended to take a hard line against autonomy and strongly promoted the swift cultural and political integration of Alsace into France.

The *Revue* also had an intimate connection to the Ligue d'Alsace Français (League of French-Alsace). In November 1918, Henry Huck founded the Ligue, which had as its president Anselm Laugel; other members included local politicians such as Senator Fréderic Eccard (of the Parti républicain-démocratique). Its overarching goal was to "assure the complete and rapid assimilation of Alsace by France from a political as well as an economic and social point of view." The group, therefore, organized patriotic groups, the fostered the French language in the region, and encouraged closer relations between French civil servants and leading Alsatians. The Ligue thereby sought to "avoid maladroit measures" that would cause problems between the government and the local population. Foremost among such goals was "to avoid all clashes stemming from the differences in religion and to work for the establishment of reciprocal tolerance." The group therefore realized that the integration of Alsace into France required some degree of patience and care on the part of French authorities.[42]

The *Revue* demonstrated its assimilationist tendencies in several ways. The paper strongly supported the expulsion of "undesirable elements," that is to say, Germans and Alsatians who supported Germany.[43] Anselm Laugel urged the French government to apply French laws fully to the region; Alsatian political regionalism was an "outmoded mindset" rooted in the politics of the prewar period. Indeed, the new motto for Alsatians, according to Laugel, should be "Alsace to France" rather than "Alsace to the Alsatians." Insofar as the paper promoted Alsatian regionalism, it did so in a limited manner. For the paper, as well as groups associated with it such as the Ligue, Alsatian regionalism was to be primarily economic. Moreover, they argued that economic regionalism should be expanded to all of France, not just Alsace. Support for administrative and political regionalism led down the "slippery slope" to "particularism, then regionalism" and was to be avoided at costs.[44]

The *Revue* also, on occasion, promoted Alsatian culture. For example, it praised the newly opened outdoor Alsatian theater, celebrated the 25th anniversary of the foundation of the Alsatian theater in Strasbourg, and promoted festivals of Alsatian costumes and traditions. In addition, the paper supported the instruments of prewar resistance to German rule, for example, announcing in glowing terms the renewed publication of Henri Zislin's *Dur's Elsass*.[45]

Near the positions of the *RdAL* and the *JAL*, as well as the Parti-radical socialiste and the Parti radical indépendent, was that of the former Social Democrats. Led by Jacques Peirotes and his paper, the *Freie Presse*, the Socialists became the only Alsatian party to join a larger French political party; specifically, the Socialists transformed into the local branch of the SFIO (Section française de l'Internationale ouvrière). In general, the party supported the swift incorporation of Alsace into the French state. Specifically, the Socialists firmly championed the introduction of secular education and the separation of church and state. The party, however, wished to preserve German municipal self-rule, and more importantly, German social welfare provisions, which it considered superior to those of France.[46]

Moving across the political spectrum, the former liberal organizations. the Liberals and the Democrats, found themselves split into several groups. The first, the Parti Républicain-démocratique, led by Charles Frey and Charles Altdorffer, had the *SNZ* as its main press organ with some support from *Revue d'Alsace et de Lorraine*. The party supported a limited regionalism; in addition to economic regionalism, the Republican-Democrats wished to retain some of the German social laws and the maintenance of German as one of the regional languages. The party, however, pushed for the introduction of interconfessional (though not secularized) schools.[47] The other heir to the liberal mantle was the Parti républicain-radical led by François Oesinger and Camille Dahlet. Garnering its support from the Protestant, petit-bourgeois of Lower Alsace, the party originally was highly assimilationist and anticlerical. By the mid-1920s, Dahlet, along with prewar Liberal leader Georges Wolf, would break away to form an organization with a more regionalist focus, the Progressive Party.[48]

The Catholic Center Party also quickly reestablished itself in the immediate months following the Armistice as the largest and most important local political organization; indeed, the majority of both deputies and senators from the region were members. Gone were some of the party leaders such as Eugène Ricklin (in confinement in Kork) and Karl Hauss (in ill health and in disgrace for joining the Schwander government). Returning leaders included Joseph Pfleger, Nicholas Delsor, Eugène Muller, Joseph Brom, and Xavier Haegy.

In a series of meetings beginning in February 1919, the party—renamed the Union populaire républicaine (hereafter, UPR)—began setting out its broad political program. In general, the party leadership agreed that protecting the linguistic and religious heritage of the region would stand as the party's primary goal. The means by which the UPR would achieve this aim, however, remained unclear.[49] Specifically, should the UPR pursue autonomy—a situation neither welcome in French political life nor in the constitution of the Third Republic—or should the party develop a regionalist program as part of the broader regionalist movement within France?

The divisions within the UPR remained relatively minor in 1919, but reflected differing visions of the region dating from the 1910–11 constitutional debates. Joseph Pfleger, leader of what would become the "right," or "nationalist" (i.e., pro-French) wing, favored a regionalist program that would defend Alsatian rights the same way that Bretons, for example, promoted their own regional cultural particularities. Pfleger, however, remained adamantly opposed to the idea of autonomy because he believed autonomy was impractical within the French constitutional framework and would generate sharp opposition from the French government. Representing the "left," or "regionalist" wing of the party were Eugène Muller, Xavier Haegy, and Jean Keppi. Haegy, a Catholic priest who controlled the Catholic press of Upper Alsace, in particular pushed for the defense of Alsatian rights. Haegy therefore argued in favor of strong autonomy and the maintenance of Alsatian "separateness." Haegy, however, was not a Germanophile. Rather, as many contemporaries noted, he placed Alsatian interests, especially in the realm of religious affairs, at the forefront of his politics.[50]

Pfleger, supported by more nationalist UPR leaders such as Emile Wetterlé and Nicholas Delsor, allowed the incorporation of the regionalist agenda but blocked calls for autonomy. The party as a whole agreed that the region's economic and religious interests should be defended; moreover, the UPR aimed to push for regional reform for the broader French state. While the internal differences within the party were papered over for the first years of French rule, these early rumblings within the organization presaged long-term problems for the party. Significantly, the UPR leadership never clearly decided on the key issue of whether Alsatians should maintain their unique culture or slowly assimilate to the French nation.[51]

The tensions within the UPR can most clearly be demonstrated by two brief examples. At a cantonal meeting in Grafenstaden (a suburb of Strasbourg), a local member of the party suggested that, although he was dedicated to France, he would not hesitate to turn to the League of Nations if France broke its promises to Alsace. The local section then voted for a resolution denouncing party members who had broken with the party's stance against the separation of church and state. A week later, a general meeting of the UPR leadership, Pfleger severely criticized the Grafenstaden resolution. When a priest questioned Pfleger and the UPR delegation to the Chamber more generally, Pfleger stormed out and tendered his resignation as head of the party. Though the entire affair was quickly patched up, the battle lines between the nationalist and regionalist wings of the party had begun to be drawn.[52]

The position of Emile Wetterlé after World War I also points to the tensions inherent within the UPR. Wetterlé's pro-French stance before the war translated into a generally proassimilationist stance. Germans should be ejected from the region. The motto "Alsace-Lorraine to the Alsatians-Lorrainers" could therefore be abandoned as it had served its purpose as a means of resisting the Germanization. Moreover, Wetterlé, however, did support a limited regionalism in the realms of language, religion, and economics; Alsatians would eventually learn French, the regional education system could slowly conform to the French national system, and the French might even benefit from adopting some of the Alsatian social laws. A "wise regionalism" would be fine, Wetterlé argued, as long as it did not entail political regionalism and served to integrate Alsace into the larger French nation. Autonomy, Wetterlé argued, was the "old school, the German school" and should be rejected out of hand.[53]

Wetterlé thus managed to isolate himself within the party. Moderates decried his willingness to compromise on issues of language and religious education. His support for the nationalist wing of the party garnered him additional enemies within the UPR. Moreover, Wetterlé, as head of the Colmar-based *Nouveau Rhin Français* (the successor *Le Nouvelliste*), engaged in a series of polemical exchanges with Xavier Haegy's *Elsässer Kurier*: the acrimony of the debate led the bishop of Strasbourg to intervene and order the two priests to resolve their differences privately. Wetterlé's polemical style seemed better suited to opposition. As a result of such ongoing disputes, Wetterlé slowly lost status in the party and decided against standing as a candidate in the 1924 elections.[54]

Despite irritations visited upon the region by the French government, Alsatian parties across the political spectrum by and large pursued some degree of a "sane regionalism." Few wanted a full and swift integration into the French state; likewise, calls for autonomy, plebiscites, and even separation from France remained limited to fringe groups. On the whole, "sane regionalism" denoted some degree of cultural protection, fair treatment in the realms of taxation and civil service, the preservation of their religious rights, and more broadly, a general reform of the French state. Clear divisions existed among Alsatian parties, and tensions marked the internal development of almost all of the regional political organizations. It was the French government that came to power in the wake of the 1924 elections, the Cartel des Gauches, which would renew the spirit of hard-charging regionalism in Alsace.

The Cartel des Gauches, Secularization, and a Renewed Kulturkampf

The election of May 1924 once again witnessed a victory for the UPR as well as their National Bloc allies, the Republican-Democrats under the leadership of Charles Frey. In the rest of France, however, the Left won the majority of seats in the Chamber.[55] This new leftist coalition, the Cartel des

Gauches under the leadership of Radical Edouard Herriot, pursued a set of policies that greatly strained Franco-Alsatian relations.

In a speech before the Chamber of Deputies on 17 June 1924, Herriot laid out the legislative program of his coalition. Among his numerous goals, Herriot declared to the Chamber:

> The idea of secularity [*laicité*], such as we conceive it, appears to us as the safeguard of national unity and fraternity. . . . The government is persuaded that it has faithfully interpreted the wishes of the dear populations finally returned to France by hastening the coming of the day when the last differences between the recovered departments and the rest of the territory of the Republic can be effaced. . . . In this view, the government will prepare the measures that will permit the introduction of the entirety of the republican legislation, while respecting the established situation and guarding the material and moral interests of the region.[56]

In addition to sounding the death knell of the Commissioner Général, as well as any other form of regional administration, the Cartel's plan threatened to dismantle confessional schools in Alsace, invalidate the place of the Napoleonic Concordat in regulating church-state relations, and remove those remaining German laws that Alsatians wished to retain.

The Catholic dailies *Elsässer Kurier* and *Elsässer* took the lead in denouncing the Herriot speech. The *Elsässer Kurier* protested vehemently, lambasting Socialist Deputies Georges Weill and Jacques Peirotes for supporting the Herriot's policies. Moreover, it accused Herriot of betraying Joffre's promise at Thann.[57] The *Elsässer Kurier* would not only continue such philippics over the next several weeks, but would also compare Herriot to Bismarck and equate the political program of the Cartel des Gauches with the Kulturkampf of the 1870s. More provocatively, the paper demanded a plebiscite in Alsace for all questions relating to the issues of schools and the church.[58]

The ire raised by Herriot's speech did not abate in the ensuing months. Although twenty-one of the twenty-four deputies of Alsace and Lorraine protested the move, it was the Catholic Church itself that stood in the frontline of resistance, not the leadership of the UPR. The Archbishop of Strasbourg, Charles Ruch, implored the parish presidents of the Catholic League of Alsace (Ligue des Catholiques d'Alsace)—formed in 1921 to safeguard Catholic interests—to protest the measures of the Herriot government. On 6 and 13 July 1924, the Ligue held demonstrations at Strasbourg's Place Kléber with approximately fifty thousand in attendance at each event. They marched in the name of "our Christian schools! for the salvation of our children's souls! for the religious future of our homeland," and accused the state of trying to "exclude God and religion from the thought and feelings" of Alsatian children. Ligue propaganda argued that the French state's neutrality was merely a cover undermining Alsatians' ability to choose a religious and moral education for their children.[59]

Throughout the summer of 1924, the UPR was united in its opposition to the Herriot declaration. At a meeting in June, the party's leadership reaffirmed the UPR commitment to religious education. Several UPR leaders participated in the summer demonstrations and criticized the government in regional publications. The party, however, did not organize in direct opposition to the new government measures, but instead deferred the question to its "Committee for Actions and Defense," and more centrally, the Catholic League under the leadership of Archbishop Ruch. The UPR's reticence was tied to the divides present since the 1910 constitutional debates and in clear evidence during the 1919 debates over the party program. The regionalist wing of the party continued to push for more strident opposition to the government. The regionalist wing of the party, in addition, wanted, but did not immediately get, a greater emphasis on regional objectives. The nationalist wing also opposed the government measures, but feared the explosiveness of the situation and argued that Alsatian Catholics should work with Catholics across France to achieve their aims.[60]

The turmoil caused within the UPR and in the region in general was reflected in the reports of local officials. For example, in August 1924, the prefect of Haut-Rhin wrote a memo laying out the political atmosphere in his department since Herriot's declaration. The prefect observed that Catholics in the Haut-Rhin, especially those close to Haegy's press empire and the Conseil Général, consistently ranted against the French. In short, the prefect noted, the new policies "irritated the largest and best-organized group in Alsace." While agreeing that it was necessary to try to dampen opposition, the prefect argued that he had to proceed "with great caution" on this "agonizing question." The prefect feared that if the government took harsh measures against the opposition, or interfered with local matters in a heavy-handed fashion, it would be compared to the German regime. Therefore, the prefect averred that openly countering the Catholic opposition was probably not a viable option. While promising to make discreet moves to counter the influence of Haegy and his supporters, the prefect urged proceeding slowly and warned against pushing too hard on the issue of language.[61]

Despite the warnings of the prefect of Haut-Rhin and against the clearly expressed wishes of the Alsatian populace, the government announced in early 1925 that it would push forward with its plans to introduce lay education. As a result, the major Catholic papers, led by Bishop Ruch, called for a strike by Alsatian parents against the French school system in mid-March 1925. The participation rates in the strike varied widely from town to town; the protests failed to deter French administrators. Shortly thereafter, the *Elsässer* published the results of a survey on the school issue. Although some historians, such as François Dreyfus, have called the results of these polls into doubt, Christian Baechler has noted that, on the whole, the surveys reflected general agreement among Alsatians in favor of religious education.⁶²

The fall of the Herriot government in April 1925 brought an end to the policy of full assimilation and the introduction of secular schools, although interconfessional schools were established in Alsace's major cities, especially Socialist-dominated Strasbourg. President Paul Painlevé's administrative decisions, however, did not calm the situation. In particular, the quasi-regional administration of the General Commissioner was formally abolished in July 1925, ending the long-lasting terminal phase of the office. In its place, the Paris-based Service d'Alsace-Lorraine was established under the direction of Paul Valot, thereby completing the centralization of the Alsatian administration in a fashion similar to that envisioned by Jules Jeanneney in 1919.

Underlying the changes in the administrative landscape were tectonic shifts within the regional parties. The divide within the UPR between its regionalist and nationalist wings became more pronounced, as we will see in chapter 7. The Catholic Party, however, was not the only political organization to undergo a process of slow division. The Socialists under Jacques Peirotes came under assault from the Left as the Communists under Karl Hueber increasingly gained strength; the local Communist program decried the "colonialist" attitude of the French authorities and pushed for complete autonomy for the region.⁶³

Perhaps the clearest sign of Alsatian dissatisfaction and the increased radicalization of Alsatian politics came with the May 1925 publication of the newspaper *Die Zukunft* (*The Future*). The paper's founders included Abbé Joseph Fashauer, René Hauss (the son of Karl Hauss), and Eugène Ricklin. One of the paper's editors, Paul Schall, had already referred to the Alsatian populace as a national minority in his other publication, the satirical weekly *Der Schliffstaan* (*The Grindstone*). The rapid expansion of the paper's printing run from five thousand to thirty-five thousand in under a year's time, and the solid subscription base of over sixteen thousand (as of fall 1925), demonstrated the resonance the paper found with the Alsatian populace.⁶⁴

Die Zukunft claimed to represent the masses of Alsatians for whom the existing press had failed to speak, especially in defense of the region's cultural, linguistic, and religious heritage. Refusing to associate itself with any party, *Die Zukunft* expressed the bitterness of the editors and all Alsatians: "We waited year after year for the fulfillment of the many promises [made] before the conclusion of the peace that had anticipated our demands." In particular, *Die Zukunft* called for the "respect of our language," the "protection of our religious particularities," and the "undisturbed development of our culture."⁶⁵ The cultural demands of the paper, taken in conjunction with its demands for greater political and economic freedom for the region, essentially called for a reinstitution of the 1911 constitution. It even invoked the motto, "Alsace-Lorraine to the Alsace-Lorrainers" as its war cry.[66]

More ominously, the paper framed its demands in terms of national minority status for Alsatians, a claim that would become more insistent as the paper engaged in prolonged polemics against other regional papers. Moreover, a strain critical of France marked many of the paper's articles. For example, in the first edition of the paper, the editors played on the French motto of "liberty, equality, and fraternity" in the following manner: "Liberty, equality, fraternity! A liberty, which gives not the slightest concern to human rights [*Menschenrechte*], is for us none. An equality, which exists on the books but not in reality, we do not need. A fraternity, which for most of us is an insult, we do not want." Although a clear anti-French streak existed in the paper, the editors nonetheless tried to stress the need for change within France. Yet the repeated demand that Alsatians be recognized as a national minority undermined for many the claim that the paper wanted regionalism "within the framework of France."

The local press and parties did not hesitate to respond to the new paper. The nationalist press, not surprisingly, attacked *Die Zukunft* and its demands for autonomy, continued religious rights, and the preservation of the German language in the region. *L'Alsace française* suggested that German capital played a role in the creation of the newspaper; indeed, it had received some money from the German government. The paper was charged as separatist, antinational, and anti-French. Socialists and Radicals argued that the paper represented yet another effort by the clerical party to defend its interests in the region. Such calumnies were heaped on *Die Zukunft* throughout 1925, yet the paper flourished.[67]

The March 1926 issue of the *La Revue d'Alsace et de Lorraine* summarized the many allegations against *Die Zukunft*. The *Revue*'s editors explained their goals to expand circulation to combat *Die Zukunft* and unite loyal Alsatians and Lorrainers for "the French regionalist cause in Alsace and Lorraine." A speech given by Anselm Laugel to a number of pro-French organizations such as the Ligue de l'Alsace française, the Association des femmes de France, and the Société de secours aux blessés militaires, was reprinted in the issue. After recalling the victory of the French military in the war, Laugel argued that "Alsace is contaminated by particularism, autonomy, indeed separatism, which *Die Zukunft* seeks to propagate." But these "false brothers who became French due to President Wilson" were not "good Frenchmen [*bons Français*]" but Prussians, Bavarians, and Badeners. Such people would allow Germany, he continued, to create difficulties for France if Germany were admitted to the League of Nations. The formation of an "Alsatian minority" therefore had to be opposed at all costs. "One should not forget," Laugel railed, "that France had sacrificed 1.4 million of its children to extract Alsace and Lorraine from Germany's claws." Laugel concluded by calling upon his fellow Alsatians to fight against the "German propaganda" and for "French Alsace."[68]

Laugel's speech was emblematic of the terms that would be used to denounce the incipient autonomist movement, over which *Die Zukunft* had established a leading role. While conceding that Alsatians might have some grounds for complaints, Laugel forcefully rejected the demands of *Die Zukunft* concerning autonomy and religious rights. Autonomists were nothing more than provocateurs of a revanchist Germany. Autonomy and particularism had no connection to legitimate complaints, but rather they served as moral fig leaves for a pro-German separatism. France had to remain firm against such assaults in memory of the sacrifices made to regain the lost provinces. As we shall see in chapter 7, these themes assumed a central role in the nationalist rhetoric against the Alsatian autonomist movement.

For the UPR, *Die Zukunft* presented a daunting problem. Many of the paper's complaints resonated with UPR members, and some of the people involved with *Die Zukunft* had ties to the party. Moreover, *Die Zukunft* advocated many similar changes to those sought by the UPR. The right wing of the party, however, denounced the call for autonomy and labeled *Die Zukunft* Germanophile and separatist. Facing a mounting crisis, the UPR leadership decided to reaffirm its regionalist program of 1919, strengthening the demand for a "sane regionalism" while simultaneously restating the party's loyalty to the French state. In particular, the UPR demanded a regional administration "to safeguard better the interests of our land," bilingualism in schools, and the continuation of religious education. The party leadership hoped that the new program would satisfy both of its wings in its commitment to nation and region. Many in the UPR also hoped the reinvigorated regionalist program would undercut the more radical *Zukunft*. As Christian Baechler has pointed out, in so doing, the party often adapted language similar, if not the same, as that of *Die Zukunft*.[69]

The greater emphasis on regionalism on the part of the UPR and the increasingly radical demands of *Die Zukunft* point to the tremendous impact of and backlash against the Cartel des Gauches program. The outrage on the part of Alsatian Catholics over the proposed measures of Herriot merged with other outstanding complaints against the government. The alienation of the region's Catholics in turn paved the way for a more radical set of regionalist aspirations, of which *Die Zukunft* would be the first, but not the last, proponent.

Conclusion

Louis XIV, who acquired Alsace for France in the decades following the Peace of Westphalia, had allowed Alsatians to retain some of their local rights and customs; indeed, the dynasty had developed the motto, "Do not touch the things of Alsace [*Ne toucher pas de choses d'Alsace*]." With few exceptions and slight changes, this approach largely prevailed throughout the subsequent French regimes. Alsatians spoke German, but they had remained loyal to France.

The French government under Herriot, in violating this principle, effectively stuck its hand in a beehive. The local populace, already disenchanted with the French government over the triage commissions, the poor performance of the regional economy, the lackluster administration of the region, and the imposition of French language upon the region, reacted sharply to the government's attempt to curtail its social, political, religious, and cultural traditions further.

The widespread discontent of Alsatians to the Cartel des Gauches' plans demonstrated the lack of mutual understanding between Alsatians and French administrators. Such a clash in visions of who Alsatians were and what Alsatians wanted had developed over fifty years of separation. The inclusion of some degree of regionalist aims in the platform of almost every party in the region, especially the dominant UPR, should also have signaled the desires of the local populace to the French government. Alsatian regionalism could have been used as an integrative force, drawing Alsatians deeper into the French *mère-patrie* through a slow period of transition. Such conceptions of regionalism, however, found only limited support within France, and absolutely none under the Herriot government.

The attempt of the Herriot government to force the pace of assimilating Alsace fully into the French nation-state backfired completely, thereby damaging the relationship between region and nation for the duration of the interwar period. The remaining years of the 1920s would in particular be marked by the rise of a vociferous autonomist movement whose demands far surpassed those of the pre-1924 parties. The publication of *Die Zukunft* was merely the opening round in a half-decade of Franco-Alsatian antagonisms bred an increasingly radicalized Alsatian regionalism.

Notes

1. "Der Einzug der Franzosen in Strassburg," *Strassburger Neuste Nachrichten* (23 Nov. 1918) clipped in ADHR 2 J 231. The file contains a large collection of newspaper clippings about the entrance of French troops into Alsace.
2. Charles Frey, "Der 22. November," *SNZ* (23 Nov. 1918) clipped in ADHR 2 J 231.
3. "Discours de M. Poincaré," *Elsässer* (12 Dec. 1918).
4. Stefan Fisch, "Assimilation und Eigenständigkeit: Zur Wiedervereinigung des Elsass mit dem Frankreich der dritten Republik nach 1918," *Historisches Jahrbuch* 117, no. 1 (1997): 111–12. The French used the idea of *"désannexion"* to denote the undoing of the "injustice" of 1871 as well as to downplay the idea of a plebiscite, or Alsatians choosing their citizenship, that would be embedded in the notion of a retaking or annexation of Alsace.
5. Jean-Jacques Becker, "L'opinion publique francaise et l'Alsace en 1914," *Revue d'Alsace* 109 (1983): 125–38; Laird Boswell, "From Liberation to Purge Trials in the "Mythic

Provinces": Recasting French Identities in Alsace and Lorraine, 1918–1920," *French Historical Studies* 23, no. 1 (2000): 129–62; Francois Dreyfus, *La vie politique en Alsace, 1919–1936* (Paris, 1969), 24–27; Stefan Fisch, "Dimensionen einer historischen Systemstransformation. Zur Verwaltung des Elsass nach seiner Ruckkehr zu Frankreich," in *Staat Verwaltung. Fünfzig Jahre Hochschule für Verwaltungswissenschaften Speyer,* ed. Klaus Lüder (Berlin, 1997), 381–98; Michael Nolan, *The Inverted Mirror: Mythologizing the Enemy in France and Germany, 1898–1914* (New York, 2005), 67–85; Julia Schroda, "Der Mythos der 'provinces perdues' in Frankreich," *Konstrukte nationaler Identität: Deutschland, Frankreich, und Grossbritannien (19. und 20. Jahrhundert)* eds. Michel Einfalt et. al. (Würzburg, 2002), 115–33; William Shane Story, "Constructing French Alsace: A State, Region, and Nation" (PhD diss., Rice University, 2001), 18–33.
6. Eugen Weber, *Peasants into Frenchmen: The Modernization of Rural France, 1870–1914* (Stanford, CA, 1976), 485–96.
7. Fisch, "Dimensionen einer historischen Systemstransformation," 381–98.
8. Karl-Heinz Rothenberger, *Die elsass-lothringische Heimat- und Autonomiebewegung* (Frankfurt, 1975), 37ff.
9. *Conférence d'Alsace-Lorraine*, 70ff, 94ff.
10. Boswell, "From Liberation," 129–62. See also David Allen Harvey, "Lost Children or Enemy Aliens? Classifying the Population of Alsace after the First World War," *Journal of Contemporary History* 34, no. 4 (1999): 537–54.
11. Harvey, "Lost Children," 548–49.
12. The inhabitants of Alsace were sorted into one of four categories and assigned identity cards accordingly. Those in category "A", some 1,082,650 persons, included Alsatians whose parents were both Alsatian. Category "B" was comprised of persons with one Alsatian parent, some 183,500 persons. In Category "C" were residents from neutral or friendly nations. Finally, Category "D" included 513,800 persons considered German or Austrian. See Irmgard Grünwald, *Die Elsass-Lothringer im Reich* (Frankfurt/Main, 1984), 29–34; Harvey, "Lost children," 548–49.
13. Denunciations took various forms. Some denunciations stemmed from economic reasons; merchants and artisans tried to eliminate competition by painting their rivals as "pro-German." Some Alsatians cited the need to rid Alsace of its "German elements"; for example, the members of the Strasbourg municipal orchestra accused the conductor and a bassoonist of poor conduct against indigenous musicians and asked that the offenders be removed from their positions. Others stood accused as denouncers of "pro-French" Alsatians. For the case of the orchestra, see AMS 43/NA/40, Letter to "M. le président de la commission municipale" dated 14 December 1918. For the more general situation, see Boswell, "From Liberation," 129–62; Harvey, "Lost Children," 537–54.
14. Few Alsatians found themselves exiled to other French departments. Prefects resented the added costs of watching and provisioning suspected Alsatians; more importantly, some officials thought it unwise to proclaim Alsatian loyalty while exposing the wider French populace to suspect Alsatians.
15. Boswell, "From Liberation to Purge Trials," 154–55.
16. For Ricklin's letters to the government, see ADBR AL 121-111. For his wife's letter, see AMS 43 NA 13, Letter to Jacques Peirotes dated 27 July 1919.
17. Stephan Fisch "Die Nationalität internationaler Unternehmen Kriegsende 1918: Ein Problem bei der Rückkehr des Elsasses nach Frankreich," in *Nachkriegsgesellschaften in Deutschland und Frankreich im 20. Jahrhundert,* ed. Pierre Guillen and Ilja Mieck (Munich, 1998), 39–47; Fisch, "Assimilation und Eigenständigkeit," 113–21; David Allen Harvey, *Constructing Class and Identity in Alsace, 1830–1945* (Dekalb, IL, 2001), 131–52; Rothenberger, *Die elsass-lothringische Heimat- und Autonomiebewegung,* 46–52.
18. Taxes on the Alsatian railroad system were higher than in the rest of France; likewise, state employees from the interior, especially members of the teaching corps, received bonus pay to move and work in Alsace.
19. Harvey, *Constructing Class,* 131–52.

20. Ibid.; Rothenberger, *Die elsass-lothringische Heimat- und Autonomiebewegung*, 46–52.
21. Fisch, "Dimensionen einer historischen Systemstransformation," 388–93.
22. Baechler, *Le parti catholique*, 264–70; Fisch, "Dimensionen einer historischen Systemstransformation," 387–91; Story, 172–200.
23. Gabriel Alapetite, "Souvenirs 1920–24," *Annuaire de la Société des amis du vieux Strasbourg*, Tome VIII (Strasbourg, 1978), 106–14; Gisela Loth, *Un rêve de France: Pierre Bucher, une passion française au coeur de l'Alsace allemand*, Editions de l'Est (Strasbourg, 2000), 282–83.
24. Fisch, "Dimensionen einer historischen Systemstransformation," 388–93.
25. "Par quoi remplacera-t-on le Commissaria," *RdAL* (January 1924); Fisch, "Dimensionen einer historischen Systemstransformation," 388–93.
26. ADHR 27 J 4, "En Alsace-Lorraine, II," dated 15 August 1919; Baechler, *Le parti catholique*, 264–78; Fisch, "Dimensionen einer historischen Systemstransformation," 388–93.
27. John E. Craig, *Scholarship and Nation Building: The Universities of Strasbourg and Alsatian Society, 1870–1939* (Chicago, 1984), 195–224.
28. Stephen Harp, *Learning to be Loyal: Primary Schooling as Nation Building in Alsace and Lorraine* (Dekalb, IL, 1998), 187–92.
29. Harp, *Learning to be Loyal*, 196–200.
30. Laird Boswell, "Franco-Alsatian Conflict and the Crises of National Sentiment During the Phoney War," *Journal for Modern History* 71 (September 1999): 552–84.
31. Baechler, *Le parti catholique*, 281–88.
32. Robert Gildea, *The Past in French History* (New Haven, CT, 1994), 166–91. For an excellent treatment of Brun's work, see Julian Wright, *The Regionalist Movement in France, 1890–1914: Jean-Charles Brun and French Political Thought* (Oxford, 2003).
33. Gildea, *Past in French History*, 166–91.
34. Christian Baechler, "La question de la neutralité de l'Alsace-Lorraine à la fin de la première guerre mondiale et pendant le congrès de paix (1917–1920)," *Revue d'Alsace* 114 (1988), 204–8.
35. The cry for a "North American" guarantee combined Wilson's promise for freedom for Alsace-Lorraine with his espousal of conception of "self-determination." AN F 7/13377, "Elsässer, Lothringer"
36. Ernst was involved in a number of organizations concerned with Alsatians who had emigrated, by choice or force, to Germany and advocated German support for Alsatian autonomists efforts to the German government throughout much of the 1920s. Grünwald, *Die Elsass-Lothringer im Reich*, 47–55, 112–128.
37. ADBR AL 121–98, Joseph Hummel to Georges Clemenceau; AN F 7/13395, Report signed "Bauer" dated 7 November 1922; AN F 7/13395, Report signed "Bauer" dated 7 January 1927.
38. Bulach enjoyed a poor personal reputation and, although surveilled and later jailed by French authorities, was considered more a cantankerous, anti-French irritant than a serious threat. Bulach was known for his antics in Strasbourg cabarets and other bizarre habits. See Philip C. Bankwitz, *Alsatian Autonomist Leaders, 1919–1947* (Lawrence, KS, 1978), 12, 132 fn. 6; Rothenberger, *Die elsass-lothringische Heimat- und Autonomiebewegung*, 69–70.
39. Monique Mombert, "Le discours assimilationniste du *Journal d'Alsace et de Lorraine* de 1919 à 1924," in *La presse en Alsace au XXe siècle: Témoin-acteur-enjeu*, ed. Hildegard Châtellier and Monique Mombert (Strasbourg, 2002), 79–81.
40. Ibid., 65–86, 71–74, 82–83.
41. Lucien Coquet, "Un nouvelle politique à Strasbourg," *RdAL* (February 1921).
42. Anselm Laugel, "La Ligue de l'Alsace Française," *RdAL* (January 1921); Anselm Laugel, "La Ligue de l'Alsace Française," *RdAL* (May 1921).
43. J. Haas, "L'Expulsion des indésirables," *RdAL* (15 April 1919).
44. Georges Géville, "Dehors des Boches," *RdAL* (November 1919); "Le bon régionalisme et . . . le mauvais," *RdAL* (November 1921); Piérre du Maroussem, "L'avènement du régionalisme," (January 1921); "Notre enquête régionale," *RdAL* (November 1920); "Le régionalisme français en Alsace et Lorraine," *RdAL* (December 1920); Anselm Laugel,

"La situation politique en Alsace," *RdAL* (March 1924); "Le discours de Anselm Laugel," *RdAL* (November 1919); "Le discours de Anselm Laugel," *RdAL* (February 1923).
45. "Au théâtre de Verdure de Dambach," *RdAL* (September 1919); R. D. "Le Théâtre alsacien à Strasbourg," *RdAL* (April 1923); Etienne Roehrich, "Grande fête alsacienne de Costumes et de Coutumes du Pays de Hanau," *RdAL* (September 1923); L. C., *"Dur's Elsass," RdAL* (April 1923).
46. Dreyfus, *La vie politique en Alsace*, 40–43; Jena M. Gaines, "The Spectrum of Alsatian Autonomism," PhD diss., University of Virginia, 1990, 118–34.
47. Camille Dahlet, "Die demokratische-republikanische Partei," *Strassburger Echo*; Dreyfus, *La vie politique en Alsace*, 39–40; Rothenberger, *Die elsass-lothringische Heimat- und Autonomiebewegung*, 64–65.
48. Dreyfus, *La vie politique en Alsace*, 41–43; Rothenberger, *Die elsass-lothringische Heimat- und Autonomiebewegung*, 64–65.
49. Baechler, *Le parti catholique*, 239–49; Gaines, "The Spectrum of Alsatian Autonomism," 92–94.
50. Baechler, *Le parti catholique*, 246–47; Gaines, "The Spectrum of Alsatian Autonomism," 92–95.
51. Gaines, "The Spectrum of Alsatian Autonomism," 95–99.
52. Baechler, *Le parti catholique*, 317–26.
53. ADHR 27 J 4, "Le Régionalisme Alsacien."
54. Christian Baechler, "L'Abbé Wetterlé, Un prêtre patriote et libéral (1861–1931)," *Archives de l'Eglise d'Alsace* (1986): 272–85.
55. Dreyfus, *La vie politique en Alsace*, 81–82.
56. "Das Program der Linksblockregierung," *Elsässer Kurier* (18 June 1924).
57. "Der Linksblock rollt die elsass-lothringische Frage auf," *Elsässer Kurier* (18 June 1924).
58. "Die Ankündigung des Kulturkampfes," *Elsässer Kurier* (19 June 1924); "Die elsass-lothringischen Abgeordneten verlangen ein Plebiszit über die Kirchen und Schulfrage," *Elsässer Kurier* (20 June 1924).
59. AN F 7/13381, Poster labeled "Elsässer Katholikenbund."
60. Baechler, *Le parti catholique*, 336–48.
61. AN F 7/13381, Letter dated 11 August 1924.
62. Baechler, *Le parti catholique*, 344–46; Dreyfus, *La vie politique en Alsace*.
63. Hueber, whose mother lived in Belfort and whose wife's family came from Mulhouse, was an activist in the labor movement before World War I. Hueber served in the German army during the war and later become involved in the worker and soldier councils in Strasbourg at war's end. His advocacy of a neutral Alsace as a "bridge" between Germany and France before the war, as Samuel Goodfellow has argued, transformed into a separatist position after the Versailles settlement. See AMS 43 NA 7, Letter from Hueber to Peirotes dated 4 November 1909 and more generally Samuel Goodfellow, *Between the Swastika and the Cross of Lorraine* (Dekalb, IL, 1999), 69–71.
64. Baechler, *Le parti catholique*, 350ff; Claude Lorentz, *La presse alsacienne du XXe siècle* (Strasbourg, 1997), 446–47, Rothenberger, *Die elsass-lothringische Heimat- und Autonomiebewegung*, 89ff.
65. *Die Zukunft* (9 May 1925).
66. Rothenberger, *Die elsass-lothringische Heimat- und Autonomiebewegung*, 89ff.
67. Dreyfus, *La vie politique en Alsace*, 95–99; Rothenberger, *Die elsass-lothringische Heimat- und Autonomiebewegung*, 92–97.
68. *RdAL* (March 1926): 61.
69. Baechler, *Le parti catholique*, 348–60.

Chapter 6

DUAL CULTURES AND CONTESTED MEMORIES
ALSACE IN THE 1920S

The cessation of war inaugurated a renewed period of cultural debate in Alsace. Concerned about the reopening of the Alsatian theater, Hansi wrote the French High Commissioner in early 1919. In a letter indicative of earlier fights with Stoskopf, and infused with a strong sense of French nationalism, Hansi opined:

> The Alsatian theater, founded fifteen years ago in Strasbourg by Monsieur Stoskopf, had a rebellious tendency at the beginning and produced plays in which the faults of the German immigrant were ridiculed. It enjoyed a great success. But very quickly the German government was able to tame it, to make it serve its designs to the point where the Germans could decorate the director, personally awarding him the *Rote Adler*. The government sought to encourage the cult of the dialect, which, lest one forget, is a German dialect; through the Alsatian theater, the government found an excellent arm for checking the diffusion of the French language.
>
> Other Alsatian theaters were founded in Colmar, in Mulhouse, and in several small towns, and these different societies formed a federation. There were Germans among the actors and among the honorary members. Official authorities attended the productions. The French administration, in contrast, does not have any interest in encouraging this movement and it is stunning to see that in the weeks after the liberation the Alsatian theater was about to resume its activities. . . . It will allow an organization to be created around which all the Germanic Alsatian groups in Alsace can gather. To those will join all those compromised Alsatians who demanded neutrality after the Armistice. They already have formed a party of revanche in Germany, a group of men who refuse to renounce Alsace-Lorraine. It is in the Alsatian theaters that these men will search and find the elements on which they will be able to depend in Alsace. It would be very easy to expand the movement.[1]

Hansi's hope to ban the theater, though unfulfilled, pointed to potential cultural clashes. In his estimation, the Alsatian theater had exhausted its importance. Why should a theater of protest continue when it would only harbor malcontents and subversives? Hansi's attack indicated a refusal to accept the Alsatian theater as a legitimate element of Alsatian culture. Hansi viewed Alsace through a distinctly French lens; in contrast, Stoskopf wished to preserve Alsatian culture, a goal that had allowed him to find a modus vivendi with the German government. Yet Stoskopf, as we will see, also believed the maintenance of a distinct Alsatian culture was compatible with loyalty to the French nation.

Much as the various political parties argued over the best means to integrate Alsace into France, so, too, did cultural debates rage over the future of Alsace's "unique" culture. In part, these debates stemmed from the prewar discussion over Alsace's "dual culture"; however, the proponents of Alsace's unique binational heritage shifted. After the war, many Francophile regionalists like Hansi championed swift assimilation. Conversely, Alsatians who had grown up in the German education system, as well as those who had assumed a moderate, compromising line in the decades before the war, stepped in as the principal defenders of Alsace's German heritage. Just as with interwar political regionalism, the Alsatian cultural regionalism built on the legacy of prewar efforts to promote local culture.

New elements, however, crept into the cultural debates. Among Francophile Alsatians, a celebration of Alsace's joyous return to the *mère-patrie* was fused with reminders of French sacrifice and German perfidy to encourage Alsatians to embrace the language and culture of their rightful nation. In contrast, the most ardent regionalists, many of whom pushed for an autonomous local regime within France, demanded recognition of Alsace's unique cultural heritage not just under the banner of a "dual culture," but also by claiming that Alsatians were a national minority, thereby drawing on the rhetoric of Wilsonian idealism. Not surprisingly, a truly pro-German vision of Alsace failed to garner support; most Germans had departed, many Alsatians had unpleasant memories of German rule, and French authorities stood prepared to quash any pro-German talk in the region.

This chapter examines these shifting debates over the meaning of Alsatian culture, focusing primarily on the issues of language and the role of the Alsatian theater. The chapter then turns to explore how political and cultural differences influenced debates over commemoration in the 1920s, specifically in the realm of monuments and holidays. To assimilate the region, the French built monuments and marked French holidays, which paralleled their efforts in education, administration, and politics; these attempts often foundered on the shoals of local opposition.

A Dual Culture? Language and Theater in the Cultural Press of the 1920s

In the decades before the First World War, Alsatians such as Pierre Bucher, Anselm Laugel, and Charles Spindler defended French elements of Alsatian culture as part of the region's unique "dual culture." This cultural movement found an analogue in the prominent if unsuccessful National Union. What became of this important discourse concerning Alsatianness once France regained control of the region? What elements of the pre-1914 conception of Alsatianness—dress, architecture, the dialect, for example—remained a part of being Alsatian? Which elements were contested? Did those who had earlier defended the French nature of the region then in turn defend the German elements of Alsatian culture under the rubric of a dual culture? Alternately, what new discourses and groups emerged in defense of Alsatian culture, language, and religious identity? Such questions are paramount to understanding both cultural and political developments in Alsace in the 1920s.

In particular, this section examines how the press, especially the cultural and literary journals, envisaged, promoted, or defended various aspects of Alsatian culture. While the broader elements of Alsatian culture such as art and history merit attention, the focus will center on the interrelated issues of language and the dialect theater. Among the nationalist camp (including the journals *Les Dernières Nouvelles*, the *Journal d'Alsace et de Lorraine*, the *Revue d'Alsace et de Lorraine*, the *Journal de L'Est*, *L'Alsace Française*, and *La Vie en Alsace*), the question of language was obvious and clear; Alsatians should learn to speak French as swiftly as possible to aid their broader assimilation into the French national community. This trend reflected the attitudes not only of official French circles but of many Alsatians, for example, members of the Conférence d'Alsace-Lorraine. This is not to say that no tolerance for the German language existed in the nationalist camp; Daniel Blumenthal, among others, advocated for a period of transition. On the whole, however, pro-French regionalists pushed for the linguistic assimilation of Alsace.

Several papers took up the task of tutoring the local populace in the French language. For example, Jean Gentzburger, a contributor to the *RAI* before the war, founded the biweekly journal *La Renaissance Alsacienne* in 1919.[2] The paper, supported by French government subsidies, offered a variety of articles in French for its Alsatian audience. Unlike most journals, however, *La Renaissance Alsacienne* tried to keep its language simple so that all readers could easily follow. The paper also offered a vocabulary guide at the bottom of each article and short language lessons in each edition, for example, explaining how to tell time in French. Finally, the articles themselves served a didactic purpose as they covered episodes of history of importance to France and Alsace (e.g., the Revolution), offered short stories from French authors (e.g., a serialized publication of Alphonse Daudet's *La dernière classe*), and discussed current issues such as the status of French colonies.[3]

Some ardently pro-French Alsatians, however, found a role for the German language. Henri Zislin, whose satirical cartoons had savaged the Germans before 1914, urged French officials to subsidize his reestablished journal, *Dur's Elsass*. Zislin argued that he "envisioned the education of the people in view of practical relations that will allow the Alsatian a rapid assimilation into the *mentalité française.*" Zislin pointed out to the head of propaganda for the French administration, Jules Jaeger, that by publishing in German he could reach the bulk of the German-speaking population. With letters of recommendation from Laugel and Hansi supporting his cause, Zislin received modest support from the government. His inability to maintain a promised production schedule led to a falling out with French officials. These publication difficulties, combined with an apparent lack of public interest in the paper, led the government to end the subsidy in 1920. Zislin's aggressive polemics and sharp satirical cartoons were better adapted to opposition: lacking government support and a sufficient readership, *Dur's Elsass* quickly collapsed.[4]

While many of these nationalist papers promoted Alsatian culture, few made it the focus of their attentions. The *RAI*, which might have transformed into such a journal, disappeared during the war, its principal editors and contributors in France and its property under sequestration by the German government. Pierre Bucher's post-1919 effort *L'Alsace française* carried on the tradition to an extent, but focused more upon current events. Instead, a new journal, the monthly *La Vie en Alsace*, assumed the place of the *RAI* as the primary nationalist cultural paper.

La Vie's mission statement reflected an openly French nationalist version of the *RAI*. The editors wanted to publish a "regional organ in French; simple, accessible, and complete," which had as its goal the rebirth of Alsatian culture "after a half-century of stagnation."[5] In addition to promoting Alsace's French heritage through biographies, the journal also, much like the *RAI*, examined art and architecture as a way of discussing the heritage of Alsace.

Unlike the *RAI*, *La Vie* made no effort to promote a mixed Alsatian heritage. Insofar as the paper dealt with issues of language, the occasional article on the development of French in the region constituted the paper's entire approach to the matter. The dog that did not bark tells the tale here. No articles appeared in German or in the dialect. Instead, the paper went to great lengths to remind its readers of some of the negative aspects of German rule, for example, Wilhelm II's attitude toward Alsace, the Zabern Affair, or the restored Hohkönigsburg.[6] Alsace's history belonged with France, not Germany, a point that *La Vie* stressed repeatedly.

While *La Vie* rarely dealt with the issue of the Alsatian theater, the nationalist press, including the *Revue d'Alsace et de Lorraine* (with articles by Laugel) and *L'Alsace Française*, often promoted the institution. Indeed, with little strong opposition, Hansi excepted, the theater quickly resumed its activities in Colmar, Mulhouse, and Strasbourg; Stoskopf returned to his position as head of the Strasbourg section. Though new plays were introduced over the course of the 1920s, works by the founding playwrights of the Strasbourg group—Stoskopf, Ferdinand Bastian, and Jules Greber—retained their popularity and served as the bedrock of the institution's repertoire.

Unlike plays in German—often performed by Swiss or German traveling groups, often amid controversy and scandal[7]—the dialect theater generally enjoyed the support of French authorities, especially when plays such as *D'Große Revolution im Elsass* (*The Great Revolution in Alsace*) linked France's glorious past to the region. The theater, however, did not completely avoid trouble; the close association of some of the members of the Colmar organization with the autonomist Heimatbund led to resignations and a loss in production quality.[8] By and large, however, the theater was supported.

Assimilationist Alsatians could accept the theater as part of the regional heritage; the French government saw no real threat in the institution. For many Alsatians, celebrating the regional culture as embodied in the theater was fully compatible with loyalty to the French state. This understanding often reflected a desire to preserve Alsace's unique culture. Politically, such groups usually paralleled moderate regionalists who wished to see some transitional period in Alsatian affairs, promoted the regional economy, and hoped to maintain some of Alsace's dual heritage. Representatives of such groups included the Republican-Democrats and their press organ, the *SNZ*, the nationalist members of the UPR, and some elements of the Radical Party. Though such groups did not actively employ the rhetoric of a dual culture, their support of the German language and of Alsatian culture were grounded in the same tradition. Several cultural journals in the 1920s, notably *Die elsässische Woche* (hereafter *DEW*) and *La Littérature Populaire* promoted this cultural vision of Alsace while criticizing the so-called "Alsatian malaise," and later, the autonomist movement.

The two journals shared a number of traits. Both were written primarily in German, both had limited audiences (neither enjoyed publication runs over five thousand at their height), both aimed to address the artistic and literary needs of Alsace's German-speaking majority, and both wanted to further the process of integrating Alsace into France.[9] Both also celebrated the regional dialect, incorporating short stories and poems into their regular fare. *La Littérature Populaire* enjoyed a greater profile; local literary notables such as Gustave Stoskopf, the playwright Ferdinand Bastian, and the poet Franz Xavier Neukirch offered their support to the journal and served as regular contributors.

Both papers also clearly displayed their cultural and political banners. The *DEW* proclaimed in its opening edition that it wanted to be an "unpolitical" organ that would "leave room in each number to sing and proclaim the Alsatian homeland [*Heimat*] . . . to create a field for literary activities in the German language." The journal, however, left no doubts about its political loyalties: "The *DEW* should be a mirror of the homeland . . . the true French homeland."[10]

To pursue this program the *DEW* focused its attentions on several issues. First, it incorporated brief political commentary, opining on issues ranging from reparations to the malaise in Alsace to French policies.[11] On this score, the paper offered occasional criticism of French educational policies, but otherwise supported Alsace's fusion into the French nation. Second, the paper wove in articles linking Alsace to France. For example, the paper dedicated several articles to the memory of Pierre Bucher's efforts to keep French culture alive in Alsace, celebrated Alsace as the birthplace of the *Marseillaise*, and honored French wartime heroes such as Marshall Lyautey. Finally, and most importantly, the *DEW* promoted Alsatian culture through articles in dialect, on local artists and traditions, as well as about current cultural events such as plays and art exhibitions.

La Littérature populaire took a less political but equally clear route, promoting Alsatian "art, culture, and literature" as a means of preserving the "literary future" of the "sons of Alsace." As such, the paper hoped to offer local writers and artists a means of communicating with one another, as well as a means of exploring larger literary trends as they influenced Alsatian writers. *La Littérature* also proclaimed its political loyalties and underlying program in clear terms: "We hold as important the partial use of the French language because we consider the further continuation of both cultures, the typical Alsatian and the French, as a fundamental element of our Program . . . to strive for the inner melding of both peoples. . . . Politically speaking we are French." *La Littérature* therefore established itself in favor of a dual culture, without placing Alsatian national loyalties in doubt.

Like the *DEW*, *La Littérature* published numerous articles and poems in dialect. To a far greater degree than the *DEW*, *La Littérature* tried to nourish Alsatian literary traditions. Young, upcoming Alsatian authors were feted alongside established writers such as Stoskopf and Bastian. The paper also focused on literary criticism and broader literary developments; as a part of the latter goal, the paper sometimes offered overviews of the French literary scene as well as translations of English literature.

Both journals gave attention to the Alsatian theater. The *DEW* argued that the dialect theater was not a reaction to French policies, but rather that it "filled a need, on one hand, of the large masses that cannot speak French, and on the other hand, gives many Alsatians a chance to engage in literary pursuits."[12] In celebration of the 25th anniversary of the theater in 1924, the paper offered a brief history before returning to the present importance of the institution: "Before the war, it arose in a certain manner out of the protest against the conqueror from 1871. Today it serves as a temporary aid for a large part of the Alsatian people that does not have a mastery of the French language so as to be able to follow its extensive literature." Later editions of the paper praised the works of Gustave Stoskopf, lauding his ability to "care for the *Heimatliche* traditions and manners" especially given the "deep chasm that had developed between the German and Alsatian culture."[13]

In comparison to the intermittently intensive coverage of the Alsatian theater in *DEW*, *La Littérature* proffered theater reviews, excerpts of new plays, and biographies of some of the principal authors of the Alsatian theater as part of its regular fare, including not just the theater in Strasbourg, but also its sister organizations in Mulhouse, Colmar, and Guebwiller. The journal's coverage generally celebrated the theater as an important and intrinsic part of the Alsatian cultural scene. The overarching attitude of the paper was best iterated in a speech by Stoskopf, reproduced (in dialect) in *La Littérature's* June 1921 edition. While Stoskopf used much of the speech to review the history of the Alsatian theater—offering kudos to numerous people in the audience who had fostered its development—he also paused to consider the role of both dialect and dialect theater in a French Alsace. Stoskopf began by ruminating on the importance of the dialect as a "mother tongue, a piece of our *Heimat*" that would not soon be replaced by French; indeed Stoskopf viewed the idea of the swift inculcation of the French language as the daily language of most Alsatians as a "pious wish." Instead, people should learn French but continue to use Alsatian just as the peoples of Brittany, Provence, and the Basque country spoke perfect French alongside their native patois. The Alsatian dialect should remain, despite political changes, a constituent element of what it meant to be Alsatian.

For this reason, the dialect theater served an important role, and, according to Stoskopf, it could replace the loss of German theater in Alsace (which had been banned by French authorities). Stoskopf warned, however, that the theater could only take limited steps in this direction as the theater could not easily put on productions of Ibsen or Schiller. Instead, he suggested that the theater possessed a higher purpose "to foster the language of the homeland, our customs, our traditions." Stoskopf argued further that the "love of the fatherland and the love of the Heimat did not exclude one another." Indeed, in Brittany and Provence, artists had proven region and nation were compatible. Alsatians could have their dialect and still be loyal Frenchmen.[14]

Through the lens of the Alsatian theater, the *DEW* and *La Littérature Populaire* promoted a vision of Alsace that maintained much of its local character. Both journals, however, viewed this Alsatian uniqueness as fully compatible with being French; their understanding of belonging to the French nation therefore was not predicated on language or ethnicity, but on membership in a civic community. This wish to square Alsatian identity with the circle of French nationalism represented one of the primary stumbling blocks between Alsatians and the French government, as well as among Alsatians whose vision of the region's cultural future differed. Moreover, as the 1920s progressed, and a greater acrimony developed between Alsatians and the French government, some Alsatians began to argue more vigorously for the protection of the region's German heritage. In parallel, these Alsatians clamored for the Alsatian theater to take up the banner of protest once again.

The autonomist newspapers saw in Alsatian theater specifically, and in Alsatian culture more generally, hope for maintaining Alsatian uniqueness. Autonomist papers argued ceaselessly for the rights of Alsatians to develop their own culture, and therefore, on behalf of all Alsatians, claimed administrative autonomy within France, and later, for the protection of Alsatian culture. Two papers in particular offer parallels to the *DEW* and *La Littérature Populaire*, the satirical weekly *Der Schliffstaan* (*The Grindstone*) and the literary bimonthly *Der Eiserne Mann* (*The Iron Man*). Like the two pro-French journals, these papers had limited press runs. Both papers wished to promote the German aspects of Alsatian culture. Both leaned toward autonomy, though *Schliffstaan*, edited until 1925 by one of the editors of *Die Zukunft*, Paul Schall, adopted a much more militant line in this regard. In addition to its heightened support for Alsatian political autonomy, *Der Schliffstaan* included in its pages articles, poems, and political cartoons in dialect, thereby linking its political aims to the importance of the local patois. *Der Eiserne Mann*, in contrast, supported the Alsatian theater, customs, and traditions, but published almost exclusively in *Hochdeutsch*.

The founders of *Der Eiserne Mann* in large part came from a population of young Alsatians who had grown up and were educated in the German cultural world and neither desired to emigrate nor to abandon this element of their heritage.[15] Politically, the paper demonstrated several tendencies. First, the editors pleaded for pacifism by especially noting the terrible impact of poison gas in the last war and by arguing that future wars would only be more horrendous as such weapons technology advanced.[16] Second, *Der Eiserne Mann* repeatedly stressed the "tragedy of a borderland" as the overarching theme of Alsatian history and pointed to such developments as the commissions de triage.[17] Out of this tragic circumstance and out of Alsace's experiences as a part of Germany sprang a healthy Alsatian particularism. In an appeal for amnesty for the "neutralists," especially René Ley, Philippe Oberlé argued that "a good, upstanding, and incorruptible Alsatian" did not get along well with either the French or the Germans, which was Alsace's "tragic undoing."[18] Nonetheless, as "two cultures, two great nations meet in Alsace," the journal would avoid the "laughable games" of nationalists "on both sides of the Rhine" and try to work for "reconciliation and understanding" in Alsace.[19]

Der Eiserne Mann, surprisingly, rarely deigned to criticize French language policy. Instead, the journal saved its vitriol to criticize the management of the Alsatian theater with Gustave Stoskopf serving as the chief bête noire. *Der Eiserne Mann*, lambasting Stoskopf's vanity, accused the theater under Stoskopf of lacking in originality. In particular, the journal argued that Stoskopf acted as "God on high" who did not want his legacy as the greatest Alsatian dialect playwright challenged. In fact, the theater critic for the journal, writing under the pseudonym "Orpheus," did not like the greatest hit of the theater, *D'r Maire*, as it depicted Alsatians, at least as embodied by the main character, in a buffoonish light.[20]

Der Eiserne Mann did not, however, want to do away with the theater, but rather demanded that the organization move beyond the "grotesque farces" that characterized the "Stoskopf School." Philippe Oberlé had nothing against comedies per se, and indeed thought the dialect well suited to comedy. Rather, the dialect theater needed to take up more serious matters especially if it wanted to be "pedagogically effective."[21] What lay behind such criticism? In part, such accusations were not new; critics such as Friedrich Lienhard had raised such accusations in the decades before World War I. In the context of interwar Alsace, when German-language theater had been severely limited, the call for elevated quality of the plays of the Alsatian theater represented a plea for an ersatz German-language theater. If the plays of Schiller, Goethe, and Lessing could not be performed, then at least the works of the Alsatian theater should go beyond the *théâtre du boulevard* style that dominated the organization's repertoire. Such arguments implied a more serious and dramatic Alsatian theater would aid Alsatians in maintaining the German half of their dual culture.

D'r Schliffstaan, in contrast to *Der Eiserne Man* as well as the other cultural journals, took an avowedly more political line by frequently commenting on current affairs. Whereas papers such as *La Vie en Alsace* tried to link French and Alsatian history, *Schliffstaan* did not dip into the well of history to justify the German heritage of the region. Indeed, the journal openly admitted that German rule had been flawed, especially as represented in moments such as the Zabern Affair. Therefore, much like the *Zukunft*, *Schliffstaan* invoked the rhetoric of preserving "rights" and "traditions." In this regard, *Schliffstaan* criticized French rule, especially as it encroached on those "Alsatian liberties" and "Alsatian traditions" that General Joffre had promised to protect. *Schliffstaan* went about its task through the use of satire and humor.

A series of cartoons entitled "A Good Child, according to the assimilated St. Nicholas" captures the range of topics that served as the objects of *Schliffstaan*'s satirical wrath, defining "a good child" as he "who supports the current regime and believes its promises," "who fully and gladly pays taxes," who "fights against the *Zukunft*. . . . who prays to the laicized God," "who fights the German language in Alsace," and "who lives and dies for the campaign slogan 'France is one and divisible.'"[22] Here and elsewhere in *Schliffstaan*, the issues that Alsatians viewed as detrimental to their own interests become clear. A highly Catholic Alsace was threatened with secularization. The false promises of the French government to respect regional traditions or rights—perhaps weak under German rule, but nonetheless present—provided reason to protest French policies. Another criticism leveled at the government was its inability to deal with Alsatians who had been civil servants under German rule; the French government had taken years determining funding levels for the pensions of these workers, leaving many in dire economic straits.[23] It should also be noted, however, that the paper did not wish for Alsace to rejoin Germany or break free of France, but rather wanted France to respect the political, social, and cultural rights of Alsatians. Criticism of German leadership was not an uncommon theme for the paper.[24] And the paper also made fun of the idea that a "free state of Alsace-Lorraine could survive" in a "United States of Europe."[25] The paper, in sum, pushed for a regional political and cultural autonomy within France.

In a similar fashion to *Der Eiserne Mann*, *Schliffstaan* stood as a firm supporter of the German language. The journal argued that "the advance of French must never, not even a bit, have as a consequence the renunciation of the mother tongue."[26] The paper also pushed for the (re)introduction of German into schools: "For elevated intellectual exchange one needs a cultural and literary language. The literary language that complements the dialect is German."[27]

Much like *Der Eiserne Mann*, *Schliffstaan* viewed the dialect theater as a constituent element of Alsatian culture. More importantly, *Schliffstaan* stressed the importance of the Alsatian theater in maintaining a unique cultural identity. For example, the editor opined that Alsatian theater

> cannot and does not wish to develop works of world literature. But for the cultivation of our dialect and *Volkstum*, for the furthering of the feeling of *Heimat*, for the understanding of the history of our land, for the strengthening of the old morals and traditions it has become indispensable, and it will remain so, as long as the leadership of the Alsatian theater itself has the desire to hold to the chosen path. The Alsatian Theater stands today in the foreground of the interests of our *Heimat*.[28]

The Alsatian theater, in the journal's opinion, served multiple purposes. It represented a means of furthering Alsatian identity by maintaining the dialect and promoting Alsatian morals and traditions in the public sphere. Less overtly, *Schliffstaan*'s support for the dialect and education in German allowed Alsatians a means to resist the Frenchification of Alsatian society.

Schliffstaan, even more than the *DEW* or *Der Eiserne Mann*, provided ongoing coverage of the theater through reviews about the plays during the theater season, including information about performance times and comments about attendance. Like *Der Eiserne Mann*, *Schliffstaan* concerned itself with the quality of the productions. The value of the works was clear: "The Alsatian theater [since 1919] has remained true to its program that it set out from its beginning. It is a workshop for the literary arts of the *Heimat*, for Alsatian uniqueness, and indigenous culture, and as such is a cultural factor that cannot be assessed highly enough."[29] Yet it was not nearly enough that the theater be a well-spring of Alsatian culture. As in the past, it should concern itself with current issues. Indeed, Paul Schall decried the fact that no one had, "in the spirit of Stoskopf," written plays that "reflect the concerns of today's Alsace." This worry was echoed by another, namely, that people only went to see the plays for "momentary, comic entertainment" and "were disappointed if they received more artistic fare."[30] According to Schall, the theater needed to serve the cultural and spiritual needs of Alsatians, thereby resisting the inroads of French assimilation, while simultaneously addressing the political concerns of Alsatians vis-à-vis France. In fact, the theater remained a symbol of Alsatianness, but neither in the 1920s nor thereafter could it assume the multiple functions assigned to it by the writers of *Schliffstaan*.

The cultural debates over the meaning of Alsatianness, as in the period before 1914, both reflected and influenced the political situation. The diversity of visions over Alsace's cultural future paralleled the numerous divisions of Alsace's political scene both before, and especially after, the Herriot speech of June 1924. The prewar polarization of Alsatian identity between its pro-French and pro-Alsatian sides continued to color political and cultural debates in the region. If particularist groups failed to garner full support in the region, it was due to the fact that, much as before the war, the proponents of Alsatianness could not bridge their own internal differences.

Assimilation and Memory: Monuments and Holidays

If language and theater provided one realm for debate, monuments and national holidays emerged as contested arena of memory and commemoration. French nationalists wanted to efface the vestiges of German rule and reshape the physical spaces of Alsace as a means of assimilating the regained province back into the French nation.[31] Commemoration, however, proved difficult. In part, local politics, often driven by party ideology, created tensions. In part, Alsatians had divergent and divided memories over the past, especially with regard to the World War. Holidays offered a period when the nation could be celebrated; in the hands of some Alsatian regionalists, however, Armistice Day, 14 July, and the holiday for Jeanne d'Arc could become moments for critical reflection on the status of Alsatian and French relations.

Almost immediately following the war, French authorities began reshaping the architectural and monumental landscape of Alsace by replacing German emblems and flags with French equivalents. Streets were renamed and often dedicated to the French generals from the Great War. Strasbourg's Kaiserplatz became the Place de la République. Moreover, French authorities undertook a process of cataloguing the historically noteworthy buildings across Alsace to determine how scarce resources could be allocated for the purposes of maintaining historically significant regional landmarks.[32]

Beyond such initial steps to erase the German past in the region, nationally minded Alsatians and French authorities began to undertake projects to promote memories of the French nation. As Stephen Harp has demonstrated, schools represented just one front in this particular battle by instructing Alsatians in the historical traditions of the French Third Republic.[33] The landscape of the cities also became an important site for re-establishing the French nation as French authorities, *revenants* (Alsatians who returned to Alsace after leaving for France in the 1870s), and ardent local nationalists sponsored monuments to French luminaries.[34] These projects paralleled the earlier efforts of Germans to reshape the Alsatian loyalties through monuments to Germany's historical past.

Local politics and interests, however, often disrupted these well-laid plans. Strasbourg provides an important example of the difficulties faced by Alsatian French nationalists, regional administrators, and the national government. In particular, the Strasbourg city council could often prove stubbornly independent on matters concerning the city's commemorative landscape. Strasbourg's city council did not undermine commemorative projects per se, but managed to alter aspects of the various projects. The motives of the Strasbourg council varied: some projects were blocked for aesthetic concerns, others for ideological reasons. As Shane Story has pointed out, inclusion of high-ranking French politicians such as Raymond Poincaré, Georges Clemenceau, and Alexandre Millerand on a monument committee did not always guarantee unimpeded development of such projects: a monument to the *Marseillaise*, written by Rouget de Lisle in 1792 as the Prussians approached the French border, was shunted off to a remote corner of the Place Broglie.[35]

Political and ideological conflict sometimes moved the city council. For example, in 1919 the Union alsacienne Jeanne d'Arc was created to promote the image of Jeanne d'Arc as a national heroine within Alsace. One of its main goals was the erection of a Jeanne d'Arc monument in Strasbourg. The Union sponsored fund-raising events in 1920 toward this end and helped secure the donation of a statue of Jeanne by the sculptor Paul Dubois in 1921. The group then only had to find an appropriate place for the monument within Strasbourg's center (they hoped for a square near the Palais Rohan), a task that proved more difficult than expected.[36]

Socialists, in control of the city council, refused to allow the monument on city property due to its religious character. After the city council rejected the placement of the statue near the Palais Rohan, the group turned to Commissioner General Alapetite for support. While Alapetite could not overturn the decision of the municipal leadership, he could offer the Union a separate location within the city on land under his authority. Alapetite therefore suggested the garden of the Palais du Rhin, formerly the German imperial residence in Strasbourg, for the statue of the "national heroine."[37] Although the Union viewed the sculpture's placement in the garden as provisional, and indeed still hoped that the statue could find a home in the "heart of Strasbourg,"[38] the monument remained in the garden until World War II when the German occupation force destroyed it.[39]

Efforts to weave more contemporary French figures into the Strasbourg landscape also encountered difficulties. In 1921, a committee led by the current and future heads of the university sought contributions for a monument to Louis Pasteur. Early in his career, Pasteur had worked in Strasbourg; the committee wished to erect a monument to the scientist as part of the planned festivities for his centenary in 1922–23.[40] One of the calls for contributions framed the monuments' purpose quite clearly:

> It is for a Strasbourg delivered from the foreign yoke that the centenary of Pasteur should be celebrated and donned as a form of glorification. The inauguration of the monument of which we have dreamed will mark the great day of the exposition, the unforgettable fête, where intellectual France, the France of fruitful labor in every domain, will be the guest of Alsace.[41]

To drive the point home further, the committee linked these positive aspects of the project to Alsace's more recent past, writing, "Alsace and Lorraine wish that this centenary monument dignify the scientist of whom the English philosopher Huxley said after the war of 1870: 'the discoveries of Pasteur sufficed to cover the ransom of 5 billion paid by France to Germany.'"[42]

Initially, the efforts of the committee seemed effective. Over 110,000 francs were raised in the 1923 drive alone, with contributions coming from both private donors and public officials.[43] The monument design chosen by the committee and executed by Larrivé, however, did not meet great approval among the broader Alsatian populace. Moreover, the choice of placement—in front of the university and opposite to the Goethe monument—angered both critics and the general populace alike. While the festivities surrounding the Pasteur centenary went off without a hitch, the placement of the monument continued to rankle local officials.[44] Indeed, the city council voted against the placement of the monument at the university and the entire work would later be displaced to the Civil Hospital.[45]

The erection of a statue of Victor Hugo and Alphonse de Lamartine—created in honor of the centenary of Romanticism—did not receive the negative responses of the Jeanne d'Arc and the Pasteur monuments. Yet much like with the Pasteur monument, the committee in charge, led by university rector Christian Pfister, did not acquire the location for the statue it desired. Efforts to create the work began in 1927 when the committee put out a call for donations for the project. The initial letter to potential donors recalled the glory of French romanticism while tying Alsace to France's cultural heritage, noting that the monument would be, "in Alsace, returned to its true destiny, a gesture of high spiritual significance, a work of patriotic communion. . . . Alsace remains, according to a contemporary of Louis XIV, 'a fervent foyer of love for France.'"[46] Rudolf Redslob, a local historian, lobbied Mayor Jacques Peirotes for the placement of the statue at the Place de la République on the site of the former equestrian statue to Wilhelm I. Paralleling the language of the letter to donors, Redslob argued,

> In effect, in our conception, the placement of this monument should be a grand, patriotic French gesture. We want to say with this monument that we are definitively French, and the German era is forgotten. It therefore seems to me that this will be a living symbol by placing the double statue in a location of the city that has memories of stone speaking of the conqueror and his happily ephemeral reign. Would it not be a grand gesture to place two poets who incarnate French genius, the France of Arts and Letters, the France of Peace, in the middle of all the palaces that the German vanquisher raised as citadels of his power? See there the imperial palace; [see there] the local parliament where one struggled for the liberty of Alsace-Lorraine but where one often felt the irresistible grip of the conqueror; see there the library, another instrument of the conqueror.[47]

Redslob continued in a similar vein in the attempt to make the Place de la République the home for the new monument. By doing so, he sought to subvert the meaning of the square as a center of German authority.[48]

The pleas of the Committee and Redslob achieved only partial success. Peirotes indicated his acceptance of the Place de la République for the statue. The city council, however, differed, especially after reviewing the various proposals for the monument for their aesthetic fit to the site. The council therefore rejected the placement of the monument at the Place de la République. In part, this rejection may have stemmed from a long-standing hope among council members that a monument to the fallen of the Great War might be erected in the same place. Instead, the Hugo-Lamartine statue would eventually be dedicated at the Orangerie Park in 1931; later requests to move the statue to the garden of the Palais du Rhin were rejected.[49]

Yet more controversial were efforts to commemorate the First World War. Much like in the rest of France and elsewhere, Alsatian commemorations often became the contentious.[50] Several issues converged to make the process of creating and dedicating monuments more difficult in Alsace. Alsatian veterans, much like their counterparts elsewhere, sometimes differed with government officials as to how the war ought to be remembered. Alsatians, however, had served on both sides of the conflict. These conflicts over memory were further exacerbated by the traditional independence of Alsatian communes. Under German rule, Alsatian communes had enjoyed a relative degree of autonomy: translated into the French case, Alsatian autonomy created difficulties for local officials as some communities demanded to have all their dead remembered, not just those who died for France.[51]

Such tensions played out in several ways. In Mulhouse, for example, veterans of the French and German armies clashed over the appropriate form of commemoration and the proper inscription for a future monument; the involvement of Souvenir Français, which did not want to honor the fallen enemy, only complicated matters. The city's mayor managed to avert a minor crisis aided in part by the project's artist, Maxime Réal del Sarte; the statue had two figures to celebrate French liberty and honor the sacrifices of fallen soldiers. A crisis of commemoration was averted.[52]

In other towns, the local community tried show its loyalty to France while also remaining mindful of the divergent experiences of the war. For example, the town of Quatzenheim dedicated its monument in 1919. The inscription on the monument, fully endorsed by the departmental head of monuments as well as by local officials from the Interior Ministry, read, "In remembrance of the liberation of Alsace, to the young men of Quatzenheim, victims of the war, 1914–1918."[53] Thus, it did not differentiate between those who fell for the Germans and those who fell for the French.

Unfortunately for French administrators, such easy-to-approve monuments were the exception rather than the rule. Some municipalities faced internal divisions over the memories of the war and threatened to have separate monuments, a prospect, as Shane Story has pointed out, which was anathema to French officials. Split commemorations would keep tensions in the various communes alive and, by reminding Alsatians of their German past, slow the progress of integration. Independent-minded communes often submitted their plans as faits accomplis to departmental authorities.[54]

At times, French officials caused their own headaches; for example, at the 1932 dedication of a memorial, Prefect Roland Marcel did not participate in the religious part of the ceremony and when he did speak, used the occasion to criticize the "mistrust and discord" present in Alsace. A local paper responded critically, opining, "Is mistrust not awakened in a deeply pious population when the highest civil servant in the department neglects the religious part of the dedication and only appears when drink and *Kugelhopf* are served?"[55] The sacred and religious aspects of the process of commemoration played an important role, and woe to the French official who disregarded local feelings over the gravity of the moment.

In Strasbourg, municipal politics and contested memories waylaid attempts to erect a World War I monument.[56] The municipal elections of May 1929 witnessed a strange alliance of autonomists, Catholic regionalists, and autonomist-minded Communists winning a narrow majority in the city council, which led to the ousting of the long-time Socialist mayor, Jacques Peirotes. In his stead the regional Communist leader Karl Hueber, who had long decried the French administration in the region as imperialist and had called for at the very minimum autonomy for Alsace, assumed the head of the city council.[57] The municipal government under Hueber not only delayed the monument's erection but also irked the French government, as we shall see shortly, with its general unwillingness to demonstrate proper support for French national holidays.

The lack of a monument did not go unnoticed; even *Die Neue Zukunft*, a weekly supplement to the fiercely autonomist *Elsass-Lothringische Zeitung*, called the situation a "shameful circumstance," and argued that "there was enough distance from the experiences of the war" to allow for the creation of a monument.[58] The displacement of the Hueber government by Charles Frey in the 1935 elections created an opportunity to rectify the issue to allow a project to go forward.

A private commission, headed by Henri Levy, raised several hundred thousand francs for the monument.[59] Léon Drivier, a Paris-based sculptor, was selected to create the statue. Drivier elected to sculpt a Pietà-like statue.[60] Instead of one fallen figure, two are cradled in the mother's arms, representing Alsatians who had fought on both sides of the war. For the inscription, the committee chose the relatively neutral "A nos morts: 1914–1918"; a German translation, however, was rejected for fear of causing a "demonstration."[61] The organizers also managed to succeed where the Hugo-Lamartine commission had failed; the monument, inaugurated in October 1936, was erected at the center of the Place de la République.[62] By choosing a monument that could commemorate the memories of all sides in Alsace, the steering committee for the war memorial managed to bridge some of the differences dividing the local community. By placing the statue at the Place de la République, the committee also managed fill a major gap in the local memorial landscape.

While local monuments could exacerbate local divisions and create tensions between communal and departmental officials, the only national monument erected in the region, the memorial complex at Hartmannswillerkopf (also known as Vieil Armand), enjoyed local support. The ridge and surrounding slopes of Hartmannswillerkopf, located near the town of Cernay, had seen hard combat, especially in 1915, and over twenty thousand soldiers from the French and German armies had died along this section of the front.[63] The monument at the site belongs to the series of large French commemoration projects like those at Douaumont, Notre Dame de Lorettes, and Dormans.

Even as efforts got underway in 1920 to collect donations for the monument, French officials had to worry about the physical preservation of the site, especially as the battlefield became a tourist destination. The head of the military in Strasbourg, General de Boisseau, demanded in 1920 that better control of visitors be exercised; in particular, a Swiss group had crossed into French territory in "wild numbers" to "profane" the battlefield with a rendition of the *Internationale*.[64] Similarly, General Commissioner Alapetite had to admonish members of the Touring-Club de France that photograph stands at the site could not be expanded; moreover, postcards were to be in French, though there could be translations under the French captions.[65] To judge by the absence of complaints in subsequent years, French authorities seemed to have regulated visits to Hartmannswillerskopf to their satisfaction. In this way, they managed stop the battlefield from being profaned by commercialization.

In the meanwhile, the committee in charge of raising funds for the monument went about the arduous task of seeking donations. Led by General Tabouis, a veteran of the campaigns in the area and a commander in the garrison at Mulhouse, the steering committee sought both public and private support.[66] As an organization associated with the Souvenir Français, the committee received some direct subsidies from the local administration. At times, the committee garnered donations in kind as when the general commissioner offered material from leftover war stocks, especially bronze, for the future construction of the site.[67] The committee also gained some popular support; for example, the Société de secours aux blessés militaires, led by Suzanne Herrenschmidt (who, along with her husband, had helped to raise money for the Musée alsacien before the war), helped to secure the support of the prefect and raise money among Strasbourg's Francophile elite.[68]

The committee sought broader public help by appealing to Alsatians' sense of duty and history. After reminding Alsatians of their desire to return to France, the committee turned to examine the sacrifice of French soldiers and Alsatian duty to remember:

> Some of them, many even, arrived and you saw them march before you in those unforgettable days of November 1918. It is in their name that we appeal to you who watched them.
>
> It concerns honoring and glorifying the memory of those who did not arrive because they fell while thinking of you. . . . Banish from your heart, from your spirit indifference, ingratitude, and forgetfulness. Give, give for the soldiers of France, who died for your deliverance.[69]

The extent to which such calls actually won over Alsatians is not clear. Much of the support in the region seems to have come from leading industrialists and business leaders.[70] Regardless of the financial bases for the project, by 1925 the committee was ready to present a model of the future monument, designed by Robert Danis, at a Parisian exposition.

The inauguration of the monument in 1932, despite the politically tumultuous incidents of the late 1920s and early 1930s when the autonomist movement reached its apogee—with accusations of treason, trials, and bitter regional political squabbles—did not evoke a storm of protest. Nor did the local press seem overly enthusiastic about the event. Rather, a measured support characterized President Albert Lebrun's October 1932 visit to Alsace, during which he led the dedication of the memorial. The ceremonies, which took place on 9 October, included a short prayer service and were attended by political leaders, members of patriotic organizations, and the Bishop of Strasbourg as well as by local cultural luminaries such as Gustav Stoskopf.[71]

In keeping with the spirit of commemoration, both the speeches and press coverage adopted a subdued tone. In particular, both politicians and newspapers stressed two elements. First, the horrors of war—and the subsequent desire for peace—were remembered in the ossuary, crypt, cemetery, and monument atop the "bloody mountain." Second, the motif of French sacrifice for the liberation of Alsace assumed a central place in the rhetoric of the day. Indeed, President Lebrun went so far as to tie the events of 1870–71 to the sacrifices of 1914–1918; France had, albeit at a high cost, not only avenged the loss of 1870–71, but had also reclaimed Alsace and its populace, which had fought valiantly against German domination for decades.[72] The elision of Alsatian sacrifices in the German Army did not spark protests, at least not as evidenced by the major Alsatian dailies.

The erection of new monuments was not the only way that French authorities tried to reestablish a French identity in Alsace after the war. Holidays, too, offered a means of celebrating the nation, especially Bastille Day. The two other major French national secular (as opposed to religiously oriented) holidays, the Fête de Jeanne d'Arc and Armistice Day (11 November) enjoyed official and popular support but also could be contested; the left did not see the purpose in the former, and the latter, given the fact the vast majority of Alsatians had served in the German military, carried a good deal of ambivalence.

All three major holidays shared certain characteristics, at least as far as official ceremonies were concerned. Departmental and municipal officials were expected to bedeck buildings in tricolor bunting. In Strasbourg, all three holidays had a military component, a troop review and parade centered on the Place de la République, though ceremonies often also took place at the Place Kléber, the city's commercial center. All had an accompanying banquet and other festivities; however, for the Armistice Day celebrations these tended to be muted. Politicians, administrators, journalists, and leading businessmen as well as the heads of the local religious communities were invited to attend; foreign dignitaries, mostly consular officials, also received invitations, especially for the Armistice Day celebrations.[73]

Each holiday naturally had its own unique features. The Bastille Day celebrations, for example, traditionally included balls on 13 July, the illumination of the Strasbourg Cathedral, and a fireworks display. While religious services played a part of each holiday, they formed a more central part of the Jeanne d'Arc festivities. In contrast to both the Bastille Day and Jeanne d'Arc celebrations, the Armistice Day ceremonies called for a more subdued tone. While commemorating the victory of France over Germany, the holiday also recalled the immense death and destruction of the war. The presence of veterans, many of whom bore the visible evidence of their experience, served as reminders of the war at the various services.[74]

Alsatian reactions to the various holidays differed according to the holiday, circumstances in the regional political situation, and ideological persuasion. Of the three holidays, the Fête de Jeanne d'Arc, celebrated in May, enjoyed the least support but suffered the least opprobrium. While officials and members of various patriotic groups celebrated the holiday, the girl of Domrémy does not seem to have grabbed the attention of the Alsatian populace.[75] The major regionalist papers, including the Catholic dailies such as the *Elsässer* and *Elsässer Kurier*, devoted little if any space to the holiday. Likewise, pro-French Socialist papers such as the *Freie Presse* not surprisingly also failed to accord the day any coverage. Indeed, only the nationalist papers such as the *Journal de L'Est* (edited by Pierre Bucher's son-in-law, Jules-Albert Jaeger) or *S' Elsass* offered substantial coverage.[76] While the historian cannot naturally rule out popular support for the holiday, the decisive lack of reporting on the holiday—especially in contrast to Bastille and Armistice Day—suggests a very limited influence for the holiday in the region.

Armistice Day emerged, in comparison to the Fête de Jeanne d'Arc, as an important holiday. In somber tones, the Alsatian press annually called on its readers to commemorate the terrible losses of the First World War. At times, Alsatian attitudes mimicked those of the larger French polity. For example, in 1921, when the French parliament tried to shift the holiday to Sunday, 13 November, Alsatian editors decried the move just as veterans across the country had.[77]

Beyond a communal moment of sorrow, the day had divergent meanings. The nationalist daily *Journal d'Alsace et de Lorraine* not surprisingly used the occasion to celebrate the return of Alsace to France and recall French suffering at the hands of the Germans. Moreover, the paper at times reminded its readers that the Germans had yet to fulfill their treaty obligations and even went so far as to charge Germans with revanchist intent with regard to Alsace.[78] The *Journal de L'Est* espoused a similar view, but underscored more clearly the links between Alsace and France by recalling the victorious days of November 1918. The issue of national sacrifice also came to the fore; for example, in 1925, the paper stressed how French soldiers had "subordinated regional and personal interests" to the war, an obvious jab at the growing regionalist movement, especially in its *Zukunft* vintage.[79]

The Socialist press, in contrast, focused upon the need for greater peace in Europe. In part, papers such as the *Le Républicain* and the *Freie Presse* wanted to see disarmament, increased moral investment in the League of Nations, and revisions to the Versailles Treaty, all of which would, in turn, increase the prospects for European peace. As such, the articles of the later 1920s praised the idea of the Locarno Treaty. The Socialists also occasionally used the issues of peace, war, and commemoration to hammer on right-wing nationalist politicians such as Raymond Poincaré and Georges Clémenceau whose "politics of hate" disturbed European peace.[80]

Much like the pro-French and Socialist press, the moderate regionalist press adopted a reverent air for its coverage of Armistice Day. Catholic, regionalist-oriented papers pushed for greater efforts toward peace; unlike the Socialists, dailies such as the *Elsässer Kurier* and the *Elsässer* focused on the need to avoid a renewal of specifically Alsatian suffering by calling attention to the unique position of the region as a borderland between two great powers. Only in the late 1920s did a critical strand creep into the commemorative articles. For example, the 11 November 1929 edition of the *Elsässer* recalled that Alsatians had fought on both sides of the war. The French government needed to realize that all Alsatians, not just those in the uniform of the *poilu*, "had died for the Fatherland. Only when the current administration took steps to include all Alsatians could the reintegration of Alsace into France be completed."[81]

If the moderate Catholic regionalist press demonstrated a measured respect for the holiday, then the autonomist press was conspicuous in its failure to offer commentary concerning the Armistice. Such an omission is not easily explained; the short-lived autonomist papers in the 1920s (the leading papers, *Die Zukunft*, *Die Volkswille*, and *Die Volksstimme* enjoyed approximately two-year press runs apiece) offer only a limited range of possible material to examine.

The central holiday on the national calendar was *Quatorze Juillet*, or Bastille Day. Government officials placed great emphasis on the importance of the holiday, and on the need to demonstrate the links between France and Alsace; the holiday became a celebration of the nation and the regained region. The basic elements of the holiday—military reviews, balls, and fireworks—enticed Alsatians to local celebrations. To judge by the annual press coverage of the holiday,[82] Alsatians took part in the festivities in large numbers. The regional administration, however, at times felt the need to outline the ties between nation and region, not only for the Alsatians, but for foreigners as well.

One curious example of this impulse came in 1921 when the Harvard Glee Club visited Strasbourg over the holiday. In a letter to the prefect's office, General Commissioner Alapetite wrote, "The Ministry for Foreign Affairs has called to my attention quite clearly the importance of the members of this society, who belong to one of the oldest American universities and who are moved by the most pro-French sentiments to take away a favorable impression of our country."[83] To satisfy the wishes of the Foreign Ministry and the general commissioner, the glee club enjoyed an exhibition of Alsatian traditional dress (with over four hundred participants) at the Orangerie Park as a part of the day's larger festivities. The organizers hoped that, along with the normal parades and speeches at the Place Kléber as well as trip to Mt. Ste. Odile, this demonstration would "make these seventy American delegates aware of happy Alsace, French Alsace." Unfortunately, the prefect did not indicate whether this display impressed the Harvard students.[84]

French officials also used the holiday to remind their countrymen of the renewed links between the mère-patrie and the newly regained province. (See Figure 6.1) In 1919, on the first celebration of 14 July following the Armistice, the departmental government of the Bas-Rhin sent a delegation of Alsatian women to Paris to participate in the festivities of the day. The young women, decked out in full traditional dress, attended the main parade and passed out bouquets—tied in tricolor ribbons—to national and foreign dignitaries.[85] The placement of the Alsatian women in traditional garb in a central place in the Parisian festivities clearly demonstrates the desire of the government to affirm the return of Alsace to the mère-patrie.

Among local observers, the holiday, much like Armistice Day, offered an opportunity to opine on national loyalty, local politics, and the quality of the French government. This trend is particularly evident in the late 1920s. The more nationalist papers in 1926, for example, pointed to the popular support for the holiday as evidence that the autonomist coalition the *Heimatbund* was "gravely mistaken" in assuming that people would support their political goals, continuing, "Alsace is French. . . . It refuses to fall in the traps of antinational agents."[86] Some papers, recalling the enthusiasm of Alsatians for the Revolution in the 1790s, argued that such demonstrations of public loyalty on holidays demonstrated the long-term support of Alsatians for France.[87]

Local disputes naturally colored Bastille Day arguments about the heritage of the nation. For example, the Strasbourg Radical-Socialist paper *La République* attacked the regionalist tendencies of its fellow Alsatians. In particular, the paper accused the clergy (and by extension, the UPR)

Figure 6.1. Bastille Day 1919, Strasbourg

of ultramontanism and of blocking the introduction of the full range of French law to the region. The paper then proceeded to tie the hostility of the Alsatian clergy to French law to the general unwillingness of the French clergy to accept the Third Republic and further likened clericalism to opposition to the Revolution. Indeed, the paper argued that until the full panoply of French laws were introduced, the "fourteenth of July could not be properly celebrated."[88]

In response, the *Elsässer* asked if 14 July had only been celebrated since Emile Combes had passed the separation laws in 1905. The paper then rejected discussing political affairs on the national holiday and instead recounted a story whereby an elderly German man who wished to visit family in Alsace had to travel to Paris to receive his visa. Germans traveling to other parts of France could simply receive permission from their local consulate. The paper then asked why Alsatians and Lorrainers were not treated equally with other members of the French republic as evidenced by the unfair treatment of visitors to Alsace and the unequal taxation of Alsatians. The *Elsässer* exhorted local representatives to force Paris to deal with Alsatian issues more energetically.[89]

Dissonant voices did not come solely from the press. Under the city council dominated by the autonomist alliance, the holiday became a source of controversy. The problems surrounding the *Fête nationale* began in summer 1929 when Karl Hueber ordered a minimum of decorations (tricolored bunting on only two windows) for Strasbourg's city hall.[90] Such a policy earned the mayor the ire of the nationalist-leaning press. The continuation of the policy on other holidays led to French nationalists in the region taking matters into their own hands; for example, during the night of 10 November 1929, a group of young men hung French flags, some with the fleurs de lys attached, from several windows of city hall.[91]

It was with the following year's celebrations, however, that fireworks really flew, or perhaps more accurately stated, almost did not fly. Rumors spread that the city would not authorize its yearly subsidy for a fireworks display and the illumination of the cathedral. In particular, the Communist members of the council averred the subsidy represented a poor use of the taxpayers' money and suggested that it was simply a bourgeois holiday anyway. Although the city council would eventually authorize the credits by a narrow majority (several autonomists abstained), the maneuver generated much concern in the press. One local paper even accused the Communist council members of wishing to see the "USSR as the *patrie*" as the grounds for their unwillingness to celebrate this "national and Alsatian holiday."[92]

The controversy did not end there. In 1931, the autonomists and Communists on the council managed to block the subsidy. Again, the press protested the move, but Hueber and his colleagues remained firm in their opposition. To counter the intransigence of city hall, a group of private citizens, led by Henri Weber, Fritz Kieffer, and Gustav Stoskopf, founded the Comité des Fêtes de la Ville de Strasbourg. With help from private donations, as well as lights lent by the prefect, the *comité* managed both to illuminate the cathedral and to hold the fireworks display. Indeed, the *comité* continued its work over the course of the next several years until Hueber's coalition fell out of power and Charles Frey reinstated the subsidy in 1935.[93]

Conclusion

Much as in the realm of education, administration, and politics, the process of cultural assimilation in Alsace proceeded at a snail's pace. The attempts to promote French culture—or to blend French and Alsatian traditions and history—achieved only limited success because a population that primarily spoke German was not prepared for a rapid changeover to the Frenchified vision of Alsatianness. French efforts to shape Alsatian culture could not overcome this basic barrier. Likewise, an Alsatian populace that had diverse political agendas and divergent experiences of the war resisted the reshaping of the region's memorial landscape by subverting the efforts of nationalistic Alsatians and French administrators.

Ironically, some Alsatians tried to marry an appreciation for Alsatian traditions such as the dialect with loyalty to the French region. This French-Alsatian particularism, not surprisingly, did not adopt the rhetoric of the dual culture from before the First World War. Instead of Alsace as a synthesis of French and German culture, the editors of *La Littérature Populaire* and the *DEW*, and one might add more distantly, dailies such as the *SNZ*, promoted a notion of Alsatianness that was simultaneously unique and fully compatible with membership in the French nation. Not surprisingly, Gustave Stoskopf remained involved in such a vision, in many ways continuing his prewar concern with the promotion of Alsatian culture.

This is not to say that a concept of a dual culture died completely. At least in the early and mid-1920s, journals such as the *Der Eiserne Mann* and editors such as Paul Schall promoted German and Alsatian culture in a similar vein to the proponents of the dual culture before 1914. Unlike the Pierre Buchers of yesteryear, these new champions of Alsace's complex cultural heritage (in contrast to Bucher's agitation for an Alsatian return to France) did not push for a return to Germany. Rather, a generation raised in German schools wanted to preserve its linguistic and cultural world. As its frustration grew, and as the French government alienated more Alsatians in the mid-1920s, implicit and explicit arguments for a dual culture faded as Alsatian regionalism took a turn toward the rhetoric of autonomy and protection for the culture of a national minority.

Notes

1. ADBR AL 121–186, Letter dated 20 January 1919.
2. ADBR AL 121–189.
3. See *La Renaissance alsacienne* 3, n. 1–19 (1923).
4. ADBR AL 121–189.
5. "A nos lecteurs," *La Vie en Alsace* (Jan. 1923).
6. Paul Bourson, "Guillaume II en Alsace et Lorraine," *La Vie en Alsace* (July 1928); Paul Bourson, "L'Affaire de Saverne," *La Vie en Alsace* (Jan. 1934); "Le Haut-Koenigsbourg et sa Reconstruction," *La Vie en Alsace* (Jan. 1935).
7. Bernhard von Hülsen, *Szenenwechsel in Elsass. Theater und Gesellschaft in Strassburg zwischen Deutschland und Frankreich, 1890–1944*. Deutsch-Französisch Kulturbiblothek 22 (Leipzig, 2003), 147–250.
8. Jean Dewitz, "Le perception du théâtre populaire alsacien dans la presse (1920/1921)," in *La presse en Alsace au XXe siècle: Témoin-acteur-enjeu*, ed. Hildegard Châtellier and Monique Mombert (Strasbourg, 2002), 87–102; Jean-Marie Gall, "Quatre-vingt ans de theatre alsacien de Colmar." *Saisons d'Alsace* 25, no. 73 (Printemps 1981): 43–56; René Muller, "Le théâtre alsacien de Mulhouse." *Saisons d'Alsace* 25, no. 73 (1981): 15–42.
9. "Einführung," *Die elsässische Woche* (18 Feb. 1922); "Zum Geleit," *La Littérature Populaire*, n. 1 (1920).
10. "Einführung," *Die elsässische Woche* (18 Feb. 1922).
11. "Schulen," *DEW* (11 March 1922); "Ein wahres Wort über Elsass," *DEW* (20 May 1922); "Deutsche Lüge," *DEW* (9 Sept. 1922); "Elsässerditsch," *DEW* (6 Jan. 1923); "Elsässer Patriotismus," *DEW* (21 July 1923).
12. "Elsässerditsch," *DEW* (6 Jan. 1923).
13. "Aus dem elsässischen Kunst und Geistleben," *DEW* (7 June 1924).
14. "Elsässisches Theater im Strasbourg," *La Littérature Populaire*, n. 9–10 (June 1921).
15. Vogler, *Histoire culturelle de l'Alsace*, 403.
16. See, for example, Philippe Oberlé, "Der Nächste Krieg," *Der Eiserne Mann* (15 March 1925).
17. Philippe Oberlé, "Die Vergiftung der Grenzlandseele," *Der Eiserne Mann* (1 Nov. 1924), 18–19.
18. Philippe Oberlé, "Amnestie für den Elsässer Ley!" *Der Eiserne Mann* (1 May 1925), 209–10.
19. Paul Buchman, "Die Anti-Kulturliga," *Der Eiserne Mann* (1 September 1925), 343–44.
20. Orpheus, "Das elsässische Theater," *Der Eiserne Mann* (15 Oct. 1924), 13–14; Orpheus, "Zur Dekadenz des elsässischen Theaters," *Der Eiserne Mann* (1 Nov. 1914), 26–28; Thomas Seltzener, "Aus dem Tagebuch des Kunstlebens," *Der Eiserne Mann* (1 Feb. 1925), 126–28; "Elsässisches Theater," *Der Eiserne Mann* (15 March 1925); "Elsässisches Theater," *Der Eiserne Mann* 415–416 (1 Nov. 1925), 415–16.
21. Ibid.
22. *Schliffstaan* (2 January 1926), 1.
23. This theme occurs repeatedly in the *Schliffstaan*. In the last six issues of 1925 and first ten of 1926, *Schliffstaan* took up this question specifically, and it made regular news throughout the entire period of late 1924 to mid-1926.
24. *Schliffstaan* (12 June 1926), 1.
25. The idea for a free state had been originally put forward by a group of Alsatians led by Klaus Zorn von Bulach, the son of the former secretary of state for Alsace under German rule. The idea had first been raised, without serious consideration being given to it by the Allies or Germany, in 1918–19. Bulach then began pushing for this idea again in early 1927 as part of the program of the Alsatian Opposition-Block party. See Philip C. Bankwitz, *Alsatian Autonomist Leaders, 1919–1947* (Lawrence, KS, 1978), 18–19, and *Die Wahrheit* (16 April 1927), 1.

26. *Schliffstaan* (22 September 1923), 2.
27. *Schliffstaan* (20 December 1924), 2.
28. *Schliffstaan* (22 May 1924), supplement, 1.
29. *Schliffstaan* (14 July 1924), 4.
30. *Schliffstaan* (22 January 1927), 3.
31. Annette Maas, "Zeitenwende in Elsass-Lothringen: Denkmalstürze und Umdeutung der nationalen Erinnerungslandschaft (November 1918–1922)," in *Denkmalsturz. Zur Konfliktgeschichte politischer Symbolik*, ed. Winfried Speitkampf (Göttingen, 1997), 79–108.
32. ADBR D 414–2039. In particular, see the circular of 7 July 1925 as well as the responses from the numerous municipalities.
33. Stephen Harp, *Learning to be Loyal: Primary Schooling as Nation Building in Alsace and Lorraine* (Dekalb, IL, 1998), 196–201.
34. William Shane Story, "Constructing French Alsace: A State, Region, and Nation," PhD diss., Rice University, 2001, 222–24.
35. Ibid., 223. See also ADBR AL 121–1091, Letter to Haut-Commissaire dated 10 February 1919.
36. ADBR AL 121–187, Report of the Commissaire spécial dated 6 July 1920.
37. ADBR AL 121–1091, Letter from Alapetite to the Sécretaire Général du Comité de l'Union alsacienne Jeanne d'Arc dated 1 June 1922.
38. "Das Jeanne d'Arc Monument," *Elsässer* (13 July 1922) clipped in AMS D IV 179/979. See also AMS D IV 179/979, Report signed "Kraft" dated 22 June 1931.
39. AMS D 700/130, George Spinner à le Ministre de l'éducation nationale, Direction d'Architecture, Bureau des Batiments civils et des palais nationaux dated 27 May 1955. Spinner had estimated that the reconstruction of the statue would cost approximately 2,000,000 francs, and the project was apparently rejected.
40. "Das Pasteurdenkmal," *SNZ* (19 December 1921); "Pasteur's Centenary," *New York Times* (9 July 1922). See generally as well the press clippings in AMS Div. IV 185/990.
41. AMS Div. IV 185/990, "Souscription pour le monument Pasteur de Strasbourg."
42. Ibid.
43. ADBR D 286–308, "Souscription pour le monument Pasteur."
44. ADBR D 286–304, Memo signed "Borrel" dated 20 November 1922; 121 AL 99, "Program for Presidential Trip"; AMS Div. IV 185/990, Report signed "Dopff" dated 22 June 1931; Y. Barry, "Le monument Pasteur," *La Vie en Alsace* (June/July 1923): 22–23.
45. AMS Div. IV 185/990, Report signed "Reyer" dated 29 December 1928.
46. AMS Div. IV 184/896, "Appel en faveur d'un monument Lamartine-Victor Hugo"
47. AMS Div. IV 184/896, Letter from Redslob to Peirotes dated 27 December 1927.
48. The Place de la République, earlier the Kaiserplatz, was a circular area framed by several important buildings built by the German administration including the Imperial Palace, University Library (adorned, as discussed in chapter 3, with the busts of German and European writers), Reichsland administrative buildings, and eventually the seat of the *Landtag* (today, the Théâtre National de Strasbourg). In the center of the square a statue to Wilhelm I had been erected in 1911.
49. AMS DIV IV 186/968, Memo of Peirotes signed 28 January 1928, Report of the 4th commission to the mayor dated 17 December 1927, Extracts of the city council meeting dated 29 April 1929, Memo for Mayor dated 27 March 1931; ADBR AL 98–708, Letter from Paul Bastier to Paul Valot dated 27 April 1931.
50. Mark Connelly, *The Great War, Memory and Ritual: Commemoration in the City and East London, 1916–1939* (Rochester, NY, 2002); Catherine Moriarty, "Private Grief and Public Remembrance: British First World War Memorials," in *War and Memory in the Twentieth Century*, ed. Martin Evans and Ken Lunn (Oxford, 1997), 123–45; Daniel Sherman, *The Construction of Memory in Interwar France* (Chicago, 1999); *War and Remembrance in the Twentieth Century*, eds. Jay Winter and Emmanuel Sivan (New York, 1999); Jay Winter, *Sites of Memory, Sites of Mourning: The Great War in European Cultural History* (Cambridge, 1995).
51. Story, "Constructing French Alsace," 228: also see generally ADBR AL 121–584.

52. Story, "Constructing French Alsace," 229–30.
53. ADBR AL 69–70, Memo from Directeur de l'Architecture et des Beaux-arts dated 25 July 1919.
54. Story, "Constructing French Alsace," 227–34.
55. *L'echo de Wissembourg* (2 Nov. 1932) clipped in ADBR D 286–304.
56. Story, "Constructing French Alsace," 234–37.
57. This political coalition had come about as the result of several years worth of mutual election favors between the Communists and the autonomists; the ties of the latter with some elements within the Catholic party helped seal the coalition. The odd alliance, while securing Karl Hueber's tenure in office until his displacement by Charles Frey in 1935, led the clerical supporters to be labeled turncoats and helped lead to the 1929 ousting of Hueber from the local Communist Party. See Samuel Goodfellow, *Between the Swastika and the Cross of Lorraine* (Dekalb, IL, 1999), 75–77; AN F7/13392, Report signed "Bauer" dated 27 September 1929.
58. *Die Neue Zukunft* (23 Feb. 1935) clipped in AMS Div. IV 179/971.
59. AMS Div. IV 178/971, Report entitled "Aufstellung eines Gefallenendenkmales auf der Place de la République" dated 1 March 1935.
60. Story, "Constructing French Alsace," 236.
61. AMS Div VI 178/971, Letter from Henry Levi to Charles Frey (19 June 1935).
62. The monument still stands in the Place de la République where, in addition to the years of the First World War the years for the Second World War, Vietnam War, and Algerian War were added.
63. Hartmannswillerkopf (le Vieil Armand), Official Website, http://www.abri-memoire.org/hwk.php. Site accessed 11 Jan. 2003.
64. ADBR AL 121–1091, Letter from General Boisseau to the General Commissioner dated 20 Aug. 1920.
65. ADBR AL 121–1091, Letter from Alapetite to the Touring-Club de France dated 8 December 1920.
66. ADBR AL 121–1091, "Monument du Hartmannswillerkopf."
67. ADBR AL 121–1091.
68. ADBR D 286–304, Projet du comité du monument national de l'Hartmannswillerkopf (1927)
69. ADBR AL 121–1091, "Monument et ossuaire du Hartmannswillerkopf."
70. ADBR D 286–304, Projet du comité du monument national de l'Hartmannswillerkopf
71. "Feierlichkeiten im Haut-Rhin," *SNZ* (10 Oct. 1932). The use of the idea of festivities here was used not to disparage the inauguration of the memorial, but rather because President Lebrun also presided over the opening of a new canal and hydro-power station during his visit.
72. "Le Président de la République sera demain l'hote du Haut-Rhin," *La France de l'Est* (8 Oct. 1932); "L'inauguration de crypte du Vieil-Armand," *La France de l'est* (9 Oct. 1932); "Feierlichkeiten im Haut-Rhin," *SNZ* (10 Oct. 1932); "Lebrun ehrt die Kriegsgefallenen," *Elsässer Kurier* (10 Oct. 1932); *Journal d'Alsace et de Lorraine* (10 October 1932); *Strassburger Neueste Nachrichten* (10/11 Oct. 1932).
73. ADBR 286 D 304 contains the official plans, as filed with the prefect for the Department of the Bas-Rhin, for each holiday for most of the 1920s. For the municipal plans, see AMS Cérémonie 24/180–183; Div. C 23/178.
74. Ibid.
75. Ibid. See also, ADBR AL 121–187, "Union alsacienne Jeanne d'arc."
76. For example, the *Journal de L'Est* (10 May 1926) gave front page coverage to the festivities, especially as Marshall Foch was in attendance. *S' Elsass* also reported on the festivities, but not always on the front page.
77. Antoine Prost, *In the Wake of War: 'Les anciens combattants' and French Society, 1914–1939*. Trans. Helen McPhail (Providence, RI, 1992), 58–61. For Alsace, see the press clippings in ADBR D 286–304.

78. "11 November 1925," *Journal d'Alsace et de Lorraine* (11 Nov. 1925); "Il y a dix ans," *Journal d'Alsace et de Lorraine* (11 Nov. 1928); "L'Alsace et le 11 Novembre," *Journal d'Alsace et de Lorraine* (12 November 1929).
79. *Journal de L'Est* (11 Nov. 1925); "11 Novembre," *Journal de L'Est* (11 Nov. 1926); "Une date," *Journal de L'Est* (11 Nov. 1927); "Strasbourg célèbre avec éclat la Fête de la Victoire," (12 Nov. 1927); "L'arrondissement de Hagenau célèbre l'anniversaire de l'armistice," *Journal de L'Est* (13 Nov. 1927); "Le commémoration de l'armistice," *La France de l'Est* (11 Nov. 1929).
80. *Freie Presse* (11 Nov. 1925); *Freie Presse* (11 Nov. 1926); *Freie Presse* (11 Nov. 1927); *Der Republikaner* (11 Nov. 1925); *Der Republikaner* (11 Nov. 1926); *Der Republikaner* (11 Nov. 1927).
81. *Elsässer* (12 Nov. 1925); *Elsässer* (12 Nov. 1926); *Elsässer* (10 November 1927); *Elsässer* (9 Nov. 1929); *Elsässer Kurier* (10 Nov. 1926); *Elsässer Kurier* (12 Nov. 1927); *Elsässer Kurier* (12 Nov. 1928).
82. The press reports are drawn from the newspaper citations in the discussion below.
83. ADBR D 286–304, Letter from Alapetite to the Prefect dated 5 July 1921.
84. ADBR D 286–304, Letter of Fritz Kieffer to the Cabinet du Prefet dated 29 June 1921; AMS Div. C 23/178, "Harvard Glee Club Program."
85. ADBR AL 121-9.
86. "La Fête Nationale a été célébrée avec éclat," *Journal de L'Est* (15 July 1926).
87. *Journal d'Alsace et de Lorraine* (15 July 1926); "Elsässische Freiheitsstimme," *Strasburger Neueste Nachrichten* (14 July 1926); "Der Quatorze Juillet in Strassburg," *Strasburger Neueste Nachrichten* (15 July 1926); "Die Feier des Nationalfestes im Straßburg," SNZ (15 July 1926).
88. "Zum Quatorze Juillet," *La République* (14 July 1926); "Zum Quatorze Juillet 1928," *La République* (14 July 1928).
89. "Hetze gegen die nationale Stimmung am Nationalfest," *Elsässer* (15 July 1926).
90. "La municipalité pavoisé aux couleurs nationales," *Journal d'Alsace et de Lorraine* (4 July 1929).
91. AN F 7/13392, Report signed "Reichart."
92. "La Mairie et la fête nationale," *Dernières Nouvelles* (12 July 1930); for the wider press coverage, see the numerous clippings in AMS Div C 23/179.
93. AMS Div. C. 23/179, Letter from Weber to Hueber dated 10 July 1931; "Die Beleuchtung," *Messager d'Alsace* (15 July 1931).

Chapter 7

THE APOGEE OF THE AUTONOMIST MOVEMENT

In July 1928, a group of local politicians gathered at Strasbourg's Palais des Fêtes. Three thousand people crammed inside, another three thousand waited outside. Those present included Eugène Ricklin, head of the autonomist Heimatbund (Homeland Union), Paul Schall and René Hauss of the autonomist Landespartei, Camille Dahlet of the autonomist Fortschrittliche Partei (Progressive Party), firm UPR regionalists such as Joseph Rossé, and several members of the Alsatian Communist Party. This eclectic coalition of political allies had gathered to celebrate the pardon and release of Rossé and Ricklin, who had been found guilty of threatening the security of the state in a closely watched May 1928 trial.[1] The July 1928 festivities marked an emblematic high point for interwar Alsatian regionalism, and more specifically, for the autonomist movement of the 1920s. Between April 1928 and May 1929, the improbable coalition of Catholics, Communists, autonomists, and Progressives scored a moderate number of electoral victories under the banner of the Volksfront (People's Front).

The years between 1926 and 1930 witnessed the rise, cresting, and incipient decline of the Alsatian autonomist movement, a grouping of diverse political parties and organizations that wished, at the very least, to attain greater protection for the cultural, linguistic, and religious heritage of the region. Frustration at French policies, especially the ill-fated program of the Cartel des Gauches, made Alsace fertile ground for a rising autonomist sentiment, for which *Die Zukunft* served as bellwether and in the mid-1920s, its loudest voice. The Alsatian autonomy movement so successfully fused discontent with developments since 1918 with the region's unique sense of identity and victimhood that it impelled local parties to consider their aims through the lens of the region.[2]

The Alsatian autonomist movement did not represent a monolithic organization. Rather, several diverse groups eventually united under the Volksfront, forming a loose coalition similar to the 1911 National Union.

Notes for this section begin on page 201.

Supporters and fellow travelers of the autonomy movement included regionalists in the UPR, Protestant liberals who wanted more protection for the regional language and culture under the guise of autonomy, as well as a faction of the local Communist Party. On its more radical fringes, minor parties such as Klaus von Bulach's Oppositionbloc and the Unabhängige Landespartei für Elsass-Lothringen (Independent Regional Party for Alsace-Lorraine), founded by key supporters of *Die Zukunft*, veered increasingly towards separatism. Collectively, these groups enjoyed limited electoral success, especially in the 1929 Strasbourg and Colmar municipal elections. Yet even at its height, the coalition never truly threatened the dominance of the regional political powerhouse, the Catholic UPR.

This chapter considers the changing fate of the autonomist movement in Alsace in the latter half of the 1920s and early 1930s. It first explores the creation and influence of the Heimatbund, a group similar in goals and nature to the National Union of 1911. The chapter then turns to the increasing radicalization of the autonomist movement and the French responses to the perceived threat it posed. Finally, the chapter examines the ephemeral political successes of the autonomy movement in 1928 and 1929 before changes in French policy and internal divisions among the various autonomist groups drove the autonomist coalition apart.[3]

The perceived strength and even mere presence of the autonomist movement created severe tension in the region, especially as it was continually believed in cahoots with German authorities. The claim of many autonomists that Alsatians were a national minority only exacerbated the problem; the radical autonomist rhetoric alienated potential allies locally while hardening the attitudes of French officials. The autonomists' success, however limited, forced a change in the political landscape of the region, often leading to divisions within the region's political organizations. Moreover, the French government, working under the presumption that the autonomists were German pawns and deeply resentful of the apparent insult to the French sacrifices of World War I, demonstrated little desire to discuss Alsatian demands. Such unwillingness was reinforced by the general suspicion of Third Republic leaders in the interwar period to countenance a special region within a "unified and indivisible" France.

A New National Union? The Heimatbund and the Growth of the Autonomy Movement

The attempt of the Herriot government to impose greater linguistic and legal unity on Alsace left massive turmoil in its wake. Few parties could avoid articulating a clear defense of regional interests. The vociferousness and radicalism of demands, though, varied greatly. The editors of the *Die Zukunft*, for example, claimed that Alsatians were a national minority; the Parti Communiste d'Alsace (PCA) called for a plebiscite to determine the international status of Alsace and Lorraine. While differing on issues of church-state relations, both groups wanted greater control for local economic affairs, protection for the regional culture, and a regional administration.[4]

In a less radical vein, the UPR sought to defend Alsatian interests, but rejected the idea of an Alsatian "national minority" and confirmed its loyalty to the French state. Laying out a coherent position, however, proved difficult. A series of contentious meetings took place between 1925 and early 1926 during which the party plotted its course. Some within the party leadership, such as Joseph Rossé, head of the teachers' union, or the priests Joseph Fashauer and Joseph Zemb, had close ties with *Die Zukunft* and urged following the newspaper's line. More moderate UPR regionalists such as Michel Walter expressed some sympathy for the goals of the newspaper, but argued that the party needed at all times to show its clear and unwavering loyalty to France. Along with Xavier Haegy, a priest who controlled a small publishing empire in Upper Alsace, Walter agitated in favor of limited regional autonomy. In contrast, the nationalist wing, led by Joseph Pfleger, supported the defense of the regional interests, especially in the realm of religion, but denounced *Die Zukunft*'s radicalism and not for the first time threatened to leave the party if its platform shifted too close to the paper's line.[5] Indeed, the scissions within the UPR between "regionalists" and "nationalists" would eventually lead to a splintering of the party as radical autonomists were expelled and the nationalist members left to form a separate party.

For the short term, members bridged their differences by calling for a restructuring of the French state. In part the UPR wanted greater political stability at the national level. More importantly, party leaders hoped that the institution of a "sane regionalism" amid general reform would afford Alsatians the opportunity to have a regional legislature, budget, and power to regulate "particular legislation owing to its unique history." While it called for general reform of the French state knowing the region would never receive special autonomy, it also laid its regional interests clearly on the table. The program stated, "In virtue of being an Alsatian party and conscious of its duty to defend with all energy the interest of our *petit pays*, the liberties, and acquired rights of a long past, the party insists with the greatest energy upon the urgency of regional reform for Alsace." The party then listed particular areas over which the regional administration should have competence including education (with an eye toward bilingual instruction and religious instruction), some social laws, and cultural affairs.[6]

The UPR program in many ways reflected a return to the situation under the Constitution of 1911—a moderate regional autonomy—though within and loyal to France.[7] The party refused to call Alsatians a national minority and therefore adopted a less combative stance than the editors of *Die Zukunft*. Other parties evinced a similar longing for a moderate course. Aside from religious differences, the Republican-Democrats under

Charles Frey probably could have supported the UPR position. In addition, Georges Wolf, a leading member of the Radical-Socialists in Strasbourg and a former Liberal, argued in favor of similar reforms. He even tried in the spring of 1926 to create a coalition to promote cultural autonomy and the use of the German language. Wolf, however, was rebuffed because other parties (including his own), and above all the UPR, did not see the utility in such an alliance.[8]

Although Wolf's coalition failed, some Alsatians viewed greater solidarity as critical to efforts to defend Alsatian rights. In early 1926, a loose coalition began to consider the creation of a nonpartisan organization to fight for the political and cultural rights of Alsace. This group, like the National Union, brought together diverse allies, most notably key leaders from *Die Zukunft* and politicians from the regionalist wing of the UPR.[9] The leaders of this budding union included Jean Keppi, a municipal employee from Hagenau and a founding member of the UPR, who convinced Eugène Ricklin to sign on. Numerous others joined the pair: Joseph Rossé, who enjoyed the support of Xavier Haegy's press organization; René Hauss, son of the former Center leader Karl Hauss and collaborator on *Die Zukunft*; and Paul Schall, editor of the *Die Zukunft*.[10] Together, they created the Heimatbund in 1926.

Several issues bound these men together. First, all had grown up under German rule and been educated in the German school system. Second, they wished to protect the linguistic and cultural heritage of the region. Third, all wanted, at least in 1926, regional autonomy for Alsace within France. Yet the Heimatbund members remained divided on several key issues. Much as with the National Union, Catholic members of the Heimatbund did not want to threaten the dominant position of the Catholic party in the region, and therefore desired to create not a party but an informal alliance. The participation of these leading Catholics ensured a program amenable to some within the UPR and promised support from some of the UPR faithful. The religious bias of the Heimatbund leadership, much like with the National Union, complicated possible alliances with secularly oriented potential partners such as the Radical Socialist Camille Dahlet, a Protestant from Zabern.[11]

After several months of discussion, the founders of the Heimatbund met in Strasbourg and published its program on 5 June 1926 with some 112 signatories. The program began by recalling the broken promises of the French regime and pointing to the threat that "fanatical assimilationists" posed to the "being, soul, and culture of the Alsatians and Lorrainers." The Heimatbund then called all "true Alsatians" to "bear the circumstances no longer" and fight "as a national minority for complete autonomy in the framework of France." In particular, the Heimatbund wanted a regional legislative and administrative body with budgetary authority, maintenance of the status quo in church-state relations, preservation of the "Christian character of the Alsatian people," and education in

German. In addition, the *Bund* demanded greater support for the Alsatian economy, local control of the railroad network, and the reinstallation of certain German laws deemed beneficial to Alsatians.[12]

The Heimatbund made it clear that it did not want to disrupt the current political landscape; rather, it merely wanted to help direct the efforts of Alsatian and Lorrainer parties to defend the interests of their region.[13] Much like the National Union, therefore, the *Bund* did not have a firm basis of organizational support but rather relied on its ability to guide the established parties in Alsace to work together.

A final issue in the manifesto concerned the international situation. Karl-Heinz Rothenberger has suggested that the Heimatbund in part arose within "the spirit of Locarno."[14] As Georges Wolf argued in his 1926 book, Germany's recognition and guarantee of the 1919 border along with its attendant renunciation of Alsace gave France the opportunity to treat Alsace more kindly because an autonomy movement no longer represented a stepping-stone to German revanchism.[15] The Heimatbund's manifesto, reflecting this spirit of conciliation, stated that its members were "enthusiastic supporters of the idea of freedom and international cooperation and opponents of imperialism and militarism." Alsace, in this conception, could return to its rightful role as a "meeting place between two cultures" and would help foster "reconciliation between Germany and France."[16] The *Heimatbündler*, as they came to be known, therefore recalled Alsace's dual culture, but did so by demanding a far-reaching autonomy—well beyond that of the Nationalbund of 1911—framed by the provocative claim that Alsatians constituted a national minority.

While scholars have pointed in recent years to the importance of regionalism within the French Third Republic,[17] and while Alsatians certainly promoted a strong regionalism, French officials in Alsace had little patience for demands for a special regime for Alsace. Beyond the self-conception of France as an "indivisible" nation, the sacrifices of the Great War loomed over Alsatian debates. Thus, the publication of the manifesto set off a firestorm that enraged the strong nationalistic elements of Alsatian society, generated forceful official reprisals, further radicalized the autonomist movement, and eventually overshadowed the aspirations of moderate regionalists.

The immediate reception of the declaration sparked a range of responses. Nationalist papers responded with outrage, especially within pro-French circles. Papers such as *France de l'Est* and the *Journal d'Alsace et de Lorraine* loudly and consistently denounced the demands of the Heimatbund, arguing that such claims went against the nature of the French nation-state. The government was called upon to quash the group swiftly and decisively, especially as many of the signatories had ties to the state. The vitriol poured on the Heimatbund in large part stemmed from the national press's clear belief that the ulterior motives of the group lay in separating Alsace from France.[18]

Two issues in particular fueled this opinion. First, some of those involved in the Heimatbund, such as Ricklin, and others who were sympathetic to it, such as Georges Wolf, had apparently shown their true colors in the years before 1918.[19] Friendly to Germany, they embraced as their ultimate goal the creation of an autonomous province "to separate Alsace morally from the fatherland [*patrie*]."[20] Second, the papers sharply disputed the idea of Alsatians being designated as a "national minority." Seeing in this rhetoric, with the implied appeal to the League of Nations and false appeal to the "spirit of Locarno," the nefarious hand of Germany, "imperialistic" and "vengeful," Anselm Laugel condemned this danger roundly.[21] In other places, Laugel decried the appeal to the League of Nations as decidedly anti-French; no other French region, not Picardy or Brittany, would invoke such a claim. Only, in Laugel's estimation, would a group with ulterior motives even hint at petitioning powers outside of France.[22]

In a repeat of the 1911 criticisms of the National Union, the nationalist press prognosticated a lack of viability for the *Bund* on several counts; its divided membership, its alleged proximity to the UPR, and its radical agenda all would serve to undermine its efforts. As Jules-Albert Jaeger, editor of the nationalist *France de l'Est*, pointed out, the manifesto was a compromise meant to satisfy UPR stalwarts like Jean Keppi, liberals like Georges Wolf and Camille Dahlet, and Communists, in addition to more independent Catholic-friendly supporters such as Ricklin and Schall. Jaeger opined that this "nonpartisan alliance" was doomed to shatter along the ideological fault lines separating these groups. Moreover, Jaeger saw the alliance as little more than a cover for the regionalist branch of the UPR. In parallel, these papers also derided the Heimatbund's demands. After all, less-ambitious projects had been presented in the Chamber only to fail miserably; therefore, the Heimatbund was at best fencing with moonbeams.[23]

Rather than simply focusing on the German threat, Socialist papers viewed the Heimatbund through the twin lenses of socialism and nationalism. Much like the earlier National Union, the Socialists saw the Heimatbund as a vehicle of the clergy to continue its *Kulturkampf* for Catholic education in the region. Beyond the attack on the religious implications of the manifesto, the *Freie Presse* also decried the "antinational" and "separatist" nature of the Heimatbund's demands; the desire to protect Alsatian "customs and traditions" was nothing more than a "Chinese wall ... which would separate the provinces of Alsace and Lorraine from the rest of France."[24] The Socialist paper of Mulhouse took a harsher stance, averring that the *Bund* was nothing more an "Alsatian Stahlhelm" that wanted nothing less than "breaking away of Alsace-Lorraine from France."[25] Socialists papers instead argued Alsatians should promote the welfare of the "working people" of Alsace in their fight against capital.[26]

The Catholic press, embodied in the Strasbourg paper *Der Elsässer* and the Colmar-based *Elsässer Kurier*, both supported the general goals of the

Heimatbund and wished to see the "homeland rights" of Alsace defended. Moreover, both papers blamed the French government for bringing Alsatians to autonomism by trying to rule Alsatians as it did the French interior and ignoring Alsatian desires with regard to language, religion, and culture. Both Catholic dailies wished for a regionalism within the context of France; neither discussed the more radical claims of the Heimatbund concerning Alsatians' status as a national minority.[27]

The two major Catholic dailies fought back against the critics of the Heimatbund, meeting the antinational charge head-on. Accusations of the Heimatbund's separatist intent, antinational attitude, and German ties, they argued, dishonored the suffering of Alsatians during the war, avoided dealing with Alsatian complaints about the French administration, and ignored the long history of Alsatians defending their regional rights. Alsatian regionalists were not "antinational"; on the contrary, they wished to see a general reform of the French system. A special statute would allow the people of the region to "secure and guarantee their cultural, linguistic, and religious traditions."[28] Simultaneously, the Catholic papers deflected the charges of the Socialist press by questioning its assimilationist tendencies and asking whether Socialists would defend Alsatian interests.

The support of the major Catholic German-language papers belied a growing rift within the UPR. The July 1926 meetings of the party were marked by renewed, heightened tensions. The national faction, led by Joseph Pfleger, wanted an open condemnation of the Heimatbund and *Die Zukunft*. Pfleger also called for the expulsion of those party members who had signed the manifesto. In contrast, the regionalist branch of the party firmly supported the Heimatbund. Other UPR leaders, suspicious of the *Bund*'s rhetoric but sympathetic to the special needs of the region, tried to find a compromise between the two wings. Eugène Muller and Michel Walter managed to avoid an open breach by reaffirming the independence of the UPR from the Heimatbund while pushing a renewal of the party's regionalist aims. The seeds of division, already sown in the first years after the war, had begun to show the first signs of sprouting into a full-fledged break.[29]

The Heimatbund also found support among some of the Radical-Socialists, mostly from the old Liberals who had thrown their lot with the Radical-Socialists instead of with the Republican-Democrats under Charles Frey. In particular, Georges Wolf supported the broad aims of the *Bund*, especially in the realm of language. A Protestant preacher who had pushed for Alsatian rights before the First World War, Wolf exhorted his fellow Radicals in the local party organization—whose loyalty to France could not be questioned—to support Alsatian "homeland rights." Arguing that France had made numerous blunders in the region, Wolf promoted a decentralized France in which a local Alsatian administration could "promote the common interests of Alsatian culture." Wolf realized the issue of confessional schools might prove difficult, but expressed hope that such issues could be resolved.[30] Wolf, however, could not bring the local party to his position. The party acknowledged the problems existent in the region and confirmed the need for local organizations to "support homeland rights in one fashion or another." Yet the party could not accept the Heimatbund's rhetoric, especially the claim to national minority status. *La République* noted that this development "marked a new stage," one that was "irredentist" and tied to clerical influence.[31] Much as with the UPR, Radicals faced an incipient splintering of the party.

The most ardent supporters of the Heimatbund included, not surprisingly, autonomist papers such as *Die Zukunft* that published nearly inexhaustible reiterations of the manifesto aims and sprang repeatedly to the defense of the Heimatbund. Jean Keppi, for example, argued that the Heimatbund did not receive foreign money but rather arose in Alsace because the French, in an "unworthy manner," had tried to repress the "legitimate demands" of Alsace. Indeed, the *Heimatbündler* had expressly stated their loyalty to France, but wanted changes in the French constitution so that Alsatians would once again harbor "the loyalty found here at the cease-fire." His line of argument pointed to the importance of the legacy of regionalism under German rule. The Heimatbund, separatist or not, wanted a strong regionalist regime for which the constitution of 1911 represented a starting point.

French officialdom responded rapidly to the Heimatbund. Much like the nationalist press in Alsace, the government viewed the Heimatbund as little more than anti-French agitators with ties to Germany.[32] The government already suspected that *Die Zukunft* had received its seed money from German sources, a suspicion that was true.[33] Yet the desire to view developments in Alsace through anti-French, pro-German lenses distorted official French understanding of the problems in Alsace. The willingness of even some of the national papers to concede that problems existed and consistent warnings from the days of the Conférence d'Alsace-Lorraine onward might have signaled to the government that the perfidious Germans were not always behind their difficulties in the region.

The French government attacked the Heimatbund at its base; 102 Alsatians had signed on to the manifesto, among whom were teachers, railroad workers, and priests, all of whom were considered state employees.[34] On 11 June, just scant days after the manifesto appeared, Labor Minister Pierre Laval ordered Alsatian state employees who had signed the document, including Joseph Rossé, to appear before disciplinary councils. Likewise, the Ministry of Religion ordered clerical signatories to be punished. Later in the summer, Raymond Poincaré would convince Bishop Ruch of Strasbourg to condemn *Die Zukunft*. While the government might have tried to quell the autonomist fire before it got out of hand, its actions only fueled the problem; French measures angered the teachers' union, alienated workers in state service, and gave the regionalist press further grist for the mill. The government's actions merely fanned greater opposition and gave greater attention to the cause of the Heimatbund.[35]

The vitriol over the Heimatbund declaration and the actions of the government did not fade over the long, hot days of the summer of 1926. Rather, the acrimony festered. Socialists and Catholics continued to fight over the religious nature of the Heimatbund's goals. The nationalist press, especially the *Journal d'Alsace et de Lorraine*, continued to inveigh against the Heimatbund as nothing more than a cover organization for German revanchism.[36] The negative chorus in the nationalist press was joined by new voices. For example, the Union Nationale des Combattants, a national veterans' association, sent letters in protest of the Heimatbund to the departmental administration and even held small demonstrations against the *Bund*.[37] The furor over the Heimatbund also generated support for Alsace's nascent extreme right-wing groups such as an Alsatian branch of Action Française.[38] This nationalist caterwaul against the autonomist movement did not deter the Heimatbund; the confluence of heightened opposition to the group and the group's determination to spread its message led to one of the few incidents of street violence in the fight over Alsatian national and regional belonging.

On 22 August 1926, Eugène Ricklin and Joseph Rossé, along with local autonomists and a group of sympathetic Communists, traveled to Colmar to protest the measures taken by the French government against the signatories to the Heimatbund Manifesto. When Ricklin arrived at the train station, he and his companions were met, as the *Elsässer* noted, by "royalists and fascists" (or, in the words of the *Journal d'Alsace et de Lorraine*, "patriots") who assaulted Ricklin. Ricklin escaped with minor injuries, but the same group conducted counter-demonstrations outside the restaurant where Ricklin and the autonomists gathered. Further violence ensued as the police, some mounted, slowly intervened.[39]

The nationalist press celebrated the incident as a welcome chastisement of the autonomists and praised the actions of the local patriots. Other papers expressed sympathy for those who demonstrated against Rossé and Ricklin: *La République*, while regretting the violence, compared the autonomists to the German Stahlhelm; Charles Frey, likewise opposed to the autonomist demonstration, opined that the autonomists and Communists had themselves aroused "rage and indignation" against a gathering with "an antinational character."[40] Other papers noted that the incident was one of the "saddest pages" of Alsatian history and accused the police and gendarmes of implicitly supporting the counter-demonstration.[41]

The German-language Catholic press immediately denounced the incident. Indeed, the *Elsässer Kurier* criticized not only the violence in Colmar, but also the "hate expressed in the French language press and certain German papers against the people of the Heimatbund and, in effect, against all those who in the first instance feel Alsatian."[42] After condemning the lack of protection provided by local police, the paper called on well-intentioned "French of the interior" to fight against the "royalists and fascists" of the "blue-white-red Stahlhelm." The *Elsässer* likewise upbraided the same groups, comparing the "Hurrah patriots" in their "fanaticism and chauvinism" to the "Prussian jackboot," decrying the inaction of the police, and questioning whether Paris would allow such "assaults on the civil peace."[43]

Ricklin personally responded to the incident in *Die Zukunft*. Publishing an open letter to the prefect of Haut-Rhin, Ricklin offered his perspective on the incident and criticized the slow response of police authorities. Ricklin also took the opportunity to request the right to carry a "weapon of self-defense" because of the police failure; the request would be denied.[44] Ricklin's compatriots at the paper also provided the chorus to Ricklin's solo by railing against not only the "incapable police" but also the "nationalists" whom the Parisian papers (not to mention some of the local papers) had praised as heroes. Continuing the philippic, the paper argued that the police's inability to defend the right of the Heimatbund to assemble, and the need of the *Bund*'s opponents to resort to violence, left the Heimatbund's members little other option than "to defend our civil rights ruthlessly."[45]

The "brawl in Colmar," as some papers referred to the incident, did not lead to more street violence. Indeed, in an age in which politics often turned violent, the debates over autonomy, regionalism, and the rights of Alsatians within France remained remarkably free of physical violence. Rhetorically, however, the debates over the Heimatbund intensified differences both within and among Alsatian parties, hardened the already distrustful and impatient attitudes of French administrators, and, as we shall see shortly, further radicalized the autonomist movement.

Much like the National Union, the Heimatbund exercised great influence over local politics. Political parties across the spectrum were forced to take positions vis-à-vis the new group. Much like the Union, the *Bund* ultimately failed to achieve its goals, lacking the ability to unify other parties as it could not overcome the divisions of its own membership and the divisiveness of its own rhetoric. Unlike the Union, the Heimatbund operated in a much different political atmosphere; French officials had little tolerance for an organization that seemed to call into question the unity of the centralized French state, and moreover, was apparently comprised of agents of the German foe. The Heimatbund, however, set the stage for greater confrontation between regional leaders and national authorities and opened the door to more radical parties.

New Parties, French Responses

The months following the incidents in Colmar brought renewed if ineffective attempts to resolve the discontent that dominated political life in Alsace. The Poincaré government seemed prepared to make some minor concessions to Alsatian sensibilities. Keeping to the party program of 1919 and 1925, the UPR resubmitted projects to introduce greater regional autonomy across France. Such efforts bore little fruit. The years following the promulgation of the Heimatbund Manifesto witnessed an increasing radicalism on the part of the autonomist movement, heightened tensions among Alsatian political parties, and a steeled government position against the "separo-autonomists" in Alsace.

The French government under Raymond Poincaré took steps to try to defuse the situation, but only after first irking local representatives. In July 1926, in response to the Heimatbund, Justice Minister Louis Barthou unsuccessfully introduced a law to repress "all political propaganda seeking to remove a part of the [national] territory from the national authority."[46] In October 1926, in correspondence with the head of the University of Strasbourg, Poincaré pursued the idea of relaxing linguistic assimilation and the expanding bilingualism in the educational and public life of Alsace. The project never got off the ground. In any case, as François Roth has pointed out, a government led Poincaré, a committed proponent of secularization, was unlikely to give ground on the key issue of religious education, thereby his gestures would not have generated sufficient goodwill.[47]

The UPR also tried to resolve tensions by submitting a project in the Chamber to create a regional administration for Alsace and Lorraine. After debating the terms of such a project for over a year, many of the original proponents, including deputies from Lorraine, refused to endorse the proposal.[48] The UPR proposal invited the government to study the possibility for a general reform of the French state through decentralization. This long-term reform was to be wed to a special statute for Alsace and Lorraine. In particular, the measure called for a regional budget subject to national approval, a regional parliament with direct elections, and required bilingual ability as well as knowledge of the region for state employees and civil servants, which UPR leaders such as Michel Walter hoped would help ameliorate the unrest among the Alsatian populace. The program received little support with the nationalist press questioning its premises and the autonomist papers excoriating its timid ambitions. The project went nowhere in the Chamber.[49]

The fact that only eight UPR deputies signed on to the party's proposal even before it went to the Chamber signaled the growing schism within the party over the future of the region. The growing division was evidenced in 1926 by the appearance of a mixed-language Catholic paper, *S'Elsass*. Supporters from the national wing of the UPR hoped that the weekly would counter the influence of the regionalist Catholic dailies, especially the *Elsässer* and the *Elsässer Kurier*. The paper denounced the autonomists and Communists. It later lambasted electoral alliances between the regionalist branch of the UPR and the various autonomist groups. *S'Elsass* never achieved broad success. Its press runs remained mostly under three thousand copies per week, whereas its rival Catholic papers averaged well over ten thousand per day.[50]

S' Elsass was not the only new paper, nor was it the most vitriolic against the autonomist movement. In early 1927, *Das Bollwark (The Bulwark)* appeared with the support of the Union de défense nationale et républicaine (Union of National and Republican Defense), a group of Alsatians who wished to fight the antinational tendencies of the autonomy movement. Written primarily in German, the paper's contributors included the fiercely nationalist satirist Henri Zislin. The monthly journal condemned the antinational nature of the autonomy movement, called for official action against first the Heimatbund and later the Landespartei and the Oppositionsbloc of Klaus Zorn von Bulach, and reveled in the scandals of the autonomist camp. For example, when Joseph Fashauer lost his position at the publishing house Erwinia due to the German provenance of certain funds, the journal cooed in delight. When it also became known that Fashauer, a priest, had conducted an affair with a young woman at the paper, the paper skewered both the priest and his lover, noting that the latter, "possessed of a German enthusiasm," had been "known to run around with German officers during the war."[51] *Das Bollwark* also denounced Ricklin's German military service (as a doctor) during the war as indicative of his loyalties. As time passed, the journal became increasingly caustic. One satirical cartoon, for example, depicted a giant Hindenburg in uniform, his arms draped around a Communist and a priest with the captions, "Onward, children of the fatherland."[52] *Das Bollwark* had limited press runs; the tenor that marked the paper, however, points to the increasingly hardened positions among not just the autonomists, but also within nationalist circles.[53]

At the same time that the UPR witnessed an evolution in its position and suffered the symptoms of an impending internal split, the autonomist camp also underwent numerous changes. In the eighteen months following the establishment of the Heimatbund, three new parties were born. One, the Oppositionsbloc of Klaus Zorn von Bulach, and its intermittently published journal, *Die Wahrheit (The Truth)*, which promoted the idea of wounded Alsatian rights and the need for a plebiscite, was based on sound and fury ultimately signifying nothing other than to earn the ire of the government as yet another source of troublemakers.[54]

More importantly, the Alsatian Radical Party, or more properly stated, its branch in Lower Alsace, experienced division within its ranks. Georges Wolf, along with Camille Dahlet, a Protestant from Zabern and friend of René Schickele, had slowly drifted from the party. Wolf wanted to push the party in a more regionalist direction, while Dahlet was an increasingly outspoken critic of the French government, especially on issues such as the commissions de triage, the seemingly privileged position of the Revenants, and infringements upon the cultural traditions of Alsatians. Both supported an expanded autonomy for Alsace within France. In contrast to the Heimatbund, neither initially supported the idea of an Alsatian minority (though Dahlet would later toy with the idea). Moreover, as Protestants and Liberals, neither placed a great emphasis on the religious question.⁵⁵ Breaking from the party, Wolf and Dahlet founded the Fortschrittliche Partei (Progressive Party) to promote their brand of regionalist politics in October 1926.

In April 1927, Wolf received financial banking for a party paper, the weekly *Das Neue Elsass* (*The New Alsace*). The newspaper, which never had press runs over ten thousand copies, served as the principal podium for Wolf's and Dahlet's arguments.⁵⁶ First, Wolf and Dahlet contended that Alsace's cultural heritage—including the German language—needed to be protected and preserved. Second, both wanted regional autonomy for Alsace with a local administration and local parliament. Taken in conjunction, these goals represented the continuation of two elements of Alsatian regionalism: the promotion of a particular Alsatian culture under the rubric of a dual culture, and the desire to reinstate the autonomy guaranteed the region in the Constitution of 1911. For Wolf especially, these goals were not at all separatist, but rather fit within a wide-ranging plan to reform the French state. Moreover, Wolf firmly believed in the Treaty of Locarno and he hoped that Alsace, with its unique cultural heritage and historical background could serve as bridge between France and Germany rather than as a casus belli.⁵⁷

Both the Progressive Party and its paper enjoyed mild success and influence in Lower Alsace. Dahlet would sit in Chamber of Deputies from 1928–1940 as a representative of the district around Zabern, a highly Protestant town. In addition, Dahlet would assume the party leadership in 1928; Georges Wolf, citing personal reasons, resigned in early 1928. Wolf wanted to return to his vocation as pastor, but also was discouraged by the crackdowns against the autonomist movement. In a letter to the head of the Lutheran Church in Strasbourg, he argued that he had only worked for regional rights for Alsace and not to "isolate Alsace from France."⁵⁸ In the wake of Wolf's departure, the Fortschrittspartei drifted in a more radical direction as Dahlet colluded with other, more separatist groups. Dahlet, however, never strayed into separatism as would the local Communists, the eventual successors to the Heimatbund, and other right-wing autonomist groups in the 1930s. Indeed, the Progressive Party eventually broke from the ever more radical line taken by the broader autonomist movement.⁵⁹

In September 1927, yet another regionalist party appeared, the Unabhängige Landespartei für Elsass-Lothringen (Independent Regional Party for Alsace-Lorraine) led by Paul Schall, Karl Roos, and René Hauss. They met at the Strasbourg restaurant L'Abbatoir with approximately three hundred in attendance. After praising the many fine qualities of the Alsatian people, Schall and Roos began to lay out a program that echoed many of the points of the Heimatbund. The party wanted greater guarantees for the German language including use of German in courts and the local administration, the maintenance of confessional schools, better economic protection, and local control over the railroads and civil service. In addition, the three speakers, especially Roos, went on the offensive, accusing France of breaking the promises of Joffre and other wartime leaders and arguing that France had only retaken Alsace and Lorraine "under the pretext of liberating them."[60]

This final point hints at the separatist notes creeping into the autonomist chords of the party. Far more than in the work of the Heimatbund, the leaders of the Landespartei, both in their inaugural meeting and in *Die Zukunft*, pushed for national minority status, the right of Alsatians to "self-determination," and the right of appeal to the League of Nations. The meeting ended with a shouting of the now familiar motto, "Alsace-Lorraine to the Alsatians-Lorrainers."[61]

The creation of the Landespartei represented the fulfillment of Schall's, Hauss's and Roos's desire to surpass the Heimatbund and actually create an autonomist party. Doing so may have been detrimental to their long-term aims. Both the regionalist wing of the UPR and Ricklin as head of the Heimatbund opposed the move as it might draw potential voters away from the regionalists in the UPR. Moreover, the Landespartei's aims seemed unrealistic and its support, mainly drawn from Upper Alsace, limited. Nonetheless, the Landespartei attracted the support of the *Die Zukunft*, which later ceased to be the main organ of the Heimatbund—a role that devolved to *Die Volksstimme* (*The Voice of the People*), which enjoyed the support of UPR-Heimatbund stalwarts Jean Keppi, Joseph Rossé, Joseph Fashauer, and Eugène Ricklin. *Die Zukunft*, in the meanwhile, ratcheted up its rhetoric, especially with regard to its claim to national minority status for Alsatians, as it adopted an agenda closer in spirit to the Landespartei.[62]

The creation of the Landespartei, and the increased stridency and vociferousness of the autonomist movement in general, prompted the French government to action. The government first banned the most radical of the papers—*Die Volksstimme*, *Die Wahrheit*, and *Die Zukunft*—in early November 1927. Using a law from 1895 concerning the control of the foreign-language press, the French government would later ban *Das Neue Elsass* and *Der Schliffstaan* as well. On a certain level, the government actions proved ephemeral as new autonomist papers such as *Die Volkswille* (*The Will of the People*) quickly sprang up as replacements.[63]

The government's action drew swift, if mixed, responses. The nationalist press firmly welcomed the measures and questioned why the bans had not come sooner.[64] Some papers hoped that the banning of these papers would "destroy anti-French propaganda."[65] The Radical German language paper *La République*, divested of the influence of Dahlet and Wolf, gave the action qualified support. The Catholic press worried that it too might become subject to government interference.[66] More nationalist papers such *Est Républicaine* in Lorraine called for the suppression of all German-language papers. Such a move, *La République* argued, would be detrimental to the

French cause in the region and did not obviate the need to deal with the problems plaguing relations between Alsace and France.[67]

Not surprisingly, the government's actions drew the ire of much of the local press. The *Elsässer* compared the ban to German plans to suppress French-language papers in 1913; the *Elsässer Kurier* went even further, arguing that such moves paralleled the old German Diktatur.[68] The Catholic press was joined in its protest by the *SNZ* of Charles Frey, who wanted some regionalist concessions. Frey thus criticized the government while condemning the papers in question. The *SNZ* also believed that the government's language-based legal justification was highly dubious given that most Alsatians spoke German. In addition, Frey raised concerns about the freedom of the press.[69] The opposition of Frey and the Catholic papers led several Catholic representatives, including Michel Walter and the national-wing leader Joseph Pfleger, Frey, and Lorrainer deputy Robert Schumann to submit a resolution in protest of the actions in the Chamber of Deputies. The resolution condemned the legal justification of the ban and not the desire to ban the papers per se.[70]

The controversy did not fade quietly. At a meeting of the UPR in November 1927, party members chided the autonomist press while echoing the concern about whether such measures were applicable to the broader German-language press. Several UPR leaders stressed their ability to combine loyalty to France with use of the German language. The party wanted guarantees and approved of the resolution of Pfleger, Walter, Frey, and Schumann. Some strains did show as Joseph Rossé and Xavier Haegy at times exchanged bitter words with their fellow UPR members. Nonetheless, the meeting came to a resolution, which read, in part:

> [The UPR] rejects the point of view of the government that holds that the law of 22 July 1895 concerning public, foreign-language journals in France is applicable to journals in the German language appearing in Alsace and Lorraine. The German language, which is the written language of the large majority of the population of Alsace and Lorraine, and is obligatorily taught in primary education, should not be considered as a foreign language in Alsace and Lorraine.[71]

The party simply wanted guarantees, long sought, for German in the region. French policy, however, left little opening for German-speaking loyal Frenchmen.

The controversy continued as Karl Hueber unleashed a tirade against the government action in the Chamber, protesting the "brutality with which the French treat the recovered provinces."[72] Moreover, Thomas Seltz, head of the UPR, sent a letter to Raymond Poincaré asking for clarification concerning the nature of the measures, especially their meaning for the German-language press of Alsace. Poincaré responded by arguing that the French government had respected the linguistic heritage of Alsace, most notably by allowing some German-language education, German-language religious education, and permission for bilingual correspondence in municipal administrations. The press ban, however, did not represent such a situation for Poincaré; instead he appealed to the need to protect the national interest, because a failure to act to defend "unity" and "indivisibility" would send the wrong messages to Germany.[73]

The conflict over the newspaper ban points to a larger clash in expectations between Alsatians and the French. As early as the Conférence d'Alsace-Lorraine and the wartime education practices of French-occupied Alsace, the government had generally supported an assimilationist line in the realm of language. Although many Alsatians had overtly or implicitly promoted the compatibility of French national loyalty and Alsatian particuliarism, French officials viewed the issue ambivalently. The fusion of language rights with the discourse of national minority rights, claims for self-determination, and demands for autonomy did not help the cause of the solidly pro-French, German-language proponents. The French government, however, had not finished trying to suppress the autonomist movement.

Local police had long kept close tabs on the activities of Alsatian parties; indeed, the pertinent files in Strasbourg and Paris would be far less illuminating if not for the reports of police (including one incident in which an inspector listened to an autonomist meeting while hidden in a restroom stall). In November 1927 the police led the charge, conducting a series of searches of homes and offices to find evidence of local connections to Germany.[74] On Christmas Eve, the French moved to quell the three main autonomist groups: the Heimatbund under Ricklin, the Oppositionbloc, and the Landespartei of Roos and Schall.[75] Twelve people were arrested and nearly a dozen more followed in the ensuing months. As with the newspaper bans, the nationalist press praised the arrests and the regionalist press decried the police actions.[76]

Before the trials of these autonomists even began, the effects of the government action could be felt. Xavier Haegy, the often outspoken head of the *Elsässer Kurier*, fearing arrest following fellow editor Joseph Rossé's imprisonment, assumed a more muted tone. In the city council of Hagenau, a motion to praise the actions of the government fell short, resulting in the dissolution of the council by the government, new elections, and a new strange alliance of the national wing of the UPR, Radicals, Socialists, and Royalists against the regionalist UPR candidates for seats on the council.[77]

The trials, which took place in May 1928, riveted the attention of the local press and brought Alsace into national focus. Ricklin, Rossé, Schall, Fashauer, Hauss, Marcel Stürmel, and ten others were tried for trying to foment a conspiracy against the government and trying to separate Alsace from France. While we know now that *Die Zukunft, Die Volksstimme,* and the publishing house Erwinia all received money from across the Rhine, and while the government had some evidence concerning these ties, the prosecution nonetheless faced an uphill battle. Not only was the government's proof weak, but the government lumped together too many disparate defendants, many of whom had promoted cultural or political autonomy, but not separatism. Indeed, with few exceptions, the government would find that its reach had exceeded its grasp.[78]

The trial itself lasted almost a month. In addition to several local lawyers, the defendants also enjoyed the services of lawyers from Corsica and Brittany and testimony from the French writer and supporter of Alsatian autonomy, Jean de Pange. The examination of the accused often lapsed into melodramatic accusation and denial; Police Inspector Bauer read over eighteen hours worth of newspaper articles to prove the connections between Germany and the autonomists. Yet even during the trial, the prosecutor Fachot had to admit that he had no proof of an actual conspiracy. In addition, Senator Eugène Muller, Deputy Médard Brogly, and Xavier Haegy (all of the UPR)—serving as witnesses for the defense—placed the autonomist movement in the historical context of traditional Alsatian particularism. A Communist deputy from Lorraine caused a stir by arguing that the Alsatians (and Lorrainers) were national minorities. And UPR deputy Michel Walter characterized the entire affair as a "national catastrophe."[79]

The verdict was announced in late May. Eleven of the defendants were acquitted; four—Joseph Fashauer, Joseph Rossé, Eugène Ricklin, and Paul Schall—were found guilty, sentenced to one year of prison, and forbidden from returning to Alsace for five years. In the wake of this verdict, the local police reported that the populace remained relatively calm. The press read the mixed decision according to its own predilections. The nationalist press praised the exposure of the true nature of the autonomist movement. The autonomists, in contrast, claimed victory in the numerous acquittals, condemned the convictions, and lambasted the actions of the government. Dahlet called the entire incident "another Zabern," painting the incident as another infringement of local rights. The Communists under Hueber renewed their demands for a plebiscite.[80] The trials, especially given the ambivalent outcome, did not harm the autonomist movement. As we shall see, both the acquitted and the condemned were viewed as heroes by autonomist forces. The publicity of the trials and a degree of public sympathy for the defendants provided the autonomists with a series of limited electoral victories.

Divided Parties and the Decline of the Autonomist Movement

The trial and conviction of some of the leading members of the autonomist movement brought the many grievances of Alsatians against the French state to the fore. Before the trial had even begun, the autonomist movement had secured a victory in the 1928 elections for the Chamber of Deputies. Using the limited success of the elections and the attention from the trial, the autonomist movement reached its height. The victories proved short lived, but their impact was felt across the region. Regional political parties, most notably the UPR, began to splinter. Division, however, also slowly beset the autonomist groups as their ideological differences and regionalist aspirations diverged.

In late April 1928, as the Colmar trial loomed heavily in the minds of Alsatians, elections for the Chamber of Deputies took place. The parties' various programs were not new and reflected the importance of regionalist concerns, much as the 1911 *Landtag* elections had been dominated by the future of Alsace. Even the local branch of the Socialist Party, one of the firmest supporters of assimilation, incorporated regionalist elements into its program by pushing more forcefully for bilingualism in official arenas (schools, courts, and public events) and French decentralization though not for autonomy. The party did not, however, give up hope for the secularization of Alsatian schools. The UPR, Communists, Progressive Party, and Landespartei all pushed for some degree of autonomy for the region. Given the similarity of the various autonomist programs, and given hints of collusion between the various autonomist groups, one nationalist paper fulminated on the eve of the election that the heavily regionalist parties wanted to confuse the public with the "mirage of autonomism" that veiled the fact the autonomists "obey the orders of Rome and Moscow."[81]

The forces of autonomy and regionalism won a limited success in the election. The UPR still took a majority of the sixteen deputies from Bas-Rhin and Haut-Rhin. Karl-Heinz Rothenberger has characterized thusly on the national and regional question; the election results included three assimilationists including Frey and Peirotes; two Catholic assimilationists including Pfleger of the UPR; eleven moderate *"Heimatrechtler"* (including Michel Walter, UPR); five radical regionalists including Dahlet, Rossé, and Ricklin (although both Rossé and Ricklin were in jail awaiting trial); the Communist Jean-Pierre Mourer, who displaced the Socialist candidate; and firm assimilationist Georges Weill. Rothenberger therefore has suggested the elections were a "protest vote." While there is some truth to this statement, this label must be qualified. First, as François Dreyfus has argued, although the electorate shifted toward the regionalists, the overall power distribution, with the UPR taking the majority of seats, remained relatively unchanged. Second, the radical and moderate camps of *Heimatrechtler* were not necessarily compatible. Third, Walter's placement in the moderate camp belies his willingness to create electoral alliances with the more radical camp. Finally, Rothenberger does not explore the losses of such autonomists such as René Hauss in Hagenau.[82]

The April elections boosted the morale and profile of the autonomist movement. The July pardon of Ricklin, Rossé, Hauss, and Fashauer only elevated the movement's sense of success.[83] Small crowds greeted the pardoned men upon their release, to the tune of the song "O, Strassburg."[84] A series of meetings at the end of the month featured Rossé, Ricklin, and Schall to promote the autonomist movement and to denounce their persecution by the French state. Over 2,500 greeted the leaders in Colmar, and over 6,000 people turned out to listen to a coterie of autonomist bigwigs in Strasbourg.[85] Although Ricklin used the meetings to thank his well-wishers and announce his withdrawal from public life for health reasons, the other autonomists took the moment to boost their cause. In Strasbourg, Dahlet of the Progressive Party, Rossé of the UPR, Schall, and Hauss all mounted the rostrum to decry the trials and argue for Alsatian rights. Mourer even argued in favor of the need for international aid from the League of Nations to secure Alsatian rights.[86] This show of autonomist unity pointed toward the growing cooperation of the various autonomist parties, which, as we shall see shortly, led to a more formal electoral alliance in the form of the Volksfront.[87]

If the autonomist parties gained a measure of unity from the elections and pardons, the same events strained the internal tensions of the UPR to the breaking point. In summer 1928, Eugène Muller, Michel Walter, and Xavier Haegy, following the party programs of 1919, 1925, and the project of 1926, pushed the party in a stricter regionalist direction. The regionalist wing was opposed to the various sanctions against Alsatians; moreover, some of its leaders such as Walter saw opportunities in an alliance of autonomist parties. A July 1928 meeting of the party served as a prelude to the party's division, as members of the national wing of the UPR lambasted fellow party members who had participated in the recent demonstrations after the release of Ricklin and Rossé. The controversy continued into the fall, when internal party dissension and alliances between the regionalist wing and autonomists influenced the outcome of the elections of the Conseils Généraux in both Alsatian departments.[88]

In a November UPR meeting, the national wing threw down the gauntlet by demanding the ejection from the party of Rossé and Walter for their ties with the autonomist movement. When the regionalist wing balked, the members of the nationalist wing set out to establish a new party. The Action Populaire Nationale d'Alsace (hereafter, APNA) was founded the same month. The new party had relatively few members, but counted among its ranks four of the six regional senators, three of the ten UPR deputies, and eighteen of the thirty-four members of the Conseil Général. To expand the party base, the APNA leaders began appealing to the local organizations of the UPR, thereby setting off an internecine fight for support within the UPR. With government subsidies the party also founded a new German-language daily paper, *Die Elsässer Bote* (The Alsatian Messenger), to promote a national, Catholic point of view. The *Bote* and the broader APNA saw themselves as regionalist *and* nationalist; they were defending Alsatian rights "with all energy" while rejecting the autonomists as "antinational." According to Bas-Rhin Prefect Borromée, by mid-1929 the

APNA had gained 3,000–4,000 adherents; the rump UPR, in contrast, had approximately 12,000–13,000 adherents.[89]

The division of the UPR allowed the remaining party leadership, all strong regionalists, to pursue electoral alliances with the other autonomist groups. A new coalition, the Volksfront, was formed by the UPR, Communists under Hueber, Progressives under Dahlet, and the Landespartei. The group's general aims comprised many of the goals of the Heimatbund including protection of the German language, administrative autonomy, and a greater promotion of the Alsatian economy. On ideological issues such as church-state relations, Volksfront members fudged by remaining largely silent. Another, more ominous set of differences lay beneath the surface of unity: the question of the ultimate aim of Alsatian regionalism and the relation of the region to the French and the German nations.[90]

The Volksfront enjoyed a modicum of temporary success in its first year along with several setbacks. Two elections in particular point to the temporary strength of the coalition. After the Chamber of Deputies refused to seat Rossé and Ricklin in light of their convictions, new by-elections were held. The Volksfront successfully ran strong autonomists, René Hauss and Marcel Stuermel, as their replacements. Yet the Volksfront success was not always guaranteed. APNA leader Joseph Pfleger defeated Xavier Haegy for an open senatorial seat in an October 1929 by-election; Pfleger's seat in the Chamber was then filled by the APNA.[91]

The municipal elections of 1929 marked the other major victory of the Volksfront. The Strasbourg elections, discussed in chapter 6, brought Karl Hueber to city hall by a narrow margin. The Volksfront also enjoyed success in the Colmar elections of the same year. The alliance had been built over several years, and the municipal elections represented the most open collaboration among the various autonomist parties.[92] The victory, however, belied other problems. Both Hueber and Michel Walter, named first deputy mayor, generated severe criticism for their unlikely alliance. The former faced formal exclusion from party branch that he had almost individually created; the latter, a Catholic, lost support in his own party.

The victories of the autonomist-Communist alliances in the municipal elections of 1929, taken in conjunction with their strong showing in the 1928 national elections, represented the electoral zenith of autonomist success. While the various groups that constituted the Volksfront had individual triumphs on par with those of 1928, the autonomist movement had entered a period of stagnation and slow fragmentation. By the mid-1930s, as Karl-Heinz Rothenberger and Samuel Goodfellow have shown, the autonomist movement had splintered into a number of increasingly radical groups and important members of the alliance had renounced cooperation with their fellow Alsatians.[93]

Central to the process of fragmentation was the increasing willingness of the Landespartei to adopt a more fascist language and show an appreciation for the growing power of the Nazi Party. Instead of focusing on the legitimate concerns of Alsatians within the French state, the party, and its new paper, *Die Elsass-Lothringische Zeitung*, frequently denounced parliamentary democracy, praised Hitler and Mussolini, and increasingly alienated local clergy with its pro-German bent. More ominously, splinter groups within the party began to form uniformed gangs similar to the SA in Germany and adopt anti-Semitic rhetoric. The external radicalization and internal divisions of the Landespartei slowly drove away key members of the Volksfront coalition.[94]

The UPR was the first to break away. The separatist tendencies of the Landespartei, combined with its adaptation of Nazi rhetoric's antireligious overtones, drove the Catholic party to dissolve its ties to the Volksfront. Such a move also allowed moderates within the party to try, albeit unsuccessfully, to bridge the gap between the UPR and the APNA, especially as Charles Didio tried to promote a "reasonable regionalism" acceptable to all within the Catholic parties. Moreover, personal disputes between UPR leader Michel Walter and Landespartei founders Paul Schall and Karl Roos further undermined the coalition, especially as the UPR as a whole assumed a critical stance toward developments in Germany.[95] The Progressive Party under Dahlet, also fearful of the growing menace across the Rhine and the radical line of the Landespartei, assumed an independent course in support of moderate autonomy in 1933.[96]

The final member of the alliance, the Communists under Hueber, did not so much drop out of the alliance as become irrelevant. Hueber's decision to align the party with the UPR alienated some of the local party faithful and caused a rupture between Alsatian Communists and the larger French Communist organization. In addition, the accusation that Hueber had accepted German money in support of the party finally led to a break between Hueber's supporters and more doctrinaire Communists in July 1929. Hueber managed to remain mayor of Strasbourg until 1935 when he lost to Charles Frey. The Communist autonomists as a whole moved steadily away from a Communist line, choosing to stay true to the autonomist element of their program. As the French Communist Party, Communist refugees from Germany, and local Communist loyalists took up the banner of anti-Fascism, these independent Communist autonomists, led by Hueber and Jean-Pierre Mourer, drifted ideologically to the right. In their stead, the Socialists, far more congenial to France, gradually regained lost ground among the Alsatian working classes.[97]

The dissolution of the Volksfront, however, was not only effected by internal differences. The increasing threat of Nazism, as we have seen, undermined its tenuous unity. In addition, the growing economic crisis in France focused attention away from the issue of regional autonomy. Of equal importance, the French government, beginning with the trial of Karl Roos in 1929,[98] had tried to adopt a more moderate attitude toward the demands of Alsatians. No autonomy was granted, the French centralized state was not reformed and decentralized, and German did not gain acceptance alongside French in the region. Nonetheless, the French administration relented in its efforts to push a hard and fast assimilation. Most importantly, the government ceased its attempts to secularize the region and took a more moderate stance on the issue of language. Under the prodding of Deputy Charles Frey, the government under Pierre Laval in the early 1930s allowed the limited use of German in the administration and in court. The prefects who had supported the suppression of the autonomist newspapers and the trials were replaced. President Gaston Doumerge pardoned those found guilty in the 1928 conspiracy trials, and thereby eroded the popularity of Rossé and his compatriots as "martyrs." Collectively, these measures helped attenuate the most egregious complaints of Alsatians against the French government.[99]

The autonomist movement, riven by ideological differences and the unwillingness of certain partners in the Volksfront to countenance a separatist regional line tinged with Nazi-like rhetoric, dissolved. Dahlet and UPR continued to push for a regional administration, but without the vigor of the earlier years as the outrage, social unrest, and deleterious French policies were subsumed to the economic turmoil of the Depression and looming threat of Nazi Germany. As Alsatian autonomist groups splintered in the thirties, and numerous right- and left-wing fringe parties sprang up, the vision of the Heimatbund, much like the earlier National Union, fell by the wayside.

Conclusion

In a similar vein to the National Union, the Heimatbund focused the attention of the entire Alsatian political and journalistic establishment on the issue of autonomy and regional rights. While, again like the National Union, the Heimatbund helped determine the framework of the debates over Alsace's future, it also introduced a higher degree of divisiveness than its prewar analogue. The alleged separatist threat hidden behind calls for national minority status and greater self-determination for the Alsatians, the suspicion of German intrigue, and the memory of French sacrifice, joined to French reprisals against Alsatian civil servants, pointed to a greater overall impact of the Heimatbund. The *Bund* not only ignited powerful responses, but also set in motion the slow convergence of an alliance of strong regionalist Catholics, autonomists, and Communists; the creation of a new autonomist party; and eventually a greater polarization of Alsatian society.

Even moderate success for the Heimatbund faced an uphill battle given the opposition within France not just to autonomy, but even to an attenuated regionalism. Alsatians such as Eugène Muller joined broader French organizations like the Fédération Régionalist to promote Alsatian interests within a broader context of French administrative reform.[100] Yet efforts to reform the French centralized state largely fell short; the creation of a number of economic regions was a far cry from the aspirations of regionalists from Brittany, Corsica, and Alsace. The governments under Herriot and Poincaré had little patience for regionalists' dreams of decentralization. As Robert Gildea has noted, it is perhaps ironic that the Alsatian demand for autonomy, and evocation of national minority status, precluded from the outset any hope of concessions.[101] The French government would not negotiate with apparent pawns of the German government.

The autonomist movement of the late 1920s, from the early days of *Die Zukunft* to the Heimatbund and beyond, was marked by four ghosts of the past. First, Alsatian autonomists had the promises of Joffre in mind for the protection of their rights. Second, the constitutional struggles of 1910–11 hung like a specter over the debates of the 1920s, reminding Alsatians of their former, if limited, regional autonomy. Third, the legacy of the dual culture, implicitly and explicitly employed by the autonomist movement, underlay many of the demands of the Alsatian autonomists. Finally, the legacy of the war and the peace marked the rhetoric and ferocity of the debates over the present and future status of Alsace. From the French nationalist perspective, the sacrifice of 1.4 million French soldiers and the ongoing perfidy of the *boche* meant that "self-determination" equaled "separatism." From the autonomist perspective, the appeal to self-determination and the authority of the League of Nations stood as a new tool in the fight for Alsatian rights.

Notes

1. AN F7/13396, Report dated 1 Aug. 1928 signed "Klein."
2. Samuel Goodfellow, *Between the Swastika and the Cross of Lorraine* (Dekalb, IL, 1999), 14–16.
3. Philip C. Bankwitz, *Alsatian Autonomist Leaders, 1919–1947* (Lawrence, KS, 1978), 4–5; Francois Dreyfus, *La vie politique en Alsace, 1919–1936* (Paris, 1969), 130–31; Jena M. Gaines, "The Spectrum of Alsatian Autonomism," PhD diss., University of Virginia, 1990, 296ff; David Allen Harvey, *Constructing Class and Identity in Alsace, 1830–1945* (Dekalb, IL, 2001), 156ff; Karl-Heinz Rothenberger, *Die elsass-lothringische Heimat- und Autonomiebewegung* (Frankfurt, 1975), 12–15, 132ff.
4. See also Gaines, "The Spectrum of Alsatian Autonomism," 182–90; Goodfellow, *Between the Swastika and the Cross*, 70–75; Rothenberger, *Die elsass-lothringische Heimat- und Autonomiebewegung*, 89–101.
5. AN F7/13881, Report on the UPR meeting of 29 November 1925 signed Sebille; AN F7/13392, Report on the UPR Congress of 17 May 1926; Baechler, *Le parti catholique alsacien*, 341–60.
6. AN F7/13881, Report on the UPR meeting of 29 November 1925 signed "Sebille." See also, Baechler, *Le parti catholique* alsacien, 341–60.
7. Baechler, *Le parti catholique* alsacien, 341–60.

8. Gaines, "The Spectrum of Alsatian Autonomism," 162–77. Wolf unsuccessfully tried the same feat in the following year.
9. *Die Zukunft* (9 May 1925).
10. Rothenberger, *Die elsass-lothringische Heimat- und Autonomiebewegung*, 103–6; see also AN F7/13382, Report of 25 May 1926. According to the police report of the meeting of the Heimatbund, the members of the *Bund* such as Ricklin went to great lengths to argue that their party was not separatist and wanted to work within France for their goals.
11. Baechler, *Le parti catholique* alsacien, 360–70; Dreyfus, *La vie politique en Alsace*, 100–103; Gaines, "The Spectrum of Alsatian Autonomism," 183–202; Rothenberger, *Die elsasslothringische Heimat- und Autonomiebewegung*, 103–6.
12. "Manifesto of the Heimatbund," 8 June 1926 in *Documents de l'Histoire*, 455.
13. Ibid.
14. Rothenberger, *Die elsass-lothringische Heimat- und Autonomiebewegung*, 103.
15. Georges Wolf, *Das Elsässische Problem: Grundzüge einer elsässische Politik im Zeitalter des Pakts von Locarno* (Leipzig, 1926), 133–35.
16. "Manifesto of the Heimatbund," 8 June 1926 in *Documents de l'Histoire*, 455.
17. Kolleen Guy, "Oiling the Wheels of Social Life: Myths of Marketing Champagne in the Belle Epoque," *French Historical Studies* 22, no. 2 (1999): 211–39; Caroline Ford, *Creating the Nation in Provincial France: Religion and Political Identity in Brittany* (Princeton, NJ, 1993), 3–8; Herman Lebovics, *True France: The Wars over Cultural Identity, 1900–1945* (Ithaca, NY, 1992), 142–49; Julian Wright, *The Regionalist Movement in France, 1890–1914: Jean-Charles Brun and French Political Thought* (Oxford, 2003), 165–98.
18. J.A. Jaeger, "Un manifeste autonomiste," *Journal de l'Est* (8 June 1926); "De quoi se plaignent-ils," *Journal d'Alsace et de Lorraine* (10 June 1926); "Échos de ce qui se passe en Alsace et en Lorraine," *La Revue d'Alsace et de Lorraine* (July 1926), 133–34.
19. Ricklin, for example, had served as a doctor in the German army and had taken an allegedly accomodationist attitude during the war. This picture ignored his regular opposition to German national designs in the region, such as in the funding of Hohkönigsburg.
20. "Les Variations de M. Georges Wolf," *France de l'Est* (29 June 1926); Anselm Laugel, "Le véritable danger des menées autonomistes," *La Revue d'Alsace et de Lorraine* (Aug. 1926).
21. Anselm Laugel, "Le véritable danger des menées autonomistes," *La Revue d'Alsace et de Lorraine* (Aug. 1926).
22. Anselm Laugel, "Un mot de réponse à la Zukunft," *Journal de l'Est* (20 June 1926).
23. Jules-Albert Jaegy, "Un manifeste autonomiste," *Journal de l'Est* (8 June 1926); "Utopie autonomiste," *Journal d'Alsace et de Lorraine* (8 June 1926).
24. "Manifest der elsässischen Sozialisten zur Heimatbewegung," *Freie Presse* (29 June 1926).
25. "Vom französischen Keppi zum elsass-lothringischen Stahlhelm," *Der Republikaner* (11 June 1926).
26. "Der Manifest der Heimattreuen," *Freie Presse* (8 June 1926); "Klerikale und Heimatbund," *Freie Presse* (24 June 1926); "Der neue Kurs im klerikalen Lager," *Freie Presse* (7 July 1926); "Ein erstes Wort zum Aufruf der Heimatsbündler," *Der Republikaner* (6 June 1926); "Die entlarvten Heimatsbündler," *Der Republikaner* (7 June 1926).
27. "Der elsass-lothringische Heimatbund," *Elsässer Kurier* (9 June 1926); "Allerhand Propagandamethoden," *Elsässer* (11 June 1926).
28. "Erklärung des Heimatbundes," *Elsässer Kurier* (1 July 1926).
29. Baechler, *Le parti catholique*, 371–80.
30. "Kurs geradeaus!," *La République* (6 June 1926).
31. "Der Heimatbund," *La République* (10 June 1926).
32. A long report, compiled by Police Inspector Bauer from numerous earlier reports that traced "anti-French activities" in Alsace, demonstrates the trend to connect Alsatian

autonomists from 1918 onward with Germany. *Die Zukunft* and later the autonomist paper *Die Volksbote* were believed to have ties to German funding. The report, written in early 1927, concluded that the latest wave of "autonomist agitators" wanted to separate Alsace from France despite their "statement to the contrary." See AN F7/13395, "La propagande anti-française en Alsace-Lorraine" (marked secret) dated 7 January 1927.

33. The accusation of German support—done both to keep German memories alive in Alsace and arguably for the purpose of disrupting the French domestically—has often been the subject of debate and has been used, by contemporaries and to a lesser degree by some historians, to question the popular support and legitimacy of the autonomist movement. Such accusations, however, are largely irrelevant. As Christian Baechler has pointed out, even if some autonomists received limited aid from German sources, this aid does not explain the rapid spread in popularity of *Die Zukunft*, nor does it mitigate the long-term strength of a powerful regionalist movement in the mid-late 1920s. This also parallels the situation before 1914 when pro-French groups had received support from France, thereby outraging German nationalists. See Baechler, *Le parti catholique*, 350–351.

34. According to Karl-Heinz Rothenberger, the breakdown of signatories was as follows: 57 people from Lower Alsace, 18 from Upper Alsace, 27 from Lorraine; professionally, there were 22 clergy (13 Catholics and 9 Protestants), 12 doctors, 4 journalists, 3 architects, 3 pharmacists, 2 writers, 1 lawyer, 10 merchants, 9 railroad employees, 6 salaried employees, 5 agricultural laborers, 4 workers, 2 civil servants, and 14 unknown. See Rothenberger, *Die elsass-lothringische Heimat- und Autonomiebewegung*, 110.

35. "Les sanctions contre les signataires du manifeste du Heimatbund," *Journal d'Alsace et de Lorraine* (29 July 1926); "Le Cabinet Poincaré et l'Alsace-Lorraine," *Journal d'Alsace et de Lorraine* (1 Aug. 1926). See also Dreyfus, *La vie politique en Alsace*, 102–5; Gaines, "The Spectrum of Alsatian Autonomism," 199–202; Rothenberger, *Die elsass-lothringische Heimat- und Autonomiebewegung*, 111–18.

36. "La France a le devoir de se défendre," *Journal d'Alsace et de Lorraine* (3 Aug. 1926); "La Condamnation de l'autonomisme," *Journal d'Alsace et de Lorraine* (6 Aug. 1926); "La projet de loi contre les menées anti-français et l'Alsace-Lorraine," *Journal d'Alsace et de Lorraine* (8 Aug. 1926); "La propagande séparatiste en progression," *Journal d'Alsace et de Lorraine* (22 Aug. 1926); "Que fait-on contre les agents de l'Allemagne en Alsace et en Lorraine," *Journal d'Alsace et de Lorraine* (21 July 1926).

37. ADBR AL 98–671, Letter from UNC-Wissembourg to the Prefect of Bas-Rhin dated 15 June 1926; ADBR AL 98–671, Letter from UNC-Metz to the Prefect of Bas-Rhin dated 29 June 1926.

38. Goodfellow, *Between the Swastika and the Cross*, 43–50.

39. "Un défaite autonomiste à Colmar," *Journal d'Alsace et de Lorraine* (23 August 1926).

40. *Der Republikaner* (23 Aug. 1926); *La République* (23 Aug. 1926); *SNZ* (23 Aug. 1926).

41. *Mülhäuser Volksblatt* (24 Aug. 1926).

42. "Ein blütiger Sonntag in Colmar," *Elsässer Kurier* (23 Aug. 1926).

43. "Der Kampf um unsere Heimatrechte," *Elsässer* (24 Aug. 1926).

44. "Offener Brief des Herrn Ricklin an den Präfekten des Ober-Elsass," *Die Zukunft* (28 August 1926).

45. "Der Knüppel regiert im befreiten Elsass-Lothringen," *Die Zukunft* (28 August 1926).

46. Quoted in François Roth, *Raymond Poincaré. Un homme d'état républicain* (Paris, 2000), 507.

47. Roth, *Raymond Poincaré*, 507–9. See also Baechler, *Le parti catholique*, 385.

48. Baechler, *Le parti catholique*, 382–83.

49. Ibid., 383–86.

50. Lorentz, *La presse alsacienne du XXe siècle* (Strasbourg, 1997), 111, 114, 120; Baechler, *Le parti catholique*, 371ff.

51. "Der Skandal des Heimatbundes," *S' Elsass* (March 1927).

52. *S' Bollwark* (Apr. 1928).
53. "Contre l'autonomisme," *S' Bollwark* (Jan. 1927); "Der Assimilation entgegen," *S' Bollwark* (Jan. 1927); "Contre l'autonomisme camouflé," (Feb 1927); "Heimatbund ist Hochverrat," *S' Bollwark* (May 1927); "Die grosse Lüge," *S' Bollwark* (Nov. 1927); "Kommunisten und Autonomisten sind unsere wirklichen Feinde," *S' Bollwark* (April 1928).
54. Rothenberger, *Die elsass-lothringische Heimat- und Autonomiebewegung*, 127–28.
55. Dreyfus, *La vie politique en Alsace*, 107–10; Gaines, "The Spectrum of Alsatian Autonomism," 165–78.
56. Dahlet had long been critical of the commissions, Revenants, and the general French treatment of Alsatians. As a consequence, Dahlet would argue that Alsatians have a "feeling for the Heimat" [*Heimatsgefühl*] but not for the *patrie*. The latter was dependent upon better treatment of Alsatians. Dahlet therefore did not see the pejorative term "conditional French," often applied to seemingly pro-French regionalists such as the left-wing of the UPR, as a negative but rather as a reflection of the state of affairs in Alsace. See "Die Bedingungsfranzösen," *Das Neue Elsass* (28 Jan. 1928).
57. Georges Wolf, "Dem Neuen Elsass zum Geleit," *Das Neue Elsass* (14 Apr. 1928); "Die Partei Spricht," *Das Neue Elsass* (14 Apr. 1927); Georges Wolf, "Elsässischer und französischer Regionalismus," (7 July 1927); "Mundart und Schriftsprache," *Das Neue Elsass* (8 Sept. 1927); Georges Wolf, "Zweisprachigkeit und Doppelkultur," *Das Neue Elsass* (29 Sept. 1927); Camille Dahlet, "Einheitsstaat und Dezentralization," *Das Neue Elsass* (22 Dec. 1927).
58. AN F7/13391, Report signed Bauer. AN F7/13387, Report dated 4 Feb. 1928 signed Bauer.
59. Rothenberger, *Die elsass-lothringische Heimat- und Autonomiebewegung*, 210–20.
60. AN F7/13395, Report dated 25 Nov. 1927 signed "Bauer." See also Rothenberger, *Die elsass-lothringische Heimat- und Autonomiebewegung*, 133–36. Rothenberger argues that the party was not necessarily separatist, it really wanted a wide-ranging autonomy and seemed willing to accept such within France. One must agree with other historians such as Samuel Goodfellow on this point: the Landespartei had already shifted from autonomism to a soft separatism, a position that would slowly grow more radical over the ensuing years.
61. AN F7/13395, Report dated 25 Nov. 1927 signed "Bauer." See also Rothenberger, *Die elsass-lothringische Heimat- und Autonomiebewegung*, 133–36.
62. Lorentz, *La presse alsacienne*, 438–40; Rothenberger, *Die elsass-lothringische Heimat- und Autonomiebewegung*, 133–37.
63. Baechler, *Le parti catholique*, 390–95; Dreyfus, *La vie politique en Alsace*, 117–33; Gaines, "The Spectrum of Alsatian Autonomism," 215ff; Rothenberger, *Die elsass-lothringische Heimat- und Autonomiebewegung*, 137–40.
64. Although the SNZ had highly ambivalent feelings toward the legal justification of the move, its article of 14 November provides a helpful overview of the press reactions to the government action. "Das Verbot der autonomistischen Zeitungen," *SNZ* (14 Nov. 1927).
65. *S' Elsass* (17 Nov. 1927).
66. *Journal de l'Est* (15 Nov. 1927); *Journal de l'Est* (17 Nov. 1927); *Journal de l'Est* (22 Nov. 1927); *Strassburger Neueste Nachrichten* (14 Nov. 1927).
67. "Die Regierungsmassnahmen gegen die Autonomistenpresse," *La République* (15 Nov. 1927); "Der 'Est Républicain' gegen die deutschsprachige Presse von Elsass und Lothringen," *La République* (19 Nov. 1927).
68. "Verbot der autonomistischen Presse," *Elsässer* (14 Nov. 1927); *Elsässer Kurier* (13 Nov. 1927).
69. "Das Verbot der autonomistischen Zeitungen," *SNZ* (15 Nov. 1927).
70. "Zum Antrag Schumann, Frey, Pfleger, Walter," *SNZ* (22 Nov. 1927); See also Rothenberger, *Die elsass-lothringische Heimat- und Autonomiebewegung*, 136–38.
71. AN F7/13386, Report dated 24 November 1927 signed "Bauer."

72. Rothenberger, *Die elsass-lothringische Heimat- und Autonomiebewegung*, 136–38.
73. "M. Poincaré répond à M. Seltz," *Le Journal d'Alsace et de Lorraine* (2 Dec. 1927).
74. Rothenberger, *Die elsass-lothringische Heimat- und Autonomiebewegung*, 137–38.
75. AN F7/13386, Memo dated 25 December 1927 signed "Bauer"; See also Rothenberger, *Die elsass-lothringische Heimat- und Autonomiebewegung*, 136–40.
76. "Die Haussuchungen bei den Autonomisten," *Strassburger Neueste Nachrichten* (27 Dec. 1927); "Die separatistische Bewegung," *Strassburger Neueste Nachrichten* (31 Dec. 1927); "Le petit Noël des autonomistes," *Journal d'Alsace et de Lorraine* (27 December 1927); *Journal d'Alsace et de Lorraine* (31 December 1927); "Die polizeilichen Untersuchungen bei den Autonomisten," (27 Dec. 1927); "Nach der Verhaftung Dr. Ricklin's," *Elsässer Kurier* (12 Mar. 1928); Camille Dahlet, "Die Zwangsjacke," *Das Neue Elsass* (21 Jan. 1928); Camille Dahlet, "Diktaturwahlen," *Das Neue Elsass* (28 Jan. 1928); Camille Dahlet, "Das alte Leid," *Das Neue Elsass* (7 July 1928).
77. Baechler, *Le parti catholique*, 387–404; Rothenberger, *Die elsass-lothringische Heimat- und Autonomiebewegung*, 154–59.
78. Baechler, *Le parti catholique*, 404–406; Bankwitz, *Alsatian Autonomist Leaders*, 23–28.
79. "Der Komplott Prozess von Colmar von 1.-24. Mai 1928: gesammelte Verhandlungsberichte (Colmar, 1928); Rothenberger, *Die elsass-lothringische Heimat- und Autonomiebewegung*, 161–65.
80. AN F7/13397, Rapport sur l'opinion publique après le procès de Colmar (Mulhouse) dated 25 May 1928; AN F7/13397, Rapport sur l'opinion publique après le procès de Colmar (Seléstat) dated 26 May 1928.
81. Dreyfus, *La vie politique en Alsace*, 117–25.
82. Ibid., 117–30; Rothenberger, *Die elsass-lothringische Heimat- und Autonomiebewegung*, 155–58.
83. AN F7/13397, Letter to the Ministry of the Interior dated 28 May 1928.
84. AN F7/13397, Rapport sur l'opinion publique après le procès de Colmar (Ricklin) dated 24 July 1928; Rapport sur l'opinion publique après le procès de Colmar (Fashauer, Rossé, Schall).
85. AN F7/13396, Report dated 27 July 1928 signed "Klein."
86. AN F7/13395, Report dated 1 Aug. 1928 signed "Klein."
87. AN F7/13395, Report dated 16 Sept. 1928 signed "Bauer."
88. Baechler, *Le parti Catholique*, 407–21.
89. Ibid.
90. Ibid., 415–42; Gaines, "The Spectrum of Alsatian Autonomism," 256–85; Rothenberger, *Die elsass-lothringische Heimat- und Autonomiebewegung*, 177–84.
91. Ibid.
92. AN F7/13392, Report dated 27 Sept. 1927 signed "Bauer."
93. Goodfellow, *Between the Swastika and the Cross*, 110–49; Rothenberger, *Die elsass-lothringische Heimat- und Autonomiebewegung*, 199–213.
94. Bankwitz, *Alsatian Autonomist Leaders*, 28–29; Goodfellow, *Between the Swastika and the Cross*, 108–15.
95. Baechler, *Le parti Catholique*, 442ff.
96. Dreyfus, *La vie politique en Alsace*, 176–79.
97. Goodfellow, *Between the Swastika and the Cross*, 75–86.
98. Karl Roos had fled to Switzerland ahead of the police during their sweep of autonomists in late 1927–early 1928 and only came to trial in 1929.
99. Dreyfus, *La vie politique en Alsace*, 167–70; Harvey, *Constructing Class*, 164ff; Rothenberger, *Die elsass-lothringische Heimat- und Autonomiebewegung*, 190–210.
100. AMS 26 NA II.24.C/4 and AMS 26 NA II.25.A/2
101. Robert Gildea, *The Past in French History*, (New Haven, CT, 1994), 196–198.

Conclusion

Visions and Divisions

Today, Alsace stands at one of the key seams of the European Union, the crossroads between France and Germany. The European Parliament sits on the edge of Strasbourg. The departments that comprise Alsace work with the neighboring German *Länder* to integrate labor markets, promote cultural bonds, build linked infrastructure, and even underwrite "people to people" projects, often supported by the European Union.[1] Workers shuttle both ways across the border to work each day; the transportation network for Strasbourg stretches across the Rhine into neighboring Kehl. Hartmannwillerskopf's monument has taken a more inclusive approach commemorating the fallen from both countries' armies. Meanwhile, German tourists flock to Strasbourg to visit the cathedrals, to Colmar to see typical Alsatian architecture, and along the *route du vin* to sample the region's finest wares. And many happily purchase souvenirs, including Hansi's postcards depicting picturesque Alsatian scenes.

This changed place of Alsace—no longer the object of Franco-German contention—reflects a number of shifts on the broader European level. Most notably, the growth of the European Community and later the European Union, with Franco-German cooperation their heart, helped obviate such longstanding disputes. Indeed, Alsace has moved beyond its status as a prize of geopolitical struggle to one of the symbols of the new Europe. Alsatians no longer have to choose between two competing national cultures, but can partake in both.

Viewed more broadly, Alsace, as with many other border regions, has seen its position in Europe transform from an object of contestation to a bridge between neighboring countries. Alsace, paralleling other border areas in western Europe, has sought cross-border cooperation economically, culturally, and (to a lesser extent) politically.[2] If frontier regions such as Alsace, the Saar, and South Tyrol marked the fractured lines of national contestation in an older Europe, slowly they have come to represent the promise of a newer Europe.

Notes for this section begin on page 212.

The ability of Alsace and other border regions to stand as bridges rather than barriers, however, has not always come easily or without cost. For example, after World War II, it took over four decades for the South Tyrolean question to be resolved, and then only after the issue came before the UN, and more sadly (albeit briefly), the area was subjected to sporadic terrorism.[3] Alsace may serve as a bridge, but much of its regional culture—so celebrated by the diverse parties studied here—is a faint palimpsest of its former self, changed by French policy, a postwar aversion to German culture, changing demographics in the region, and broader changes in cultural tastes. Alsatian regionalism has found occasional voice in cultural revival— an Alsatian theater still exists in Strasbourg—as well as in the environmental movement, but more often finds its expression in the restaurants and shops catering to tourists.[4] Thus, there is an irony that now that Alsace and other border regions no longer need to hide or contest their identities, those self-same identities are less poised to take advantage of the new situation.

In contrast, the old modes of cross-border contestation actually served to encourage Alsatian regionalism. As local politicians, intellectuals, businessmen, and clergy sought to come to terms not simply with the demands of French or German nationalism, but mass political parties, industrialization, and increasing secularization, they employed regionalism as framework through which to negotiate their place within Germany and later France. Thus, regionalism served the Alsatians as a political language, as a cultural vision, and as a central community of identity. An incipient identity had existed in Alsace before German annexation, and a sense of Alsatian uniqueness continued far into the post-1945 period, highlighted by the trial of Alsatian conscripts for their actions at Oradour-sur-Glane.[5] German annexation, German policies, the Great War, French reannexation, and French policies all helped spur Alsatian regionalism on toward becoming a strong movement. Internal divisions over national loyalty, religion, political ideology, and the very meaning of Alsatianness splintered this movement into a variety of competing regionalisms.

From the Volkspartei of Daniel Blumenthal to the autonomist Landespartei of Karl Roos and Paul Schall, the rallying cry of "Alsace to the Alsatians" rang out. In part, this motto reflected a protest against German, then French policies. But Alsatian regionalism was not simply a movement against the nationalist, assimilationist policies of the German and French nation-states. It was also a positive assertion of Alsatian cultural uniqueness, the region's economic development, and improved political rights for the Alsatian populace. Alsatians across the regionalist spectrum and throughout the region's changing political status argued in favor of preserving the unique heritage of the region. Some agreement on how Alsace should be envisioned existed. Yet the multiple, often subtle contrasts of regional visions gave rise to regionalist divisions.

Several factors contributed to the multifaceted nature of Alsatian regionalism. Divergent responses to German, then French demands for conformity to the nation-state imparted upon Alsatian regionalism a Janus-like quality. Alsatian German nationalists such as Friedrich Lienhard, or arguably later Germanophiles such as Paul Schall and Karl Roos, represented a small minority. Conversely, French nationalists such as Hansi, Emile Wetterlé, or Joseph Pfleger also advocated a minority point of view. They benefited, in the backward glance of history, from promoting and conforming to a French nationalist vision of Alsace. French victory in 1918 seemed to confirm their perspective. A red thread tied Francophile Alsatian resistance to harsh German rule and France's triumph in World War I to a heroic narrative of French/Alsatian ultimate ascendance over Germany and vengeance for the German misdeeds of 1871 and 1914–1918. But to many Alsatians, they—as much as their land—stood between the two nations, attracted yet repulsed by both, secure perhaps only in their unique, if seemingly tragic position as a borderland.

Ideologies other than nationalism, however, also splintered Alsatian regionalism. The Alsatian Left divided over tactics and goals in the 1920s as a nascent Communist Party quickly grew to challenge the Socialist Party. Religion, moreover, ran as a chasm between Alsatian parties. Parties of the Left, such as the Social Democrats and the Liberals before 1914, and the Socialists, Parti Radical indépendante, and Radical-Socialists after 1918, squared off against the Center/UPR over the issue of religion. At no point was this divide clearer than during the constitutional and election debates of 1910–11. The parties contended over issues of electoral procedure while jockeying for political power. However, the desire for the parties of the Left to diminish the preponderant power of the Catholic party and to secularize Alsatian society represented a real, often unbridgeable divide. The rhetorical warfare surrounding this ongoing *Kulturkampf* helped undermine both the National Union and Heimatbund and was evident in the bitter exchanges between the Socialist and Catholic press.

Religion may have divided Alsatian parties, but it also fueled Alsatian ambitions. The continually dominant position of the Catholic party, whether in its Center or UPR incarnation, points not just to the prominent social and political role of the clergy in Alsace, especially in the wake of the departure of many French secular leaders in the 1870s, but also to the enduring importance of religion among the Alsatian populace. The ability of Catholic leaders to rally their supporters around the nexus of region/religion also underscores the importance of overlapping identities. The firestorm of protest following the Herriot speech of June 1924 announcing the government's intention to introduce the *lois laïques* into Alsace demonstrates this fact. Although concerns over other issues also fostered Alsatian discontent, and later French reprisals caused more trouble than not, the issue of religion and the position of the Catholic parties (even after the UPR/APNA split) determined the relative strength of the regionalist movement. Religious and regional identities overlapped.

Despite such nationalist and ideological splits, Alsatians often shared a common vision of the region even if the various factions failed or refused to admit that fact. Nowhere were the commonalities and continuities as well as the Janus-faced character of Alsatian regionalism clearer than in the formation of the National Union and the Heimatbund. Despite the pro-French leanings of the former and the autonomist (and potentially separatist) leanings of the latter, both had similar ambitions. Both wanted to unify Alsatian parties to defend Alsatian interests; both wanted to maintain Alsace's unique cultural blend; both desired greater autonomy for Alsace; and both placed themselves in opposition to the national government. Both, furthermore, failed on two counts: through their inability to bridge differences between the Center/UPR and other parties, and their ineffectiveness in drawing a larger Alsatian populace into their specific iterations of Alsatianness. Finally, both groups shared massive influence disproportionate to their political success; each framed the regionalist debates in 1910–1913 and 1926–1929 respectively.

Underlying the political plans and cultural visions of both groups was the idea of an Alsatian double culture. The idea of a Franco-German blend forming a unique regional culture influenced the National Union, the Heimatbund, and many of the political and cultural organizations throughout the period. Disagreements reflecting varying regional and national loyalties weighted French versus German influences differently from group to group. But the debates of the decades before 1914 and those of the 1920s point to the idea as a common, if contested, battleground among Alsatian regionalists. The cultural visions of Alsace pushed into politics, indirectly through the process of commemoration and directly in the aims of the various political parties. Herein lie the intertwined and inextricable links of culture and politics within the realm of Alsatian regionalism.

A subvariant of the dual-culture conception of Alsatian regionalism might be termed the "Stoskopf ideal," which, while acknowledging the tensions and mutual influences of French and German culture on the region, framed the issue as one between Alsace/Germany and later Alsace/France. Stoskopf and like-minded individuals did not see an automatic antipode between the Alsatian and the respective national cultures; rather, they understood them as complements. Proponents of Alsatian culture in this vein before and after World War I worried about regional customs, traditions, and dialect. While wanting a regime that would preserve and foster Alsatian uniqueness, such cultural regionalists also wanted equality for the Reichsland before 1914 and integration into France after 1918. Such a moderate position, moreover, foresaw a potentially complementary relationship between region and nation.

The moderate position, especially in this dyad of region-nation, raises the larger question about the broader nature of regionalism. Do regions serve to integrate the local populace into the nation, as in the case of the Palatinate or Württemberg, by making the local national? Or do regions serve to inhibit national integration? Alsace proves both cases or neither, depending on one's perspective and which groups one chooses to investigate. Before 1914, Germans clearly hoped that Alsatian regionalism would undermine loyalties to France and eventually bring Alsatians into the national fold. Francophile regionalists fought a valiant and vigorous rhetorical battle to inhibit this process, while some Alsatian regionalists moved toward integration, often obstructed by German nationalist blundering. After 1918, some Alsatians wanted regionalism within France: others wanted autonomy, even if they had to claim Alsatians as a national minority and appeal to the League of Nations. Divided national loyalties gave Alsatian regionalism both an integrating and resistant nature, thereby undermining Alsatian attempts to preserve their own culture and protect the regional economic and political situation. The multifaceted nature of Alsatian regionalism also confused, vexed, and stymied German then French officials.

The complex relations between Alsace and Germany, then France, point to the many ironies of the Alsatian situation. If Alsatians had distrusted Germany in 1871 and misunderstood the meaning of 1918, then German and French nationalists were united in their failure to comprehend Alsatian prerogatives. Both German and French officials viewed Alsatians as easily convertible or as loyal members of their respective national communities. The Alsatians proved both the Germans and French, in the main, wrong. Alsatians were not simply Germans by language and custom who had had the misfortune of falling prey to the dynastic ambitions of the Bourbon dynasty. Conversely, although some Alsatians had protested and resisted German rule, and celebrated the war's end with relief, they were not prepared to become part of the unified, secularized *mère-patrie* of 1918. Such mutual misperceptions created an atmosphere for conflict. The ironic similarity of German and French governance—linguistic assimilation, religious restrictions, administrative and nationalist arrogance, vacillation between repression of and liberty for Alsatian regionalism, and a simple inability to decide whether Alsatian particularism was good or bad—forms a continuity in the history of Alsace as well.

German-Alsatian and French-Alsatian conflict, however, springs out of yet another irony, one that returns us to the issue of the integrative power of regionalism. Both before and after the First World War, the respective German and French governments could have used Alsatian regionalism to win over the local populace, but foundered on their own conceptions of the nation. German nationalists could not concede that Alsatians culture be interwoven with the culture and language of the *Erbfeind* France, and therefore would not accord Alsatians an equal place within the German nation-state. French nationalists, at least those in power for most of the 1920s such as Herriot and Poincaré, found themselves in a double-bind. Many Alsatians wanted to be French, but also German-speaking, intensely Catholic, and with a regional administration. This offended not only the form of the nation-state, secular France "one and indivisible," but also, as Laird Boswell has suggested, the ethnic definition of France, French-speaking and without those of German blood. Alsatians were prized yet mistrusted objects of German and French national designs.[6]

No event radicalized the clash of Alsatian regionalism with German, then French, nationalism like the First World War. German martial law was not impelled solely by military considerations for securing a borderland, but also by the deep distrust of German officers for the political loyalty of the Alsatian populace. Franco-Alsatian culture had to be stamped out. For French nationalists, the influence of the Great War was both subtle and direct. The long decades of French propaganda that had portrayed Alsace as a lost French province—a view strengthened by the works of Hansi, efforts of Emile Wetterlé, and outcry over the Zabern Affair—in combination with the celebrations of November 1918, led French officials to believe they had regained a loyal province. The growth of Alsatian discontent, punctuated by an autonomist movement that claimed national minority status, brought the legacy of the war to full bloom. France had sacrificed over 1.4 million men in the long and bitter struggle to the Germans; Alsatians who did not understand France's sacrifice were ungrateful, antinational, and most likely German agents. The war, then, left Alsatians more aware of their unique position, gave some Alsatians a new means of protesting their fate, and hardened French attitudes toward the particular difficulties of the Alsatian situation.

Alsatian regionalism had a powerful allure, if varying success, in providing Alsatians with a means of protest, a sense of agency, and a form of community against the tides of fortune as a border region between two great powers. Both Germany and France tried to impose their own vision of the nation upon Alsace. Yet Germany, with its federalized conception of the nation-state, could not countenance the French heritage of Alsace and thus denied the Alsatians full membership in the German nation. The French, in contrast, wished to include Alsace in a centralized French Third Republic. Yet the Alsatian desire to have a regional administration and to speak German flew in the face of the prevailing notion of nationhood. Alsatians wanted to be French, but not on terms acceptable to the French.

Alsatian regionalism was tinged with numerous ironies: the similarities of French and German administrative policies and mistakes, the continuities of regionalist demands despite divergent motives, as well as the repeated failures to find unity in division because of an unresolved *Kulturkampf* and split national loyalties. Perhaps the greatest irony, however, was the inability of Alsatians to reconcile their dual culture with either the German or French nation-state despite their desire to so. For many Alsatians, "Alsace to the Alsatians" could also mean "Alsace within Germany" or "Alsace within France." France, however, saw the German face of the Alsatian Janus, Germans the French. The fractured vision of "Alsace to the Alsatians" ironically only furthered Alsace's divided destiny.

Notes

1. "Regional Policy: INTERREG III A—Saarland-Moselle/Lorraine-Western Palatinate," http://ec.europa.eu/regional_policy/country/prordn/details.cfm?gv_OBJ=ALL&gv_PAY=FR&gv_reg=ALL&gv_THE=ALL&gv_PGM=2000RG160PC011&LAN=5#zone (Accessed 25 August 2006).
2. Stefan Wolff, *Disputed Territories: The Transnational Dynamics of Ethnic Conflict Settlement* (New York, 2003), 1–33.
3. Antony E. Alcock, *The History of the South Tyrol Question* (London, 1970); Wolff, *Disputed Territories*, 115–49.
4. Michael Essig, *Das Elsass auf der Suche nach seiner Identität* (München, 1994), 166–218; Wolff, *Disputed Territories*, 68–77.
5. Sarah Farmer, *Martyred Village: Commemorating the 1944 Massacre at Oradour-sur-Glane*, (Berkeley, CA, 1999), 135–70.
6. Laird Boswell, "From Liberation to Purge Trials in the "Mythic Provinces": Recasting French Identities in Alsace and Lorraine, 1918–1920," *French Historical Studies* 23, no. 1 (2000): 159–61.

BIBLIOGRAPHY

Archival Sources

Archives Départementales du Bas-Rhin

Abteilung des Innern

AL 22–23/1
    22–23/2
    22–32
    22–40
    22–59
    22–75
    22–77/ Vol. 1–4
    22–79
    22–80
    22–84
    22–99
    29–9
    30–131
    30–66
    47–29/1
    47–29/2
    47–46/1
    47–88
    69–436
    69–463 (139)
    71–21

Bureau des Statthalters

AL 27–180
    27–371
    27–665
    27–840a-g

Landtag

AL 39–443
   39–464
   39–468
   39–470

Statthalter

AL 87–879
   87–5372
   87–5602

Fonds Valot

AL 98–250
   98–634
   98–639
   98–641
   98–661
   98–671
   98–691
   98–700
   98–1089
   98–1090
   98–1091

AL 121 Fonds du Commissariat Général

AL 121–9
   121–34/74
   121–74/89
   121–98
   121–99
   121–102
   121–111
   121–184
   121–185
   121–186
   121–187
   121–188
   121–189
   121–326
   121–359
   121–363/64
   121–579
   121–584
   121–675
   121–891

Polizeipraesidium Strassburg

AL 116–123
    116–124
    116–154
    116–228

Presse

AL 132–17
    132–18
    132–21
    132–25

Series D (Bezirkspräsident/Prefecture)

D 247–23 (b)
   286–308
   388–677
   700–130
   700–131

W 1146 Direction Régional des Affaires culturelles d'Alsace

Devis, pieces comptables et registres de visiteurs concernat le château du HK
W   1146–23
    1146–24
    1146–25

Collection Heitz

J   38–481
   38–486

Archives Départementales du Haut-Rhin

Collection Heitz

2 J 198
2 J 204

Papiers de Paul Albert Helmer

2 J 208–235

Collection Waltz

9 J 79–99

Papiers Wetterlé

27 J 1–13

Papiers Pfleger

27 J 14–17

Fonds Haeggni

40 J 1–7

Sous-prefectures (1870–1918)

Kreis Colmar

3 AL 1/833
3 AL 1/834
3 AL 1/3541
3 AL 1/3557
3 AL 1/3457
3 AL 1/1554
3 AL 1/1556
3 AL 1/1557

Kreis Guebwiller

4 AL 1/1
4 AL 1/3
4 AL 1/4
4 AL 1/5–8

Bezirkspräsidium (1870–1918)

8 AL 1/199–247
8 AL 1/436
8 AL 1/9408
8 AL 1/9409
8 AL 1/9410
8 AL 1/9508

World War I

AJ 30/40–1 (Purg. 11699)
AJ 30/40–2 (Purg. 11699)
AJ 30/41–1 (Purg. 11700)
AJ 30/53 (Purg. 11713)
AJ 30/58 (Purg. 11728)
AJ 30/74 (Purg. 11734)
AJ 30/75 (Purg. 11735)
AJ 30/77 (Purg. 11737)
AJ 30/84 (Purg. 11744)

AJ 30/85 (Purg. 11745)
AJ 30/88 (Purg. 11748)

Prefecture 1918–1940

Purg. 200157
Purg. 200158
Purg. 200159
Purg. 200160

Archives du Musée alsacien

The files of the Musée are organized into several boxes containing press clips, programs, and other correspondence from the years before 1914. I thank once again Madame Malou Schneider, head curator of the Musée, for her permission to access these files.

Bilder aus dem elsässischen Museum

Archives Municipales de Strasbourg (AMS)

Événements Historiques (1789–1919)

16–53
19–65
19–66
19–67
19–68
20–72
21–74

Cérémonies, Salles, Expositions, Fêtes

22/169
23/178
23/179
24/180
24/181
24/183

Musées Municipaux

D IV 320/1763
D IV 326/1799
D IV 326/ 1800 4/99
D IV 326/1801
D IV 326/1802 4/99

D IV 327/1804 23/104
D IV 327/1805 2/99
D IV 327/1806 6/99
D IV 327/1807 8/108
D IV 328/1808
D IV 328/1809
D IV 328/1810 7/105
D IV 328/1811
D IV 328/1812
D IV 329/1813
D IV 329/1814
D IV 329/1815 2/105
D IV 329/21/132
D IV 329/492/3117
D IV 329/492//3118

20th Division—Alsatica

1/22 Satzungen des litterarische Vereine "Alsabund" (1893)
2/31 Bulletin de la société pour la conservation des monuments historiques d'Alsace 1956/1892
6/80 Vogensenclub 1895/1950
8/105 Strasburger Verschönerungsverein

Division VI—Travaux Municipaux

Div. VI 178/971
Div. VI 179/975
Div. VI 179/979
Div. VI 184/986
Div. VI 185/190
Div. VI 185/995

Fonds Peirotes

43 NA 1–51

Fonds Dollinger

Boîte 1–Boîte 13

Fonds Eugène Muller

26 NA II/1–17

Archives Nationales (France)

Series F7 13377–13404 Rapports et pièces diverses concernant la situation politique en Alsace-Lorraine, l'activité des partis, la propagande communiste, autonomiste, et antimilitariste, le mouvement syndicaux.

Bundesarchiv-Militarisches Archiv (Freiburg)

PH 5 IV/13
PH 5 I/75
PH 5 IV 4
PH 5 IV/18

Contemporary Press

Bilder aus dem elsässischen Museum
S' Bollwark
Cahiers Alsaciens
Echo de Wissembourg
Der Eiserne Mann
S' Elsass
Elsässer
Elsässer Kurier
Die elsässische Woche
Elsässische Landeszeitung
Elsass-Lothringische Zeitung
Elsässische Volksbote
L'Express de Mulhouse
Frankfurter Zeitung
Die Freie Presse
Jahresbericht für neuere deutsche Literaturgeschichte
Journal de Colmar
Journal d'Alsace- Lorraine
Journal d'Alsace et de la Lorraine
La Littérature Populaire
Le Matin
Le Nouvelliste
Das Neue Elsass (Editor Theodor Heuss, 1910–11)
Das Neue Elsass (Editor Camille Dahlet, 1927–28)
La Renaissance alsacienne
Revue Alsacienne Illustrée
Revue Politique et Parlementaire
Schlettstader Tagesblatt
Der Schliffstaan
Strassburger Burgerzeitung
Strassburger Korrespondenz
Strassburger Neueste Nachrichten
Strassburger Neue Zeitung
Strassburger Post
Strassburger Zeitung
La Vie en Alsace
Die Volksstimme
Die Volkswille
Der Volksfreund

Weissenburger Zeitung
Die Zukunft

Printed Sources

Administration Militaire de l'Alsace. Rapport sur l'organisation des territoires (1914–1916). Thann, 1917.
The Annexation of Alsace-Lorraine and its Recovery. Paris, 1918.
Procès Verbaux de la Conférence d'Alsace-Lorraine. Paris, 1917.
Stenographisches Protokoll des Landesausschusses
Stenographisches Protokoll des Landtags

Contemporary Works

Der Komplott-Prozess vom Colmar 1.-24. Mai 1928. Gesammelte Verhandlungsberichte. Colmar, 1928.
Petition des Vogesen Hotel-Besitzer Vereins und die Bewilligung des Wiederaufbaus der Hohkönigsburg, Bibliothèque Nationale et Universitaire (BNUS), Côte MeIIIHK
Abel, Hans Karl, ed. *Briefe eines elsässische Bauernburschen aus dem Weltkriege an seinem Freund 1914–1918.* Stuttgart, 1922.
Alapetite, Gabriel. "Souvenirs 1920–24." *Annuaire de la Société des amis du vieux Strasbourg,* Tome VIII, 106–14. Strasbourg, 1978.
Barrès, Maurice. *Mes Cahiers.* Paris, 1929.
Borries, Emil von. *Die deutsche Seele des Elsass.* Basel, 1918.
Fleurent, Joseph. "L'idée de patrie en Alsace." *Revue politique et parliamentaire* 14 (January/February/March 1907): 327–33.
Herrenschmidt, Suzanne. *Memoirs pour la petite histoire. Souvenirs d'une Strasbourgeoise.* Strasbourg, 1972.
Husser, Philippe. *Un Instituteur Alsacien. Entre France et Allemagne, journal, 1914–1951.* Edited by Alfred Wahl. Strasbourg, 1989.
Laugel, Anselm. "L'Avenir intellectuel de l'Alsace." *Revue politique et parliamentaire* 14 (July/August/September 1908): 245–71.
———. *Oberlin: Roman aus der Revolutionszeit im Elsaß.* Hamburg, 1933.
Laurent, Francois. *1914–1918. Des Alsaciens-Lorrains otages en France. Souvenirs d'un Lorrain interné en France et en Suisse pendants la guerre.* Edited by Camille Maire. Strasbourg, 1998.
Lienhard, Friedrich. *Jugendjahre. Erinnerungen von Friedrich Lienhard.* Stuttgart, 1918.
———. *Où appartient l'Alsace-Lorraine?* Zurich, 1915.
Meinecke, Friedrich. *Erinnerungen, 1901–1919. Strassburg, Freiburg, Berlin.* Stuttgart, 1949.
Ritleng, Georges. *Souvenirs d'un vieux strasbourgeois, L'alsatique de poche.* Strasbourg, 1973.
Rudrauf, Charles. *Le drame de la mauvaise frontière. Lettres d'un Alsacien (1914–1916).* Strasbourg, 1924.

Ruland, Heinrich. *Deutschtum und Franzosentum in Elsass-Lothringen. Eine Kulturfrage*. 2. Auflage. Colmar, 1909.
Spindler, Charles. *L'Alsace pendant la guerre*. Strasbourg, 1926.
Schweitzer, Albert. *Out of My Life and Thought*. New York, 1933; trans. 1949; reprint 1950.
Stoskopf, Gustave. *D'r Herr Maire: Luschtspiel in dreij Akt*. Strassburg, 1902.
———. *D'r Hoflieferant: elsässische Komodie in drei Aufzugen*. Strassburg, 1904.
———. *D'r Prophet: Drama in fünf Aufzugen*. Strassburg, 1900.
———. *D'r Verbotte Fahne: elsässische Komodie in drei Aufzugen*. Strassburg, 1905.
———. *E Demonstration: elsässische Komodie in drei Akten*. Strassburg, 1904.
———. "In der Gewerej Stoskopf." *Revue alsacienne de littérature*, no. 2 (1983): 7–10.
———. *In Ropfer's Apotheke: Schwank in drei Aufzugen*. Strassburg, 1907.
Waltz, Jean-Jacques [Hansi]. *L'Alsace Heureuse. Le Grand Bonheur du Pays d'Alsace aux Petit Enfants par l'Oncle Hansi*. Paris, 1918; reprint, Besancon, 1990.
———. *L'Histoire d'Alsace. Recontee aux petites enfants d'Alsace et de France par l'Oncle Hansi*. Paris, 1913; reprint 1915.
———. *Mon Village. Ceux qui n'oublient pas; images et commentaires par l'Oncle Hansi*. Paris, 1913.
Wolf, Georges. *Das elsässische Problem: Grundzüge einer elsässische Politik im Zeitalter des Pakts von Locarno*. Leipzig, 1926.

Secondary Sources

Agulhon, Maurice. "The Center and the Periphery." *Rethinking France: Les Lieux Des Mémoire*. Vol. 1, *The State*. Edited by Pierre Nora, 53–76. Chicago, 2001.
Alcock, Antony E. *The History of the South Tyrol Question*. London, 1970.
Anderson, Benedict. *Imagined Communities: Reflections on the Origin and Spread of Nations*. New York, 1983; revised edition, London, 1991.
Anderson, Margaret, *Practicing Democracy: Elections and Political Culture in Imperial Germany*. Princeton, NJ, 2000.
Andreas, A. *Charles Spindler. Aus dem Leben und Schaffen eines elsässichen Künstlers*. Strassburg, 1934.
Applegate, Celia. "A Europe of Regions: Reflections on the Historiography of Sub-National Places in Modern Times." *American Historical Review* (1999): 1157–82.
———. "Heimat and the Varieties of Regional History." *Central European History* 33, no. 1 (2000): 109–15.
———. *A Nation of Provincials: The German Idea of Heimat*. Berkeley, CA, 1990.
Baechler, Charles, and Jean-Pierre Kintz. 1982—. *Nouveau dictionnaire de biographie alsacienne* (48 volumes). Strasbourg, France: La Fédération des Sociétés d'Histoire et d'Archéologie d'Alsace.
Baechler, Christian. "L'Alsace entre la guerre et la paix. Recherches sur l'opinion République (1917–1918), Vols. 1–3." Thése du troisième cycle, Université de Strasbourg, 1969.
———. "La question de la neutralité de l'Alsace-Lorraine à la fin de la première guerre mondiale et pendant le congrès de paix (1917–1920)." *Revue d'Alsace* 114 (1988): 242–85.

———. *Le parti catholique alsacien 1890–1939, du Reichsland à la République jacobine.* Paris, 1982.

———. "La question de la neutralité de l'Alsace-Lorraine à la fin de la première guerre mondiale et pendant le congrès de paix (1917–1920)." *Revue d'Alsace* 114 (1988): 185–208.

Baker, Keith. *Inventing the French Revolution.* Cambridge, 1990.

Balibar, Etienne. "The Nation Form: History and Ideology." In *Becoming National,* edited by Geoff Eley and Robert Suny, 151–78. New York, 1996.

Bankwitz, Philip C. *Alsatian Autonomist Leaders, 1919–1947.* Lawrence, KS, 1978.

Baridou, Laurent and Nathalie Pintus. *Le Château du Haut-Koenigsburg. À la recherche du Moyen Âge.* Paris, 1998.

Baumann, Georges. "Le Théâtre Alsacien, 1900 à 1950." *Saisons d'Alsace* 3 (1950): 345–47.

Becker, Jean-Jacques. *1914: Comment les Français sont entrés dans la guerre.* Paris, 1977.

———. "L'opinion publique francaise et l'Alsace en 1914." *Revue d'Alsace* 109 (1983): 125–38.

Berghahn, Volker. *Imperial Germany: 1871–1914.* Providence, RI, 1994.

Bhabha, Homi. "DissemiNation: Time, Narrative, and the Margins of the Modern Nation." In *Nation and Narration,* edited by Homi Bhahba, 291–322. London, 1990; reprint, 1994.

Bischoff, Georges. "L'Invention de l'Alsace." *Saisons d'Alsace,* no. 119 (Printemps 1993): 35–70.

Blackbourn, David. *The Long Nineteenth Century: A History of Germany, 1780–1918.* Oxford, 1997.

Blackbourn, David, and Geoff Eley. *The Peculiarities of German History.* Oxford, 1985.

Bodner, Jay. "Public Memory in an American Society: Commemoration in Cleveland." In *Commemorations: The Politics of National Identity,* edited by John R. Gillis, 74–89. Princeton, NJ, 1994.

Bopp, Marie-Joseph. "Le premier procès de Hansi." *Saisons d'Alsace* 3, no. 1 (Hiver 1952): 65–73.

Boswell, Laird. "Franco-Alsatian Conflict and the Crises of National Sentiment During the Phoney War." *Journal for Modern History* 71 (September 1999): 552–84.

———. "From Liberation to Purge Trials in the "Mythic Provinces": Recasting French Identities in Alsace and Lorraine, 1918–1920." *French Historical Studies* 23, no. 1 (2000): 129–62.

Brustein, William. *The Social Origins of Political Regionalism. France, 1849–1981.* Los Angeles, 1988.

Candir, Rene and Steinman, Paul. *Hansi a travers ses cartes postales, 1985–1951.* Obernai, 1992.

Ciampani, Andrea. "Die Elsässer Katholiken und der heilige Stuhl zwischen nationaler Identität und universalistischem Selbstverständnis: Die "Querelen" um den Strassburger Koadjutor 1879–1881." In *Grenzregionen im Zeitalter des Nationalismus,* edited by Angelo Ara, 116–51. Berlin, 1998.

Colley, Linda. *Britons: Forging the Nation, 1707–1837.* New Haven, CT, 1992.

Confino, Alon. *The Nation as Local Metaphor: Württemberg, Imperial Germany, and National Memory, 1871–1918.* Chapel Hill, NC, 1997.

Connelly, Mark. *The Great War, Memory and Ritual: Commemoration in the City and East London, 1916–1939.* Rochester, NY, 2002.
Craig, Gordon. *The Politics of the Prussian Army, 1640–1945.* New York, 1955; reprint 1964.
Craig, John E. *Scholarship and Nation Building: The Universities of Strasbourg and Alsatian Society, 1870–1939.* Chicago, 1984.
Dewitz, Jean. "Le perception du théâtre populaire alsacien dans la presse (1920/1921)." In *La presse en Alsace au XXe siècle: Témoin-acteur-enjeu,* edited by Hildegard Châtellier and Monique Mombert, 87–102. Strasbourg, 2002.
Dollinger, Philippe, ed. *Documents de l'Histoire de l'Alsace.* Toulouse, 1972.
Dorpalen, Andreas. *Heinrich von Treitschke.* New Haven, CT, 1957.
Dreyfus, Francois. *La vie politique en Alsace, 1919–1936.* Paris, 1969.
Duara, Presenjit. "Historicizing National Identity, or Who Imagines What and When." In *Becoming National,* edited by Geoff Eley and Robert Suny, 151–78. New York, 1996.
Eley, Geoff and Ronald Suny. "Introduction." In *Becoming National,* edited by Geoff Eley and Ronald Suny, 16–17. Oxford, 1996.
Ertz, Michel. *Friedrich Lienhard und René Schickele: Elsässische Literaten zwischen Deutschland und Frankreich.* Hildesheim, 1990.
Essig, Michael. *Das Elsass auf der Suche nach seiner Identität.* München, 1994.
Farcy, Jean-Claude. *Les camps de concentration français de première guerre mondiale (1914–1920).* Paris, 1995.
Farmer, Sarah. *Martyred Village: Commemorating the 1944 Massacre at Oradour-sur-Glane.* Berkeley, CA, 1999.
Farrar, Lancelot. *The Short War Illusion: German Policy, Strategy, and Domestic Affairs, August–December 1914.* Santa Barbara, CA, 1973.
Fisch, Stefan. "Assimilation und Eigenständigkeit: Zur Wiedervereinigung des Elsass mit dem Frankreich der dritten Republik nach 1918." *Historisches Jahrbuch* 117, no. 1 (1997): 111–28.
———. "Dimensionen einer historischen Systemstransformation. Zur Verwaltung des Elsass nach seiner Rückkehr zu Frankreich." In *Staat Verwaltung. Fünfzig Jahre Hochschule für Verwaltungswissenschaften Speyer,* edited by Klaus Lüder, 381–98. Berlin, 1997.
———. "Die Nationalität internationaler Unternehmen Kriegsende 1918: Ein Problem bei der Rückkehr des Elsasses nach Frankreich." in *Nachkriegsgesellschaften in Deutschland und Frankreich im 20. Jahrhundert,* ed. Pierre Guillen and Ilja Mieck, 39–47. Munich, 1998.
Fleurent, Joseph. "Hansi. Sa vie, son oeuvre." *Saisons d'Alsace* 3, no. 1 (Hiver 1952): 17–38.
Fontana, Josef. *Geschichte des Landes Tirols, Band 3: Vom Neubau bis zum Untergang der Habsburgermonarchie (1848–1918).* Innsbruck, 1987.
Ford, Caroline. *Creating the Nation in Provincial France: Religion and Political Identity in Brittany.* Princeton, NJ, 1993.
Gaines, Jena M. "Alsatian Catholics against the State, 1918–25." *Contemporary European History* 2, no. 3 (1993): 207–24.
———. "The Politics of National Identity in Alsace." *Canadian Review of Studies in Nationalism* 21, no. 1–2 (1994): 99–109.
———. "The Spectrum of Alsatian Autonomism." PhD diss., University of Virginia, 1990.

Gall, Jean-Marie. "Quatre-vingt ans de theatre alsacien de Colmar." *Saisons d'Alsace* 25, no. 73 (Printemps 1981): 43–56.
Gall, Lothar. "Das Problem Elsass-Lothringen." *Reichsgründung, 1870/71. Tatsachen, Kontroversen, Interpretationen*, edited by Theodor Schieder and Ernst Deuerlein, 365–85. Stuttgart, 1970.
Gellner, Ernest. *Nations and Nationalism*. Ithaca, NY, 1983.
Gelvin, James. *Divided Loyalties and Mass Politics in Syria at the Close of Empire*. Berkeley, CA, 1998.
Gildea, Robert. *The Past in French History*. New Haven, CT, 1994.
Gemie, Sharif. *Brittany 1750–1950: The Invisible Nation*. Cardiff, 2007.
Gerson. Stéphane. *The Pride of Place: Local Memories & Political Culture in Nineteenth-Century France*. Ithaca, NY, 2003.
Goodfellow, Samuel. *Between the Swastika and the Cross of Lorraine*. Dekalb, IL, 1999.
Guy, Kolleen M. "Oiling the Wheels of Social Life: Myths of Marketing Champagne in the Belle Epoque," *French Historical Studies* 22, no. 2 (1999): 211–39.
———. *When Champagne Became French: Wine and the Making of a National Identity*. Baltimore, 2003.
Green, Abigail. "The Federal Alternative? A New View of Modern German History." *The Historical Journal* 46, no. 1 (2003): 187–202.
Greenfeld, Liah. *Nationalism: Five Roads to Modernity*. Cambridge, MA, 1992.
Grünwald, Irmgard. *Die Elsass-Lothringer im Reich*. Frankfurt/Main, 1984.
Haefs, Hanswilhelm. *Die deutsche Heimat-museen*. Frankfurt, 1984.
Haenggi, Charles. "Hansi, journaliste." *Saisons d'Alsace* 3, no. 1 (Hiver 1952): 79–82.
Hall, Stuart. "Cultural Identity and Diaspora." In *Identity: Community Culture and Difference*. London, 1990.
Harp, Stephen. *Learning to Be Loyal: Primary Schooling as Nation Building in Alsace and Lorraine*. Dekalb, IL, 1998.
Harter-Feist, Christiane. "Le problème d'Alsace et les relations franco-allemands dans l'ouevre de Friedrich Leinhard." PhD diss., Université des Sciences Humaines de Strasbourg, 1998.
Harvey, David Allen. *Constructing Class and Identity in Alsace, 1830–1945*. Dekalb, IL, 2001.
———."Lost Children or Enemy Aliens? Classifying the Population of Alsace after the First World War." *Journal of Contemporary History* 34, no. 4 (1999): 537–54.
Harvie, Christopher. *The Rise of Regional Europe*. Historical Connections, edited by Geoffrey Cossick, Tom Scott et al. London, 1994.
Hiery, Herman. *Reichstagwahlen im Reichsland: Ein Beitrag zur Landesgeschichte von Elsass-Lothringen und zur Wahlgeschichte des deutschen Reiches, 1871–1918*. Beitrage zur Geschichte des Parlamentarismus und der politischen Parteien, Band 80. Düsseldorf, 1986.
———. "Zwischen Scylla und Charybdis: Carl Graf von Wedel als Statthalter im Reichsland Elsass-Lothringen (1907–1914)." *Revue d'Alsace* (1986): 299–328.
Hobsbawm, Eric. *Nations and Nationalism since 1780: Myth, Program, and Reality*, 2nd. ed. Cambridge, 1992; reprint, 1993.
Hülsen, Bernhard von. *Szenenwechsel in Elsass. Theater und Gesellschaft in Strassburg zwischen Deutschland und Frankreich, 1890–1944*. Deutsch-Französisch Kulturbibliothek 22. Leipzig, 2003.

Igersheim, François. *Alsace des Notables (1870–1914)*. Strasbourg, 1981.
———. *L'Alsace et ses historiens, 1680–1914. La fabrique des monuments*. Strasbourg, 2006.
Jahr, Christoph. *Gewöhnliche Soldaten: Desertion und Deserteure im deutschen und britishen Heer, 1914–1918*. Göttingen, 1998.
Jenkins, Jennifer. *Provincial Modernity: Local Culture and Liberal Politics in Fin-de-Siècle Hamburg*. Ithaca, NY, 2003.
Kaes, Anton. "Germany as Memory." In *From Hitler to Heimat: The Return of History as Film*. Cambridge, MA, 1989.
Kahn, Bonnie Menes. *My Father Spoke French: Nationalism and Legitimacy in Alsace, 1871–1914*. Harvard Studies in Sociology. New York, 1990.
Karasek, Erika. *Die volkskundlich-kulturhistorisch Museen in Deutschland. Zur Rolle der Volkskunde in der bürgerliche-imperialistischen Gesellschaft*. Berlin, 1984.
Keating, Michael. *The New Regionalism in Western Europe*. Cheltenham, UK, 1998.
Kocka, Jürgen. *Klassengesellschaft im Krieg. Deutsche Sozialgeschichte, 1914–1918*. 2nd ed. Vol. 8, *Kritische Studien zur Geschichtswissenschaft*. Göttingen, 1978.
Koshar, Rudy. *Germany's Transient Pasts: Preservation and National Memory in the Twentieth Century*. Chapel Hill, NC, 1998.
Kramer, Alan. "*Wackes* at War: Alsace-Lorraine and the Failure of German National Mobilization, 1914–1918." In *State, Society, and Mobilization in the Europe during the First World War*, edited by John Horne, 107–21. New York, 1997.
Kurlander, Eric. *The Price of Exclusion: Ethnicity, National Identity, and the Decline of German Liberalism, 1898–1933*. New York, 2006.
Lammers, Benjamin J. "National Identity on the French Periphery: The End of Peasants into Frenchmen?" *National Identities* 1, no. 1 (1999): 81–87.
Laurent, Francois. *1914–1918. Des Alsaciens-Lorrains otages en France. Souvenirs d'un Lorrain interné en France et en Suisse pendant la guerre*. Edited by Camille Maire. Strasbourg, 1998.
Laven, David, and Baycroft, Timothy. "Border Regions and Identity." *European Review of History—Revue européenne d'histoire* 15, no. 3 (June 2008): 255–75.
Lebovics, Herman. "Creating the Authentic France: Struggles over French Identity in the First Half of the Twentieth Century." In *Commemorations: The Politics of National Identity*, edited by John Gillis. Princeton, NJ, 1994.
———. *True France: The Wars over Cultural Identity, 1900–1945*. Ithaca, NY, 1992.
Loth, Gisela. *Un rêve de France: Pierre Bucher, une passion française au coeur de l'Alsace allemand, Editions de l'Est*. Strasbourg, 2000.
Lorentz, Claude. *La presse alsacienne du XXe siècle*. Strasbourg, 1997.
Maas, Annette. "Kriegerdenkmäler und Gedenkfeiern um Metz: Formen und Funktionen kollektiver Erinnerung in einer Grenzregion." In *Stadtentwicklung im deutsch-französisch-luxemburgischen Grenzraum (19. u 20. Jh.)*, edited by Rainer Hudemann and Rolf Wittenbrock, 89–118. Saarbrücken, 1991.
———. "Zeitenwende in Elsass-Lothringen: Denkmalstürze und Umdeutung der nationalen Erinnerungslandschaft (November 1918–1922)." In *Denkmalsturz. Zur Konfliktgeschichte politischer Symbolik*, edited by Winfried Speitkampf, 79–108. Göttingen, 1997.
Mayeur, Jean-Marie. *Autonomie et politique en Alsace. La Constitution de 1911*. Paris, 1970.
Mitchell, Allan. "'A Real Foreign Country': Bavarian Particularism in Imperial Germany, 1870–1918." *Francia* 7 (1979): 587–96.

Mombert, Monique. "Le discours assimilationniste du *Journal d'Alsace et de Lorraine* de 1919 à 1924." In *La presse en Alsace au XXe siècle: Témoin-acteur-enjeu*, edited by Hildegard Châtellier and Monique Mombert, 65–86. Strasbourg, 2002.
Mommsen, Wolfgang. *Imperial Germany, 1867–1918: Politics, Culture, and Society in an Authoritarian State*. London, 1995.
Moriarty, Catherine. "Private Grief and Public Remembrance: British First World War Memorials." In *War and Memory in the Twentieth Century*, ed. Martin Evans and Ken Lunn, 123–45. Oxford, 1997.
Morley, David, and Robins, Kevin. "No Place like *Heimat*: Images of Home(land) in European Culture." *New Formations* 12 (Winter 1990), 1–23, reprinted in *Becoming National*, edited by Geoff Eley and Ronald Suny, 456–80. New York, 1996.
Morrison, Jack. G. "The Intransigents: The Alsace-Lorrainers against the Annexation, 1900–1914." PhD diss., University of Iowa, 1970.
Muller, René. "Le théâtre alsacien de Mulhouse." *Saisons d'Alsace* 25, no. 73 (1981): 15–42.
Nachtigal, Reinhard. "Loyalität gegenüber dem Staat oder zur *Mère-Patrie*? Die deutschen Kriegsgefangenen aus Elsass-Lothringen in Russland während des Ersten Weltkrieges" *Zeitschrift für die Geschichte des Oberrheins* 154 (2006): 395–428.
Nohlen, Klaus. *Baupolitik im Reichsland Elsass-Lothringen, 1871–1918*. Berlin, 1982.
Nolan, Michael C. *The Inverted Mirror: Mythologizing the Enemy in France and Germany, 1898–1914*. New York, 2005.
Peer, Shanny. *France on Display: Peasants, Provincials, and Folklore in the 1937 Paris World's Fair*. New York, 1998.
Pflanze, Otto. *Bismarck and the Development of Germany*. Vol.1, *The Period of Unification, 1815–1871*. 2nd ed. Princeton, NJ, 1990.
Prost, Antoine. *In the Wake of War: 'Les anciens combattants' and French Society, 1914–1939*. Trans. Helen McPhail. Providence, RI, 1992.
Renouvin, Pierre. "Die öffentliche Meinung in Frankreich, 1914–1918," *Vierteljahrshefte für Zeitgeschichte*, no. 3 (July 1970).
Richez, Jean-Claude. "L'Alsace revue et inventée. La Revue alsacienne illustrée, 1895–1914." *Saisons d'Alsace*, no. 119 (Printemps 1993): 83–94.
Richez, Jean-Claude. "Le château du Haut-Koenigsburg: Frontière, mémoire, et illusion," *Revue des Sciences Sociales dans la France de l'Est*, no. 18 (1993): 249–54.
Rimmerle, Eva. *Sprachenpolitik im Deutschen Kaiserreich vor 1914: Regierungspolitik und Veröffentliche Meinung in Elsass-Lothringen und den östlichen Provinzen Preussens*. Vol. 17, *Müncher Studien zur neueren und neuersten Geschichte*. Frankfurt/Main, 1996.
Robertson, Eric. *Writing Between the Lines: René Schickele, 'Citoyen francais, deutscher Dichter' (1883–1940)*. Vol. 11, *Internationale Forschungen zur Allgemeinen und Vergleichenden Literaturwissenschaft*. Amsterdam, 1995.
Rossé, Joseph, et al. *Das Elsass von 1870–1932. I Band. Politische Geschichte*. Colmar, 1938.
———. *Das Elsass von 1870–1932. IV Band. Karten, Graphiken, Tabelle, Dokumente, Sach- und Namenregister*. Colmar, 1938.
Roth, Elizabeth. "Heimatkunde als Grundlage in Geschichtsbewusstsein," in *Heimat, Tradition, Geschichtsbewusstsein*. Hrsg. Klaus Weigelt. Mainz, 1986.

Roth, François. *Raymond Poincaré. Un homme d'état républicain* (Paris, 2000)
Roth, Martin. *Heimatmuseum: zur Geschichte einer deutscher Institution*. Berlin, 1990.
Rothenberger, Karl-Heinz. *Die elsass-lothringische Heimat- und Autonomiebewegung.* Frankfurt, 1975.
Sahlins, Peter. *Boundaries: The Making of Spain and France in the Pyrenees*. Berkeley, CA, 1989.
Schneider, Camille. "Gustave Stoskopf: zélateur, fondateur, et animateur des arts au seuil du siècle." *Saisons d'Alsace*, no. 274–84 (1954).
Schoenbaum, David. *Zabern 1913: Consensus Politics in Imperial Germany*. London, Boston, 1982.
Schroda, Julia. "Der Mythos der 'provinces perdues' in Frankreich." *Konstrukte nationaler Identität: Deutschland, Frankreich, und Grossbritannien (19. und 20. Jahrhundert)* eds. Michel Einfalt, et. al., 115–33. Würzburg, 2002.
Sherman, Daniel. *The Construction of Memory in Interwar France*. Chicago, 1999.
Silverman, Daniel. *Reluctant Union: Alsace-Lorraine and Imperial Germany, 1871–1918*. University Park, PA, 1972.
Skurski, Julie. "The Ambiguities of Authenticity in Latin America: *Doña Bárbara* and the Construction of National Identity." In *Becoming National*, edited by Geoff Eley and Ronald Suny, 371–402. Oxford, 1996.
Steinhoff, Anthony. "Protestants in Strasbourg, 1870–1919. Religion and Society in Late Nineteenth Century Europe." PhD diss., University of Chicago, 1996.
Story, William Shane. "Constructing French Alsace: A State, Region, and Nation." PhD diss., Rice University, 2001.
Stoskopf, Charles-Gustave. *Stoskopf, le peintre: 1896–1944*. Colmar, 1976.
Stoskopf, Nicolas."Un étudiant alsacien à Paris." *Saisons d'Alsace*, no. 4 (1999): 32–37.
Taacke, Charlotte. *Denkmal im sozialen Raum: Nationale Symbole in Deutschland und Frankreich im 19. Jahrhundert*. Göttingen, 1995.
Thiesse, Anne-Marie. *Ecrire la France: Le littéraire régionaliste de langue française entre la Belle Epoque et la Libération*. Collection "Ethnologies." Paris, 1991.
———. *Ils Apprenaient La France : L'exaltation des Régions dans le discours patriotique*. Paris, 1997.
Umbach, Maiken. "Introduction." *European Review of History—Revue européenne d'histoire* 15, no. 3 (June 2008): 235–42.
Vassberg, Liliane M. *Alsatian Acts of Identity: Language Use and Language Attitudes in Alsace*. Multilingual Matters 90. Edited by Derrick Sharp. Clevedon, UK, 1987.
Verhey, Jeffrey. *The Spirit of 1914: Militarism, Myth, and Mobilization in Germany*. New York, 2000.
Vicari, Eros. *L'histoire de la littérature en Alsace*. Strasbourg, 1985.
Vogler, Bernard. *Histoire culturelle de l'Alsace*. Strasbourg, 1994.
———. *Histoire politique de l'Alsace*. Strasbourg, 1995.
Wahl, A. and Jean-Claude Richez. *L'Alsace entre France et Allemagne, 1850–1950*. Strasbourg, 1994.
Walker, Mack. *German Home Towns: Community, State, and General Estate, 1648–1817*. Ithaca, NY, 1971.
Weber, Eugen. *Peasants into Frenchmen: The Modernization of Rural France, 1870–1914*. Stanford, CA, 1976.
Wehler, Hans-Ulrich. *The German Empire, 1871–1918*. New York, 1985.

———. *Krisenherde des Kaiserreiches: Studien zur deutschen Sozial- und Verfassungsgeschichte*. Göttingen, 1970; Second edition, 1979.

Weichlein, Siefried. "Saxons into Germans: The Progress of the National Idea in Saxony after 1866." Paper presented at Memory, Democracy, and the Mediated Nation. Political Cultures and Regional Identities in Germany, 1848–1998, Toronto, 18–20 September 1998.

White, Dan S. "Regionalism and Particularism." In *Imperial Germany: A Historiographical Companion*, edited by Roger Chickering, 131–55. Westport, CT, 1996.

Wilcken, Niels. *Architektur im Grenzraum: das öffentliche Bauwesen in Elsass-Lothringen, 1871–1918*. Saarbrücken, 2000.

Wilkinson, James. "The Uses of Popular Culture by Rival Elites: The Case of Alsace, 1890–1918." *History of European Ideas* 11 (1989): 605–18.

Winter, Jay, and Jean-Louis Robert. *Capital Cities at War: Paris, London, Berlin, 1914–1919*. Vol. 1. New York, 1997.

Winter, Jay and Sivan, Emmanuel, eds. *War and Remembrance in the Twentieth Century*. New York, 1999.

Winter, Jay. *Sites of Memory, Sites of Mourning: The Great War in European Cultural History*. Cambridge, 1995.

Wolff, Stefan. *Disputed Territories: The Transnational Dynamics of Ethnic Conflict Settlement*. New York, 2003.

Wright, Julian. *The Regionalist Movement in France, 1890–1914: Jean-Charles Brun and French Political Thought*. Oxford, 2003.

Young, Patrick. "Of Pardons, Loss, and Longing: The Tourist's Pursuit of Originality in Brittany, 1890–1935." *French Historical Studies* 30, no. 2 (2007): 269–304.

INDEX

"Alsace to the Alsatians" 1–2, 73, 75, 82, 84–5, 118, 139, 142, 146, 192, 207
"Alsace-Lorraine to the Alsatians-Lorrainers" See "Alsace to the Alsatians"
Action Française, 187
Action Populaire Nationale d'Alsace (APNA), 197–99, 209
Alapetite, Georges, 134, 163, 167, 171
Alsatian constitution (1879), 13, 74–5
Alsatian constitution (1911), 75–81, 84, 94–5, 141, 145–6, 186, 191
Alsatian Renaissance, 10, 20–2, 29, 61, 64
Alsatian Social Democratic Party, 47, 67, 77, 81–6, 91, 119–21
Alsatian Theater, 22, 25, 28–36, 46–7, 60, 83, 139–40, 153–55, 156–62, 207
  criticism of, 34–5, 152–53, 159–61
  origins of, 29–30
Altdeutsche, 31–2, 35, 45, 77, 91, 100–1
Altdorffer, Charles, 140
Anderson, Margaret L., 74
Applegate, Celia, 4–5, 9, 16 n. 10
Armistice, 64, 100, 119, 128, 131, 140, 152, 162, 169–72
Armistice Day [Fête de la Paix], 170–3
Autonomist Movement, 2, 8, 11, 27–8, 58, 136–38, 147–8, 150 n. 38, 156, 158, 166–67, 171–73, 177 n. 57, 179, 181–201
  French government suppression of, 183, 186
  splits in, 190–91, 198–200
Autonomy, 3–4, 8, 11, 13, 21, 25, 47, 75–8, 80–2, 85, 95, 115, 117–20, 136, 141–2, 145–47, 153, 158–59, 161, 165–66, 180–82, 184, 188–91, 194, 196, 198–201, 210
  See also Autonomist Movement

Baechler, Christian, 107, 119, 144, 147
Barrès, Maurice, 23, 61, 79, 129, 137
Bartholdi, Auguste, 65
Barthou, Louis, 66, 189
Basque region, 3, 5, 158
Bastian, Ferdinand, 29, 33–4, 155–57
Bastille Day, 43, 169–74
Bavaria, 3, 5, 13, 26, 40, 46, 146
Bebel, August, 13
Besançon Trial, 10
Bethmann-Hollweg, Theobald von, 73, 75–6, 92, 94
Biographies alsaciennes, 25, 27, 155
Bismarck, Otto von, 12–14, 75, 143
Bissingen-Nippenburg, Graf, 67
Blackbourn, David, 74
Blumenthal, Daniel, 58, 65, 77–8, 80–3, 86–8, 97 n. 43, 101, 115, 138, 154, 207
Boll, Léon, 77, 80–3, 87, 96 n. 16, 138
Das Bollwark, 190
Bonaparte, Napoleon, 20, 25, 62
Bordeaux (protest), 15, 50 n. 88, 129
Borderland, 6–7, 159, 171, 208, 211
Borries, Emil von, 27, 107
Boswell, Laird, 131–32, 211
Brant, Sebastian, 25
Breton, See Brittany,
Brittany, 4–5, 141, 158, 184, 195, 201
Brom, Joseph, 118, 140

Brun, Jean-Charles, 137
Bucher, Pierre, 20–5, 37, 44, 53, 60–3, 84, 86–8, 101–2, 109, 120, 134, 153, 155, 157, 170, 174
Bulach, Hugo Zorn von, 61, 75, 92–3
Bulach, Klaus Zorn von, 138, 150 n. 38, 175 n. 25, 180, 190
Bundesrat, 13–4, 57, 75–6, 79–80, 85, 116

Carte tricolore, 112–113, 125 n. 84
Cartel des Gauches, 130, 142–43, 147–48, 180
Center Party (Alsace), 16, 76–7, 80–3, 85–8, 92–3, 97 n. 33, 104, 117–20, 127 n. 117, 136, 140, 182, 208–9
  See also Union Populaire Républicaine (UPR)
Center Party (Germany), 80
Chatrian, Alexandre, 30, 63
Chronique d'Alsace-Lorraine, 23
Church-state relations, 78–9, 86–7, 115–16, 130, 136, 143, 181–82, 198
Civil-military relations, 89–90, 91, 94, 96 n. 10, 102, 106–7, 110
  See also Zabern Affair
Clemenceau, Georges, 133, 137, 163, 170
Colmar Trial, 10, 196–97
Colmar trio, 78, 97 n. 43
Colmar, brawl in, 187–8
Commemoration, 52–68, 162–175
Commisariat général, 132–34, 143, 145, 152, 163, 167–68, 171
Commission des Alsacien-Lorrains et Ôtages, 112, 125 n. 84
Commissions de triage, 131–32, 134–36, 139, 148, 159, 190
Communist Party (Alsatian), 133, 138, 145, 166, 173, 177 n. 57, 179–80, 184, 187, 189-91, 195–96, 198–200, 208
Conférence d'Alsace-Lorraine, 115, 130–31, 138, 154, 186, 194
Confino, Alon, 4, 9, 26
Conseil Général, 144, 197
Coquet, Lucien, 139
Criqui, Eugen, 29

Dahlet, Camille, 140, 179, 182, 184, 190, 191–92, 195–200
Dallwitz, Johann von, 94, 116

Danis, Robert, 168
Daudet, Alphonse, 129, 154
Deimling, Berthold von, 92
Delsor, Nicolas, 65–6, 83, 87, 140–41

E Demonstration, 32–4
Deutsche Tageszeitung, 36
Dialect (Alsatian), 5–6, 8–9, 12, 15–16, 20–3, 26–31, 33–5, 45–7, 112, 135, 152, 154–61, 174, 209
Dictatorship paragraph, 13, 82, 96 n. 8
Dieckmann, Albert, 54–5
Dollinger, Ferdinand, 25, 53, 60–1, 63, 86
Dollinger, Léon, 25, 53, 60–1, 63, 86
Doré, Gustave, 25
Dreyfus, François, 144, 196
Drivier, Léon, 167
Dual Culture, 8–9, 22, 24–5, 83, 152–54, 156–7, 160–61, 174, 183, 191, 201, 209, 211
Dubois, Paul, 163
Dur's Elsass, 140, 154–55

Ebhardt, Bodo, 55
Eccard, Fréderic, 139
Education system, 82, 84, 86, 105, 111, 115, 134–6, 138, 143–4, 163, 182
Der Eiserne Mann, 159–61, 174
Elections:
  Colmar, 180
  French National Assembly (1871), 15
  Landtag (1911), 73, 81–88, 95
  Landtag (general), 75, 78, 80–1
  parliamentary (French), 132, 142, 189, 195–98
  Reichstag (1887), 13
  Strasbourg, 166–67, 180
Eley, Geoff, 74
Die elsässische Monatsschrift, 26
Die Elsässische Woche, 156–59, 161, 174
Ensfelder, Eugen, 25
Erckmann, Émile, 30, 63
Ernst, Robert, 137, 150 n. 36
Ertz, Michael, 28
Erwinia, 26
Erwinia (publisher), 190, 194
Erzberger, Matthias, 117
European Community, See European Union

European Union, 3, 206
Executive Committee of the Free Republic of Alsace-Lorraine, 137

Falkenhayn, Erich von, 92
Fashauer, Joseph, 145, 181, 190, 192, 194–96
Fecht Valley, 113
Fédération Régionaliste Française, 137, 200
First World War, See World War I,
Flake, Otto, 24
Fleurent, Joseph, 45–6
Folklore museums, 63
Ford, Caroline, 9
Forstner, Gunther von, 91–94
France:
　"Indivisible", 10, 180, 183, 211
　Chamber of Deputies, 128, 141–3, 184, 189, 191, 193, 195–6, 198
　High Commissioner in Alsace, 132–33, 152
　language policy in Alsace, 82, 84, 105–6, 111, 114–15
　Third Republic, 2, 4–5, 141, 163, 173, 180, 183, 211
　transition of control in Alsace, 128–36, 143, 162
Franco-Prussian War, 7, 12
French Regionalism, See Regionalism, France,
Frey, Charles, 84, 128, 140, 142, 167, 174, 177 n. 57, 182, 185, 187, 193, 196, 199–200

Germany, Kaiserreich, 63, 74, 84, 129
Germany, language policy in Alsace, 40–1, 80, 84–5, 106–7
Sonderweg, 74
Gneisse Affair, 38, 75, 97 n. 43
Grad, Charles, 1, 75
Grafenstaden Affair, 99 n. 101, 141
Great Depression, 10
Great War, See World War I
Greber, Jules, 29, 34, 60, 155

Haegy, Xavier, 85, 138, 140–42, 144, 181–82, 194–95, 197–98
Hans von Schnakenloch, 32–3

Hansi, See Jean-Jacques Waltz
Harp, Stephen, 136, 162
Hartmannswillerkopf [Vieil Armand], 102, 167–69
Harvey, David A., 108, 131
Hauss, Karl, 30, 65, 75, 78, 83, 88, 96 n. 8, 118–19, 138, 140, 145, 182
Hauss, René, 145, 179, 191–92, 194, 197–98
Die Heimat, 28
Heimatbund, 156, 172, 179–80, 182–92, 194, 198, 200–1, 208–9
Helmer, Paul, 111
Henner, Jean-Jacques, 25
D'r Herr Maire, 30, 34–5, 79, 159
Herrenschmidt, Suzanne, 168
Herriot, Éduoard, 7, 64, 134, 137, 143–45, 147–48, 162, 180, 201, 208, 210
Hessler, Alexander, 29–30
Heyler, Théophile, 89
Historical preservation, 55–56
D'r Hoflieferant, 31–2, 34, 36
Hohkönigsburg, 37–8, 53–60, 64–5, 68–9, 155
Horsch, Adolf, 29
Hueber, Charles [Karl], 133, 137, 145, 151 n. 60, 166–67, 174, 177 n. 57, 193, 195, 198-89
Hummel, Joseph, 138
Husser, Philippe, 1, 101, 110

Images Alsaciennes, 21–2

Jahr, Christoph, 103
Jahrbuch für Geschichte, Sprache, und Literatur (JfGSL), 26–8, 52, 107
Jeanneney, Jules, 133–34, 145
Joan d'Arc, 163–64, 169–70
Joffre, Joseph, 64, 102, 110, 116, 122 n. 12, 130, 135, 143, 160, 192, 201

Kablé, Jacques, 15
Kaiserplatz, See Place de la République
Keating, Michael, 3
Keppi, Jean, 141, 182, 184, 186, 192
Kiener, André, 65
Kiener, Fritz, 24
Kléber, Jean-Baptiste, 36, 66
Koshar, Rudy, 47 n. 2, 55

Kramer, Alan, 106, 127 n. 122
Kulturkampf, 7, 14, 142–44, 184, 208, 211

L'Histoire d'Alsace, 38–40
    See also Waltz, Jean-Jacques (Hansi)
Landesausschuss, 13, 37, 54, 56–9, 65, 75, 78–9, 82
Landespartei für Elsass-Lothringen (Independent Regional Party for Alsace-Lorraine), 179–80, 190–92, 194, 196, 198–99, 204 n. 60, 207
Language, 7–9, 11, 28, 30–31, 39, 41, 46, 47, 63, 65, 80, 82, 85, 107
    See also dialect (Alsatian),
Laugel, Anselm, 10, 21–4, 30, 35, 46–7, 53, 56, 58, 60, 65, 68, 78, 81–3, 86–9, 101, 109, 115, 120, 139–40, 146–7, 153, 155, 184
League of Nations, 8, 141, 146, 170–1, 184, 192, 197, 201, 201
Lebrun, Albert, 168–9
Levy, Henri, 167
Ley, René César, 137, 159
Liberal Party (Alsace), 16, 35–36, 55, 58, 61, 63, 67–8, 74, 77–88, 96 n. 14, 104, 115, 118–19, 128, 140, 182, 184–85, 191, 208
Lienhard, Friedrich, 21, 27–8, 35, 47, 59, 107, 160, 208
Ligue d'Alsace Française [League of French Alsace], 139
Lisle, Rouget de, 163
La Littérature Populaire, 156–9, 174
lois laïques, 130, 208
Lorraine, 2, 10, 12–13, 16 n. 2, 58–9, 64, 69, 86–88, 93, 95, 112, 131, 133, 143, 146, 164, 173, 181–82, 184, 189, 192–93, 195
Louis XIV, 27, 147, 164

malaise alsacien, 7, 130, 136
Marseillaise, 32–33, 36, 67, 89, 104, 157, 163
Maurras, Charles, 137
Mayeur, Jean-Marie, 74, 87
Meinecke, Friedrich, 18 n. 33, 26
Mère-patrie, 2, 8, 66, 120–21, 148, 153, 172, 210
Millerand, Alexandre, 64, 132, 134, 163
Möller, Eduard von, 13

Mon Village, 39, 41–44
    See also Waltz, Jean-Jacques (Hansi),
Moroccan Crises, 87, 120
Mourer, Jean-Pierre, 196–97, 199
Muller, Eugène, 137, 140–1, 185, 195, 197, 200
Musée alsacien, 22–3, 53, 58, 60, 62, 64–5, 68, 107, 109, 168
Muth, Henri, 137

Naeger, Émile, 110, 124 n. 67
Napoleon, Louis (Napoleon III), 12
Napoleonic Concordat, 78, 115, 143
National Council [National Rat], 119, 128, 130
National Socialism, 10, 27, 199–200
National Union (Union nationale), 74, 81–88, 95, 96 n. 14, 154, 179, 180, 182–84, 188, 200, 208, 209
Nationalism, 3–5, 47 n. 2, 65, 77–78, 184, 208
    French, 7, 22–23, 39, 47, 63, 73, 83, 88–89, 102–3, 105, 152, 158, 207, 211
    German, 7, 18 n. 29, 26–8, 37, 45, 47, 73, 75, 78, 88–89, 92, 106–7, 116, 207, 211
Neissen, Xavier, 64
Nora, Pierre, 52

Oberlé, Philippe, 159–60
Oberpräsident, 13
Oesinger, François, 140
Oppositionsbloc, 138, 190
Oradour-sur-Glane, 207

Palatinate, 26, 33, 209
Pange, Jean de, 195
Paris Peace Conference, See Treaty of Versailles
Parti radical indépendent, 140
Parti républicain-démocratique [Republican-Democratic Party], 139–40
Particularism, 4, 9, 13, 35, 45–6, 86, 110, 139, 146–47, 159, 174, 195, 210
Pasteur, Louis (monument), 164–5
Payer, Friedrich von, 117
Peer, Shanny, 9

Peirotes, Jacques, 67, 77, 82, 119, 128, 132–33, 140, 143, 144, 164–66, 196
Pfister, Christian, 164
Pfleger, Joseph, 85, 119, 140–1, 181, 185, 193, 196, 198, 208
Place Broglie, 66, 160, 163
Place de la République, 62, 54, 162, 164–5, 167, 169
Place Kléber, 143, 169, 171
Poilu, 100, 120–21, 171
Poincaré, Raymond, 128–29, 137, 146, 148, 163, 170, 186, 188–89, 193, 201, 210
Preiss, Jacques, 66, 70 n. 24, 77–78, 81–82, 84, 86–87, 89, 98 n. 59, 116
Professor Knatschke, 37–38
  See also Waltz, Jean-Jacques (Hansi)
Progressive Party [Fortschrittliche Partei], 140, 179, 191, 196–99
Protestaires, 15
Protestler, 10
Puttkamer, Alberta von, 22

Quatorze Juillet, See Bastille Day

Radical-Socialist Party, 139, 172, 182, 185, 208
Rapp, Charles, 137
Redslob, Rudolf, 164–5
Regional Identity, definition, 5–6, 11
Regionalism:
  Regionalism, cultural, 21–2, 153–162, 185–6, 209
  Regionalism, French, 7, 9–11, 20, 183, 189, 210
  Regionalism, German, 9–11, 44–47, 210
Reichsland, 13, 22, 26, 54, 73–76, 80–81, 84, 90–95, 108, 116–18, 209
Reichstag, 13, 15, 30, 37, 56, 65–66, 75–76, 80–81, 83, 87, 92, 94, 110, 112, 119, 127 n. 117
La Renaissance Alsacienne, 154
Reuter, Adolf von, 91–3
Revue alsacienne illustrée (*RAI*), 22–29, 35, 27, 45, 57, 52, 61–63, 65, 69, 83, 88, 109, 154–55

Revue d'Alsace et de Lorraine, 139–40, 146, 154–55
Richez, Jean-Claude, 20, 25
Ricklin, Eugène, 58, 65–69, 179, 182, 184, 187–8, 190, 192, 194–8, 202 n. 10
Riff, Adolph, 63
Roos, Karl, 27, 191–2, 194, 199, 205 n. 98, 207–8
Rossé, Joseph, 126 n. 110, 167, 179, 181–82, 186–87, 193–98, 200
Roth, François, 189
Rothenberger, Karl-Heinz, 131, 183, 196, 198
Rulard, Heinrich, 45

Saar, 206
Sarte, Maxime Réal del, 166
Schall, Paul, 145, 159, 161, 174, 179, 182, 184, 191–2, 194–5, 197, 199, 207–8
Schickele, René, 33, 35, 79, 88, 190
Der Schliffstaan, 145, 159–62, 192
Schmitt, Christian, 28
Schneegans, August, 15
Schoenbaum, David, 74
Schultz, Albert, 65
Schumann, Robert, 183
Schwander, Rudolf, 77, 117, 126 n. 110, 137–8, 140
Schweitzer, Albert, 112
Section française de l'Internationale ouvrière [SFIO], See Socialist Party (Alsatian). See also Alsatian SPD
Sélestat city council, 54–5
Self-determination, 8, 85, 150 n. 35, 187, 192, 194, 200–1
S'Elsass, 189
Seltz, Thomas, 193
Service d'Alsace-Lorraine, 134, 145
Sherman, Daniel, 52
Socialist Party (Alsatian), 133, 136–7, 139–40, 143, 145–6, 163, 166, 170–2, 184–5, 187, 194, 196, 199, 208
Société des amis des arts d'Alsace, 29
South Tyrol, 3, 5–6, 206–7

Souvenir d'Alsace, 89
Souvenir Français, 64, 83–4, 88–89, 166, 168
Spindler, Charles, 10, 20–23, 28–9, 47, 60–1, 107–109, 153
Spinner, Antoine, 66–8
Spirit of 1914, 100–1, 121 n. 1
St. Leonard Group, 22, 30, 60
St. Odile, 23, 171
Statthalter, 13, 54–55, 58, 75, 77–81, 85, 89, 93–95, 116–18, 137
Stoeber, Adolphe, 30
Stoeber, Auguste, 30
Stoeber, Daniel, 30
Story, Shane, 163, 166
Stoskopf, Gustave, 10, 20–3, 25, 29–37, 45, 47, 60–1, 77–9, 88, 152–3, 155–161, 168, 173–4, 209
Strassburger Neue Zeitung, 35–6, 77–9, 81, 83, 88, 118, 140, 156, 174, 193
Stuermel, Marcel, 198

Thirty Years' War, 54
Treaty of Frankfurt, 7, 15
    See also Franco-Prussian War,
Treaty of Versailles, 2, 137, 151 n. 63, 170
Treitschke, Heinrich von, 12, 18 n. 29

Union Nationale des Combattants, 187
Union Populaire Républicaine (UPR), 136, 138–45, 147, 156, 172, 179–82, 184–85, 188–90, 192–200, 208–9
    See also Center Party (Alsace)
University of Strasbourg, 16, 26–8, 44, 53–4, 116, 118, 135, 164, 189

Valot, Paul, 134, 145
D'r Verbotte Fahne, 32
La Vie en Alsace, 154–5, 160
Vogler, Bernard, 20
Volksfront [People's Front], 179, 197–200
Volkspartei, 77, 82, 207
Die Volkstimme, 171, 192, 194

Wackes, 90–1
Die Wahrheit, 190, 192
Walter, Michel, 138, 181, 185, 189, 193, 195–99
Waltz, Jean-Jacques (Hansi), 21, 25–6, 36–44, 47, 52, 79, 87–8, 94–5, 96 n. 16, 97 n. 43, 101–2, 120, 129, 134, 152–3, 155, 206, 208, 211
Wedel, Karl von, 38, 65–6, 73, 75, 89–92, 94–5
Wegerlin Affair, 89–90
Wehler, Hans-Ulrich, 74, 126 n. 110
Weill, Georges, 143, 196
Wendel, Hermann, 121
Wetterlé, Émile, 37–8, 44, 57–8, 65–68, 70 n. 24, 77, 80–83, 85–9, 95, 96 n. 25, 97 n. 43, 99 n. 101, 101–2, 106, 115–6, 120, 129–31, 134, 141–2, 208, 211
Wilhelm I, 27, 53–4, 59 165
Wilhelm II, 54–5, 57–8, 60, 155
Wissembourg (monument), 53, 64–9, 73, 75, 83
Wittich, Werner, 24, 26, 44–5
Wolf, Georges, 77–8, 83, 118, 138, 140, 182–6, 190–2
Workers, 2, 15, 131, 133, 160, 186, 206
World War I, 7, 8, 9, 44, 63, 68, 100–121, 153, 163, 165, 174, 183, 185, 207, 210–11
    Alsatian veterans of, 166–71
    civil internées, 112–14
    commemoration of, 166–71
    evacuations of Alsace, 113–14
    food supply in Alsace, 107–8, 111–12
    martial law in Alsace, 100, 106–7, 114
    outbreak, 101–102
    political consequences of in Alsace, 180, 184
    postwar planning, 115–119
    POWs, 104–5
    pre-war attitudes in Alsace, 120–121
    propaganda (French), 122 n. 87
    propaganda (German), 107
    security measures against, 108–120, 122 n. 16
    special measures against Alsatian soldiers, 100, 103–4

volunteers in French army, 101, 104–5, 122 n. 4, 123 n. 32
volunteers in German army, 101, 104, 122 n. 15
See also Armistice Day
See also Commissions de triage
See also Conférence d'Alsace
Württemberg, 13, 26, 210

Young Alsace, 45

Youngest Alsace, 35

Zabern Affair, 8, 73–75, 88–95, 100, 102, 120, 155, 160, 195, 211
Zemb, Joseph, 181
Zislin, Henri, 68, 87, 89, 96 n. 16, 120, 129, 140, 154–55, 190
Die Zukunft, 145–48, 159–60, 170–71, 179–82, 185–86, 188, 192, 194, 201, 202 n. 32

www.ingramcontent.com/pod-product-compliance
Lightning Source LLC
Chambersburg PA
CBHW072150100526
44589CB00015B/2166